Distant Views

Program Authors
Richard L. Allington
Camille Blachowicz
Ronald L. Cramer
Patricia M. Cunningham
G. Yvonne Pérez
Constance Frazier Robinson
Sam Leaton Sebesta
Richard G. Smith
Robert J. Tierney

Instructional Consultant
John C. Manning

Program Consultants
Teresa Delgadillo
Rose Marie Delgadillo-Reilly

Critic Readers
Mary Jo Brick
Gloria M. Brown
Judy A. Credicott
Barbara Hayes
Carolyn Lawson
Evelyn Vera

Scott, Foresman and Company

Editorial Offices:
Glenview, Illinois

Regional Offices:
Sunnyvale, California
Tucker, Georgia
Glenview, Illinois
Oakland, New Jersey
Dallas, Texas

Scott, Foresman Reading: An American Tradition

Acknowledgments

Text

Page 9: Adapted from "The Pugnacious Pussycat" by A. R. Swinnerton, *Boys' Life*, May 1976. Reprinted by permission of the author.

Page 19: "A Pet Trout" adapted from *Angling in America* by Charles E. Goodspeed. Copyright 1939 by Charles E. Goodspeed. Copyright © renewed 1967 by George T. Goodspeed. Reprinted by permission of Houghton Mifflin Company.

Page 21: Adaptation of "In the Middle of the Night" from *What the Neighbors Did and Other Stories* by Philippa Pearce (Thomas Y. Crowell). Copyright © 1972 by Philippa Pearce. Reprinted by permission of Penguin Books Ltd. and Harper & Row, Publishers, Inc.

Page 34: Adaptation of "The C Chord Misery Blues" by E. M. Hunnicutt, *Boys' Life*, August 1984. Reprinted by permission of the author.

Page 46: From *Get Lost, Little Brother* by C. S. Adler. Copyright © 1983 by C. S. Adler. Reprinted by permission of Ticknor & Fields/Clarion Books, a Houghton Mifflin Company and Carol Mann Literary Agent for the author.

Page 58: "Jigsaw Puzzle" by Russell Hoban from *Allsorts 3*. Copyright © 1970 by Russell Hoban. Reprinted by permission of Harold Ober Associates Incorporated.

Page 63: Adapted from *Our World: Lands and Cultures*, p. 317, *Scott, Foresman Social Studies* by Joan Schreiber et al. Copyright © 1983, Scott, Foresman and Company.

Page 64: Adaptation from *Barbara Jordan: The Great Lady from Texas* by Naurice Roberts. Copyright © 1984 by Regensteiner Publishing Enterprises, Inc. Reprinted by permission of Childrens Press.

Page 72: Excerpt by Daniel K. Inouye from the introduction to *Journey to Washington* by Senator Daniel K. Inouye with Lawrence Elliot. Copyright © 1967 by Prentice-Hall, Inc. Reprinted by permission.

Page 76: Adaptation of "The Making of a Scientist" by Robert W. Peterson, *Boys' Life*, September 1982. Reprinted by permission of the author.

Page 84: "To Look at Any Thing" by John Moffitt. Copyright © 1961 by John Moffitt. Reprinted from his volume *The Living Seed* by permission of Harcourt Brace Jovanovich, Inc.

Page 86: Adaptation of chapter 2, "Miracle at the Pump House" from *The Helen Keller Story* by Catherine Owens Peare (Thomas Y. Crowell). Copyright © 1959 by Catherine Owens Peare. Reprinted by permission of Harper & Row, Publishers, Inc.

ISBN 0-673-71513-2

Copyright © 1987,
Scott, Foresman and Company, Glenview, Illinois.
All Rights Reserved. Printed in the United States of America.

45678910–RRW–96959493929190898887

Acknowledgments continued on page 582

Contents

Imagine having your own bodyguard to protect you from the neighborhood bully. See how Bryan's care and feeding of Harry the cat brings Bryan benefits that he's never dreamed of.

HARRY
THE
HEAVYWEIGHT

by A.R. Swinnerton

This kid Bruno Schroder always seemed to be a million steps ahead of everyone else—including me. He was bigger, tougher, and louder than any of us other kids. He was always ready to lean on one of us. He'd give you a quick little shove from behind, scatter your books, or grab your hat right off your head. Then he'd dare you to start something. So I kept my profile low, hoping that Bruno never got me cornered.

I was thinking about this very thing while I was delivering papers on the last day of school in June.

My last house was the Biddle place. Two kids lived there. They were meaner than Bruno but small enough for me to handle. They had a big, scroungy dog that was as grouchy as a scorpion with a hotfoot.

I tossed the paper on the porch lightly, keeping an eye out for the dog. Just as I was turning away, the front door crashed open. Out came a burst of angry shouts along with a large cat. I don't know whether he was thrown out or what, but by the time he hit the steps he was streaking, tail up and ears back.

The cat shot by me like an F-4 phantom jet,[1] a rippling, grayish blur. The door slammed shut. I backed away, looking for that high-speed cat. He was waiting for me at the corner, sitting on a low stone wall, washing himself as if nothing had happened. Was he a rough-looking brute—a battle-scarred King Kong of cats! Both ears above his wide, flat face were chewed up and cauliflowered. He had a healed-up cut over his right eye. The scar pushed his eyebrow down until it

---

1. F-4 phantom jet: A U.S. Air Force fighter plane that can fly faster than twice the speed of sound. Sound waves travel about 760 miles (1,220 kilometers) an hour.

almost covered his eye. This gave him a cockeyed squint. His coat was either dirty gray with white spots or dirty white with gray spots. I couldn't decide which.

From my pocket I dug out a piece of soft candy still wrapped in paper. I pushed it toward him. He sniffed it and ate the whole thing, paper and all. "Let's go, Harry," I said. The name just popped up. I suppose because of my Uncle Harry who plays professional hockey.

I hung my paper sack in the garage, waiting for Harry He strolled in and gave my legs a rub-around. I went inside.

"Mom," I said, "a big cat followed me home."

"Never mind about the size," she said. "I hate cats. And we're not interested in such an animal, Bryan."

"But he's hungry, Mom! Harry ate a piece of candy, paper and all."

"What about Harry?" asked Pop, coming in just then, on the tail end of it.

"He eats candy," said Mom, laughing. "Paper and all."

"Yeah," I said. "He's sitting on the hood of our car right now, washing his feet."

"My brother Harry?"

"No—Harry the cat. Take a look, Pop."

In the garage Harry eyed Pop. Then he flicked his tail and gave Pop's legs a rubbing. "He's an ugly brute," said Pop, "but friendly. Where'd you get him?"

I told Pop. He rubbed Harry under the chin, and the cat hissed like a viper. "Hey," said Pop. "He can't meow. You've got a speechless beast here, Bryan."

"I know," I said, as Harry curled up his front paws into furry fists and jabbed at Pop with his left. "Something else is weird too. After he ate the candy, he belched a lot. I never heard a cat belch—never. Do you think there's something wrong with him?"

Pop grinned and said, "No, but, of his nine lives, I'd say it's six down and three to go."

"He needs someone to look after him," I suggested. "Do you suppose I can keep him, Pop?"

"Well, if you can't find his real owner—and if he'll stay—but he belongs in the garage. Your mother has her opinion of cats, so don't expect any improvement when she sees this one. Feed him, Bryan."

I put a lost-and-found ad in the paper about Harry. I spent a whole dollar doing it. But no one called or came to claim him. So Harry stayed. By August, after eating regularly, he weighed almost seventeen pounds. We got used to his hissing, which he couldn't help, and his belching, which he seemed to enjoy.

I was the only kid in town with a pet like Harry. I tied a piece of old throw rug over the rear carrier on my bike. Harry would ride along, hanging on with his claws and hissing at passing cars. Other times we guys would form a circle and hiss at him. Harry would stand up on his hind legs, double up his front paws, and jab away like a heavyweight. I've had three dogs, and I was crazy about each one. But, believe me, I loved that Harry.

Then along came Labor Day. I'd be starting sixth grade and going to the new school that had been built. Opening day was supposed to be something special. Pop made me dress up a little more, which I hated. The mayor herself and a lot of other bigwigs were all over the place. In the afternoon there was a special assembly and we got our class assignments. Afterwards, at about two-thirty, everyone headed home.

I was jogging along, anxious to get out of my school clothes. Suddenly I heard this "Clomp! Clomp!" behind me. I didn't have to look. I knew who it was—Bruno Schroder, looking bigger and meaner than he had last June. He was closing in fast.

"Hey, pretty-boy Bryan," he hooted, coming up beside me. "Your shoes are on backwards. You're going to trip and hurt yourself, dummy." Slick as a whistle he put one foot down right in my path. I tripped on it, falling flat in the dirt, losing my glasses. Angry and scared, I looked up at Bruno. "Told you," he said, grinning. "Warned you, but—"

I never saw Harry, but I heard his hiss. Next thing I knew, he was up on Bruno's back and shoulders, clawing away at his head ratatat-tat, triple time. When Bruno turned his head to see what was after him, Harry leaned over and let go a combination belch, hiss, and scream right in Bruno Schroder's ear. I could see the blood drain from Bruno's face. Bruno ran, old Harry hanging on, still using his head for a bongo drum.

"Harry!" I called. Harry let go of Bruno's shoulder and jumped to the ground. He came loping back to me, still hissing softly.

I told Mom and Pop about what had happened. Pop said, "I hope Harry didn't hurt Bruno."

"No," I said, "but he sure scared him."

Then Mom said something that made me think she wasn't the cat-hater she pretended to be. "Bryan, let's ask the vet why Harry can't meow," she suggested. "It's the least we can do for him."

On the way I held Harry in the car. When we got out, he was jumpy. I put him on the examining table and held him down. Just then the vet walked in. She took one look at the cat and yelled, "Hey, where did you find him, Bryan?"

"Find who?" My heart sank. "Did she recognize Harry?" I wondered.

"Rocky, my crazy cat! He hung around here for a couple of years. I tried to find a home for him, but, of course, no one wanted him. Finally he got so frightful I had to put him in a cage. He wasn't cockeyed then, but one way I'd always recognize him. He couldn't meow, so he hissed. Say there, old Rocky! Want to hiss for me?"

Old Harry sat crouched on the table. His ears were twitching, and his eyes were flashing. No doubt he was thinking about his time in the cages out back. Then he straightened up, flicked his crooked tail, opened his mouth, and meowed. Just once, no more.

The vet scratched her head in amazement. "Well, I never! Boy, he sure looks like Rocky. Why did you bring him in to see me?"

"Never mind," I said, picking Harry up carefully. "Let's go, Mom."

Harry never meowed again, but that once was enough. You'll never find a cat smarter than old Harry. In my book, he was a heavyweight in more ways than one.

1

Getting Along

Joining forces. Working as a team. Cooperating. Getting along. When you work with others, you can often succeed—whether you're dreaming a dream, solving a problem, or seeking a goal.

The characters in this section all come to know the value of getting along. Brothers and sisters join forces. Two friends share a dream. And a young boy seeks help to achieve his plan.

Understanding Plot

What story is being told in these pictures about children getting along? A good guess would be that a group of children want a place to play baseball, but they find that the vacant lot where they want to play is a mess. They decide to clean it up to create a baseball field. The last picture shows that the children now have a fine, clean place in which to play.

As you can see, one event leads to another event in the story. A series of related events that make up a story is called the **plot.** Most plots are made up of a **goal** (what the character or characters want), a series of attempts to reach the goal, and an **outcome** (the end that tells whether the character or characters finally get what they want).

Think about the plot of "Harry the Heavyweight."

1. What are Bryan's goals in the story?
2. What happens to help Bryan reach his goals?
3. What is the outcome of the story?

By answering the questions, you can figure out the plot of "Harry the Heavyweight." When you put together the answers, you can retell the plot in this way: (1) Bryan wants Bruno to stop bothering him. He wants to keep Harry, a cat that he finds while on his paper route. (2) Harry comes to the rescue. He jumps on Bruno's back and scares Bruno away. (3) Bruno doesn't bother Bryan anymore, and Bryan gets to keep Harry.

Practicing Plot

Read this tall tale about a man and his loyal pet trout. Look for the important events that make up the plot. Then answer the questions that follow the story.

Once there was a man who had a pet trout named Tommy, which he kept in a barrel. But the trout grew pretty big and had to have the water changed a good deal to keep him alive. The man was too lazy to do that, and so he thought he would teach the trout to live out of water. So he did. He began by taking Tommy out of the barrel for a few minutes at a time. He did that pretty often. Soon he took him out more often and kept him out longer. By and by Tommy could stay out a good while if he was in the wet grass. Then the man found he could leave him in the wet grass all night. Pretty soon the trout could live in the shade whether the grass was wet or not. By that time the trout had become pretty tame, too, and he would follow the man around a good deal. When the man would go out to dig worms for the trout, Tommy would go along and pick up the worms for himself. The man thought everything of that fish, and when Tommy didn't need water at all anymore and could go anywhere—even down the dusty road in the hot sun—you never saw the man without his trout. Circus people wanted to buy Tommy, but the man said he wouldn't sell a fish like that for any money. The man would come to town with Tommy following along in the road, just like a dog. Of course the trout traveled a good deal like a snake, and almost as fast.

Well, it was pretty sad the way the man lost his trout, and it was curious, too. He started for town one day with Tommy coming along behind, as usual. When the man came to a bridge in the road, he saw there was a plank missing, but he went on over it without thinking. By and by he looked around for Tommy, and Tommy wasn't there. He went back a ways and called, but he couldn't see anything of his pet. Then he came to the bridge and saw the hole. He thought right away that maybe his trout had fallen through it. So he went to the hole and looked down, and sure enough, there was Tommy, floating on the water, bottom-side-up. He'd tumbled through that hole into the brook and drowned.

1. What is the man's goal?
2. What does the man do to achieve his goal?
3. How did the man's goal become a hazard for Tommy?
4. What is the outcome of the story?
5. In a few sentences, tell the plot of the story.

Tips for Reading on Your Own
- Find out what the main characters want to achieve.
- Trace the related events that help the characters or hinder them from reaching their goals.
- Decide whether the main characters achieve their goals and how.

Brothers and sisters really can get along, especially if their goal is eating paradise cakes in the middle of the night! One by one the children get involved in a series of events that make up the plot of this story. Notice how they join forces to put their secret plan into action.

In the Middle of the Night

by Philippa Pearce

In the middle of the night a fly woke Charlie. At first he lay listening, half-asleep, while it swooped about the room. Sometimes it was far; sometimes it was near—that was what had woken him; and occasionally it was very near indeed. It was very, very near when the buzzing stopped: the fly had alighted on his face. He jerked his head up; the fly buzzed off. Now he was really awake.

Charlie pulled his head down under the bedclothes. All of him under the bedclothes, he was completely protected; but he could hear nothing except his heartbeats and his breathing. He was overwhelmed by the smell of warm bedding, warm pajamas, warm himself. He was going to suffocate. So he rose suddenly up out of the bedclothes; and the fly was waiting for him. It dashed at him. He beat at it with his hands. At the same time he appealed to his younger brother, Wilson, in the next bed: "Wilson, there's a fly!"

Wilson, unstirring, slept on.

Now Charlie and the fly were pitting their wits against each other: Charlie pouncing on the air where he thought the fly must be; the fly sliding under his guard toward his face. Again and again the fly reached Charlie; again and again, almost simultaneously, Charlie dislodged him. Once he hit the fly—or, at least, hit where the fly had been a second before, on the side of his head; the blow was so hard that his head sang with it afterward.

Then suddenly the fight was over; no more buzzing. His blows—or rather, one of them—must have told.

He laid his head on the pillow, thinking of going to sleep again. But he was also thinking of the fly, and now he noticed a tickling in the ear he turned to the pillow.

It must be—it *was*—the fly.

He rose in such panic that the waking of Wilson really seemed to him a possible thing, and useful. He shook him repeatedly: "Wilson—Wilson, I tell you, there's a fly in my ear!"

Wilson groaned, turned over very slowly like a seal in water, and slept on.

The tickling of Charlie's ear continued. He could just imagine the fly struggling in some passageway too narrow for its wingspan. He longed to put his finger into his ear and rattle it round, like a stick in a rabbit hole; but he was afraid of driving the fly deeper into his ear.

Wilson slept on.

Charlie stood in the middle of the bedroom floor, quivering and trying to think. He needed to see down his ear, or to get someone else to see down it. Wilson wouldn't do; perhaps Margaret would.

Margaret's room was next door. Charlie turned on the light as he entered: Margaret's bed was empty. He was startled, and then thought that she must have gone to the lavatory.

Wilson asleep; Margaret vanished; that left Alison. But Alison was bossy, just because she was the eldest; and, anyway, she would probably only wake Mum. He might as well wake Mum himself.

Down the passage and through the door always left ajar. "Mum," he said. She woke, or at least half woke, at once: "Who is it? Who? Who? What's the matter? What?—"

"I've a fly in my ear."

"You can't have."

"It flew in."

She switched on the bedside light, and as she did so, Dad plunged beneath the bedclothes with an exclamation and lay still again.

Charlie knelt at his mother's side of the bed and she looked into his ear. "There's nothing."

"Something crackles."

"It's wax in your ear."

"It tickles."

"There's no fly in there. Go back to bed and stop imagining things."

His father's arm came up from below the bedclothes. The hand waved about, settled on the bedside light, and clicked it out. There was an upheaval of bedclothes and a comfortable grunt.

"Good night," said Mum from the darkness. She was already allowing herself to sink back into sleep again.

"Good night," Charlie said sadly. Then an idea occurred to him. He repeated his good night loudly and added some coughing, to cover the fact that he was closing the bedroom door behind him—the door that Mum kept open so that she could listen for her children. They had outgrown all that kind of attention, except possibly for Wilson. Charlie had shut the door against Mum's hearing because he intended to slip downstairs for a drink of water—well, for a drink and perhaps a snack. That fly business had woken him up and also weakened him: he needed something.

He crept downstairs, trusting to Floss's good sense not to make a row. He turned the foot of the staircase toward the kitchen, and there had not been the faintest whisper from her, far less a bark. He was passing the dog basket when he had the most unnerving sensation of something being wrong there—something unusual, at least.

"Floss?" he whispered, and there was the usual little scrabble and snuffle. He held out his fingers low down for Floss to lick. As she did not do so at once, he moved them toward her, met some obstruction—

"Don't poke your fingers in my eyes!" a voice said, very low-toned and cross.

He took an uncertain little step toward the voice, tripped over the obstruction, which was quite wrong in shape and size to be Floss, and sat down. Two things now happened. Floss, apparently having climbed over the obstruction, reached his lap and began to lick his face. At the same time a human hand fumbled over his face, among the slappings of Floss's tongue, and settled over his mouth. "Don't make a row! Keep quiet!" said the same voice. Charlie's mind cleared: he knew, although without understanding, that he was sitting on the floor in the dark with Floss on his knee and Margaret beside him.

Her hand came off his mouth.

"What are you doing here anyway, Charlie?"

"I wanted a drink of water."

"There's water in the bathroom."

"Well, I'm a bit hungry."

"If Mum catches you . . ."

"Look here," Charlie said, "you tell me what you're doing down here."

Margaret sighed. "Just sitting with Floss."

"You can't come down and just sit with Floss in the middle of the night."

"Yes, I can. I keep her company. Only on weekends, of course. No one seemed to realize what it was like for her when those puppies went. She just couldn't get to sleep for loneliness."

"But the last puppy went weeks ago. You haven't been keeping Floss company every Saturday night since then."

"Why not?"

Charlie gave up. "I'm going to get my food and drink," he said. He went into the kitchen, followed by Margaret, followed by Floss.

They all had a quick drink of water. Then Charlie and Margaret looked into the larder: the remains of a roast, a very large quantity of mashed potato, most of a loaf, eggs, butter, cheese . . .

"I suppose it'll have to be just bread and butter and a bit of cheese," said Charlie. "Else Mum might notice."

"Something hot," said Margaret. "I'm cold from sitting in the hall comforting Floss. I need hot cocoa, I think." She poured some milk into a saucepan and put it on the hot plate. Then she began a search for the cocoa. Charlie, standing by the cooker, was already absorbed in the making of a cheese sandwich.

The milk in the pan began to steam. Given time, it rose in the saucepan, peered over the top, and boiled over on to the hot plate, where it sizzled loudly. Margaret rushed back and pulled the saucepan to one side. "Well, really, Charlie! Now there's that awful smell! It'll still be here in the morning, too."

"Set the fan going," Charlie suggested.

The fan drew the smell from the cooker up and away through a pipe to the outside. It also made a loud roaring noise. Not loud enough to reach their parents, who slept on the other side of the house—that was all that Charlie and Margaret thought of.

Alison's bedroom, however, was immediately above the kitchen. Charlie was eating his bread and cheese, and Margaret was drinking her cocoa, when the kitchen door opened and there stood Alison. Only Floss was pleased to see her.

Charlie muttered something about a fly in his ear, but Margaret said nothing. Alison had caught them red-handed. She stood there. She liked commanding a situation.

Then, instead of taking a step backward to call up the stairs to Mum, she took a step forward into the kitchen. "What are you having, anyway?" she asked. She glanced with scorn at Charlie's poor piece of bread and cheese and at Margaret's cocoa. She moved over to the larder, flung open the door, and looked searchingly inside. In such a way must Napoleon have viewed a battlefield before victory.

Her gaze fell upon the bowl of mashed potato. "I shall make potato cakes," said Alison.

They watched while she brought the mashed potato to the kitchen table. She switched on the oven, fetched her other ingredients, and began mixing.

"Mum'll notice if you take much of that potato," said Margaret.

But Alison thought big. "She may notice if some potato is missing," she agreed. "But if there's none at all, and if the bowl it was in is washed and dried and stacked away with the others, then she's going to think she must have made a mistake. There just can never have been any mashed potato."

Alison rolled out her mixture and cut it into cakes; then she set the cakes on a baking-tin and put it in the oven.

Now she did the washing up. Throughout the time they were in the kitchen, Alison washed up and put away as she went along. She wanted no one's help. She was very methodical, and she did everything herself to be sure that nothing was left undone. In the morning there must be no trace left of the cooking in the middle of the night.

"And now," said Alison, "I think we should fetch Wilson."

The other two were aghast at the idea, but Alison was firm in her reasons. "It's better if we're all in this together, Wilson as well. Then if the worst comes to the worst, it won't be just us three caught out, with Wilson hanging on to Mum's apron strings, smiling innocence. We'll all be for it together, and Mum'll be softer with us if we've got Wilson."

They saw that, at once. But Margaret still objected. "Wilson will tell. He just always tells everything. He can't help it."

Alison said, "He always tells everything. Right: we'll give him something to tell, and then see if Mum believes him. We'll do an entertainment for him. Get an umbrella from the hall and Wilson's sou'wester and a blanket or a rug or something. Go on."

They would not obey Alison's orders until they had heard her plan; then they did. They fetched the umbrella and the hat, and lastly they fetched Wilson, still sound asleep, slung between them in his eiderdown. They propped him in a chair at the kitchen table, where he still slept.

By now the potato cakes were done. Alison took them out of the oven and set them on the table before Wilson. She buttered them, handing them in turn to Charlie and Margaret and helping herself. One was set aside to cool for Floss.

The smell of fresh-cooked, buttery potato cake woke Wilson, as was to be expected. First his nose sipped the air, then his eyes opened, his gaze settled on the potato cakes.

"Like one?" Alison asked.

Wilson opened his mouth wide and Alison put a potato cake inside, whole.

"They're paradise cakes," Alison said.

"Potato cakes?" said Wilson, recognizing the taste.

"No, paradise cakes, Wilson," and then, stepping aside, she gave him a clear view of Charlie's and Margaret's entertainment, with the umbrella and the sou'wester hat and his eiderdown. "Look, Wilson."

Wilson watched with wide-open eyes, and into his wide-open mouth Alison put, one by one, the potato cakes that were his share.

But, as they had foreseen, Wilson did not stay awake for very long. When there were no more potato cakes, he yawned, drowsed, and suddenly was deeply asleep. Charlie and Margaret put him back into his eiderdown and took him upstairs to bed again. They came down to return the umbrella and the sou'wester to their proper places, and to see Floss back into her basket. Alison, last out of the kitchen, made sure that everything was in its place.

The next morning Mum was down first. On Sunday she always cooked a proper breakfast for anyone there in time. Dad was always there in time, but this morning Mum was still looking for a bowl of mashed potato when he appeared.

"I can't think where it's gone," she said. "I can't think."

"I'll have the bacon and eggs without the potato," said Dad, and he did. While he ate, Mum went back to searching.

Wilson came down, and was sent upstairs again to put

on a dressing gown. On his return he said that Charlie was still asleep and there was no sound from the girls' rooms either. He said he thought they were tired out. He went on talking while he ate his breakfast. Dad was reading the paper and Mum had gone back to poking about in the larder for the bowl of mashed potato, but Wilson liked talking even if no one would listen. When Mum came out of the larder for a moment, still without her potato, Wilson was saying: ". . . and Charlie sat in an umbrella-boat on an eiderdown-sea, and Margaret pretended to be a sea serpent, and Alison gave us paradise cakes to eat. Floss had one too, but it was too hot for her. What are paradise cakes? Dad, what's a paradise cake?"

"Don't know," said Dad, reading.

"Mum, what's a paradise cake?"

"Oh, Wilson, don't bother so when I'm looking for something . . . When did you eat this cake, anyway?"

"I told you. Charlie sat in his umbrella-boat on an eiderdown-sea and Margaret was a sea serpent . . ."

"Wilson," said his mother, "you've been dreaming."

"No, really—really!" Wilson cried.

But his mother paid no further attention. "I give up," she said. "That mashed potato: it must have been last weekend. . . ." She went out of the kitchen to call the others: "Charlie! Margaret! Alison!"

Wilson, in the kitchen, said to his father, "I wasn't dreaming. And Charlie said there was a fly in his ear."

Dad had been quarter-listening; now he put down his paper. "What?"

"Charlie had a fly in his ear."

Dad stared at Wilson. "And what did you say that Alison fed you with?"

"Paradise cakes. She'd just made them, I think, in the middle of the night."

"What were they like?"

"Lovely. Hot, with butter. Lovely."

"But were they—well, could they have had any mashed potato in them, for instance?"

In the hall Mum was finishing her calling: "Charlie! Margaret! Alison! I warn you now!"

"I don't know about that," Wilson said. "They were paradise cakes. They tasted a bit like the potato cakes Mum makes, but Alison said they weren't. She specially said they were paradise cakes."

Dad nodded. "You've finished your breakfast. Go up and get dressed, and you can take this"—he took a coin from his pocket—"straight off to the sweetshop. Go on."

Mum met Wilson at the kitchen door. "Where's he off to in such a hurry?"

"I gave him something to buy sweets with," said Dad. "I wanted a quiet breakfast. He talks too much."

Meet the Author

Asked how she got the idea for her story, "In the Middle of the Night," Philippa Pearce said, "When I was an adult, I went to stay for a weekend with my parents. They still lived in the house in which I had been brought up. In the middle of the night I began to be pestered by a gnat or fly. I took the usual defense action, more or less as described in the story. Then the fly was no longer there, *but* there was what seemed an ominous tickling in my ear. (I remember thinking then that it sounded as loud as a pigeon flapping in a chestnut tree.) In the end, I got up and went to my parents' bedroom and woke my mother. Obligingly she looked in my ear and assured me there was nothing there. So I went back to bed and to sleep.

"And that's really all. The rest is invention/imagination.

"A few further details, perhaps. Potato cakes are a specialty of Lancashire, where my mother came from. She made them for us, especially in winter. Delicious; but terribly fattening."

Philippa Pearce is a popular and respected author of books for children. Her book *Tom's Midnight Garden* won the Carnegie Medal for 1958. Her other books include *A Dog So Small* and *The Way to Sattin Shore*. She also writes short stories. She lives with her family in Cambridge and sometimes broadcasts for the B.B.C.

Checking Comprehension and Skills

Thinking About What You've Read

1. How do the children get along with one another when they have a common goal?
2. Why does Charlie go downstairs?
3. How does Charlie's trip to the kitchen change Margaret's goal?
4. In what way is Alison's behavior different from what Charlie and Margaret expect?
5. What plan do the children decide to carry out?
6. Why do they decide to include Wilson?
7. Why doesn't Mum believe the story that Wilson tells the next morning?
8. If you were one of the older children, how would you act when you came down for breakfast? Begin by stating the goal the three older children have. Why?
• 9. Tell the plot of this story in a few sentences.
• 10. Were the children successful in achieving their goal? What makes you think so?

Talking About What You've Read

Does Dad know about his children's nighttime adventure? Why do you think as you do? If he doesn't know, what might he think went on in the middle of the night? If he does know, why doesn't Dad express his feelings about what happened? Why would he send Wilson out instead? What could be going on in Dad's mind?

Writing About What You've Read

Either Dad knows what happened, or he doesn't know. Choose one point of view. Then write one or two sentences that tell what Dad is thinking based on the point of view you have chosen.

• Literary Skills: Plot

Sometimes a friendship can be sorely tested when people's plans don't work out smoothly at first. Sabrina and Ria get along very well until they try out a plan to earn money for a favorite hobby. Notice how and why working toward this goal causes their feelings toward each other to change.

THE
C CHORD MISERY
B·L·U·E·S

by E. M. Hunnicutt

The cost of albums was ruining us. Even when we shared records, Sabrina Peabody and I couldn't keep up with all the new releases.

"Other hobbies are cheaper, Ria," Sabrina said. We were standing in the Record Emporium, looking at the new double album by Electricity, our favorite rock group. One record we could have handled. There was no way we could spring for two, even with all the baby-sitting and grocery bagging we'd done. "If I didn't have music in my blood," Sabrina went on, "I'd look for another hobby."

I knew she was working up to something, talking her way into it, as she always does.

"My dad played trumpet in school," she said. "My mom plays the violin. Even my grandmother was a singer and dancer on stage years ago."

"Right, Sabrina." My family was different. If we have any talent, I guess it's for mathematics. Dad is an accountant, and Mom teaches high school math.

"Ria, let's go see my grandmother."

"OK." I figured she was going to ask her grandmother to advance the money for the album.

But instead, she walked in, kissed Mrs. Peabody on the cheek, and said, "You still have your guitar, Grams? Ria and I are going to form a rock group."

"Sabrina!" I said. "You can't play the guitar; I can't play one. How are we going to form a rock group?"

"Par-tic-i-pate!" she sang. "Participate" was Electricity's latest hit song. "Begin with a vi-sion. And be ready when your sea-sea-season comes." That was part of the lyric, and I began to see where this scheme had come from.

"Ria," Sabrina continued, "you've got a good voice, and anybody can play the tambourine."

"I have a tambourine, too," Mrs. Peabody said.

She'd been after Sabrina for years to take up music and carry on the family tradition. Before you could say stereo multiplex, she had the guitar out and was sitting there playing a song. She smiled at my surprise. "In the old days we had to be versatile," she said. "My career began when I learned to play the ukulele to accompany friends dancing the Charleston. I can play several instruments. Sabrina will learn quickly, with her natural talent."

"We'll make a demo," Sabrina said, "a demonstration tape, and send it to record companies. Then we'll sign a contract, cut some records, and go on tour." Not just money for albums, but fame and fortune were almost ours.

Were we totally dreaming? Two gals who'd never had a lesson, and already we were cutting records? Maybe we were dreaming, but I trust Sabrina. When she gets going, she can make me believe anything. It sounded great.

Until Sabrina picked up the guitar. First she couldn't remember the names of the strings. The fifth time Mrs. Peabody said, "E, A, D, G, B, E," I butted in.

"Sabrina, it's a pattern of skips, 4, 4, 4, 3, 4." Number patterns are easy for me.

"Skips?" Sabrina said weakly.

"We'll come back to that," her grandmother said. "Let's talk about reading notes. Music is measured in bars," she explained . . . and explained, and explained.

I said, "Like the inches on a ruler. See?" But Sabrina didn't see.

"We'll just do a basic C chord," Mrs. Peabody said, but after an hour she was still the only one doing the chord. The F and G chords didn't work out either.

"Mrs. Peabody," I said, "let me see if I've got this straight. The name of the chord is its basic note, but you can combine the notes in any order, and when you change keys you keep the same ratio of space between notes." To me it looked like equations, patterns of letters and numbers.

"That's an unusual way of putting it, Ria," she said. "Most people just follow the chord charts, but you're right. Music is very mathematical."

I was amazed. "Sabrina, I'll help you!" I'd helped her with her math plenty of times.

But she shook her head. Then she handed the guitar to *me*. "Let me see that tambourine." It didn't even sound like Sabrina's voice. She went outside, and the next time I looked, she'd disappeared.

I should have gone after her. She was my best friend, and she'd had a bad blow. But once that guitar was in my hands, I couldn't seem to think of anything else. Mrs. Peabody was excited too. When people start playing music, it's easy to forget about the rest of the world.

That afternoon she taught me the major chords and basic strumming. "Ria, you have a remarkable talent."

"Talent? Me? It's so easy!"

She taught me tuning and sent the guitar home with me to practice. And that's what I did: practice—and practice some more. The guitar opened a whole new world to me. Mrs. Peabody helped me every day. She said she'd never seen anyone learn so fast.

My folks were surprised—and skeptical. Dad said, "I never expected musical talent in this family. It's great, but are you sure you'll stick with it, Ria?"

Why are parents always asking questions like that? I wondered that to myself, but out loud I answered, "I don't know, Dad. I just know I like to play."

Somehow, my mom was impressed I was so frank, so the next Saturday they bought me my own guitar. I was so happy I promised I'd practice every day. It was an easy promise to keep.

The days passed quickly, and I suddenly realized Sabrina hadn't been around to see me in a while. I mentioned this to Sabrina's grandmother on my next visit.

"Ria, go and see her," Mrs. Peabody said. "Her mother says she just sits in her room."

So I went over, kicking myself for being such a lousy friend. I found her sprawled across her bed, surrounded by countless sheets of paper.

"Sabrina, . . ." I started.

But she cut off the apology I'd rehearsed, and when she turned, I saw the familiar grin. "Ria, don't worry! I've been putting my misery to practical use."

We were back to normal. Sabrina was up to something, and I didn't know what it was—yet.

She turned thoughtful. "Ria, when I handed the guitar over to you, that was the lowest I've ever felt. Then it hit me, that's what music is all about. How people feel."

"Feelings?"

"Sure, Ria."

The sheets of paper were songs she'd written, setting down the words and composing the tunes by ear. The first

one needed no explanation. "The C Chord Misery Blues."
She sang it for me, and it was a great song. There are
different kinds of music talent. Sabrina was a composer.

The second song was "Lost and Lonesome."

"That's how I felt," Sabrina said, "watching you play the
guitar. I don't mean the songs are about me *really*, but the
feeling in them is mine. And once the misery was in the
music, it wasn't in me anymore."

"Upriver Rock" was a happy, upbeat tune. She had a
dozen first-rate songs. I'd been a rock music fan long
enough to know the difference between quality material and
kids' stuff.

Later, when Mrs. Peabody heard the songs, she agreed. I
guess I shouldn't have been surprised. Sabrina may change
course, but she never quits.

"I don't know what to say, Sabrina!"

"Don't say anything. Sing. We have to rehearse."

She'd even come up with a name for the group. The
Mathematics. Lead guitar and tambourine with both of us
on vocals.

I don't really want to talk about the demo we made, but I will anyway. We sent it to every record company we'd ever heard of—and nothing happened. Nothing at all. Zero. Zip. When people tell you the record business is tough, they aren't kidding.

Then a funny thing happened. We got a helping hand from—of all people—the post office. Sabrina got a call from the manager of the local radio station.

"We've got your demo over here," he said. "The post office got it mixed in with a stack of tapes coming to the station. We played it by mistake, really—and you two aren't bad. We didn't know there was a local rock group. That's real news." He wanted to play the tape on the air. "Have you tried getting local jobs?" he asked. "The county fair? The youth center?" We hadn't. "A lot of people who aren't in the big time still earn money playing music."

He was right. After we'd been on local radio, we began getting jobs around town. Our first job was a pancake supper, and they paid us in pancakes. We ate so many I haven't been able to look at a pancake since. But after that, we started getting small checks, enough to keep us in albums with a little left over for movies.

"It's experience," the manager said. His name was Mr. Al, and he was getting to be a good friend. "You're improving. The Mathematics just might make it to the top some day."

There was more. Mr. Al knew the music business. He taped some of our material and sent it out, not to big record companies, but to small bands.

"Bands are always looking for new material," he said.

Last week a band out West paid Sabrina for permission to record "The C Chord Misery Blues." I don't mean they paid her a million dollars, but the check was nice.

So we keep learning, and hoping. In the meantime, it's a lot of fun playing music for people in our hometown.

Still, I couldn't get the check for the song off my mind.

"Sabrina," I said, one day when we were rehearsing, "I've known suffering. When we were sending out the first demo, I experienced real misery. So maybe I could be like you and write songs too. What would you think of 'I Almost Lost My Best Friend Because of an Unfortunate Misunderstanding . . . Blues'?"

She shook her head and grinned. "You're a great guitar player, Ria. Stay with the strings."

"Strings," I said. "Right." I mean, I trust Sabrina.

Meet a Reader

"I like to listen to music on the radio, and I like soft rock music best," says Jon Windness about his taste in music. But unlike the characters in "The C Chord Misery Blues," he does not play an instrument nor does he collect records.

Jon Windness from Illinois is a student in the sixth grade. Why does Jon like to read? "Because it's fun!" He likes to read articles about real sports heroes, science fiction in which the events could really happen, and solve-it-yourself mystery stories. A favorite classic is *The Wind in the Willows.* Jon says, "It's funny, and I like the animal characters who talk like people."

Jon also likes sports. He prefers playing games to being a spectator at them. Many sports appeal to him—baseball, soccer, floor hockey, golf, and tennis.

Checking Comprehension and Skills

Thinking About What You've Read

1. How does the way Ria and Sabrina get along with each other change during the story?
- 2. Why do the girls want to form a rock group?
3. What talents does each girl think she has?
4. What do the girls discover while visiting Mrs. Peabody that puts their friendship to the test?
5. If you were Ria, would you follow Sabrina and try to talk to her? Why or why not?
- 6. Why are the girls finally able to form a rock group? What effect does this have on their friendship?
- 7. What leads to the playing of The Mathematics' tape on the local radio station?
8. In a few sentences, tell the plot of this story.
9. In what two ways does Mr. Al help Sabrina receive a check for "The C Chord Misery Blues"?
10. Do you think the girls' friendship will last? Tell why.

Talking About What You've Read

Sabrina discovers that her musical talent is her ability to write songs. She knows that really good songs tell something about personal experience and feelings. What important experiences does Sabrina have in this story about which she could write a song? What feelings would she want to express? For example, how was she feeling about her plan to form a rock group? Why did Sabrina write "Lost and Lonesome?" What experience brought about these feelings?

Writing About What You've Read

List three events about which Sabrina had strong feelings. Write a song title that she might write to express her feelings about each of these events.

• Comprehension Skill: Cause and effect relationships

On Which Day of the Week Were You Born?

In "The C Chord Misery Blues," Ria was good at math. See how good you are. Birthdays are special occasions for sharing with family and friends. Follow the formula to find the day of the week on which you were born. If you already know the day, find out the day for a friend or a relative.

1. Write the last two digits of the year in which you were born. Call this number A.
2. Divide that number (A) by 4, and drop the remainder if there is one. This answer, without the remainder, is called B.
3. Find the number for the month in which you were born in the Table of Months. Call this number C.
4. On which date of the month were you born? Call this number D.
5. Add the numbers from the first four steps: A + B + C + D.
6. Divide the sum you got in step 5 by the number 7. What is the remainder from that division? (It should be a number from 0 to 6.) Find this remainder in the Table of Days. That table tells you on which day of the week you were born.

This method works for any date in the twentieth century. You can't use it to find out days before 1900. It *will* help you to find out on which day of the week a certain holiday or your next birthday will fall. In many almanacs there is a perpetual calendar. That calendar will help you see if you did the math correctly.

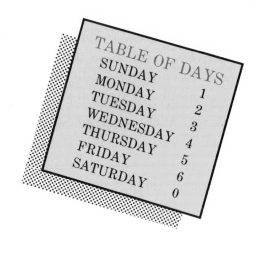

TABLE OF MONTHS

JANUARY	1 (0 in a leap year)
FEBRUARY	4 (3 in a leap year)
MARCH	4
APRIL	0
MAY	2
JUNE	5
JULY	0
AUGUST	3
SEPTEMBER	6
OCTOBER	1
NOVEMBER	4
DECEMBER	6

TABLE OF DAYS

SUNDAY	1
MONDAY	2
TUESDAY	3
WEDNESDAY	4
THURSDAY	5
FRIDAY	6
SATURDAY	0

Getting the Picture

Pretend you are Charlie getting up in the middle of the night. You want to slip downstairs for a drink of water or perhaps a snack. You know your way well in the dark. You hold on to the bannister and creep silently down. You hardly dare breathe. You are careful not to make any noises so that you won't disturb Floss whose bed is near the foot of the stairs. It is so dark there that you can't see her. It is pitch dark at the foot of the stairs.

As you read this, were you able to put yourself in Charlie's place? Could you picture what Charlie saw and felt and heard? Did you feel as if you were really there?

You will get more out of stories and articles you read if you try to picture what's described. Pretend you are there. Use as many of your senses as you can: see, hear, taste, smell, and touch. The more clearly you can picture what you read, the more you'll get from your reading.

Todd Lewis has a goal in mind and a wonderful plan to achieve it, but he must get support from his older brothers, his parents, and a public official. How does getting along with others help Todd to achieve his goal? As you read about Todd's plan, think about the theme of the story.

Get Lost, Little Brother

by C. S. Adler

Todd lay in bed trying to bring the day into focus. Even though it was Saturday, he had awakened with a sense of urgency. He struggled to untangle himself from the dream of the night—something to do with curling up in a dark burrow for safety. Guppies were in it too, swimming past his eyes. His prettiest guppy mother had had her babies last night, and he'd stayed up late seeing to it they were secure.

He rolled out of bed and went to check the tank. It was perking along nicely, thermostat working, air bubbling. The babies were swimming pinheads in the fry crib Todd had improvised out of wire and nylon mesh. Now what was it he had to do today? The island—the town offices—the rowboat. Oh, yeah.

"Mom says if you want any pancakes you'd better get downstairs fast," Michael said from the doorway. He was wearing his baseball cap. He and Leon had a game this morning. Todd made a sudden connection. The town offices were right behind the ball field. He already had found out they were open Saturday mornings. He could hitch a ride with whoever drove his brothers to the game. Good. That solved one problem.

"Leon, how could you take the last of that syrup?" Mother was asking when Todd entered the kitchen. "Now there isn't any left for Todd. How can you be so selfish?"

"Maybe it'll teach Todd to get up on time," Dad said, and to his youngest son, "Good morning, slugabed."

"Good morning," Todd mumbled.

"Dad, are you going to watch us play this morning?" Leon asked. "You said you would last time, remember?"

• Can you picture the
scene in the kitchen?

Their father put down the agricultural supplies ad he was studying from the Saturday paper and looked at Leon. "I'm sorry, son. I told you I was short on time this weekend."

"But, Dad, all the other kids' fathers watch. Last week I pitched a no-hitter."

"Good," Dad said dryly. "Someday you'll be a pro ballplayer and make a fortune, no doubt, but meanwhile I've got a job to do if we want to eat."

"Mom works too," Leon mumbled.

"Her job has different demands. Mine is time-consuming. I'm not any fonder of the traveling I'm required to do than you are, but we'll just have to live with it," Dad said. Then his lip quirked up and he added, "I'm sorry about the ball game, Leon. I'm going to the plant. I'll try to get home in time to repair that part of the front lawn that the truck tore up."

"Can you drop Leon and Michael off at the ball field on your way to work?" Mother asked. "I could pick them up on my way back from food shopping."

"Agreed," Dad said. With a felt-tipped marker, he circled a lawn fertilizer on sale.

"Can I go too?" Todd asked casually. "To the ball field."

"How come you want to go to a baseball game?" Leon wanted to know. "You said baseball was boring. You want to watch us play?"

"Sort of," Todd said.

"Yeah?" Leon sounded as if he didn't believe it, but when he got up to take his dishes to the dishwasher, he gave Todd a brotherly whack on the back. It was the kind of whack he often gave Michael, a Leon love tap. Todd was startled, pleased, surprised, and embarrassed. He was surprised that his interest in Leon's activities should matter to Leon, pleased at Leon's token of affection, and embarrassed because he had earned it falsely. He wanted to go to the baseball field only so that he could sneak off to the town offices without anybody knowing it.

Todd sat in the back of the station wagon, leaning against the rear seat behind his brothers and facing backward. As usual, he had to watch where they'd been instead of where they were going. He was trying to figure out what to do about the rowboat. It was sure to get overlooked in Dad's long list of weekend activities.

Besides fixing the lawn, Mom wanted Dad to work on their income tax today. That would take him forever. So would reading the Sunday *Times* tomorrow. Sunday afternoon Dad and Mom were going to a reception at the museum. Todd wondered if he and his brothers could launch the rowboat alone.

Leon and Michael were talking their father's ear off about what their baseball coach had said and how the lineup was changing and whether they'd get to go to Atlanta this summer as last year's winning team had. Dad wasn't saying much in response. The country road unreeled in a long green alley behind the car.

"Hey, Dad," Todd put into a breathing space between his brothers' chatter. "How about the rowboat? Can't we get it out of the garage today?"

"Sorry, Todd. It'll have to wait."

"We could get it out ourselves," Leon said. "Some of the guys are coming over this afternoon. Four of us could handle it easy."

"No doubt, but I want to make sure of your rowing ability before I let you loose on the river."

"Boy, Dad," Leon said, "you never have time to do anything that's fun!"

Todd remembered the lawn repair job and asked, "Leon, do you think you and Michael and I could help Dad fix those ruts on the lawn? *Then* he'd have time left for the boat."

Leon turned around and eyed him narrowly. "What's with you today? You take some kind of goody pill?"

"Those ruts are so deep, I'm going to have to add soil before I seed them," Dad said.

"We could dig up sod from the river edge and sod it," Leon said. He never could resist getting involved when a job needed doing.

"Well, if you think you can," Dad said grudgingly. "I want the job done right. It's—"

"Don't worry, Dad. Michael and I can do it," Leon said.

"And me," Todd said.

"Yeah, and Todd," Leon agreed, including Todd as an afterthought.

It wasn't hard to slip away from the spotty crowd made up mostly of parents who'd come fully equipped with toddlers and dogs and babies in strollers to watch the ball game. Once the game started, Leon was concentrating too hard on his pitching to notice who was on the sidelines, and Michael was watching two teenage girls chasing a dog back in the outfield where he was stationed.

The town offices were in a low brick building not far from the ball field. As soon as Todd entered the paneled hall, he was faced with a choice of doorways, most forbiddingly closed. An arrow pointed toward the county clerk's office, which was the only door open. A woman behind a counter there directed Todd to the tax assessor's office.

There he had to work up the courage to knock. A rumble answered Todd. He knocked again. The rumble got louder. He opened the door cautiously, poised for a fast getaway if need be. A very large man at a very small desk covered with papers glared at him.

"I said, come in." The man's voice rose from the volcanic depths of his huge body. "I don't want to buy any raffle tickets, candy for good causes, or tickets to things I never plan to go to either."

"I just want to find out about an island," said Todd. "They sent me to you."

"They did, hey?" the man said. "What do you want to find out about an island?"

"Whether anybody owns it. If nobody owns it, I'd like to claim it, please."

The man sat still as a photograph. Then he set down the papers he was holding and began to heave with silent laughter. Todd was fascinated watching all the rolls from his chin down his chest to his belly shake. Finally a "hee hee" leaked out. The man wiped his eyes and his face with a clean pocket handkerchief.

- Can you picture the scene at the baseball field?

- Can you picture the tax assessor?

"Well," he said. "Well, that's the best I've heard yet. How old are you, kid—eleven, twelve?" Todd nodded. "And you're thinking of claiming an island, eh? You kids today! . . . What for?"

"So I can camp on it."

"Can't you camp on it without owning it?"

"But that'd be trespassing," Todd said.

The man nodded. "It certainly would. You're a law-abiding boy. Well, that's a point in your favor. Where is this island?"

He used the desk to push himself to his feet and walked to a wall-sized aerial photographic blowup of the town. It showed the river clearly, even the ripples out in the middle. Houses appeared as square rooftops, some dark, some light, strung out in the patterns of developments or spotted like street lamps along roads. Even the white, foaming edge of the rapids alongside the lock downriver from Todd's house was visible. The lock looked like a pair of dark dittos.

Todd said, "The island's right in front of my house on the river, but I'm not sure which square is my house."

"What's your address? We have a card to match every parcel of land in town, and that'll tell us who owns it."

A minute later the tax assessor laid a plump finger on a roof. "This is your house," he said. "But I don't see any island, do you?"

"No," Todd said. "But there's one there."

"Kind of a mystery, huh? Can you figure out how it could be there and not here on this map?"

"Maybe it's not a photograph? It's somebody's drawing?"

"Good try, good, but you missed it. No, this photograph was taken five years ago. Cost the town a pretty penny too. Your island is probably just a sandbar the river threw up since."

"But it's got a tree on it and grass," Todd said.

"Yes, well, grass doesn't take any time to grow. A tree, now—how big is it?"

"A little taller than I am."

"Well, it could be two, three years old," the tax assessor estimated.

"But can I claim the island?" Todd asked breathlessly.

The man did his silent heaving laugh again. "I don't know," he said. "I can see a grown man wanting to get away from it all, but a kid your age—what do you want to get away from?"

"My brothers."

"Your brothers? What do they do to you?"

"Plenty."

"I see. Well, you understand that island is likely to disappear one of these days. The river will take it away, just like it built it up. Maybe a flood or a storm or just a wet spring. But so long as it's there, I don't see that anyone's going to mind your taking charge of it."

"Can I put in an official claim so no one can take it away from me?" Todd asked.

"You'd have to maintain it, keep it clean, make good and proper use of it. We don't want to turn public property over to private use and have it become an eyesore. I don't want phone calls coming in from irate citizens about the scenery being spoiled."

"I'll take good care of it," Todd promised, looking the tax assessor in the eye.

"All right, then." The man's eyes squeezed shut and Todd thought he was going to laugh again, but instead he moved lightly over to a file cabinet. "Let's see now. Seems to me I have some kind of form here that fits. 'Course, your being a minor, it's not going to stand up in court, you understand. But for the purpose at hand—Here it is." He read aloud. "'The undersigned,' that's you. Sign here." He handed Todd his pen. "'. . . is hereby laying claim to the property owned by the State Department of Transportation and described hereinafter as follows.' Now you describe the island in your own words right there."

Todd described the island as shaped like a shoe and having a tree on it and being in front of property owned by Mr. and Mrs. Warren Lewis, about twenty feet off their shoreline. "All right, now," the tax assessor said. "I'll keep this on file here so I'll know who to get after if we run short on tax money this year." He smiled hugely. "Shake, son. You're now a landowner, semiofficially, and I wish you luck with your island."

"I'll be careful with it," Todd said. "Can I have a copy of that form I signed?"

"Right you are. Got to hang on to important legal documents." With a single shake of his belly, the tax assessor tore off the bottom sheet of the three and handed it to Todd. It was not too legible, but it made Todd feel secure to have the pink sheet folded in his shirt pocket.

He returned to the ball field in time for the last inning and watched Leon pitch a hitter out.

"Hurray, Leon!" Todd jumped up and yelled in an excess of good humor. "Yay, yay, yay."

Leon looked over at him and grinned. Neither he nor Michael even asked if Todd had been there the whole time. Mother came promptly at twelve. Todd squeezed in among the bags of food crammed in the rear of the small hatchback. Leon and Michael sat up front with Mother.

"Did you have a good game, boys?" she asked.

"Wicked good," Leon said.

"And how was your morning, Todd?"

"Excellent," Todd said, thinking of the signed claim in his pocket.

After lunch, Leon set to work on the lawn, with Michael and Todd following his direction uncomplainingly. Leon cut out one-foot squares of soggy lawn with a knife and used the square-edged shovel to lift each piece up with enough dirt attached to allow the grass to root easily in the new location.

Michael prepared the ruts in the front lawn by filling in the deepest parts with loose dirt dug from the back of the rosebed. Todd transported the sod in the wheelbarrow to the front yard, where he and Michael fitted it into place. By the time their father got home, the job was done.

"How's it look, Dad?" Leon asked eagerly.

"Not bad, not bad at all." Dad peered at the reasonably level expanse of sodded lawn. He nodded approval.

"Can we get the rowboat out now?" Todd asked.

"All right. Let's do it before I put my car in the garage."

Todd exulted silently. Today he had gotten everything he wanted—the island, the transportation to it—everything! Now, if only Leon didn't get too interested, it would all work out. Maybe.

Checking Comprehension and Skills

Thinking About What You've Read

1. How does getting along with others help Todd achieve his goal?
• 2. Choose one of the sentences below and explain why it is a theme of this story.

    a. If you are not afraid to try, sometimes you can do what seems impossible.

    b. When everyone works together, the benefits can be greater than you might expect.
3. Why does Todd want a place of his own? What events in the story make you think so?
4. How does the tax assessor's attitude toward Todd change during their meeting? Why?
5. How does working together help the brothers' and their father's ability to achieve their goals?
6. Which of these words would you use to describe Todd: **a.** resourceful, **b.** selfish, **c.** cooperative? Tell why.
7. If you could have your own special place, what would it be like? Tell about it.

Talking About What You've Read

Think about why Todd wants a place of his own. How do you think Todd will feel when he is finally alone on his island? How will this feeling differ from his feeling at home? What kinds of things might Todd do when he spends time on the island?

Writing About What You've Read

Imagine that you are Todd. You have just spent your first day on your island. How did you feel when you arrived? What did you do there? Write an entry in your diary. Include a sentence to describe your feelings about your first day on your island. List four activities that you carried out there.

• Literary Skills: Theme

JIGSAW PUZZLE

by Russell Hoban

My beautiful picture of pirates and treasure
Is spoiled, and almost I don't want to start
To put it together; I've lost all the pleasure
I used to find in it: there's one missing part.

I know there's one missing—they lost it, the others,
The last time they played with my puzzle—and maybe
There's more than one missing: along with the brothers
And sisters who borrow my toys there's the baby.

There's a hole in the ship or the sea that it sails on,
And I said to my father, "Well, what shall I do?
It isn't the same now that some of it's gone."
He said, "Put it together, the world's like that too."

LOOKING BACK

Thinking About the Section

In this section you have read three stories about characters who work together to reach goals. The outcome of each plan is successful because the characters are able to get along with others. The chart below shows what some of the characters did to cooperate. On a separate sheet of paper, write the information given on the chart. Then fill in the missing information about the other characters by determining what they did to cooperate.

Goal	How the Characters Cooperated	Outcome
make potato cakes and keep it a secret	Allison—cooked and cleaned up, decided how to involve Wilson Margaret— Charlie—	made potato cakes and kept their secret
form a rock group	Ria— Sabrina—wrote lyrics for rock songs Mrs. Peabody—	
	Todd— Tax Assessor— Michael and Leon—	

Writing About the Section

Now, imagine how the outcome of each story would have been different if any of the characters had refused to cooperate. Suppose that Alison had not cleaned the kitchen carefully. Suppose that instead of writing lyrics, Sabrina had just sulked and stopped talking to Ria. What might have happened if the tax assessor had thought that Todd was too young to own an island? Write a sentence that describes a different ending for each story.

2

Turning Points

Each time you reach a fork in the road your life may take a new direction. How do you react at these turning points—these times of change and uncertainty? Do you slow down, wanting to keep things as they are? Or do you rush forward, eager for something new?

In this section you'll read about the turning points faced by some special people—a Hawaiian boy who becomes a U.S. senator, an inquisitive youth who becomes a research scientist, and a deaf and blind girl who is helped by a dedicated teacher.

Finding the Main Idea and Supporting Details

In a few words, what is the picture about? Your answer will be the **topic.** The picture is about a girl studying. You can tell by the books on the table.

What is the most important idea about the topic? Is it a girl is researching career choices, is it a girl is taking notes on *Going to Law School*? The first choice is the most important, or **main idea** of the picture. The second choice gives some information about the main idea. It is a **supporting detail.**

The main idea can be implied or stated. It is always implied in a picture, but it can also be implied or stated in a paragraph or an article. When the main idea is implied, you must determine it from the information and then state it in your own words. If the main idea is stated clearly in a sentence, then you simply have to find that sentence.

The signing of the Constitution marked a turning point in our history. As you read the next passage, find the main idea and the supporting details. If the main idea is not stated, you need to determine it.

The Constitution, written in 1787, says that the President of the United States must be chosen by the voters and that elections must be held every four years. An amendment to the Constitution states that a President may hold office for no more than two full terms. If the President dies in office, or resigns, or cannot perform his or her duties for any other reason, there is no confusion about who then becomes President. An amendment to the Constitution clearly states who is next in line. That person is the Vice President. The Executive Office of the United States government has always passed from one President to the next according to the Constitution.

1. In a word or two, what is the topic of the passage?

To answer question 1, ask yourself, "What is the passage about?" The answer is the Constitution because all of the sentences tell about the Constitution.

2. What is the main idea? State it in your own words.

To answer question 2, decide what is the most important idea about the topic. For this passage, the main idea is implied, so you must determine it. Ask yourself what idea all the sentences tell about the Constitution. Here is one way to state the main idea: *The Constitution states the rules that govern the selection of the President.*

3. What are the details that support this main idea?

Practicing the Main Idea and Supporting Details

Read the paragraphs below to find out the main idea.

When Barbara Jordan was in the tenth grade, she heard a speech by a lawyer from Chicago. She was very impressed. She decided to become a lawyer just like the speaker, Edith Spurlock Sampson. Her speech marked a turning point in Barbara Jordan's life.

Jordan studied law at Boston University in Boston, Massachusetts. After graduation from law school in 1959, she could have stayed in Boston and enjoyed an easy life. But Jordan decided to return home to Texas. The civil rights movement had started. Many blacks and whites were working together to end segregation. They were working to make certain the law would be equal for everyone, black or white. Barbara Jordan wanted to take part in this struggle. As a lawyer, she knew she could help change things.

1. What is the topic of the article?
2. What is the main idea of the article?
3. What are the details that support this main idea?

Tips for Reading on Your Own

- Ask yourself what the paragraph or article is all about. Your answer will be the topic.
- Look for a sentence that gives the most important, or main, idea about the topic. If you can't find it, decide what is the important idea that all the sentences state about the topic. Put that idea into a sentence, which will be the main idea.
- Look for details—small pieces of information—that support or tell more about the main idea.

What kind of event do you think can change a life, perhaps forever? Several turning points shaped the life of Daniel Inouye (in nō′wā), U.S. senator from Hawaii. Determine the main idea of this article as you read.

Go for Broke:
DANIEL INOUYE

by Teri Crawford

The first elected representative from the new state of Hawaii was ready to take the oath of office. The Speaker of the House began the ceremony by saying, "Raise your right hand and repeat after me." Daniel Inouye raised his left hand instead and repeated the words, "I, Daniel Ken Inouye, do solemnly swear that I will support and defend the Constitution of the United States."

Raising his left hand instead of his right was symbolic of the long road Inouye had traveled before he became a member of Congress in 1959. As a U.S. soldier he had been seriously injured in a battle during World War II and had lost his right arm as a result. But this didn't stop him. He continued to live up to his combat team's motto, "Go for Broke!"

Early Education

Inouye showed perseverance even when he was a young boy in Hawaii. Born in 1924, Inouye was the oldest child in a poor Japanese-American family. He took seriously the fact that he was expected to look after his younger brothers and sister. He earned money by baby-sitting, mowing lawns, and cutting his friends' hair. He also taught tourists how to stand on a surfboard and ride the waves to the shore. He went to both an American school and a Japanese school, where he learned about the history and the customs of Japan.

Hawaii was a beautiful place in which to grow up, but it also had its problems. Even though Hawaii was a U.S. territory, it had been settled by many different groups— Polynesians, Japanese, Chinese, and Europeans. All of them considered themselves to be Americans, but there were conflicts between the darker-skinned Asian people and the white people in charge of the government. Some whites made it hard for Asians to find good jobs and housing. Many white children were not allowed to play with *Nisei* (nē′sā′), the children of Japanese immigrants.

It was difficult for Asian children to get good schooling. Around the age of twelve, all children were given a test to see how well they spoke English. Those who passed were sent to the English standard schools, which were far superior to other schools. Most white children had no trouble passing this test. Most Nisei children, however, had learned English as a second language, and many of them spoke a combination of English and a primary language such as Japanese or Hawaiian. Only a few were able to pass the test.

Daniel K. Inouye, sister Mae Masako (mä'ā mä sä'kō), and brothers John and Robert (from left to right)— taken in 1934

Inouye failed the test, but he did not let this stop him. He was determined to become a surgeon. He had been impressed by two doctors. One doctor had taken care of his grandmother, and another doctor had treated him when he broke his arm and needed surgery. He also attended a first-aid class every day after school.

As Inouye became a young man, however, he found his boyhood dream tragically interrupted.

The World Goes to War

In 1941, when Daniel Inouye was seventeen years old, World War II was raging in Europe. The United States was one of the few Western nations not involved in it. But the country soon found itself hurled into the conflict on the morning of December 7, when the Japanese attacked and bombed the U.S. naval base in Pearl Harbor, Hawaii. Most of the ships anchored in the harbor were either sunk or severely damaged. More than ten thousand people were killed.

The attack was especially painful for Japanese-Americans. They were shocked and angered that their ancestral country attacked their adopted country. They were also fearful that other Americans might question the loyalty of Americans of Japanese descent. They were right to worry. On the mainland, many Japanese-Americans were treated badly, and hundreds were forced to leave their homes and live in internment camps often far from where they lived.

The situation in Hawaii was not so difficult since more than half of the population was of Asian descent. At first, however, Nisei who wished to prove their loyalty by fighting for the United States were not allowed to enlist in the armed forces. Inouye was only one of the many who wanted to serve. The Nisei were able to find different ways to help their country. In addition to taking premed courses at the university, Inouye volunteered as a medical aide and began to work long hours.

He saw a further opportunity to become involved when, in 1943, the decision was made to allow Nisei to enlist in the army. On the first day the new ruling took effect, Inouye, along with more than a thousand other Nisei, enlisted. But because he was a medical student and an aide, he was considered too valuable to become a soldier. His enlistment request was refused.

Inouye was now forced to make a decision. Should he continue with his medical studies or find a way to join the army? It didn't take him long to make up his mind. He quit his studies at the university and his job as a medical aide. Two days later he was accepted into the army. He temporarily set aside his goal to become a surgeon.

Inouye became a member of the 442nd Combat Team, which was made up entirely of Nisei. Throughout the war in Europe, the 442nd held true to its motto, "Go for Broke!" They gave it all they had and became known as one of the bravest, most highly decorated units in the United States Army.

Inouye began his service as a private, but he moved up quickly. He received a battlefield commission as a second lieutenant and eventually became a captain.

The war ended for Inouye in April 1945, only eleven days before the enemy surrendered in Europe. Inouye's

Review at the presentation of awards to the 442nd Regiment Combat Team in Locco, Italy, July 4, 1945

division was on a rescue mission of the 1st Battalion of the 141st Infantry, which was surrounded by the Germans. As Inouye led his men up a hill held by German soldiers, bullets struck his abdomen, his leg, and his right elbow. Even though he was hurt badly, Inouye used his left hand to fire his gun. He did not seek medical help until he was sure the hill had been won. For his bravery, he received many medals, including the Distinguished Service Cross, the Bronze Star, and the Purple Heart. His arm was so badly injured the doctors were forced to amputate it to save his life.

Forming New Goals

As he lay in his hospital bed, Inouye realized he had to decide what to do with his life. He had reached a major turning point. He could no longer become a surgeon, but he still wanted a career in which he could help people. He decided to go back to school and study law. He knew there were many injustices a good lawyer could fight against. He even thought he might enter politics. Many changes could be made by changing the laws.

Inouye had chosen another long road. Two years passed before he was well enough to reenter the University of Hawaii. His time in the hospital was well spent. His many friends helped him with his English. They also brought him many books they thought he should read. When he at last went back to school, he became active in student government and in veterans' organizations. He also became active in politics to help Asian-Americans gain rights to education and jobs, which he realized would be especially important when Hawaii was granted statehood. During his student days, Inouye changed his life in another way. He met and fell in love with Margaret Awamura (ä'wä mu̇ r'ä), a Japanese-American teacher. They soon married.

After graduating from the University of Hawaii, Inouye wanted a firsthand look at national politics. The Inouyes traveled to Washington, D.C., where he studied for a law degree. When he graduated, he returned to Hawaii and entered the political world.

By the time Inouye returned home, the population of Asian-Americans in the Hawaiian territory had become the largest single voting group. Inouye's friends encouraged him to run for election to the territorial House of Representatives even though he was not yet thirty years old. He was at first reluctant to try, but his old determination told him to go for broke. In 1954 he became a representative.

That was only the beginning of Inouye's political career. After four years, he ran for the territorial Senate and was easily elected.

The Road to the Senate

In 1959 Inouye believed that an even greater opportunity lay ahead of him. In March Congress passed a bill making Hawaii the fiftieth state. The Hawaiian people were then able to elect two senators and a representative to the U.S. Congress. Inouye ran for the House and got 111,733 votes, the highest number of votes ever received by a candidate in Hawaii. Daniel Inouye became Hawaii's first representative and the first Japanese-American member of Congress.

Inouye's first move as a representative surprised many people. He turned down an offer to serve on the powerful and influential Foreign Affairs Committee. Instead, he agreed to serve on the Committee on Agriculture. More than anything else, Inouye wanted to help the people of his state. Much of Hawaii's economy was based on the huge sugar and pineapple industries. This made agriculture a very important matter.

September 1964—Senator and Mrs. Daniel K. Inouye and Daniel K. Inouye, Jr. Daniel, Jr., was two months old.

Another opportunity to help the Hawaiian people came in 1962, when Inouye was elected to the Senate. As a senator, he worked to pass laws protecting civil rights and giving welfare benefits to people of all races. The people rewarded him by voting for him every time he ran for the Senate.

Daniel Inouye expressed his feelings in a book he wrote for his son, Ken, who was born in 1964. In *Journey to Washington,* Inouye tells the story of his struggles and his triumphs. In the foreword he says, "My life is really not so very different from all the millions of others that have contributed to the American melting pot. My forebearers came from the Orient and it is true that their facial characteristics set them apart from Americans whose roots are in the Western world. But their problems of assimilation were exactly the same: to find work, to maintain a pride in their heritage while adapting to the culture of a strange new land, and slowly, step by painful step, to work their way up the social and economic ladder toward independence and full acceptance by their fellow countrymen."

Checking Comprehension and Skills

Thinking About What You've Read

1. Name three events that were turning points in Inouye's life. Tell how each one changed his life.
• 2. What is the topic of this article? State the main idea in your own words.
3. What was Inouye's boyhood ambition? What experiences influenced this choice?
4. Why did Inouye choose to study law? What personal qualities does this decision reveal?
5. How did statehood for Hawaii give Inouye an even greater opportunity to help people?
6. Give three details from the article that show that Daniel Inouye is a man of determination.
7. What do Inouye's three career choices—surgeon—lawyer—politician—have in common?
8. What does the motto "Go for Broke!" mean? How does Inouye *live* by this motto?
9. Which of Daniel Inouye's qualities would you most like to have? Tell why.

Talking About What You've Read

Think about the qualities that make Daniel Inouye "a man of determination." Make a list of words that describe him. You might include the words *loyal*, *brave*, and *ambitious*. Which of Inouye's actions support each word in the list?

Writing About What You've Read

If your class were going to elect a president, you would probably choose someone with qualities like Inouye's. Using one of the words above, write a campaign slogan that would help the person get elected. Make a poster using your slogan to help your candidate become known.

• Comprehension Skill: Main idea and supporting details

Using a Dictionary to Find Appropriate Meaning

Judge Rules Fairly on Each Case

Look at the above illustration. Does it match the title of this selection? The artist probably had a question about how to illustrate the headline. By looking in a dictionary or a glossary, the artist could have found the answer.

Look in the glossary at the back of your book to find the entry word *case*. Notice that there are two entries for *case* with a small raised number 1 after the first entry and a raised 2 after the second entry. *Case¹* and *case²* are called **homographs.** Homographs are words that have the same spellings but different meanings and word origins. Sometimes homographs have different pronunciations. The entry also tells the part of speech for each meaning. The *n* in italics at the end of an entry is an abbreviation that stands for noun. The *v* in italics at the end of an entry stands for verb.

Read the definitions for *case¹*. The second definition fits the meaning in the sentence about the judge. Read the definition for *case²*. The first definition of *case²* is the one the judge was confused about in the sentence. This meaning is a noun also. The second definition for *case²* is a verb.

Two phrases are listed under *case¹*, *in any case* and *in case*. These phrases are **idioms.** Notice that the meaning of an idiom is not the same as the ordinary meanings of the words that make up the phrase.

Now look for the entry word *present*. *Present* is a homograph. Homographs are words that are spelled the same but are pronounced differently. Read these sentences:

1. Everyone was *present* for the ceremony.
2. We watched the President *present* the award.

In the first sentence, *present* has the meaning of definition 1 in the entry for *present¹*. It is an adjective. In the second sentence, *present* has the meaning of definition 1 in *present²*, and is a verb.

Practicing Finding Appropriate Meanings

Look in a dictionary or the glossary of your book for the underlined words in the sentences below. Decide which numbered definition in the entry fits each sentence. Also find the part of speech for that definition.

1. We looked at the <u>cells</u> through a microscope.
2. We had spread them on small glass <u>slides</u>.
3. Make sure to balance the <u>scales</u>.
4. <u>Light</u> the Bunsen burner.

Look at the idioms after the entry for *light²*. What does *make light of* mean in this sentence?

5. Please don't <u>make light of</u> this serious situation and joke about it.

Tips for Reading on Your Own

- When you use a dictionary or a glossary, read all the definitions for each entry word to find the appropriate meaning.
- If an entry word is a homograph with a small raised number, look for another entry word with the same spelling but a different origin or meaning.
- Remember that other dictionary features may help you, too. Idioms follow entries, and parts of speech labels help you to choose an appropriate meaning.

In 1966, when Richard Ebright was in second grade, he read a book that opened the world of science to him. The book marked a turning point for Ebright—one that would lead to his lifetime career choice. Note how the use of a list and a graph in this article gives you additional information about Ebright's work.

The Making of a Scientist

by Robert W. Peterson

At the age of twenty-two, a former "scout of the year" excited the scientific world with a new theory on how cells work. Richard H. Ebright and his college roommate explained the theory in an article in the *Proceedings of the National Academy of Science.*

It was the first time this important scientific journal had ever published the work of college students. In sports, that would be like making the big leagues at the age of fifteen and hitting a home run your first time at bat. For Richard Ebright, it was the latest in a long string of achievements in science and other fields. And it all started with butterflies.

An only child, Ebright grew up north of Reading, Pennsylvania. "There wasn't much I could do there," he said. "I certainly couldn't play football or baseball with a team of one. But there was one thing I could do—collect things."

So he did, and did he ever! Beginning in kindergarten, Ebright collected butterflies with the same determination that has marked all his activities. He also collected rocks, fossils, and coins. He became an eager astronomer, too, sometimes stargazing all night.

From the first he had a driving curiosity along with a bright mind. He also had a mother who encouraged his interest in learning. She took him on trips, bought him telescopes, microscopes, cameras, mounting materials, and other equipment and helped him in many other ways.

"I was his only companion until he started school," his mother said. "After that I would bring home friends for him. But at night we just did things together. Richie was my whole life after his father died when Richie was in third grade."

She and her son spent almost every evening at the dining room table. "If he didn't have things to do, I found work for him—not physical work, but learning things," his mother said. "He liked it. He wanted to learn."

And learn he did. He earned top grades in school. "On everyday things he was just like every other kid," his mother said.

By the time he was in second grade, Ebright had collected all twenty-five species of butterflies found around his hometown. (See list below.) "That probably would have been the end of my butterfly collecting," he said. "But then my mother got me a children's book called *The Travels of Monarch X.*" That book, which told how monarch butterflies migrate to Central America, opened the world of science to the eager young collector.

Species and Subspecies of Butterflies Collected in Six Weeks in Reading, Pennsylvania

Gossamer-Winged Butterflies
white M hairstreak
acadian hairstreak
bronze copper
bog copper
purplish copper
eastern-tailed blue
melissa blue
silvery blue

Snout Butterfly

Wood Nymphs and Satyrs
eyed brown
wood nymph (grayling)

Monarchs
monarch or milkweed

Whites and Sulphurs
olympia
cloudless sulphur
European cabbage

Brush-Footed Butterflies
variegated fritillary
Harris's checkerspot
pearl crescent
mourning cloak
painted lady
buckeye
viceroy
white admiral
red-spotted purple
hackberry

At the end of the book, readers were invited to help study butterfly migrations. They were asked to tag butterflies for research by Dr. Frederick A. Urquhart of the University of Toronto, Canada. Ebright's mother wrote to Dr. Urquhart, and soon Ebright was attaching light adhesive tags to the wings of monarchs. Anyone who found a tagged butterfly was asked to send the tag to Dr. Urquhart.

The butterfly collecting season around Reading lasts six weeks in late summer. (See graph below.) If you're going to chase them one by one, you won't catch very many. So the next step for Ebright was to raise a flock of butterflies. He would catch a female monarch, take her eggs, and raise them in his basement through their life cycle, from egg to caterpillar to pupa to adult butterfly. Then he would tag the butterflies' wings and let them go. For several years his basement was home to thousands of monarchs in different stages of development.

"Eventually I began to lose interest in tagging butterflies. It's tedious and there's not much feedback," Ebright said. "In all the time I did it," he laughed, "only two butterflies I had tagged were recaptured—and they were not more than seventy-five miles from where I lived."

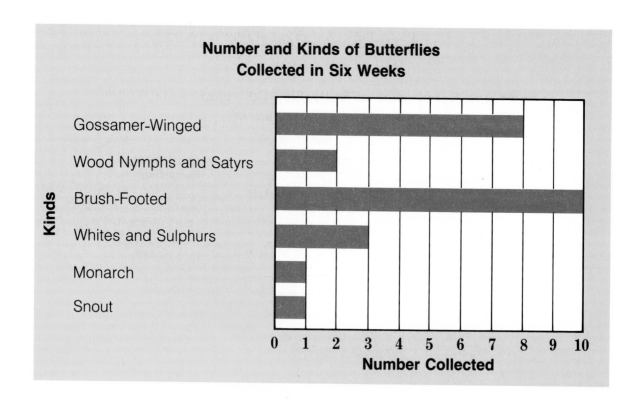

Number and Kinds of Butterflies Collected in Six Weeks

Then in seventh grade he got a hint of what real science is when he entered a county science fair—and lost. "It was really a sad feeling to sit there and not get anything while everybody else had won something," Ebright said. His entry was slides of frog tissues, which he showed under a microscope. He realized the winners had tried to do real experiments, not simply make a neat display.

Already the competitive spirit that drives Richard Ebright was appearing. "I knew that for the next year's fair I would have to do a real experiment," he said. "The subject I knew most about was the insect work I'd been doing in the past several years."

So he wrote to Dr. Urquhart for ideas, and back came a stack of suggestions for experiments. Those kept Ebright busy all through high school and led to prize projects in county and international science fairs.

For his eighth grade project, Ebright tried to find the cause of a viral disease that kills nearly all monarch caterpillars every few years. Ebright thought the disease might be carried by a beetle. He tried raising caterpillars in the presence of beetles. "I didn't get any real results," he said. "But I went ahead and showed that I had tried the experiment. This time I won."

The next year his science fair project was testing the theory that viceroy

Can you distinguish the monarch butterfly, top, from the viceroy butterfly, bottom?

butterflies copy monarchs. The theory was that viceroys look like monarchs because monarchs don't taste good to birds. Viceroys, on the other hand, do taste good to birds. So the more they look like monarchs, the less likely they are to become a bird's dinner.

Ebright's project was to see whether, in fact, birds would eat monarchs. He found that a starling would not eat ordinary bird food. It *would* eat all the monarchs it could get. (Ebright said later research by other people shows viceroys probably do copy the monarch.) This project placed first in the zoology division and third overall in the county science fair.

In his second year in high school, Richard Ebright began the research that led to his discovery of an unknown insect hormone. Indirectly, it also led to his new theory on the life of cells.

The question he tried to answer was simple: What is the purpose of the twelve tiny gold spots on a monarch pupa?

"Everyone assumed the spots were just ornamental," Ebright said. "But Dr. Urquhart didn't believe it."

To find the answer, Ebright and another excellent science student first had to build a device that showed that the spots were producing a hormone necessary for the butterfly's full development.

See the tiny gold spots on a monarch pupa.

This project won Ebright first place in the county fair and entry into the International Science and Engineering Fair. There he won third place for zoology. He also got a chance to work during the summer at the entomology (en'tə mol'ə jē) laboratory of the Walter Reed Army Institute of Research.

As a high school junior, Richard Ebright continued his advanced experiments on the monarch pupa. That year his project won first place at the International Science Fair and gave him another chance to work in the army lab during the summer.

In his senior year, he went a step further. He grew cells from a monarch's wing in a culture and showed that the cells would divide and develop into normal butterfly wing scales only if they were fed the hormone from the gold spots. That project won first place for zoology at the International Fair. He spent the summer after graduation doing further work at the army lab and at the U.S. Department of Agriculture's laboratory.

The following summer, after his freshman year at Harvard University, Ebright went back to the Department of Agriculture's lab and did more work on the gold spots' hormone. Using the lab's sophisticated instruments, he was able to identify the hormone's chemical structure.

A year-and-a-half later, during his junior year, Ebright got the idea for his new theory about cell life. It came while he was looking at X-ray photos of the chemical structure of a hormone.

When he saw those photos, Ebright didn't shout, "Eureka!" or even, "I've got it!" But he believed that, along with his findings about insect hormones, the photos gave him the answer to one of biology's puzzles: how the cell can "read" the blueprint of its DNA. DNA is the substance in the nucleus of a cell that controls heredity. It determines the form and function of the cell. Thus DNA is the blueprint for life.

Ebright and his college roommate, James R. Wong, worked all that night drawing pictures and constructing plastic models of molecules to show how it could happen. Together they later wrote the paper that explained the theory.

Surprising no one who knows him, Richard Ebright graduated from Harvard with highest honors, second in his class of 1,510. Ebright went on to become a graduate student researcher at Harvard Medical School. There he began doing experiments to test his theory.

If the theory proves correct, it will be a big step toward understanding the processes of life. It might also lead to new ideas for preventing some types of cancer and other diseases. All of this is possible because of Ebright's scientific curiosity. His high school research into the purpose of the spots on a monarch pupa eventually led him to his theory about cell life.

Richard Ebright has been interested in science since he first began collecting butterflies—but not so deeply that he hasn't time for other interests. Ebright also became a champion debater and public speaker and a good canoeist and all-around outdoorsperson. He is also an expert photographer, particularly of nature and scientific exhibits.

In high school Richard Ebright was a straight-A student. Because learning was easy, he turned a lot of his energy toward the Debating and Model United Nations clubs. He also found someone to admire, Richard A. Weiherer, his social studies teacher and adviser to both clubs. "Mr. Weiherer was the perfect person for me then. He opened my mind to new ideas," Ebright said.

"Richard would always give that extra effort," Mr. Weiherer said. "What pleased me was, here was this person who put in three or four hours at night doing debate research besides doing all his research with butterflies and his other interests.

"Richard was competitive," Mr. Weiherer continued, "but not in a bad sense." He explained, "Richard wasn't interested in winning for winning's sake or winning to get a prize. Rather, he was winning because he wanted to do the best job he could. For the right reasons, he wants to be the best."

And that is one of the ingredients in the making of a scientist. Start with a first-rate mind, add curiosity, and mix in the will to win for the right reasons. Ebright has these qualities. From the time the book *The Travels of Monarch X* opened the world of science to him, Richard Ebright has never lost his scientific curiosity.

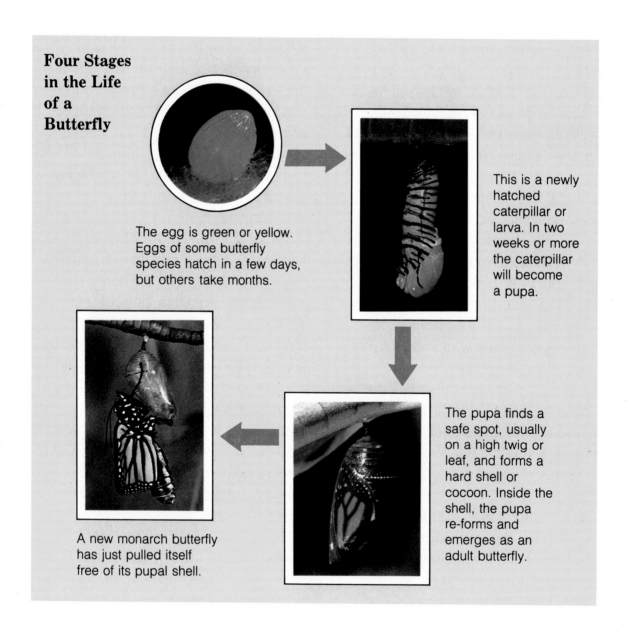

Four Stages in the Life of a Butterfly

The egg is green or yellow. Eggs of some butterfly species hatch in a few days, but others take months.

This is a newly hatched caterpillar or larva. In two weeks or more the caterpillar will become a pupa.

The pupa finds a safe spot, usually on a high twig or leaf, and forms a hard shell or cocoon. Inside the shell, the pupa re-forms and emerges as an adult butterfly.

A new monarch butterfly has just pulled itself free of its pupal shell.

Checking Comprehension and Skills

Thinking About What You've Read

1. How did a book cause a turning point in Richard Ebright's life? What is the name of the book?
2. If you lived in an isolated area, how would you spend your free time? Why?
3. Give two examples of how Dr. Urquhart influenced Ebright.
• 4. Using the list on page 77, determine the number of butterfly species that Ebright collected. How many subspecies of brush-footed butterflies did he collect?
• 5. Use the graph on page 78. How many more brush-footed than gossamer-winged butterflies did Ebright collect?
6. When Ebright first studied the gold spots on the monarch pupa, what question was he trying to answer about them? What discovery did his research lead to?
7. What question has Ebright's latest work tried to answer? What effects might his theory have, if it is correct?
8. What three qualities helped Ebright become a successful scientist?

Talking About What You've Read

Imagine that you have been assigned to write a newspaper article about Richard Ebright when he was an eighth grader and won the science fair. What questions would you ask, using the words *who, what, where, when, why,* and *how*?

Writing About What You've Read

Write three questions you would ask Richard about his experiment and about winning the prize. Write two questions you would ask the judges about their decision. Now answer the questions. Revise your work so that it resembles a news article. Write a one-line headline for your article.

• Study Skills: Graphs and lists

To Look at Any Thing

by John Moffitt

To look at any thing,
If you would know that thing,
You must look at it long:
To look at this green and say
"I have seen spring in these
Woods," will not do—you must
Be the thing you see:
You must be the dark snakes of
Stems and ferny plumes of leaves,
You must enter in
To the small silences between
The leaves,
You must take your time
And touch the very peace
They issue from.

Checking Your Progress

Camilla was already a talented figure skater, but she wanted to get better. So she found a good coach. During the first lesson, the coach shouted instructions to Camilla as she skated. "Keep your ankles straight. Watch your posture! Bend your knees before you jump!"

During the next lesson, Camilla tried to recall everything the coach had said. As she was skating, she asked herself, "Are my ankles straight? How's my posture? Am I bending my knees?" This time the coach said things like, "That's right, your ankles are absolutely straight."

Camilla became a superior skater because she kept checking on her progress. As she skated, she did all the things the coach had instructed her to do.

If you remember to check on your progress, you can get better at almost anything, even reading. As you read, you can ask yourself questions to make sure that you comprehend what you're reading. Try asking questions like these: Do I know what all the words mean? Does each sentence make sense to me? Am I following the main idea of the article or action of the story? Do I understand what the author is saying?

If you are unsure of your answers, try getting help. Camilla had a coach to help her, and you have coaches, too. Your teacher is the best coach, but you can also get help from a dictionary, an encyclopedia, or even a friend. If you remember what the coach tells you, you'll be more certain of your answers the next time you read.

You're a pretty talented reader already. Why not try to get a little better? Check yourself!

Can you imagine what learning would be like if you could neither see nor hear? The silence and darkness of Helen Keller's world made her life very difficult until a teacher helped her reach a major turning point. Notice how the author of this biography uses facts to describe this major event in Helen's education.

Miracle at the Pump House

by Catherine Owens Peare

"Phantom"—Helen Keller's own name for herself as a child—stood in the doorway sensing the excitement of a new arrival. She felt the vibration of a strange footstep on the porch, then another footstep coming closer. Strangers were often enemies. She bent her head down and charged into the newcomer, and the newcomer fell back. Again the footsteps came toward her, and the stranger tried to put arms around her. Helen drove off Miss Sullivan's embrace with kicks and punches.

She discovered that the stranger had a bag, and she grabbed the bag and darted into the house. When her mother caught up with her and tried to take the bag away, she fought. She knew Mother would give in. Mother always gave in.

But Anne Sullivan encouraged her to keep the bag and carry it upstairs. Soon a trunk was brought into the room. Helen flung herself against it, exploring the lid with her fingers until she found the lock. Miss Sullivan gave her the

Helen and Teacher,
Miss Anne Sullivan

key and allowed her to unlock the trunk and lift the lid.
Helen plunged her hands down into the contents, feeling
everything.

The newcomer lifted a doll out of the trunk and laid it in
Helen's arms. After that she did something very strange
indeed. She held one of Helen's hands and formed curious
figures in her palm. First she held her thumb and middle
finger together while her index finger stood upright. Then
she formed a circle by joining her thumb and first finger.
Finally she spread her thumb and index finger as far apart
as they would go.

• Do you understand
what Miss Sullivan
is doing?

With a sudden, wild leap Helen darted for the door. But the stranger caught hold of her and brought her back, forcing her into a chair. Helen fought and raged, but the stranger was strong. She did not give in the way family and servants did. Helen was startled to feel a piece of cake being placed in her hand. She gobbled it down quickly before it could be taken away. The stranger did another trick with her fingers. On Helen's palm she formed an open circle with her thumb and first finger; next she closed her fist for a moment. She followed that by placing her thumb between her second and third fingers and curling her last two fingers under. Finally she held all her fingertips together against her thumb.

That was enough! Helen tore loose and bolted out of the room and down the stairs—to Mother, to Father, to her half brother, to the cook, to anybody whom she could manage.

But at dinner the stranger sat next to her. Helen had her own way of eating, and no one had ever tried to stop her. She stumbled and groped her way from place to place. She snatched and grabbed from other people's plates, sticking her fingers into anything at all. When Helen came to the visitor, her hand was slapped away. She reached out for the visitor's plate again. Another slap! She flung herself forward and was lifted bodily back. Now she was forced into her own chair again and made to sit there. Once more she was raging, fighting, kicking. She broke away and found all the other chairs empty. Her family had deserted her, left her alone with this enemy!

Again the enemy took hold of her, made her sit down, forced a spoon into her hand, made her eat from her own plate.

When the ordeal finally ended, she broke away and ran out of the dining room—to Mother, to Mother's arms. Mother's eyes were wet. Mother was crying. Mother was sorry.

Every day there were battles with the newcomer. There were battles when she had to take her bath. There were battles when she had to comb her hair and button her shoes. And always those finger tricks; even Mother and Father were doing them. Since the trick for cake usually brought her a piece of cake, Helen shrewdly began to learn others.

If battles with her new governess grew unbearable, Helen could seek out Martha Washington, a child her own age, daughter of their cook, and bully and boss her. Martha's pigtails were short because Helen had once clipped them off with a pair of scissors.

Or Helen could simply romp with her father's hunting dogs and forget there was such a thing in the house as a governess. She could help feed the turkey gobblers or go hunting for the nests of guinea hens in the tall grass. She loved to burrow her way in among the big flowering shrubs, where she felt safe and protected.

There was real comfort in revenge. Helen knew about keys and locks, and she found a day when she could lock the awful intruder in her room and run away with the key. The big day of revenge came when, in one of the enemy's unguarded moments, she raised her fists in the air and brought them down on Miss Sullivan's face. Two teeth snapped off.

Helen's parents, Arthur and Kate Keller

Helen Keller when she
was six years old

An abrupt change occurred in Helen's life right after that.

Miss Sullivan took her by the hand, and they went for a carriage drive. When the carriage stopped, they alighted and entered a different house. Helen groped her way about the room, recognizing nothing until her companion placed one of her own dolls in her arms. She clung to the familiar thing. But soon Helen realized that she was alone with the stranger in a strange place. No amount of rubbing her cheek would bring Mother. Then she flung the doll away in a rage. She refused to eat, refused to wash, and gave the governess a long, violent tussle when it came time to go to bed.

- Do you understand why Miss Sullivan took Helen away?

The governess did not seem very tall, but she was strong and stubborn. For the first time in her life, Helen began to experience defeat. She grew tired, wanted to lie down and sleep, but still she struggled against the stranger's will. She would sleep on the floor or in the chair! But each time she was dragged back to the bed. At last Helen felt herself giving in. Exhausted by her own efforts and huddled close to the farthest side of the big double bed, she fell asleep.

When Helen awoke in the morning, she flung herself out of bed prepared to give further resistance. But somehow her face was washed with less effort than the night before. And after she had dressed and eaten her breakfast, she felt her companion's determined but gentle hands guiding her fingers over some soft, coarse yarn, guiding them again along a thin bone shaft with a hooked end. In a very little while Helen had grasped the idea of crocheting. As she became interested in making a chain, she forgot to hate Anne Sullivan.

- Are you following the action here? How is Helen changing?

Each day in the new house brought new skills to be learned—cards to sew, beads to string.

After about two weeks Helen had begun to accept her routine, her table manners, her tasks, her companion. The whole world seemed to grow gentler as her own raging disposition subsided.

She cocked her head suddenly one afternoon and sniffed the air, detecting a new odor in the room, something familiar—one of her father's dogs! Helen groped about until she found the silken, long-haired setter, Belle. Of all the dogs on the farm, Belle was Helen's favorite, and she quickly lifted one of Belle's paws and began to move the dog's toes in one of the finger tricks. Miss Sullivan patted Helen's head, and the approval made her feel almost happy.

Miss Sullivan soon took her by the hand and led her out the door, across a yard, to some front steps. Instantly Helen realized where she was. She was home! She had been in the little annex near home all this time. Mother and Father had not been far away. She raced up the steps and into the house and flung herself at one adult after another. She was home! Scrambling up the stairs to the second floor, she found her own room just the same. Then she felt Miss Sullivan standing behind her. Helen turned impulsively and pointed a finger at her and then at her own palm. Who was she?

"T-e-a-c-h-e-r," Anne Sullivan spelled into her hand. But the finger trick was too long to be learned at once.

Every day after that, Teacher and Helen were constant companions indoors and out, and gradually Helen learned to see with her fingers. Teacher showed her how to explore plants and animals without damaging them—chickens, grasshoppers, rabbits, squirrels, frogs, wild flowers, butterflies, trees. Grasshoppers had smooth, clear wings, but the wings of a butterfly were powdery. The bark of a tree had a curious odor, and a gentle, humming vibration ran through its huge trunk.

Hand in hand they wandered for miles over the countryside, sometimes as far as the Tennessee River, where the water rushed and churned over the dark Muscle Shoals.

For everything Helen felt or did there was a finger trick—wings, petals, riverboats, walking, running, standing, drinking.

Helen Keller reading

One morning when she was washing her face and hands, Helen pointed to the water in the basin. Teacher spelled into her hand, "W-a-t-e-r." At the breakfast table later Helen pointed to her mug of milk, and Teacher spelled, "M-i-l-k." But Helen became confused. *D-r-i-n-k* was milk, she insisted. Helen pointed to her milk again, and Teacher spelled, "M-u-g." Was *mug drink?* In another second Helen's mind was a jumble of wiggling fingers. She was frustrated, bewildered, angry—a bird trapped in a cage and beating its wings against the bars.

Quickly Teacher placed an empty mug in her hand and led her outdoors to a pump that stood near a shed in the yard. Helen stood before the pump, mug in hand.

• Are you following the action here?

Suddenly she felt cold water rushing over her hands. Teacher took one of Helen's hands and spelled, "W-a-t-e-r." While water rushed over one hand, Helen felt the letters *w-a-t-e-r* in the other.

Suddenly Helen was transfixed. She let the mug crash to the ground forgotten. A new, wonderful idea . . . back into her memory rushed that infant's word she had once spoken: *Wah-wah.* Helen grew excited; her pulse raced as understanding lighted her eager mind.

Wah-wah was *w-a-t-e-r.* It was a word! The finger tricks were words! There were words for everything. That was what Teacher was trying to tell her.

She felt Teacher rush to her and hug her. Teacher was as excited as she, crying and laughing, because at last Helen understood the concept of words.

Joyfully they ran back into the house, and Helen was surrounded by an excited household. All the rest of the day she demanded words, words, words. What was this? What was that? Even the infant Mildred—what was that? "B-a-b-y." And once more Helen pointed a persistent finger at Anne Sullivan and demanded the word that would identify *her.*

"T-e-a-c-h-e-r," Miss Sullivan spelled. "T-e-a-c-h-e-r."

The last shred of hostility and hate vanished from Helen's soul as she glowed with her sudden happiness. She felt her fingers being lifted to Teacher's face to explore its expression. The corners of the mouth were drawn up, and the cheeks were crinkled. Helen imitated the expression. And when she did, her face was no longer blank, because Helen Keller was smiling.

When bedtime finally arrived, she put her hand willingly into Teacher's and mounted the stairs. Before climbing into bed, she slipped her arms around Teacher's neck and kissed her—for the first time.

• Do you understand what the author is saying?

The following letter gives another account of the event that took place in the pump house. The letter was written by Anne Sullivan, Helen Keller's teacher. Compare the information in the biography with that in the letter.

A Letter from Anne Sullivan

April 5, 1887

I must write you a line this morning because something very important has happened. Helen has taken the second great step in her education. She has learned that *everything has a name, and that the manual alphabet is the key to everything she wants to know.*

• Do you know why the nouns *mug* and *milk* could be confused with the verb *drink?*

In a previous letter I think I wrote you that "mug" and "milk" had given Helen more trouble than all the rest. She confused the nouns with the verb "drink." She didn't know the word for "drink," but went through the pantomime of drinking whenever she spelled "mug" or "milk." This morning, while she was washing, she wanted to know the name for "water." When she wants to know the name of anything, she points to it and pats my hand. I spelled "w-a-t-e-r" and thought no more about it until after breakfast. Then it occurred to me that with the help of this new word I might succeed in straightening out the "mug-milk" difficulty. We went out to the pump house, and I made Helen hold her mug under the spout while I pumped. As the cold water gushed forth, filling the mug, I spelled "w-a-t-e-r" in Helen's free hand. The word coming so close upon the sensation of cold water rushing over her hand

Helen Keller and
Anne Sullivan

seemed to startle her. She dropped the mug and stood as one transfixed. A new light came into her face. She spelled "water" several times. Then she dropped on the ground and asked for its name and pointed to the pump and the trellis, and suddenly turning around and asked for my name. I spelled "Teacher." Just then the nurse brought Helen's little sister into the pump house, and Helen spelled "baby" and pointed to the nurse. All the way back to the house she was highly excited, and learned the name of every object she touched, so that in a few hours she had added thirty new words to her vocabulary. Here are some of them: *Door, open, shut, give, go, come,* and a great many more.

P.S.—I didn't finish my letter in time to get it posted last night, so I shall add a line. Helen got up this morning like a radiant fairy. She has flitted from object to object, asking the name of everything and kissing me for very gladness. Last night when I got in bed, she stole into my arms of her own accord and kissed me for the first time, and I thought my heart would burst, so full was it of joy.

Meet a Reader

"I thought it was exciting when Helen finally discovered that her teacher was talking to her with her fingers." That's Dennis Aldana's reaction to "Miracle at the Pump House." He continued, "I always took for granted that I could hear and speak and see. This story really made me appreciate how fortunate I am."

Dennis from Illinois is in the sixth grade. Dennis likes to read because he finds reading interesting and learns lots of things. He especially likes history books about Abraham Lincoln and his times.

When asked if he had ever had a teacher who reminded him of Anne Sullivan, he replied he had. It was his third grade teacher. Dennis said, "In that class I understood what school was really about and I started paying attention." He also said that when the teacher asked for volunteers to help teach English to an Asian-American boy, he was the first to help. The boy could not speak English and could not write using the English alphabet.

Dennis himself not only speaks English but also speaks and reads Spanish.

Checking Comprehension and Skills

Thinking About What You've Read

1. What was the major turning point in Helen's life? How did this event change her life?
2. Since Helen could neither see nor hear, what senses did she use to understand things?
3. Think about how Helen's mother and Anne Sullivan reacted to Helen. How did each woman help Helen?
4. Name two of Helen's habits that Anne Sullivan tried to correct. Was she successful, and how?
- 5. How do the two accounts of the pump house vary?
- 6. What kind of information does Anne Sullivan provide in her letter that the biographer does not?
7. How would you describe Anne Sullivan, based on the biography? How does your feeling about Miss Sullivan change after reading her letter? Why?
8. If you could have interviewed Helen Keller, what questions would you most likely have asked her? Why?

Talking About What You've Read

Suppose that you have just made a new friend who cannot see. Your friend wants to know what the color red is like. How would you describe red to your friend? What other senses would you rely on to do so? For example, if red had a smell, what would that smell be? If it had a taste, how would it taste?

Writing About What You've Read

Use your imagination. Think of as many descriptive words for the color red as you can. Make sure that your friend could use his or her other senses to understand those words. Make a list of five words and phrases that you feel describe the color red.

- Literary Skills: Types of literature—nonfiction

LOOKING BACK

Thinking About the Section

The lives of Daniel Inouye, Richard Ebright, and Helen Keller followed different roads, but each one was marked by turning points—points at which the "traveler" had to make a choice. Courage, determination, and curiosity are what make each of these people special. All three of them made wise choices and so helped direct the course of their lives.

Choose one of these people to receive a special award. Decide what quality would make this person most deserving of the award. Then consider the events in the person's life as you answer these questions:

1. Who should receive this award?
2. What quality makes this person deserving of an award?
3. What is one turning point in this person's life, when he/she showed this outstanding quality?
4. How did this event change this person's life?
5. Name one other person who influenced this person's life or who helped him/her at a turning point.

Writing About the Section

Write a paragraph about the person you have chosen to receive the special award. Copy and fill in the statement below and use it as the main idea of your paragraph. The answers you have given for the questions above will be the supporting details.

"This award is presented to _____
(insert person's name)
for showing great _____ at the turning
(insert a quality)
points in his/her life, when _____."
(describe turning point)

3

Finding Out

A painting . . . a bicycle . . . a stuffed animal. How do these items come to be? Does the process begin in the creator's mind? Does it follow a design that has been perfected through many years of use? Whether the item is original and unique or ordinary and mass-produced, probably a lot went into creating it that you may not have thought about before.

This section will help you find out what happens behind the scenes. You'll find out what goes into creating a story, how goods are produced both in a factory and by hand, and why an imitation can never be made to equal the real thing.

Drawing Conclusions

You are looking at a piece of very old sculpture. What do you think the sculpture must be like when you see all of it? Look carefully at the parts that you can see to help you find out about those that you can't see.

If you think it is horses and riders, you are right. You have just drawn a conclusion. A **conclusion** is a decision or an opinion reached after thinking about some facts and details. Conclusions are based on the facts that are given to you and on other information that you already know. You can draw conclusions from facts when you are looking at pictures, reading stories, or studying information.

In the next passage you will find out some interesting facts about the coelacanth (sē′lə kanth′). Scientists had believed this huge fish was extinct until a living example was caught in 1938. To draw conclusions about the passage, think about the facts that are given.

The discovery of one coelacanth triggered a great search for others. But it wasn't until 1952 that another was caught. Again, the fish was brought up from deep in the Indian Ocean near the Comoro Islands. Since then, more than eighty coelacanths have been caught there.

All the coelacanths have been caught on lines some 200 meters (about 650 feet) long. As one expert suggests, the Comorans may be the only people who regularly fish with such long lines. Maybe coelacanths live in other seas, and we just haven't found them.

In appearance, a coelacanth is bluish-gray with white flecks. The fish grow to about 1.5 meters (5 feet) and can weigh about 70 kilograms (150 pounds). They have tough, armorlike scales and are ferocious animals. With sharp teeth and powerful jaw muscles, a coelacanth is able to catch a rather large fish and swallow it whole.

1. What can you conclude would be a good way to search for coelacanths in other parts of the world? Explain.

To answer question 1, ask yourself what has been special about the way coelacanths have been caught near the Comoro Islands. The answer is that they have all been caught on lines some 200 meters (650 feet) long. So you could conclude that a good way to search for them in other areas would be by using lines of this length.

2. What conclusions can you draw about why the coelacanth has survived? Why do you think so?

To answer question 2, ask yourself why the coelacanth is able to protect itself. You could conclude that the coelacanth's large size, tough, armorlike scales, sharp teeth, powerful jaws, and ferocious nature probably helped it to survive.

3. What can you conclude is the reason the discovery of one coelacanth triggered a search for others? Explain.

Practicing Drawing Conclusions

When you read the story below, use details to draw conclusions and answer the questions.

The old woman toiled in the fields from dawn to dusk. Although her three sons were strong and tall, they refused to work. The old woman became so troubled about what was to become of her sons that she fell desperately ill. She summoned her sons to her bedside and told them about a hidden pot of gold. It was buried near the house, she said, but she couldn't remember exactly where. The sons would have to find it.

Soon after their mother died, the sons had no money. They began to dig near the house and then in the fields, but they couldn't find any treasure. One of the sons suggested to his brothers that since they had already dug up the land, they should plant grapevines. In a short time they had a rich vineyard with a large harvest. The brothers sold the grapes for a handsome profit. They then agreed they had found the pot of gold spoken of by their mother.

1. Why did the mother tell her sons about the gold?
2. Based on her tale, what conclusions can you draw about the mother?
3. Did the sons find what they were looking for? How do you know?
4. Did the mother really bury a pot of gold? Explain.

Tips for Reading on Your Own

- Think about the facts and details that are given. Use common sense and what you already know to come up with information that is not stated.
- Ask yourself if your conclusion makes sense.
- Back up your conclusion with information from the selection or with reasons of your own.

Do you have a favorite story—one that you enjoy hearing over and over again? As you read one of Pura Belpré's favorites, see what conclusions you can draw about the story of the Stone Dog. Then read to find out how Pura Belpré became a storyteller.

THE STONE DOG

by Pura Belpré

In Puerto Rico many years ago near the Condado Lagoon, there lived a poor fisherman. He lived alone in a hut. His only companion was his dog.

The fisherman and his dog were devoted to each other. They might be seen strolling on the white sandy beach. Or they might be seen coming through the tangle of vines along the road that led to San Juan. However, there was one place where nobody saw them together. That was in the fisherman's boat. The man never took the dog along with him.

But the dog was always beside his master as the fisherman made his little boat ready to sail. When the man pulled out to sea each morning, the dog would scamper up on the high ridge that separated the Condado Lagoon from the open sea. There he would sit and watch all day. The dog never moved until late afternoon when he saw the little boat return. Then he would race back to the shore to greet his master, and together the man and the dog would set off for San Juan to sell the fresh-caught fish.

As the years went by, the fisherman grew older, and so did the faithful dog. The fisherman still went out to sea. The dog still watched for his return, sitting on the high ridge above the lagoon.

One morning early in September, the fisherman was getting his little boat ready. All at once the dog began to bark and howl. He circled around the fisherman and tugged at his trousers. The fisherman could not remember when he had seen his dog act so strangely. He patted the dog's back, thinking the dog wanted to play, but nothing made any difference. The dog kept barking. The fisherman laughed and continued getting ready. Finally he gave the dog another pat. Then the man climbed into the boat and sailed away. The dog went to his watching place, still barking and howling.

There were numerous fishing boats out that morning. The sky was blue and the breeze gentle and fresh.

Suddenly the soft breeze changed; it began to blow wildly. The fisherman's boat was seized by the wind and whirled around. The sky darkened, and rain began to fall in torrents.

"It's a hurricane!" said the fisherman. "A hurricane blowing onshore!"

The man thought of his dog at once. Had the dog left the ridge and run home, or was he still sitting patiently there? The fisherman tried to steer his boat and veer it toward the shore. Suddenly a great wave swept over his head and tossed the boat away.

When dawn came the next morning, the hurricane was over. The sky was blue once more. The sea was so calm it was hard to believe it was the same sea that had roared and raged the night before. When the sun rose over the mountains, the families of the other fishermen ran to the shore. They watched for the return of the boats. They waited and waited, but none returned.

Then the people went slowly back to their homes to endure their grief and start a new life. As they rebuilt their village, no one gave a thought to the fisherman's dog.

Several months later a group of villagers was out gathering sea grapes. They noticed what appeared to be the figure of a dog sitting high on the ridge above the lagoon.

"Look," said one. "Isn't that the old fisherman's dog?"

"How could it be, after all this time?" said another.

To prove his point, the first man climbed the ragged stony ridge to get hold of the dog. But when he reached the spot, he found only a rock—a rock shaped like a dog. The man came down quickly. But as soon as the people looked up again, they saw the stone dog. His head was held high. His body was alert, as if ready to spring into the sea. He just sat there on top of the ridge, waiting, waiting. . . .

And there he sits today for anyone to see.

Planting Story Seeds

by Pura Belpré[1]

I grew up in a home of storytellers in Puerto Rico. The stories I heard from my family had been handed down by word of mouth for generations. These stories had once been told by the island's early settlers. Their cultures have blended to make the culture we now know as Puerto Rican.

The first people on the island were Taino Indians. They had their own kind of stories about the island. When the Spanish arrived in the 1500s, Puerto Rico was the first island they settled. Most of their stories came from Spain. Some of their stories had roots in the Orient, brought to Spain by Arab people. African people who had been brought to the island had their own beloved tales. By constant retelling, and by the creative additions of island storytellers, these stories now form the folklore background of Puerto Rico. This beautiful island has a culture enriched by old, old stories gained from many people.

As a child I enjoyed telling many of the tales that I had heard. The characters became vividly real to me. I remember that during school recess some of us would gather under

---

1. (pü'rä bel prä')

the shade of a tamarind tree. There we would take turns telling stories.

These stories came with me to the United States. I thought of myself as a storyteller. I wished to be like Johnny Appleseed, who in the United States was famous for planting apple seeds across the land. I had read about him in a book in Puerto Rico. And so I wished to plant my story seeds across the land.

Then something wonderful occurred. I began to work in the New York Public Library. Soon I was sent to its library school for further training. In a storytelling class the teacher asked the students to write a story. I recalled that when I was in the library, I had found folk and fairy tales from all over the world, but not one from Puerto Rico. How I wished that the stories I knew were among them. Here was an opportunity to do something about this lack.

So I wrote down a tale my grandmother had told me about a mouse and a cockroach, called "Perez and Martina." It was my first story seed to be planted in the United States. It became my first picture book. I planted more story seeds, and they grew too. Today I am pleased to find Puerto Rican folklore alongside the other folklore of the world.

Once I went back to Puerto Rico to do research for some Taino Indian stories. From this trip came the book *Once in Puerto Rico.* In the book appears "The Stone Dog." While working on this story, I took a taxi to the University of Puerto Rico in Rio Piedras. The driver had taken me there before. He was curious about what I was doing. I told him and said that I was working on a story I knew as a child, called "The Stone Dog."

"Have you seen it?" he asked.

"No," I answered in surprise.

"I'll show it to you. It's on our way."

He drove on, out of San Juan toward the Condado Lagoon. By and by he slowed down. Pointing to a ridge of rocks separating the lagoon from the sea, he said, "There it is. Can you see it?"

To tell the truth, I couldn't. He turned the wheel slowly, until he had the car at the right angle. "Now can you see it?" he asked.

I could not believe my eyes. Suddenly what had seemed just rocks on a ridge now had the shape of a dog. It was facing the sea, alert and ready to spring. A strange feeling came over me. It was as if I had stepped into the past. Indeed, this story had a basis in fact! I sat transfixed. The driver must have sensed my feelings. Without another word he drove on toward the university.

As I said, Puerto Rico is a beautiful island, with a culture enriched by old, old stories gained from many people. Traces of this culture are everywhere. And there are still many more story seeds waiting to be planted. . . .

Meet the Illustrator

The illustrator of "The Stone Dog," Rodrigo (rō drē′gō) Shopis, was born in New York City but lived briefly in Puerto Rico as a child. He has traveled throughout Puerto Rico as well as Mexico and Central America, and so he is well qualified to do drawings about Puerto Rican fishers.

Rodrigo Shopis doesn't feel it's necessary to go to art school to be an artist, although he attended the Cranbrook Academy of Art. As a child, his primary interest was drawing. He always carried a notebook with him, and he drew things mostly from his imagination. When he was a boy, he spent much time in museums. Two of his favorite places were the Museum of Natural History and the Museum of Modern Art; both are in New York City. Rodrigo Shopis is also a photographer. He feels that art and photography offer an opportunity to develop ideas. Creating art is more important to him than the finished art object.

Now that he is so familiar with the story, "The Stone Dog," Rodrigo Shopis has said that on his next trip to Puerto Rico he will go see the dog on the rocky ridge.

Checking Comprehension and Skills

Thinking About What You've Read

1. How did Pura Belpré come to write the story of the Stone Dog?
2. Why did Pura Belpré become a storyteller and then a writer of Puerto Rican folktales?
3. What different cultures contributed stories to form the folklore background of Puerto Rico?
4. In what way is writing stories like planting apple seeds?
5. In what ways are the fisherman and the dog devoted to each other?
6. Why doesn't the fisherman ever take the dog along with him on the boat?
• 7. Why does the dog begin to bark and howl on that early September morning?
• 8. What happens to the old fisherman?
9. For what other story would you like to know where the author got his or her idea?

Talking About What You've Read

Suppose the fisherman had paid closer attention to what the dog seemed to be trying to tell him on the day of the hurricane. How would the fisherman's actions have been different? What feelings would he have felt toward his dog? Why? How would these new developments change the story?

Writing About What You've Read

Imagine that instead of going out to sea, the fisherman had stood with his dog on the rock and watched the hurricane. The fisherman would then know that the dog had saved his life. Write three sentences that tell how the fisherman might have described this event and his feelings to his neighbors.

• Comprehension Skill: Drawing conclusions

Have you ever wanted to find out how everyday things are made? A lot of work by many people goes into making things, even something as common as a pair of jeans. Let this article take you into a factory and follow the steps in the process of turning a piece of denim into a pair of jeans.

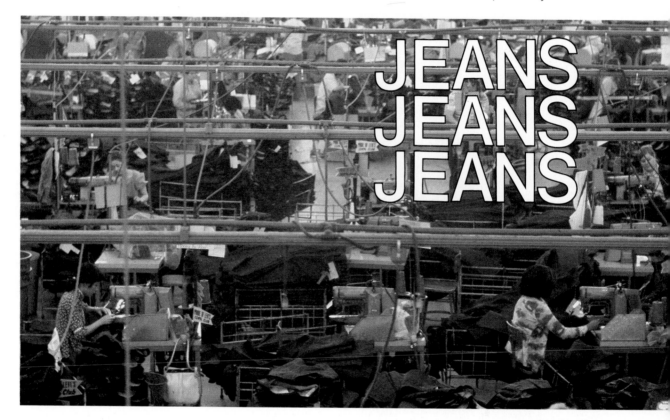

JEANS JEANS JEANS

by Luz Santana

In a city in Texas there's a big factory where my aunt makes jeans. Well, actually, she doesn't make the entire pair of pants; she sews back pockets on them. Many people work together to make one complete pair of pants.

I had an opportunity to tour the factory, and I took some pictures. All of this may look like a jumbled mess to you, but as the old saying goes, "There's method in their madness." That means the making of jeans is quite an orderly process. I hope my pictures help you understand this.

The pants begin with the pattern. The pieces for one size of pants are carefully traced onto paper.

At the same time, dark blue denim cloth is being laid out on hundred-foot long tables. Back and forth the machine rolls out the denim, until there are twenty or more layers. Any cloth that's imperfect is removed.

The pattern paper is laid over the top of the denim. Cutting machines are used to cut around each pattern, and through all the layers.

The picture below shows you what the cut pieces look like. Did you know that the word *denim* is supposed to have come from Nîmes (nēm), France? A tough cloth, called *serge de* (sėrj′ də) *Nîmes,* was made there long ago. Do you see that the word *denim* came from that name?

Next, the pieces go to be finished. The pockets are bound, that is, stitched around. This worker sews on the arcuate stitch, or one that looks like a bow. This has sometimes been nicknamed the flying seagull. Can you find it?

Another worker operates a machine that sews orange trademark tabs on back pockets.

Then the back pockets are sewn to the back part of the pants. That's the job my aunt does. There are many workers who do just this one job, just as many workers do each of the other jobs.

Then the pants get sewn together, each worker sewing together parts or adding stitching. After that, the pants are inspected for flaws. If there is a flaw, the pants go back to be redone. The workers try hard not to make mistakes, for the more pieces they turn out, the more they get paid.

Next, the final touches are added, such as belt loops and size tags. The pants go through a last inspection, and finally they are sent to be packed in boxes for shipping.

Does the making of these pants still seem a jumble to you? Take a look at the flow chart diagram on the next page. It shows you some of the steps in making the pants. It will also help you see how orderly the process is.

Putting It All Together

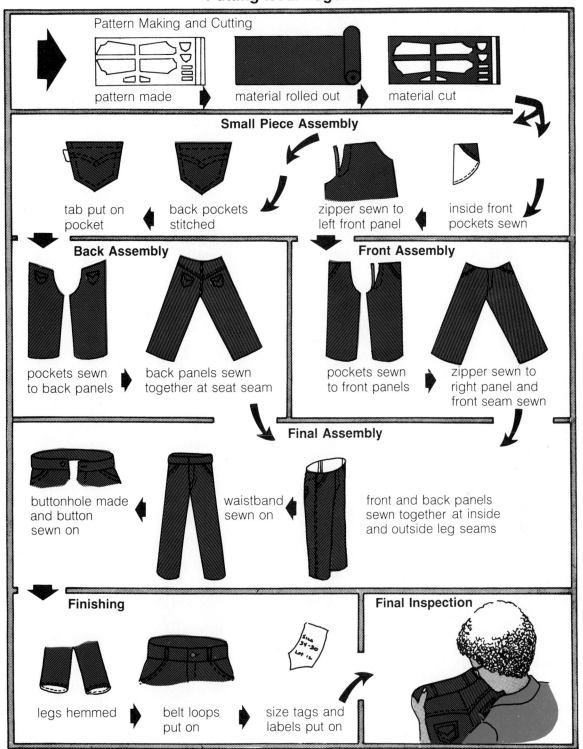

Pattern Making and Cutting

pattern made → material rolled out → material cut

Small Piece Assembly

tab put on pocket ← back pockets stitched ← zipper sewn to left front panel ← inside front pockets sewn

Back Assembly

pockets sewn to back panels → back panels sewn together at seat seam

Front Assembly

pockets sewn to front panels → zipper sewn to right panel and front seam sewn

Final Assembly

buttonhole made and button sewn on ← waistband sewn on ← front and back panels sewn together at inside and outside leg seams

Finishing

legs hemmed → belt loops put on → size tags and labels put on

Final Inspection

Now that you've found out about one process for making something, you might like to try making something yourself. Find out about a traditional Native American clown. Then follow the steps to make a paper figure that uses gravity to tumble.

The Tumbling Koshare

A Cut-Out-and-Make-It Paper Figure
by Ron Rundstrom and Pat Rosa

Have you ever watched clowns at a circus? Usually they make their audience laugh, but sometimes they teach little lessons as well.

The Pueblo Indians of the American Southwest have clowns too. They're called Koshare (ko sha′rā), and they wear black and white banded costumes. Their funny antics can be seen on many feast days and at ceremonial dances in the villages along the Rio Grande in New Mexico. The Koshare are "contrary" persons who act in ways that people should not. Their clowning exaggerates happenings in the village or copies the behavior of people at the dance. Their antics serve to point out wrongdoers and keep villagers happy. The Koshare use humor to make village life run smoothly.

You can make your own tumbling paper figure based on the Koshare.

To make a Koshare figure, place a thin piece of blank paper on page 119, and trace the Koshare figure. Then retrace it onto heavier paper or poster board. Cut it out.

Next, curl the pattern. To do this, lay the pattern upside down on a hard surface. Take a pencil and hold it flat on top of the pattern at one end. Then carefully pull the pattern out from under the pressure of the pencil while lifting the toy up. Do this with both ends until there is a curved roll in the paper.

Place one or two marbles, smooth, round stones, or a ball bearing into the box. Close up the other side, and insert that side flap under the box face. Put glue or tape on the top of both flaps if you want more strength.

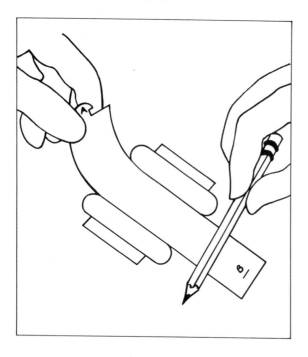

Now fold one of the side flaps and insert it under the box face. See the figure at the top of column 2. Cut slot "B." Insert tab "A" into slot "B." Glue or tape if you desire.

To make your figure tumble, place your clowns upright on a slanting surface, and let them go. If they slip, it means the slope is either too smooth or too steep. If the surface is too smooth, place a towel or a piece of cloth over it. Now watch your Koshare's funny antics.

Checking Comprehension and Skills

Thinking About What You've Read

1. What did you find out about the work that goes into making jeans?
• 2. Put in order these steps in the process:
   a. The pieces are cut.
   b. The denim is laid out.
   c. The pants are sewn together.
   d. The pockets are bound.
   e. The pattern is placed on the cloth.
3. From where is the word *denim* supposed to have come?
4. How is the arcuate stitch like a flying seagull?
5. Which step do you think is the most difficult? What information led you to draw this conclusion?
6. Why does each worker in a factory do only one job?
7. What is the role of the Koshare in Pueblo village life?
8. Why is it necessary to follow the steps carefully in order to make a tumbling Koshare figure?
• 9. Pick another process that you understand, and list the steps necessary to carry it out.

Talking About What You've Read

You have found out about the steps in two processes. You can see how important it is for each worker in the jeans factory to know his or her job. How does the flow chart help workers carry out the process of making jeans? How would a flow chart simplify the process of making a tumbling Koshare?

Writing About What You've Read

Suppose that you and your classmates were going to start a factory to produce tumbling Koshare. You would need to organize the process and make sure that each worker understood his or her job. Using the flow chart on page 117 as a guide, make a similar flow chart that shows the steps for making a tumbling Koshare.

• Comprehension Skill: Steps in a process

Michael Built a Bicycle

by Jack Prelutsky

Michael built a bicycle
unsuitable for speed,
it's crammed with more accessories
than anyone could need,
there's an AM-FM radio,
a deck to play cassettes,
a refrigerator-freezer,
and a pair of TV sets.

There are shelves for shirts and
    sweaters,
there are hangers for his jeans,
a drawer for socks and underwear,
a rack for magazines,
there's a fishtank and a birdcage
perched upon the handlebars,
a bookcase, and a telescope
to watch the moon and stars.

There's a telephone, a blender,
and a stove to cook his meals,
there's a sink to do the dishes
somehow fastened to the wheels,
there's a portable piano,
and a set of model trains,
an automatic bumbershoot
that opens when it rains.

There's a desk for typing letters
on his fabulous machine,
a stall for taking showers,
and a broom to keep things clean,
but you'll never see him ride it,
for it isn't quite complete,
Michael left no room for pedals,
and there isn't any seat.

Ask Purpose-Setting Questions

When you go shopping for jeans, you have a specific purpose in mind. You know what you are going to look for. You know the size, the price you want to pay, and perhaps the brand. You probably know in what store or stores you will shop. You will not have to spend much time shopping because you know what you want.

But suppose it's your sister's birthday and you don't know what to get her. You wander around the store or go from store to store, trying to find just the right present. You'll probably spend a lot of time looking because you don't know what you want. You don't have a specific purpose in mind.

A good reader is like a good shopper. You can be a good reader if you have a purpose for reading. Your purpose can be different for each thing you read. If you read a story, your purpose might be to enjoy yourself. If you read an article, your purpose might be to learn facts.

Before you begin reading, ask yourself, "What do I want to find out?" After you finish, think about your purpose. Did you do what you set out to do? Did you find what you were looking for?

Like a good shopper, you can become a good reader if you remember to set your purpose.

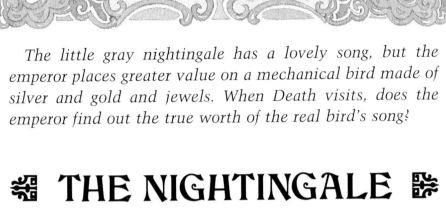

The little gray nightingale has a lovely song, but the emperor places greater value on a mechanical bird made of silver and gold and jewels. When Death visits, does the emperor find out the true worth of the real bird's song?

❈ THE NIGHTINGALE ❈

by Hans Christian Andersen

In China, as you know, the emperor is Chinese, and so are his court and all his people. This story happened a long, long time ago; and that is just the reason why you should hear it now, before it is forgotten. The emperor's palace was the most beautiful in the whole world. It was made of porcelain and had been most costly to build. It was so fragile that you had to be careful not to touch anything and that can be difficult. The gardens were filled with the loveliest flowers; the most beautiful of them had little silver bells that tinkled so you wouldn't pass by without noticing them.

Everything in the emperor's garden was most cunningly arranged. The gardens were so large that even the head gardener did not know exactly how big they were. If you kept walking you finally came to the most beautiful forest, with tall trees that mirrored themselves in deep lakes. The forest stretched all the way to the sea, which was blue and so deep that even large boats could sail so close to the shore that they were shaded by the trees. Here lived a nightingale who sang so sweetly that even the fisherman, who came every night to set his nets, would stop to rest when he heard it, and say: "How beautifully it sings!" But he couldn't listen too long, for he had work to do, and soon he would forget the bird. Yet the next night when he heard it again, he would repeat what he had said the night before: "How beautifully it sings!"

From all over the world travelers came to the emperor's city to admire his palace and gardens; but when they heard the nightingale sing, they all declared that it was the loveliest of all. When they returned to their own countries, they would write long and learned books about the city, the palace, and the garden; but they didn't forget the nightingale. No, that was always mentioned in the very first chapter. Those who could write poetry wrote long odes about the nightingale who lived in the forest, on the shores of the deep blue sea.

These books were read the whole world over; and finally one was also sent to the emperor. He sat down in his golden chair and started to read it. Every once in a while he would nod his head because it pleased him to read how his own city and his own palace and gardens were praised; but then he came to the sentence: "But the song of the nightingale is the loveliest of all."

"What!" said the emperor. "The nightingale? I don't know it, I have never heard of it; and yet it lives not only in my empire but in my very garden. That is the sort of thing one can only find out by reading books."

He called his chief courtier, who was so very noble that if anyone of a rank lower than his own, either talked to him, or dared ask him a question, he only answered, "Puh." And that didn't mean anything at all.

"There is a strange and famous bird called the nightingale," began the emperor. "It is thought to be the most marvelous thing in my empire. Why have I never heard of it?"

"I have never heard of it," answered the courtier. "It has never been presented at court."

"I want it to come this evening and sing for me," demanded the emperor. "The whole world knows of it but I do not."

"I have never heard it mentioned before," said the courtier, and bowed. "But I shall search for it and find it."

But that was more easily said than done. The courtier ran all through the palace, up the stairs and down the stairs, and through the long corridors, but none of the people whom he asked had ever heard of the nightingale. He returned to the emperor and declared that the whole story was nothing but a fable, invented by those people who had written the books. "Your Imperial Majesty should not believe everything that is written. A discovery is one thing and artistic imagination something quite different; it is fiction."

"This book I have just read," replied the emperor, "was sent to me by the great Emperor of Japan; and therefore, every word in it must be the truth. I want to hear the nightingale! And that tonight! If it does not come, then the whole court shall have their stomachs thumped, and that right after they have eaten."

"*Tsing-pe!*" said the courtier. He ran again up and down the

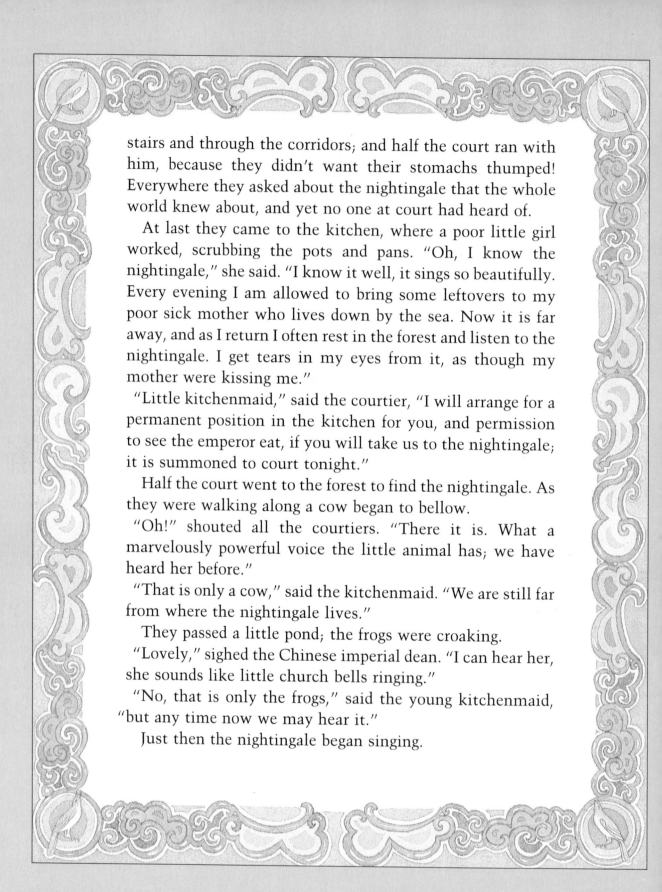

stairs and through the corridors; and half the court ran with him, because they didn't want their stomachs thumped! Everywhere they asked about the nightingale that the whole world knew about, and yet no one at court had heard of.

At last they came to the kitchen, where a poor little girl worked, scrubbing the pots and pans. "Oh, I know the nightingale," she said. "I know it well, it sings so beautifully. Every evening I am allowed to bring some leftovers to my poor sick mother who lives down by the sea. Now it is far away, and as I return I often rest in the forest and listen to the nightingale. I get tears in my eyes from it, as though my mother were kissing me."

"Little kitchenmaid," said the courtier, "I will arrange for a permanent position in the kitchen for you, and permission to see the emperor eat, if you will take us to the nightingale; it is summoned to court tonight."

Half the court went to the forest to find the nightingale. As they were walking along a cow began to bellow.

"Oh!" shouted all the courtiers. "There it is. What a marvelously powerful voice the little animal has; we have heard her before."

"That is only a cow," said the kitchenmaid. "We are still far from where the nightingale lives."

They passed a little pond; the frogs were croaking.

"Lovely," sighed the Chinese imperial dean. "I can hear her, she sounds like little church bells ringing."

"No, that is only the frogs," said the young kitchenmaid, "but any time now we may hear it."

Just then the nightingale began singing.

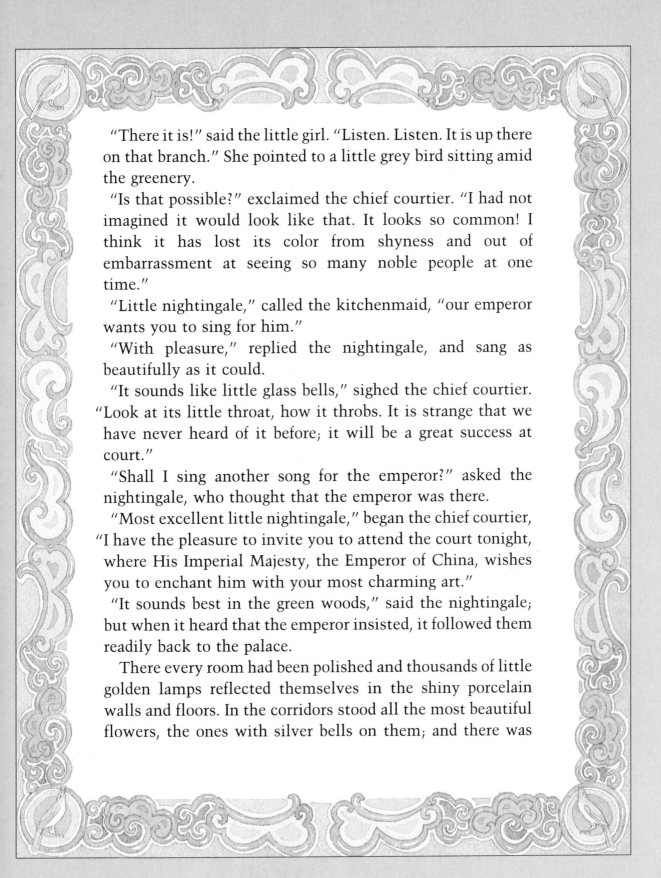

"There it is!" said the little girl. "Listen. Listen. It is up there on that branch." She pointed to a little grey bird sitting amid the greenery.

"Is that possible?" exclaimed the chief courtier. "I had not imagined it would look like that. It looks so common! I think it has lost its color from shyness and out of embarrassment at seeing so many noble people at one time."

"Little nightingale," called the kitchenmaid, "our emperor wants you to sing for him."

"With pleasure," replied the nightingale, and sang as beautifully as it could.

"It sounds like little glass bells," sighed the chief courtier. "Look at its little throat, how it throbs. It is strange that we have never heard of it before; it will be a great success at court."

"Shall I sing another song for the emperor?" asked the nightingale, who thought that the emperor was there.

"Most excellent little nightingale," began the chief courtier, "I have the pleasure to invite you to attend the court tonight, where His Imperial Majesty, the Emperor of China, wishes you to enchant him with your most charming art."

"It sounds best in the green woods," said the nightingale; but when it heard that the emperor insisted, it followed them readily back to the palace.

There every room had been polished and thousands of little golden lamps reflected themselves in the shiny porcelain walls and floors. In the corridors stood all the most beautiful flowers, the ones with silver bells on them; and there was such a draught from all the servants running in and out, and opening and closing doors, that all the bells were tinkling and you couldn't hear what anyone said.

In the grand banquet hall, where the emperor's throne stood, a little golden perch had been hung for the nightingale to sit on. The whole court was there and the little kitchenmaid, who now had the title of Imperial Kitchenmaid, was allowed to stand behind one of the doors and listen. Everyone was dressed in their finest clothes and they all were looking at the little grey bird, towards which the emperor nodded very kindly.

The nightingale's song was so sweet that tears came into the emperor's eyes; and when they ran down his cheeks, the little nightingale sang even more beautifully than it had before. Its song spoke to one's heart, and the emperor was so pleased that he ordered his golden slipper to be hung around the little bird's neck. There was no higher honor. But the nightingale thanked him and said that it had been honored enough already.

"I have seen tears in the eyes of an emperor, and that is a great enough treasure for me. There is a strange power in an emperor's tears and I know that is reward enough." Then it sang yet another song.

"That was the most charming and elegant song we have heard," said all the ladies of the court. And from that time onward they filled their mouths with water, so they could make a clucking noise, whenever anyone spoke to them, because they thought that then they sounded like the nightingale. Even the chambermaids and the lackeys were

satisfied; and that really meant something, for servants are the most difficult to please. Yes, the nightingale was a success.

It was to have its own cage at court, and permission to take a walk twice a day and once during the night. Twelve servants were to accompany it, each held on tightly to a silk ribbon that was attached to the poor bird's legs. There wasn't any pleasure in such an outing.

The whole town talked about the marvelous bird. Whenever two people met in the street they would sigh; one would say, "night," and the other, "gale"; and then they would understand each other perfectly. Twelve delicatessen shop owners named their children "Nightingale," but not one of them could sing.

One day a package arrived for the emperor; on it was written, "Nightingale."

"It is probably another book about our famous bird," said the emperor. But he was wrong; it was a mechanical nightingale. It lay in a little box and was supposed to look like the real one, though it was made of silver and gold and studded with sapphires, diamonds, and rubies. When you wound it up, it could sing one of the songs the real nightingale sang; and while it performed, its little silver tail would go up and down. Around its neck hung a ribbon on which was written: "The Emperor of Japan's nightingale is inferior to the Emperor of China's."

"It is beautiful!" exclaimed the whole court. And the messenger who had brought it had the title of Supreme Imperial Nightingale Deliverer bestowed upon him at once.

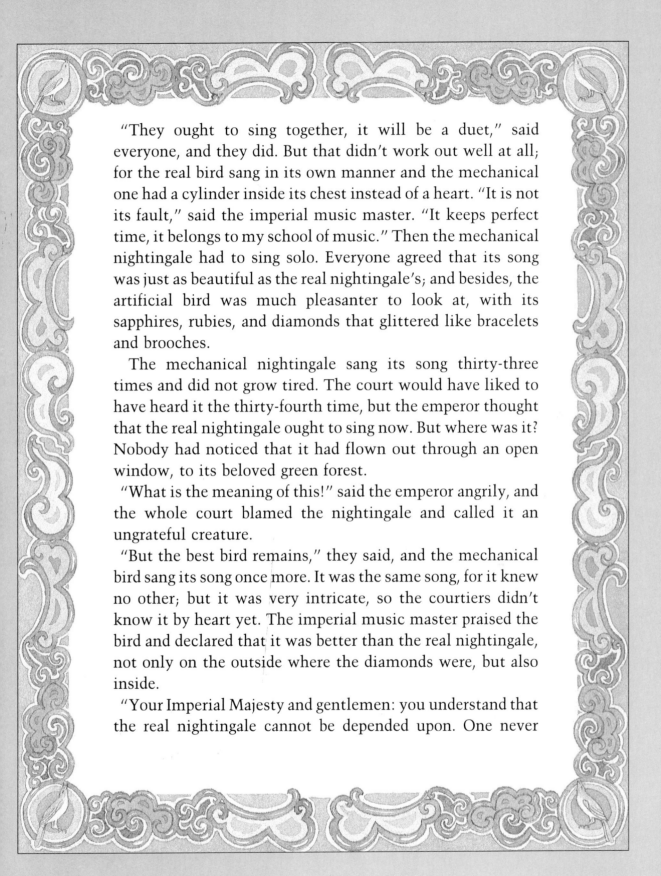

"They ought to sing together, it will be a duet," said everyone, and they did. But that didn't work out well at all; for the real bird sang in its own manner and the mechanical one had a cylinder inside its chest instead of a heart. "It is not its fault," said the imperial music master. "It keeps perfect time, it belongs to my school of music." Then the mechanical nightingale had to sing solo. Everyone agreed that its song was just as beautiful as the real nightingale's; and besides, the artificial bird was much pleasanter to look at, with its sapphires, rubies, and diamonds that glittered like bracelets and brooches.

The mechanical nightingale sang its song thirty-three times and did not grow tired. The court would have liked to have heard it the thirty-fourth time, but the emperor thought that the real nightingale ought to sing now. But where was it? Nobody had noticed that it had flown out through an open window, to its beloved green forest.

"What is the meaning of this!" said the emperor angrily, and the whole court blamed the nightingale and called it an ungrateful creature.

"But the best bird remains," they said, and the mechanical bird sang its song once more. It was the same song, for it knew no other; but it was very intricate, so the courtiers didn't know it by heart yet. The imperial music master praised the bird and declared that it was better than the real nightingale, not only on the outside where the diamonds were, but also inside.

"Your Imperial Majesty and gentlemen: you understand that the real nightingale cannot be depended upon. One never knows what it will sing; whereas, in the mechanical bird, everything is determined. There is one song and no other! One can explain everything. We can open it up to examine and appreciate how human thought has fashioned the wheels and the cylinder, and put them where they are, to turn as they should."

"Precisely what I was thinking!" said the whole court in a chorus. And the imperial music master was given permission to show the new nightingale to the people on the following Sunday.

The emperor thought that they, too, should hear the bird. They did and they were as delighted as if they had drunk too much tea. They pointed with their licking fingers toward heaven, nodded, and said: "Oh!"

But the poor fisherman, who had heard the real nightingale, mumbled, "It sounds beautiful and like the bird's song, but something is missing, though I don't know what it is."

The real nightingale was banished from the empire.

The mechanical bird was given a silk pillow to rest upon, close to the emperor's bed; and all the presents it had received were piled around it. Among them were both gold and precious stones. Its title was Supreme Imperial Night-table Singer and its rank was Number One to the Left. The emperor thought the left side was more distinguished because that is the side where the heart is, even in an emperor.

The imperial music master wrote a work in twenty-five volumes about the mechanical nightingale. It was not only long and learned but filled with the most difficult Chinese

words, so everyone bought it and said they had read and understood it, for otherwise they would have been considered stupid and had to have their stomachs poked.

A whole year went by. The emperor, the court, and all the Chinese in China knew every note of the supreme imperial night-table singer's song by heart; but that was the very reason why they liked it so much: they could sing it themselves, and they did. The street urchins sang: "Zi-zi-zizzi, cluck-cluck-cluck-cluck." And so did the emperor. Oh, it was delightful!

But one evening, when the bird was singing its very best and the emperor was lying in bed listening to it, something said: "Clang," inside it. It was broken! All the wheels whirred around and then the bird was still.

The emperor jumped out of bed and called his physician but he couldn't do anything, so the imperial watchmaker was fetched. After a great deal of talking and tinkering he repaired the bird, but he declared that the cylinders were worn and new ones could not be fitted. The bird would have to be spared; it could not be played so often.

It was a catastrophe. Only once a year was the mechancial bird allowed to sing, and then it had difficulty finishing its song. But the imperial music master made a speech wherein he explained, using the most difficult words, that the bird was as good as ever; and then it was.

Five years passed and a great misfortune happened. Although everyone loved the old emperor, he had fallen ill; and they all agreed that he would not get well again. It was said that a new emperor had already been chosen; and when people in the street asked the chief courtier how the emperor was, he would shake his head and say: "Puh."

Pale and cold, the emperor lay in his golden bed. The whole court believed him to be already dead and they were busy visiting and paying their respects to the new emperor. The lackeys were all out in the street gossiping, and the chambermaids were drinking coffee. All the floors in the whole palace were covered with black carpets so that no one's steps would disturb the dying emperor; and that's why it was as quiet as quiet could be in the whole palace.

But the emperor was not dead yet. Pale and motionless he lay in his great golden bed; the long velvet curtains were drawn, and the golden tassels moved slowly in the wind, for one of the windows was open. The moon shone down upon the emperor, and its light was reflected in the diamonds of the mechanical bird.

The emperor could hardly breathe; he felt as though someone were sitting on his chest. He opened his eyes. Death was sitting there. He was wearing the emperor's golden crown and held his gold saber in one hand and his imperial banner in the other. From the folds of the curtains that hung around his bed, strange faces looked down at the emperor. Some of them were frighteningly ugly, and others mild and kind. They were the evil and good deeds that the emperor had done. Now, while Death was sitting on his heart, they were looking down at him.

"Do you remember?" whispered first one and then another. And they told him things that made the cold sweat of fear appear on his forehead.

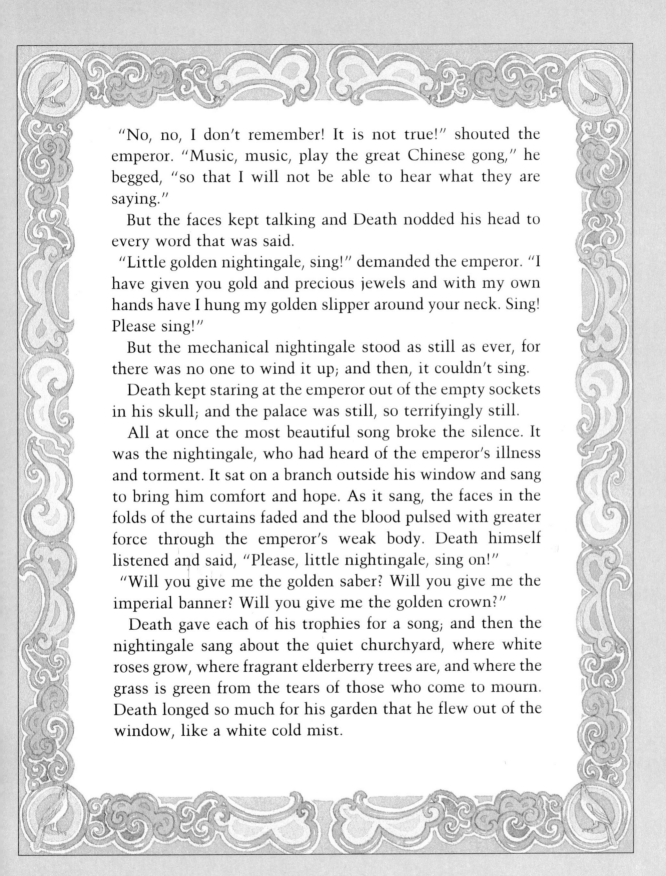

"No, no, I don't remember! It is not true!" shouted the emperor. "Music, music, play the great Chinese gong," he begged, "so that I will not be able to hear what they are saying."

But the faces kept talking and Death nodded his head to every word that was said.

"Little golden nightingale, sing!" demanded the emperor. "I have given you gold and precious jewels and with my own hands have I hung my golden slipper around your neck. Sing! Please sing!"

But the mechanical nightingale stood as still as ever, for there was no one to wind it up; and then, it couldn't sing.

Death kept staring at the emperor out of the empty sockets in his skull; and the palace was still, so terrifyingly still.

All at once the most beautiful song broke the silence. It was the nightingale, who had heard of the emperor's illness and torment. It sat on a branch outside his window and sang to bring him comfort and hope. As it sang, the faces in the folds of the curtains faded and the blood pulsed with greater force through the emperor's weak body. Death himself listened and said, "Please, little nightingale, sing on!"

"Will you give me the golden saber? Will you give me the imperial banner? Will you give me the golden crown?"

Death gave each of his trophies for a song; and then the nightingale sang about the quiet churchyard, where white roses grow, where fragrant elderberry trees are, and where the grass is green from the tears of those who come to mourn. Death longed so much for his garden that he flew out of the window, like a white cold mist.

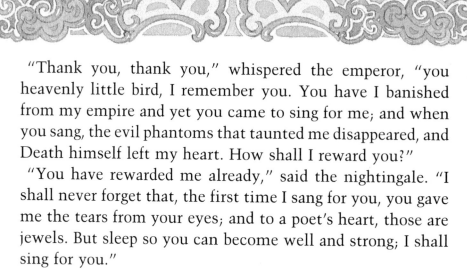

"Thank you, thank you," whispered the emperor, "you heavenly little bird, I remember you. You have I banished from my empire and yet you came to sing for me; and when you sang, the evil phantoms that taunted me disappeared, and Death himself left my heart. How shall I reward you?"

"You have rewarded me already," said the nightingale. "I shall never forget that, the first time I sang for you, you gave me the tears from your eyes; and to a poet's heart, those are jewels. But sleep so you can become well and strong; I shall sing for you."

The little grey bird sang; and the emperor slept, so blessedly, so peacefully.

The sun was shining in through the window when he woke; he did not feel ill any more. None of his servants had come, for they thought that he was already dead; but the nightingale was still there and it was singing.

"You must come always," declared the emperor. "I shall only ask you to sing when you want to. And the mechanical bird I shall break in a thousand pieces."

"Don't do that," replied the nightingale. "The mechanical bird sang as well as it could; keep it. I can't build my nest in the palace; let me come to visit you when I want to, and I shall sit on the branch outside your window and sing for you. And my song shall make you happy and make you thoughtful. I shall sing not only of those who are happy but also of those who suffer. I shall sing of the good and of the evil that happen around you, and yet are hidden from you. For a little songbird flies far. I visit the poor fisherman's cottage and the peasant's hut, far away from your palace and your court. I love your heart more than your crown, and yet I feel that the crown has a fragrance of something holy about it. I will come! I will sing for you! Only one thing must you promise me."

"I will promise you anything," said the emperor, who had dressed himself in his imperial clothes and was holding his golden saber, pressing it against his heart.

"I beg of you never tell anyone that you have a little bird that tells you everything, for then you will fare even better." And with those words the nightingale flew away.

The servants entered the room to look at their dead master. There they stood gaping when the emperor said: "Good morning."

Meet the Author

Hans Christian Andersen's life turned out to be like one of the fairy tales he is still remembered for. His family was very poor and lived in a one-room cottage. Andersen, at the age of fourteen, left his home town of Odense to seek his fortune in the theater in Copenhagen. He tried singing, acting, and dancing, but he was so unsuccessful that he almost starved.

An influential friend helped Andersen get a scholarship so that he could continue his education. After graduation, Andersen began a career of writing poems and novels and plays. But he wasn't successful in this either. Then he wrote four fairy tales and published them in a pamphlet, which was an immediate success.

While visiting a noble at the noble's country home, Andersen got to thinking about his life. Once he had been an ugly duckling in Odense and now he was like one of the swans that floated in the moat around the house. And so he wrote one of his most famous fairy tales, "The Ugly Duckling," which was really the story of his life.

LOOKING BACK

Thinking About the Section

From the selections in this section you have found out that many steps lead to creating something. Whether the final product is a story or a pair of jeans, a lot of work, time, and effort go into making it. Even when the result is a valuable lesson, a lot goes into learning it. Think about the Emperor in "The Nightingale," for example. He discovers a beautiful bird. Then a mechanical copy is sent to him. He banishes the real bird in favor of the copy. But the copy breaks and lets him down. The real bird returns and saves the day. The Emperor learns that a copy can never take the place of the real thing.

Think about the other processes you read about. How does the end result come to be? Then copy the chart below onto a sheet of paper and complete it for the selections you read. In the last column, list the steps in a process that you know about.

"Planting Story Seeds"	"Jeans, Jeans, Jeans"	"The Tumbling Koshare"	Your choice
These events led Pura Belpré to write stories of her culture: 1. 2. worked in a U.S. library 3. 4.	The main steps in making a pair of jeans are the following: 1. 2. laying out the denim 3. 4.	To make a Koshare, you follow these main steps: 1. making the pattern 2. 3. 4.	To make _____, these things should be done: 1. 2. 3. 4.

Writing About the Section

Use the information you entered in the last column of the chart. Write a paragraph explaining the process that leads to creating this item of your choice.

Books to Read

Nothing Stays the Same Forever by Gail Radley,
Crown © 1981

Carrie finds that she need not be afraid of changes. For
example, when her elderly friend and neighbor becomes ill,
help comes to Carrie from an unexpected source.

Mine for a Year by Susan Kuklin, Coward © 1984

Doug, a Labrador puppy, will be a dog guide for a blind
person one day. George has a year to give Doug tons of love
and get him ready for training. "He likes me!" shouts George
the day Doug is put into his arms. Will George be able to
give Doug up at the end of their year together?

How to Be an Inventor by Harvey Weiss,
T. Y. Crowell © 1980

Not all inventions have to be useful. The fun is in the
building of a thing and getting it to work. This book can help
you get started once a great idea has hatched. Your idea
could come out of a junk drawer. The book even tells how to
apply for a patent.

Who is Carrie? by James Lincoln Collier and Christopher
Collier, Delacorte © 1984

Carrie, a young black girl living in New York City in the late
eighteenth century, tries to solve the mystery of her own
identity. In the process, many historic events take place
around her. She even meets President George Washington.

4

Justice for All

If everyone had the same notion of justice, there would be no need for umpires. We'd all agree without discussion that the ball was fair or foul. But people don't always agree, even when the rules are written down and decided in advance. When the game is life, not baseball, justice becomes even more difficult to define.

Justice is at the center of each story in this section. A young woman challenges a braggart. A king learns the value of being honest. And in the town of Atri, the plight of a unique citizen receives special attention.

Recognizing Types of Literature: Myth, Legend

Stories of long ago that tell of amazing feats and adventures can hold the reader captive. You know that the events as written could never have happened. Even so, it's exciting to let your imagination wander freely and pretend that the events actually *did* happen.

The picture above shows an event from a myth. A **myth** is an old story handed down by word of mouth. It often explains something about nature. Myths are made-up stories

Long ago in England, when King Henry VIII ruled over the land, there lived in the town of Westminster, just outside London, a young girl named Margaret. No one ever called her Margaret, though, except maybe her mother when she was angry. To everyone else, throughout Westminster and all around the countryside, she was known quite simply as Long Meg.

And that was because she was tall. Strikingly, stunningly tall. What had happened was this.

When Margaret was twelve, she'd started to grow. I mean *really* grow. And in less than a year she'd shot up right past her oldest brother, Will. At fourteen she was as tall as her father. And by the time she was fifteen, she was gaining on her Uncle Ben, who was so tall he had to stoop to get through doorways.

Margaret's father began to worry. "Another inch," he fretted each time he measured her against the doorjamb. And he confided to his wife, "She's got to stop this growing soon. We're almost up to the top of the door!"

But Margaret's mother only gave a little smile and said, "Never mind. She'll stop when it's time."

And she did, of course. When she was sixteen, she stopped growing as suddenly as she had started. By then, though, she was as tall as the tallest man in Westminster. And that is why everyone called her Long Meg.

Now, contrary to what you might expect, Margaret didn't mind being called Long Meg. She didn't mind being tall, either. Not even when rude children stared and pointed and giggled. Not even when her elders gasped and said, "My, you've grown like a weed!"

In fact, she found being tall quite handy for certain things. Like seeing over other people's heads . . . or reaching up to the top shelf. It didn't hurt a bit to be as big as her brothers. Meg could run as fast as Will, throw as far as Tom, and wrestle Jack to the ground before he could count to twenty.

Meg's father worried about that, too." 'Tisn't proper, madam!" he said to his wife at least once every day. "Tongues are wagging about our Meg. It's a disgrace the way she runs about in breeches and wrestles with the boys. And worst of all is her sword fighting. She's at that fencing every spare moment, I tell you."

It was at fencing, though, that Meg really shone. With her long arms and legs, she could outthrust, outlunge, outparry, outduck, and outdodge not only Will, Tom, and Jack, but anyone else who dared to take her on—including Sir James of Castile, the most famous sword fighter in Westminster and about the biggest braggart in all England.

Sir James bragged at court about his distinguished ancestors from Spain. He bragged in the shops about his satin suits from France. And he bragged at Meg's father's inn about his surpassing skill with a sword. If Meg had heard him once, she'd heard him a hundred times. Then one day she decided she'd heard enough.

"There's not a man in all England can match me with a sword," he was boasting for at least the fifth time that day just as Meg arrived with his tray of food. "Send me any and all comers," he bellowed. "I promise to make quick work of them."

Meg plunked his plate down on the table and stifled an urge to make quick work of Sir James right then and there. Instead she smiled sweetly and looked deep into his eyes.

"Indeed, sir," she cooed, as politely as she could manage, "I know of someone who might be a fair match for you. And you will find him at five o'clock this very evening out walking by the windmills in St. George's Fields. He wears a blue coat and a broad-brimmed hat, and I'll warrant he would welcome your challenge."

"Touché!"[1] cried Sir James, always glad for a chance to show off. "And," he added, jumping to his feet so that everyone could hear, "if this fine champion should be the

---

1. touché (tü shā'), used to acknowledge a hit in fencing.

winner, I'll pay for his supper tonight and wait on him at table myself."

Later that afternoon, just before five, Meg stole away to the small, low rooms in the attic where she and her family lived. She pulled on a pair of her father's close-fitting breeches and slipped into an old blue coat of his. She borrowed his second-best boots and tucked her hair up tight under a broad-brimmed hat. Then she grabbed up her sword and hurried away to St. George's Fields.

Sure enough, when she got there Sir James of Castile was waiting. As soon as he saw her, he strode straight up and threw down his glove.

It's a pity, thought Meg as her eyes ran over his fine silk hose and his fur-trimmed doublet, to have to mess up that nice suit of clothes.

But before she could think anymore, Sir James reached for his weapon, *"En garde!"*[2] he shouted, and Meg pulled out her sword. The next moment the air was filled with the ringing of blade against blade.

Sir James was superb with his sword, all right, but it was clear he had met his match. Whichever way he thrust, there was Meg blocking his stroke. And her footwork was so neat and so nimble he grew dizzy just trying to keep up. So, up and down the fields they went, whacking and banging and slicing the air until at last Meg gave Sir James such a blow that his sword flew out of his hand.

Sir James had lost his fencing match.

That night half of Westminster must have crowded inside the inn to watch Sir James of Castile serve the mysterious stranger who had beaten him. Still in her disguise, Meg sat at a table all by herself right in the middle of the room. Sir James stood behind her, gazing contemptuously out at the crowd from under half-lowered eyelids. After all, he was still Sir James of Castile, descended from a long line of splendid Spanish ancestors. Yet with his nose turned up

2. en garde (ôn gärd), on guard.

and his mouth turned down and his chest stuck out as far as it would go, he looked as if he might just as well have come from a long line of bulldogs.

At last the dinner began. With a haughty flick, Sir James shook out a great linen napkin and tied it around Meg's neck.

"Humph!" he snorted and stomped off to the kitchen. And it was then his troubles turned from bad to worse.

On his way back to the table he dodged to miss a lady's elbow, and Meg's pickled eels slipped off the plate and down the front of Mistress Wiggleworth's bodice. On his next trip from the kitchen he dribbled the gravy down Bartholomew Belcher's collar. And when he tried to carve the pheasant, its drumstick shot off and into Friar Dominic's Sunday cassock.

All this time Meg never said a word. She ate her supper quietly while Sir James hurried back and forth, slipping and dripping and dropping his way into deeper and deeper disgrace—much to the delight and amusement of everyone who had gathered to watch.

With all the merriment, no one wondered why the mysterious stranger ate his supper with his hat on. No one troubled to ask. And no one pointed out that the twinkle in the stranger's eye looked just a little bit familiar. Everyone was laughing too hard at Sir James to notice. So you can imagine the shouts of surprise when at last the mysterious stranger stood up and pulled off his hat and turned out to be none other than Long Meg, the innkeeper's daughter!

And imagine Sir James's shame. He turned from pink to rose to scarlet, crimson, and purple. And from that moment on he never again bragged about his surpassing skill with a sword, he didn't have much to say about his satin suits from France, and he only mumbled now and then about his distinguished ancestors from Spain.

As for Meg, from that day on, no one in Westminster ever teased her about being tall or gossiped about her sword fighting again. The townspeople all said wasn't it wonderful the way she'd taught that upstart a thing or two. And the rude children who had stared and pointed and giggled before now followed her about the town and begged for tips on how to handle a sword.

Meg thought it was fine to be admired, but more than anything else her duel with Sir James had given her a taste of adventure—a taste that was delicious. And she yearned for more.

Checking Comprehension and Skills

Thinking About What You've Read

1. Does Meg "serve the cause of justice"? Explain your answer.
2. Why is Margaret called Long Meg? In what ways does Meg's height help her?
3. Why is Sir James so unpopular? Find two examples in the story to support your answer.
4. When Meg arranges the sword match with Sir James, what secret does she keep from him? Why?
5. Why do you suppose Meg keeps on her disguise throughout dinner?
6. How does Sir James react when he learns of the stranger's identity? How does his behavior change?
7. How do people react to Meg after she outfences Sir James?
• 8. Explain why this story is a legend.
• 9. What events in this story do you think are likely to have happened? Which ones do you think have been added? Why?

Talking About What You've Read

At the end of this story, the author states that Long Meg yearned for more adventure. Suppose Meg were living today. In what other kinds of adventures can you imagine her? What kinds of heroic deeds would you expect Meg to carry out? How would she use her great skills and her courage to do so?

Writing About What You've Read

Assume that Long Meg is a real person living today. Write a paragraph that tells about a specific situation in which you could imagine Meg serving the cause of justice.

• Literary Skills: Myth, legend

Using Context to Figure Out Unfamiliar Words

Matthew and his friend were working together on a class project about the Supreme Court. They went to the library to do research on the topic.

"I'll be in the *periodicals* area," said his friend.

"What's that?" Matthew asked, looking puzzled.

"I need to look at *The New York Times*. Also, I want some back copies of *Newsweek* and *U.S. News and World Report*."

"Let's see," Matthew thought. "It must be the department where the newspapers and magazines are kept."

Matthew figured out the word he did not know by using clues from his friend. You can also use clues to figure out the meanings of unfamiliar words in your reading. Sometimes the context—the words or sentences around the unfamiliar word—gives clues that explain, define, or give an example of an unfamiliar word. The context could also give a synonym or an antonym for the unfamiliar word. These clues may be in the same sentence, or you might need to re-read or read further. At other times, the context does not give any clues. Then you must use common sense to figure out the word. If you still have trouble, use a dictionary.

Figure out the meanings of the underlined words below.

CAR <u>CAREENED</u> OFF ROAD TO AVOID <u>BOULDER</u>; <u>CATAPULTED</u> OVER CLIFF: DRIVER <u>UNSCATHED</u>

A car headed west on I84 yesterday swerved from side to side to avoid a large rock that slid on to the road during last night's storm. The car hurled downward, then landed upside down in the river below. Surprisingly, the driver was unharmed.

The context explains the word *careened* as "swerved from side to side."

1. What is the meaning of *boulder?* Which words in the context are clues to the meaning?

When you read on, you saw that the words *large rock* mean the same thing as *boulder*.

2. What is the meaning of *catapulted?* Which words in the context are clues to its meaning?

The words *hurled downward* explain the word *catapulted*.

3. Are there any clue words that tell you the meaning of *unscathed?* How can you figure out this word?

Practicing Using Context Clues

Use context clues to figure out the meanings of the underlined words in the sentences below. Notice which words in the context help you get the meanings.

1. Derek yearned so much for his missing pet that he took no interest in other animals.
2. Sue felt compassion for her grief-stricken friend. Sue's sympathy caused her to take action.
3. She tried to console her friend by cheering him up.
4. Derek lamented his pet's absence. In time he mourned less for his pet.

Tips for Reading On Your Own

• When you see an unfamiliar word, look for context that defines, explains, or gives a synonym or an antonym for the word.
• If the context doesn't give enough clues, use your common sense or a dictionary to figure out the meaning.

King Fflewddur Fflam is in the habit of stretching the truth. Can a special harp teach him a thing or two about truth and a lesson that will serve the cause of justice? Note the details that the king adds as he tells of his adventures, and see how the harp responds to each new detail.

the truthful harp

by Lloyd Alexander

This is the tale of King Fflewddur Fflam[1] and his truthful harp, as the bards tell it in the Land of Prydain.

And this is the beginning of it.

Fflewddur Fflam ruled a kingdom so small he could almost stride across it between midday and high noon. The fields and pastures grew so near his castle that sheep and cows ambled up to gaze into his bedchamber; and the cottagers' children played in his Great Hall, knowing he would sooner join their games than order them away.

"My crown's a grievous burden!" Fflewddur cried. "That is, it would be if I ever wore it. But a Fflam is dutiful! My subjects need me to rule this vast kingdom with a firm hand and a watchful eye!"

Nevertheless, one secret wish lay closest to his heart. He yearned to adventure as a wandering bard.

"A Fflam is eager!" he declared. "I'll be as great a bard as I am a king!"

So he puzzled over tomes of ancient lore, striving to gain the wisdom every true bard must have. And he strained and struggled with his harp until his fingers blistered.

---

1. Fflewddur Fflam (flü′dər fläm).

"A Fflam is clever!" he exclaimed. "I'll soon have the knack of it, and play my harp as well as I rule my kingdom!"

At last he fancied himself ready to stand before the High Council of Bards to ask to be ranked among their number.

"A Fflam goes forth!" cried Fflewddur. "Gird on my sword! Saddle my charger! But have a care, she's wild and mettlesome."

All his subjects who could spare the time gathered to cheer him on, to wave farewell, and to wish him good speed.

"It saddens them to see me go," Fflewddur sighed. "But a Fflam is faithful! Even as a famous bard, I'll do my kingly duty as carefully as ever."

And so he journeyed to golden-towered Caer Dathyl[2] and eagerly hastened to the Council Chamber.

"A Fflam is quick-witted!" he cried confidently. "Prove me as you please! I've got every morsel of learning on the tip of my tongue, and every harp-tune at my fingers' ends!"

However, when the Council and the Chief Bard questioned him deeply, all that Fflewddur had learned flew out of his head like a flock of sparrows. He gave the right answers to the wrong questions, the wrong answers to the right questions; and worst of all, when he fumbled to strike a tune on his harp it slipped from his grasp and shattered in a thousand splinters on the flagstones. Then Fflewddur bowed his head and stared wretchedly at his boots, knowing he had failed.

"Alas, you are not ready to be one of us," the Chief Bard regretfully told him. But then, with all his poet's wisdom and compassion, the Chief Bard pitied the hapless king,

2. Caer Dathyl (ker dath'əl).

and spoke apart with a servant, desiring him to bring a certain harp which he put in Fflewddur's hands.

"You still have much to learn," said the Chief Bard. "Perhaps this may help you."

Seeing the harp, Fflewddur's dismay vanished in that instant, and his face beamed with delight. The beautiful instrument seemed to play of itself. He needed only touch his fingers to the strings and melodies poured forth in a golden tide.

"Good riddance to my old pot!" Fflewddur cried. "Here's a harp that shows my true skill. A Fflam is grateful!"

The Chief Bard smiled within himself. "May you ever be as grateful as you are now. Come back when it pleases you to tell us how you have fared."

High-hearted, Fflewddur set out from Caer Dathyl. His new harp gladdened him as much as if he were in fact a bard, and he rode along playing merrily and singing at the top of his voice.

Nearing a river he came upon an old man painfully gathering twigs for a fire. Winter had hardly ended, and a chill wind still bit sharply, and the old man's threadbare garments gave no comfort against the cold. He shivered in the gale, his lips were bitter blue, and his fingers were so numb he could scarcely pick up his twigs.

"A good greeting, friend," called Fflewddur. "Brisk weather may be good for the blood, but it seems to me you're ill-garbed for a day like this."

"No warmer clothing do I have," replied the old man. "Would that I did, for I'm frozen to the marrow of my bones."

"Then take my cloak," urged Fflewddur, doffing his garment and wrapping it about the old man's shoulders.

"My thanks to you," said the old man, wistfully fondling the cloak. "But I cannot take what you yourself need."

"Need?" exclaimed Fflewddur. "Not at all," he added,

though his own lips had begun turning blue and his nose felt as if it had grown icicles. "Take it and welcome. For the truth of the matter is, I find the day uncomfortably hot!"

No sooner had he spoken these words than the harp shuddered as if it were alive, bent like an overdrawn bow, and a string snapped in two with a loud twang.

"Drat that string!" muttered Fflewddur. "The weather's got into it somehow."

Knotting up the string, he set out on his way again, shivering, shaking, and playing for all he was worth to keep himself warm.

He wandered on, following the swiftly flowing river. Suddenly he heard a child's voice crying in distress and terror. Clapping heels to his horse's flanks he galloped down the riverbank. A small girl had tumbled into the water and the hapless child struggled vainly against the current already sweeping her away.

Fflewddur leaped from his mount and plunged with a great splash into the river, flailing his arms, thrashing his legs, striving with all his might to reach the drowning child.

"This would be an easy task," he gasped, "if only I could swim!"

Nonetheless, he pressed on, choking and sputtering, until he caught up with the child. Keeping afloat as best he could, he turned shoreward; at last his long shanks found footing on the riverbed, and he bore the girl safely to dry land.

Comforting her all the while, though water streamed from his nose, ears, and mouth, he made his way to the cottage from which she had strayed. There, the husbandman and his wife joyously threw their arms about their daughter and the bedraggled Fflewddur as well.

"Poor folk are we," cried the farm wife. "What reward can we give? All we have is yours, and small payment for saving our greatest treasure."

"Don't give it a thought," Fflewddur exclaimed, his face lighting up as he warmed to his tale. "Why, to begin with, it was in my mind to have a dip in the river. As for the rest—a trifle! A Fflam swims like a fish!"

The harp twitched violently and a pair of strings gave way with an ear-splitting crack.

"Drat and blast!" muttered Fflewddur. "What ails these beastly strings? The dampness, I'll be bound."

Taking his leave of the family, for some days he wandered happily to his heart's content, finding himself at last before the stronghold of a noble lord. To the guards at the gate, Fflewddur called out that a bard had come with music and merriment, whereupon they welcomed him and led him to the lord's Great Hall.

No sooner had Fflewddur begun to play than the lord leaped angrily from his throne.

"Have done!" he burst out. "You yelp like a cur with its tail trodden, and your harp rattles worse than a kettle of stones! Away with you!"

Before Fflewddur could collect his wits, the lord snatched up a cudgel, collared the harper, and began drubbing him with all his strength.

"Ai! Ow! Have a care!" cried Fflewddur, struggling vainly to escape the blows and shield his harp at the same time. "A king am I! Of the mightiest realm in Prydain! You'll rue this day when you see my battle host at your gates! A thousand warriors! Spearmen! Bowmen! A Fflam at their head!"

While the harp strings broke right and left, the lord seized Fflewddur by the scruff of the neck and flung him out the gate, where he landed headlong in the mire.

"A Fflam humiliated!" Fflewddur cried, painfully climbing to his feet. "Affronted! Beaten like a knave!" He rubbed his aching shoulders. "Yes, well, it's clear," he sighed. "Some people have no ear for music."

His bones too sore for the saddle, he made the best of his way afoot, with his horse joggling after him. He had trudged a little distance when the selfsame lord and his train of servants galloped by.

"What, are you still in my domain?" shouted the lord. "Begone, you spindle-shanked scarecrow! If once again I see that long nose of yours, you'll have a drubbing better than the first!"

Fflewddur held his tongue as the horseman rode past, fearing more for his harp than his skin. "Stone-eared clot!" he grumbled under his breath. "A Fflam is forgiving, but this is more than any man can bear." And he consoled himself with delicious dreams of how he would even the score—should he ever have a host of warriors at his command.

Suddenly he realized the clash of arms and noise of battle came not from his imaginings but from a short way down the road. A band of robbers, lying in ambush, had set upon the riders. The servants had fled bawling in terror and the lord himself was hard pressed and sorely in danger of losing his head as well as his purse.

Snatching out his sword and shouting his battle cry, "A Fflam! A Fflam!" Fflewddur rushed into the fray, and laid about him so fiercely and ferociously the robbers turned and fled as if a whole army of long-legged madmen were at their heels.

Shamefaced, the lord knelt humbly before him, saying: "Alas, I gave you a cudgel to your back, but you gave me a bold sword at my side."

"Ah—yes, well, for the matter of that," replied Fflewddur, a little tartly now the danger was past, "the truth is a Fflam is hotblooded! I'd been itching for a good fight all this day. But had I known it was you," he added, "believe me, I'd have kept on my way—Oh, not again!

Drat and blast the wretched things!" He moaned as three harp strings broke one after the other, and the instrument jangled as if it would fall to bits.

More than ever dismayed at the state of his harp strings, Fflewddur left the lord's domain and turned back toward Caer Dathyl, journeying to stand once again before the Chief Bard.

"A Fflam is thankful," he began, "and not one to look a gift horse—in this case, harp—in the mouth. But the strings are weak and worn. As for my wanderings, I was dined and feasted, welcomed and treated royally wherever I went. But the strings—there, you see, they're at it again!" he exclaimed, as several broke in two even as he spoke.

"I've only to take a breath!" Fflewddur lamented. "Why, the wretched things break at every word—" He stopped short and stared at the harp. "It would almost seem—" he murmured, his face turning sickly green. "But it can't be! But it is!" He groaned, looking all the more woebegone.

The Chief Bard was watching him closely and Fflewddur glanced sheepishly at him.

"Ah—the truth of it is," Fflewddur muttered, "I nearly froze to death in the wind, nearly drowned in the river; and my royal welcome was a royal cudgeling.

"Those beastly strings," he sighed. "Yes, they do break whenever I, ah, shall we say, adjust the facts. But facts are so gray and dreary, I can't help adding a little color. Poor things, they need it so badly."

"I have heard more of your wanderings than you might think," said the Chief Bard. "Have you indeed spoken all the truth? What of the old man you warmed with your cloak? The child you saved from the river? The lord at whose side you fought?"

Fflewddur blinked in astonishment. "Ah—yes, well, the truth of it is: it never occurred to me to mention them. They were much too dull and drab for any presentable tale at all."

"Yet those deeds were far more worthy than all your gallant fancies," said the Chief Bard, "for a good truth is purest gold that needs no gilding. You have the modest heart of the truly brave; but your tongue, alas, gallops faster than your head can rein it."

"No longer!" Fflewddur declared. "Never again will I stretch the truth!"

The harp strings tightened as if ready to break all at once.

"That is to say," Fflewddur added hastily, "never beyond what it can bear. A Fflam has learned his lesson. Forever!"

At this, a string snapped loudly. But it was only a small one.

Such is the tale of Fflewddur Fflam, the breaking of the strings, and the harp he carried in all his wanderings from that day forward.

And such is the end of it.

Meet the Author

Some years ago, Lloyd Alexander bought an ancient Welsh harp and tried unsuccessfully to learn to play it. In time, the strings broke, one after another, but the author will not tell what might have caused them to break.

Lloyd Alexander was born and brought up in Philadelphia, where he still lives. When he was a child, he read every book he could find, and he graduated from high school when he was sixteen. Because he could not afford to go to college, Alexander went to work as a bank messenger during the day. At night he studied and wrote, hoping to become a poet. One night, in a bookstore, he discovered a copy of *King Arthur and His Knights.* This was the beginning of his interest in tales of legendary heroes.

When Alexander was serving in the armed forces, his company was sent to Wales. The legendary home of King Arthur fascinated him, and he could easily picture the king and his knights traveling by horseback around the countryside. Years later, Alexander found a collection of Welsh legends, which brought back memories of his childhood interest in knights and heroes. He began to create his own imaginary kingdom, and this was the beginning of his series of books about Prydain, which included Newbery runner-up, *The Black Cauldron.*

Checking Comprehension and Skills

Thinking About What You've Read

1. What does the Chief Bard's harp teach Fflewddur about the truth? How does this lesson serve the cause of justice?
2. Why is the idea of being a bard so appealing to Fflewddur?
3. In what way is the Chief Bard's harp magical?
4. How does Fflewddur stretch the truth? Find three examples in the story to support your answer.
• 5. What two details does Fflewddur tell the Chief Bard about his adventures? Why are these details important?
6. What does the Chief Bard mean when he tells Fflewddur that "a good truth is purest gold that needs no gilding"?
7. How do you know that Fflewddur learns his lesson?
• 8. Give two details that support the idea that Fflewddur is a true hero.
9. Do you think there is ever any good reason to stretch the truth? Why do you think as you do?

Talking About What You've Read

Think about the truly brave deeds Fflewddur performed. He claimed he never bothered to mention them to the Chief Bard because "they were much too dull and drab." What details would you include to describe these heroic acts in a lively way? How would you stress Fflewddur's bravery?

Writing About What You've Read

Write a paragraph describing one of Fflewddur's deeds. Use details to point out how truly brave he was. For example, if you choose to describe the deed in which Fflewddur saved the drowning child, you may wish to start your description with this sentence: King Fflewddur was so brave that he threw himself into the icy water the second he heard a child crying.

• Comprehension Skill: Details

TRUE

by Lilian Moore

When
the green eyes
of a cat
look deep into
you

you know
that
whatever it is
they are saying
is
true.

Ask Yourself

You've just come home from school and you find your little brother and sister arguing. What has happened? How can you help settle their differences? You want to be a fair judge, and so you start asking questions such as, "What is this argument about?" Then you ask each child his and her side of the story. Asking questions can help you become a better judge.

Asking questions helps you read better, too. Suppose you were going to read an article about Francis Perkins, the first woman cabinet member in the United States. Before beginning to read, you might ask yourself:

What do I want to know about Francis Perkins?

In what cabinet post did she serve?

Under what President did she serve?

What was her greatest contribution?

Keep your questions in mind as you read. You will be able to answer many of them, but you'll probably be surprised to discover that the answers will often lead to new questions.

Suppose you were going to read an article about the humanitarian work of Eleanor Roosevelt. Before beginning to read, what questions might you ask yourself? On a separate sheet of paper, write four questions you would keep in mind as you read.

Remember that good readers ask questions.

A Queen establishes a system to ensure that all her subjects receive fair treatment—old and young, rich and poor. Predict what will happen to the Queen's subjects in this play about justice for all. As you read this play, predict what will happen to the once-brave knight of this fair town.

The Bell of Atri

Adapted by Adele Thane from an Italian Folk tale

CHARACTERS:

PETER

CHILDREN: *three girls*

TOWNSPEOPLE: *three women, two men*

HERALD

QUEEN

MAGISTRATE

ATTENDANTS: *one woman, one man*

SIR ROLFO, *Knight of Atri*

TROJAN, *Sir Rolfo's horse*

SCENE I

TIME: *Many years ago*

SETTING: *The marketplace in the town of Atri, in medieval Italy. Up center is a bell tower; fastened to the bell is a long rope that reaches to the ground.* HERALD *is pulling the rope.* PETER, CHILDREN, *and* TOWNSPEOPLE *enter.*

PETER: Come on! It's the Queen's bell; she had it hung here in the marketplace.

FIRST CHILD: What's it for?

PETER: I don't know. There's never been a bell like that in the town before.

FIRST WOMAN: Why does the town of Atri need a bell?

HERALD *(stops ringing bell):* The Queen is coming here to Atri to tell you herself about the bell. *(QUEEN enters with MAGISTRATE and ATTENDANTS. TOWNSPEOPLE fall back curtsying and bowing.)*

QUEEN *(to MAGISTRATE):* Are all the townspeople assembled?

MAGISTRATE: All but Sir Rolfo, the Knight, Your Majesty.

QUEEN: And where is he?

MAGISTRATE: Away on a quest, with his noble steed, Trojan.

QUEEN: A magnificent horse. Very well, Magistrate, I shall address the people. *(fanfare)* People of Atri, you are undoubtedly wondering about this handsome bell. You can see that its rope reaches to the ground so that even a little child can ring the bell. This bell is to be rung by anyone who is ill-treated or wronged. The Magistrate will come and see that justice is done.

MAGISTRATE *(nodding solemnly):* Aye, Your Majesty.

QUEEN: Rich and poor, old and young, all alike may come, for this is the bell of justice.

TOWNSPEOPLE *(together):* Long live the Queen! (QUEEN *and* MAGISTRATE *exit, followed by* HERALD *and* ATTENDANTS. PETER *and* SECOND CHILD *cross center.)*

SECOND CHILD: Come and play, Peter.

PETER *(shaking head):* I can't; I must wait for Sir Rolfo.

THIRD CHILD: You're lucky to be Sir Rolfo's stableboy, Peter. He has so many fine horses!

PETER: Yes, a hundred! And the finest one of all is Trojan, his favorite horse, who has carried Sir Rolfo safely through all his battles and daring exploits. *(looks off to the right, pointing)* That's Trojan now! Sir Rolfo is back! (SIR ROLFO *enters, leading* TROJAN. PETER *takes charge of the horse.* CHILDREN *surround* SIR ROLFO.)

SECOND CHILD: Did you slay any dragons, Sir Rolfo? How many battles did you win?

SIR ROLFO *(wearily):* All of that life is behind me. Get out of my way, children. I've no time for your foolishness. What is this bell in the marketplace?

FIRST CHILD: It's the bell of justice, sir; the Queen had it hung here.

SIR ROLFO *(bitterly):* Justice, eh! I've experienced enough of the world to know that only the rich get justice.

THIRD CHILD: But you are a very wealthy man, Sir Rolfo.

SIR ROLFO: Not wealthy enough! I want to have a fortune bigger than anyone else's in the world, and I mean to get it! *(to* PETER) Come, take Trojan to the stable.

PETER *(patting* TROJAN): You'll have some oats and hay.

SIR ROLFO *(sharply):* Don't feed him too much, Peter; oats are costly! (SIR ROLFO *exits, as* PETER *follows, leading* TROJAN *off.)*

• Can you predict what might happen to Trojan?

FIRST MAN: Sir Rolfo has changed.

SECOND WOMAN: Once he sought adventure and gallant and noble deeds, but not any longer, it seems. *(Curtain.)*

SCENE II

SETTING: *The same marketplace one year later. The rope on the bell is shorter.* TOWNSPEOPLE *are busy preparing for market day.* PETER *and* CHILDREN *wander about while* THREE WOMEN *assemble downstage.*

FIRST WOMAN: It's a year ago today that the bell of justice was hung in the marketplace.

SECOND WOMAN: I'd almost forgotten about the bell; nobody has rung it for such a long time.

THIRD WOMAN: Yes, in the beginning, the bell was rung nearly every week, and each time the Magistrate came and tried the case.

SECOND WOMAN: The Magistrate has done his job so successfully, there's no need to ring the bell now. All the wrongs in Atri have been made right.

THIRD WOMAN: The Queen will be pleased, and she'll undoubtedly reward the Magistrate.

● Do you think all the wrongs have been made right? Why?

SECOND CHILD *(reaching for rope):* The bell rope has worn thin and broken off. I can't reach it.

SECOND MAN: This will never do! The rope must be replaced. *(turning to* FIRST MAN*)* Go and get the strong rope in your shop.

FIRST MAN: I sold the last of my rope yesterday to a ship's captain who was on his way to sea.

THIRD WOMAN: Isn't there any way to mend the old rope?

PETER *(runs over to hanging vine on trellis):* Tie this grapevine onto the bell rope. It's long and strong.

FIRST MAN: Good idea. Get a ladder and help me with this vine. (CHILDREN *pull vine off trellis.* SECOND MAN *exits and re-enters with a ladder.* SECOND MAN *climbs the ladder and fastens the vine to the bell.)*

FIRST WOMAN: That's better; now even a child can reach it. (SIR ROLFO *enters, wearing shabby clothes.)*

• Can you predict who might ring the bell this time?

FIRST CHILD: Greetings, Sir Rolfo!

SIR ROLFO: Don't bother me with your chatter! *(exit)*

SECOND WOMAN: Sir Rolfo is unkind and miserly. He no longer goes on adventures, and he thinks of nothing but his hoard of gold.

FIRST WOMAN: They say that on one of his adventures he came upon a cavern where he found buried treasure—chest upon chest of gold coins. He fought for that treasure but he lost. He vowed that one day he would have a fortune of his own.

SECOND WOMAN: I hear he has sold all his possessions for gold—his castle, his flocks and herds, his orchards and vineyards.

FIRST MAN: He lives in a small cottage now.

PETER: He sold all his horses, too, all except Trojan, but he keeps that poor horse half-starved.

• What do you think is going to happen now?

THIRD CHILD: What will become of Trojan? *(Curtain.)*

SCENE III

SETTING: *The next day. The marketplace is deserted except for* TROJAN, *who limps to the grapevine hanging from the bell, whinnies happily, and starts to nibble the leaves. As he nibbles, he pulls on the vine and the bell begins to ring.* CHILDREN *and* TOWNSPEOPLE *enter.*

CHILDREN: The bell is ringing! What is wrong?

FIRST MAN: Why, it's only a horse!

SECOND WOMAN: Whose horse is it? See how thin the poor creature looks!

PETER *(bursting onstage):* Trojan! It's Trojan! He's run away!

HERALD *(entering):* Make way for the Queen! Her Majesty has heard the ringing of the bell and has come to see that justice is done.

TOWNSPEOPLE: The Queen! *(QUEEN, ATTENDANTS, and* MAGISTRATE *enter.)*

MAGISTRATE: People of Atri, the Queen has heard the bell.

QUEEN: What injustice has been done, good people?

SECOND MAN: Your Majesty, a horse has rung the bell!

MAGISTRATE: Your Majesty, this is a mistake. You should not have come, for the horse cannot grasp the meaning of the bell.

PETER: No, wait! Your Majesty, you said that all may come to ring the bell, if there has been an injustice. Surely, even a horse may call for justice, and this horse has been cruelly treated.

QUEEN: The boy is right, so let's investigate this, Magistrate.

MAGISTRATE: Whose horse is this?

FIRST MAN: It belongs to Sir Rolfo, the Knight of Atri.

THIRD WOMAN: Sir Rolfo has treated the animal most shamefully. He gives the poor creature scarcely enough food to keep him alive.

QUEEN: I've heard enough. Send for Sir Rolfo. *(ATTENDANTS bow and exit.)*

• Can you predict what the Queen is going to do?

QUEEN: Good people of Atri, this pitiful horse deserves justice, and justice he shall receive. *(ATTENDANTS re-enter with* SIR ROLFO.*)*

MAGISTRATE: People of Atri, does anyone here recognize in this miserable creature the brave and noble steed that bore Sir Rolfo safely through many a danger?

TOWNSPEOPLE *(shouting):* No, no!

MAGISTRATE: Sir Rolfo, what have you to say?

SIR ROLFO: I can no longer afford to keep the horse. It costs more to feed him than he's worth, for his usefulness is over. He'll just have to shift for himself.

MAGISTRATE: What of your hoard of gold?

CROWD: Yes, yes, you miser!

MAGISTRATE: Sir Rolfo, your heart has grown cold and hard as the gold you hoard. You have forgotten the days when Trojan saved your life and helped bring you victory and honor. Now hear my judgment: I command that one half of your gold be set aside to provide shelter and food for this horse. *(All cheer.)*

QUEEN: By royal decree, you shall be known henceforth as Rolfo, the Unknightly. Go and live alone, in disgrace, with your gold, and never attend my court again. *(SIR ROLFO goes off, as QUEEN crosses to TROJAN.)* People of Atri, each year we will celebrate this day as a holiday to mark the occasion. The Bell of Atri has brought justice even to a poor creature that could not speak for itself. *(Crowd cheers. Curtain.)*

Checking Comprehension and Skills

Thinking About What You've Read

1. How does the bell of Atri provide justice for all?
2. According to the Queen, why does the bell's rope reach to the ground?
3. What conclusions can you draw from the fact that the bell's rope is worn after one year?
4. Why can't a new rope be hung immediately? How does Peter solve the problem?
5. Why does the Knight let his horse starve? How would you describe the Knight based on his behavior?
6. Do you think the Magistrate's punishment of Sir Rolfo is a fair one? Why do you think as you do?
7. Do you think the Queen's treatment of Sir Rolfo is just? Explain your answer.
• 8. Based on Sir Rolfo's behavior, how do you predict he will treat his next horse?
• 9. Based on the horse's case, what kind of bell "rope" do you predict the townspeople of Atri will hang? Why?

Talking About What You've Read

If the events of the play took place today, a reporter would probably go to Atri to find out whether the horse received justice. What questions might a reporter ask the townspeople about Sir Rolfo's behavior, the horse's treatment, and why the bell was hung in the marketplace? What main events would the reporter want the story to cover? Why? State the most important idea of the play.

Writing About What You've Read

Pretend that you are a reporter in Atri. You have been sent to cover the highlights of this unusual decision in the cause of justice. Write a five-line story that presents these highlights. Include a headline that summarizes the main idea of your article.

• Comprehension Skill: Predicting outcomes

LOOKING BACK

Thinking About the Section

Think about how justice was served in each of the selections in this section. What is the lesson to be learned from each story? Who learned the lesson of each story? Who taught the lesson? What object helped promote justice? Copy the chart below onto a sheet of paper. Fill it in by answering the questions.

	What lesson is learned?	Who learned the lesson?	Who taught the lesson?	What object helped promote justice?
"Long Meg"			Long Meg	
"The Truthful Harp"	The truth is better than exaggeration.			
"The Bell of Atri"				the bell

Writing About the Section

Write a plan for a story in which one of the characters learns a lesson about justice. First, think of the lesson you want your story to teach; for example: All people are equal. Then use the chart you began above by answering questions about the selection. This will be your story plan.

	What lesson is learned?	Who learned the lesson?	Who taught the lesson?	What object helped promote justice?
Your story				

Complete your story plan by adding details about the characters, the setting, and the plot. These questions will help: How do the characters think, feel, and act? Describe the setting. What are some events in the plot? What is the outcome?

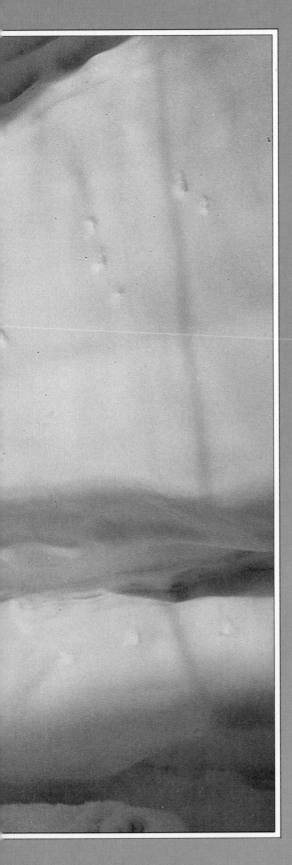

5

Meeting Challenges

Some challenges in life are major; others are less important. Sometimes you are challenged to face physical danger. Other times you are challenged within—a struggle with your conscience or the need to make a serious decision.

In this section you'll meet characters who face challenges. Two boys risk their lives on a rescue mission, a girl must overcome her fear, and another girl takes over her father's duties to protect her family in a storm. You'll discover that when the goal is worthwhile, people push themselves to meet challenges.

Understanding Personification, Simile, Metaphor

Look at the picture. What does the dandelion remind you of? Now read the poem to see what it suggests to the poet. What challenge does she say the dandelion faces?

Dandelion
by Hilda Conkling

O little soldier with the golden helmet,
What are you guarding on my lawn?
You with your green gun
And your yellow beard,
Why do you stand so stiff?
There is only the grass to fight!

In the poem a comparison is made. The poet could have made a direct statement such as, "There is a dandelion in the grass." Instead, she chose to describe the dandelion by comparing it to a soldier. A comparison helps the reader form a picture. Notice how the poet gives the dandelion the appearance of a soldier with such details as a helmet, a gun, and a beard.

In this poem the comparison is not directly stated. Such a comparison is called a metaphor. A **metaphor** is a comparison of two things that are somewhat alike. If you call grass a carpet or say that a needle is "a tiny worm creeping through material," you are using a metaphor. The word *like* or *as* is not used in metaphors.

A **simile** is a comparison made between two unlike things that is signaled by the word *like* or *as*. Some examples are the following: a sandwich as high as a skyscraper, a voice as rough as sandpaper, a runner as fast as a greyhound. Similes and metaphors can make ideas clear and writing fresh.

Giving human characteristics to things, animals, or ideas is called **personification.** Some examples are the following: the whispering pines, the frogs serenading, and opportunity calling. Of course pines do not really whisper, frogs do not really serenade, and opportunity has no voice. Personification, however, can make nonhuman things seem real and writing more lively.

The use of comparisons is not limited to poetry. Both fiction and nonfiction often contain examples of metaphor, simile, and personification.

Read the paragraphs on page 188 from "The White Cloud" by G. L. Carefoot. The story tells of the challenges one boy faces in trying to observe the mysterious trumpeter swan. What types of comparison does the author use to describe the swans?

It was three days before the boy could get back to the lake. As he peeped through the rushes, he gasped. The nest was *empty!* He was on his feet in a second. Then quickly he dropped down again. There they were! Just like a line of ships. The cob swan was in front, the pen behind. The five babies were stretched out in single file between them. The boy's eyes shone as he watched the little ones.

One baby was as white as the shining snow that hung on the great mountain far away beyond the lake. The other four were as gray as the sticks in the old muskrat house. The family of swans circled slowly around the bay. Then the cob and the pen stretched their long necks down to the muddy bottom. Five balls of fluff darted about the glassy surface.

The boy went to the lake every day the next week. And every day the little birds grew bigger and bigger.

1. Find the comparison in the first paragraph. What two things are being compared?

To answer question 1, ask yourself, "In what way are two things alike? What is the clue word?" The swans and the line of ships are alike because both can move through water gracefully. The clue word *like* signals that it is a simile.

2. The first sentence in the second paragraph contains a simile. In what way are things alike?

To answer question 2, find the things that are being compared. Look for the clue word. One baby swan is like the snow—they are the same color. The clue word *as* is used in the comparison, and it signals a simile.

3. The last sentence in the second paragraph contains a metaphor. What is being compared? In what way does the author mean they are alike?

Practicing with Literary Language

Look for literary language in this poem.

Sun

by Valerie Worth

The sun
Is a leaping fire
Too hot
To go near,

But it will still
Lie down
In warm yellow squares
On the floor

Like a flat
Quilt, where
The cat can curl
And purr.

1. Find the metaphor. In what way are the two things that are being compared alike?
2. Find the simile. What two things are being compared? How are they alike?
3. Find the personification. What human trait does the poet give to the sun?

Tips for Reading on Your Own

- As you read, think about the language the writer used. Did the author use personification, simile, or metaphor?
- To understand the meaning of any comparison, decide what two things are being compared and in what way(s) the writer meant they are alike.
- Picture what is happening. Think about how the comparisons helped you form the picture.

Matthew and Kayak[1] are meeting the challenge of the harsh Canadian tundra as they risk their lives to rescue Matthew's father. Watch for the author's use of comparisons and personification in his description of the Canadian landscape.

FROZEN FIRE

by James Houston

Matthew's father, a geologist traveling by helicopter on a prospecting trip, fails to return after a storm. Matthew and his Inuit friend, Kayak, take part in an air search. Bad weather grounds the rescue planes, but not before Kayak spots the wreckage of the helicopter. When the search plane cannot go out again, the boys follow a different plan of their own. Will Kayak's skills and his watchful eye be enough to help them rescue Matthew's father?

1. Kayak (kī′ak).

Next morning Matthew was at the tower the minute it was turning light.

"Worse today than yesterday," said Johnny, the air traffic controller. His face looked gray.

Matthew could not even see the Air Force search planes standing out on the strip.

"I checked with Lake Harbour and Arctic Bay. This whole part of the island's blanketed with fog. I'm sorry for you, kid. I know you must be sick with worry about your dad. But there's nothing any of us can do but wait."

Matthew ran quickly along the road and as he came to the Government House, he could hear a snowmobile engine roaring. The sound was distorted by the heavy fog. In a minute, Kayak drove up on his cousin's snowmobile.

"Tie your sleeping bag so you can sit on it," said Kayak, "just in front of that big red can of gasoline. I've got the gas tank full. You got the tent and food?" he asked. He checked his father's rifle to see that it was lashed on tight.

"I have," said Matthew. "Enough food for two days, maybe three."

"I'll help you lash it on this sled. We'll tow it behind to bring back the pilot and your father."

They worked together, quickly, quietly, their voices muffled by the fog.

"Put on your dark glasses and pull up your hood over your cap. Hang on tight, but be ready to jump clear fast. We're going down there," said Kayak pointing toward huge piles of jagged pressure ice along the shore. "Be careful. That's the kind of rough ice that broke my father's leg. We've got to find a path out onto the flat ice of the bay. This fog makes it hard to see. Hurry, I don't want some uncle of mine saying, 'Kayak, where are you going with all that stuff packed on your cousin's snowmobile?' I'm no good at telling lies."

Kayak pulled the starting cord and the engine roared into life again. They ran down the long snow slope toward the bay.

The rough pressure ice was piled higher than Matthew's head. There were huge slabs of it heaved up by the daily force of the tide. So narrow was their passage that they had to kneel on the seat to protect their legs. As the snowmobile lurched across a deep crack in the ice, beneath him Matthew could see the icy blue-green water choked with slush.

"We're on the sea ice. Don't worry, it's about nine feet thick," Kayak called to Matt, as they huddled together. "We go that way," he said, looking back to see that their load was still lashed tightly to the small sled.

Matthew stared ahead but saw nothing except a blank wall of drifting fog. Looking behind him, he saw that the buildings of Frobisher had disappeared. So hard was the wind-packed snow upon the sea ice they scarcely left a track.

They stopped at noon while Kayak relashed the sled, and between them they ate two pilot biscuits and shared a chocolate bar. Matthew ate some snow.

"Don't eat much of that," said Kayak. "It only makes you thirsty. Later we chip some ice and boil it into water."

They traveled on across the ice until they saw the moon shining weakly through the fog, lighting the ghostly hummocks that stood before them.

Kayak stopped the snowmobile and walked back to the sled. Matthew got off to follow. Kayak pulled a short hardwood staff out of the load on the sled. It had a piece of iron jammed into both ends.

"What's that?" asked Matthew.

"It's an old harpoon," answered Kayak. "The head and line are in my bag. I use its chisel end to feel the ice beneath the snow before I take a step. This is a very bad place."

He ran it two feet down until it struck hard ice. "Sometimes the snow hides wide cracks. If you're not careful, then you drown! You wait here," said Kayak. "We are across the bay now. There are dangerous tide cracks between the ice and the land."

Kayak disappeared in the fog. Matthew stood in the silence waiting. When at last he saw the ghostlike figure of Kayak hurrying back toward him through the fog, he let out his breath of relief.

"It's going to be hard to get off the ice," said Kayak. "We have to be careful. No old tracks to follow. That snowstorm hid everything."

They got on the snowmobile and Kayak drove on once more through the fog, following his own faint footprints in the moonlight until they came to a high barrier of ice.

"The land's on the other side. Can you drive this snowmobile?" asked Kayak.

"Yes, I think so," said Matthew. "I've been watching how you do it."

"Then follow me. But go slow. I'm going to climb through that pressure ridge. If you feel that machine start to sink through the snow, you jump far away from it, lie flat, spread out like this." He held his arms and legs spread wide.

Matthew didn't like the sound of that, but he turned the handles until the machine inched forward, then eased the steering bars right and left to test the control he needed, and followed Kayak's path.

The first icy slope was broken in the middle by a long jagged crack, and as he passed over it, he could see black water beneath him. The crack was only a foot wide, but it had an evil look. Ahead of him Kayak climbed through a narrow gap formed by two chunks of ice as big as trailer trucks. On the icy downslope the snowmobile slithered sideways and the small sled bumped the back, and Matthew almost lost control.

"Come on, hurry," said Kayak. "I hate this hanging in the middle between the sea ice and the land."

Matthew had never worked so hard in all his life as he struggled to force the heavy machine forward. Suddenly he heard the slowly turning snow track grind as though it would tear itself to pieces.

Kayak ran back and threw his full weight against its side and shouted, "Sharp rocks!"

Matthew jumped off and cut the engine and together they lay breathless against the machine.

"We made it," Kayak said. "We're . . . on the land."

Matthew saw Kayak snatch off his mitt and run his hand along the hard rubber links of the snowmobile's track.

"We loosened them right here, but they didn't break."

Cautiously Kayak gunned the motor and eased the snowmobile up the wind-swept beach. Around them, ominous black stones the size of crouching soldiers stood exposed. Matthew felt a light wind rising and saw it tear away the last remaining shreds of silver fog. Before him to the northwest lay the mountains gleaming in eerie moonlight.

"My grandfather used to say that right through that gap," Kayak pointed upward, "is the best way through these mountains. In summer a river flows down there with many waterfalls. It is frozen now and should have enough snow on top of the ice to make a good winter trail."

"It looks hard to me," said Matthew, staring at the steep white cliff faces on each side of the narrow river's mouth.

"Who can tell unless we try?" said Kayak. "We can just hope," he said, "that the river ice is not blown clear of snow."

"We could put up the tent and sleep here," said Matthew. His muscles trembled with exhaustion and he hated the thought of the twisted frozen river hiding like a white serpent in the dark shadows of the mountains.

"No," said Kayak. "I'd be afraid to

stay here. Feel that wind rising? You see how it has blown most of the snow off the beach? If that wind gets strong, it will tear your tent to pieces and kill you. I want to get safe in those mountains where we can hide from the wind. Come on, move fast. Let's go right now."

He gunned the engine and Matthew sat close behind him. They made their way cautiously through a short roll of hills, hearing the engine echo off the slopes. They followed the frozen river course into the protection of the mountains. In the path of moonlight ahead of him, Matthew saw a cruel glint of ice. It was a monster waiting to get them.

"It's going to be bad at first," said Kayak. "But maybe better later. When we get through those mountains, I think tomorrow we find your dad and the pilot over that way. That's where I saw something red."

"You think the Air Force will be flying tomorrow?" Matthew asked.

"I don't know," said Kayak looking up at the night sky and the moon. "The wind is from the south tonight. That may bring fog blowing off the open water. But we don't care too much about the fog," he said. "That's only bad for *tingmiaks*[2]—for airplanes!"

Deep in the mountains they could feel the river sloping upward. Sometimes they avoided frozen rapids where ice had formed in rough bumps. It grew colder and the moon hid behind the steep white cliffs that stood on both sides of the narrow river. Matthew sat shivering on the snowmobile, his head buried deep in his parka. He watched ahead, past Kayak's fur-trimmed hood. He could see a frozen waterfall rising like a white-walled fortress against them.

"We're going to take a rest at the bottom of the falls before we try the worst part."

When they reached its base, Kayak shut off the engine. "I hate that noise," he said, as he stood up and stretched his arms. "I just want to go to sleep."

"Me too," Matthew mumbled. "We've been going more than fourteen hours." Together they took the tent and sleeping bags off the sled.

"We won't take time to put up the tent," said Kayak, as he unrolled his bag beside the snowmobile. "We can just wrap it under us and on top of us and sleep in our bags. That way we can go quickly in the morning."

They lay down and in an instant Matthew could see that Kayak was sound asleep.

In the utter silence Matthew peered around, staring into the ghostly shadows of the mountains. It was a dead world where no creature moved or breathed. But somewhere high above him he could hear the wind sighing through the mountain passes. The wind seemed to move the night stars on their lonely course, spinning each one, causing it to send out light signals that flickered bright as icy diamonds. Matthew pulled his sleeping bag and the orange tent over his head and slept.

Kayak woke him in the morning and, although they lay in shadows, the sky above them was a brilliant azure blue umbrella and the early sunlight lit the highest peaks with a glaring golden light.

"The planes should be out today," Kayak said. "Maybe we'll see them. Maybe they'll be there when we find your father."

Matthew was so warm in his eiderdown sleeping bag that he could

_____

2. tingmiaks (ting'mē aks).

scarcely force himself out into the snow.

Kayak broke a chocolate bar and gave half to Matthew. "You'll need all your strength today," he said, as he walked over to a rock face and snapped off a hanging icicle. "I don't want to take the time to light a fire," he said. "You suck a little piece of this for water."

They shared a small box of raisins and Kayak started to plan their course up the side of the frozen waterfall. He unhitched the small sled and packed all of their gear on it.

"The snowmobile will never pull this sled. We will have to go and feel the path for bad rocks and drag the sled up ourselves. Rest when you need to. Don't sweat too much. I'm going to check the gas tank first though."

Kayak unscrewed the gas cap, put a little stick inside, and said, "*Ayii!* She needs gas very badly."

He untied the big spare can from the sled and for the second time since Frobisher filled the tank.

"Easier than feeding dogs," he said, as he screwed the cap back on.

They tied two lines to the sled and harnessed themselves to it like dogs.

When they reached the top, at last,

they sagged against the sled exhausted.

Matthew found that in spite of the cold his shirt was wet inside his nylon parka. He unzipped it.

"Be careful," said Kayak. "You'll get cold too fast. If you are too hot, you take off one mitt. That will slowly cool your whole body. When your hand gets cold, you put it back on quick."

Together they made their way back down the side of the frozen fall. Kayak gunned the snowmobile engine into life, but they did not mount the long black seat. They walked one on either side climbing the steep rough trail that they had made, each pushing as hard as he could.

When they finally climbed over the upper edge of the falls and drew up beside the sled, Matthew collapsed on his hands and knees in sheer exhaustion.

"Uggh," he gasped. "I never thought we'd make it. The top seemed as high as Mount Everest."

"That frozen waterfall was the worst part of our trail, Mattoosie. We should be near the place where I saw the helicopter sometime this afternoon."

They slithered along the upper reaches of the icy river toward the lake that was its source. Matthew sat behind Kayak and stared in wonder at the mountains sheathed in snow and ice. Kayak wove the machine from side to side, trying to travel on every patch and drift of snow, avoiding ice.

"Look over there," he called.

Above the cliffs, Matthew could see the great white spine of the Grinnell Glacier, humped like the back of some frozen dinosaur. Long spumes of snow were blowing from its western summit, whirling and shimmering like spun silver against a sky as cold and blue as hard steel.

"There's a long lake out there in front of us," said Kayak. "*Tessikotak*[3] we call it. From there we will see the highlands."

They struggled on until they reached the shore of the lake and relaxed as they crossed its smooth snow surface.

"There's a lot of wind out there," said Kayak, "but we're not so far from where I saw the helicopter."

They stopped and Kayak went back to the sled to draw his grandfather's old-fashioned brass telescope from its sealskin case.

Matthew heard him groan and saw him fall to his knees and pound the sides of his head.

"What's the matter?" shouted Matthew.

Kayak did not answer. He could only point along the trail behind him. A thin, faint yellow-colored line strung out after them. It stretched across the whole length of the lake like a yellow rope.

---

3. Tessikotak (tes'ə kō'tak).

"*Peetahungitoalook!*"[4] screamed Kayak. "It's all gone. Our gasoline's all gone. The cap came off. I tried to screw it tight, but it shook loose and came off on that waterfall!"

He leaped up off his knees and ran to the snowmobile, unscrewed the tank cap, and measured.

"Gone," he wailed. "It's all gone. Just enough for maybe a mile—or two at most. And we're more than seventy-five miles from Frobisher.

Maybe fifteen miles from where I think I saw the helicopter."

Just then a savage blast of swirling snow whistled along the lake and filled their hoods with wind. Behind them a huge snow slide rumbled in the mountains.

Struggling against the cold and a lack of food and gasoline, the two boys now must fight for survival. Rather than rescue Matthew's father, they themselves are now stranded and must be rescued.

---

4. Peetahungitoalook (pē'tə hung' ə tō'ə lŭk).

Meet the Author

In many ways James Houston's life is like the adventure stories he writes. His introduction to the Arctic, for instance, has all the earmarks of a good adventure tale. It was 1948, and he was on the last day of a brief holiday in northern Ontario. Frustrated because he had not been able to get any farther north, he jumped at the chance to fly to the east coast of Hudson Bay with a doctor on a medical mission. When it was time to return to Ontario, he did not want to go: He wanted to spend more time in the Inuit village. Equipped with only a sleeping bag, sketching materials, and a can of peaches and knowing nothing of the language, James Houston stayed on in the remote community, making friends with the Inuits and learning about their culture.

Since 1948, James Houston's life has been devoted to the art and legends of the native and Inuit (in'ü it, in'yü it) people of Canada. Although James Houston no longer lives in the Arctic, he has not forgotten the North or what it meant to him. He makes numerous trips there each year, and his love for the Arctic—for the land and the people who live there—is preserved for his readers in his growing list of books. In addition to *Frozen Fire*, he has written such such books as *River Runners* and *Long Claws*. Two of his books, *Tikta'-liktak* and *The White Archer*, have won the Canadian Library Association's Book of the Year Award as well as the American Library Association's Notable Book Award.

Checking Comprehension and Skills

Thinking About What You've Read

1. What kinds of physical challenges do Matthew and Kayak meet as they try to rescue Matthew's father?
2. Why is Kayak better suited for this trip than Matthew? Find two examples in the story to support your answer.
3. If you were Matthew, what thoughts would go through your mind as you waited for Kayak to return from out of the fog? What plans might you make?
• 4. The author says that the crack in the icy slope has an evil look. What kind of literary language has he used? Why do you think he used it?
• 5. Before Matthew falls asleep, he looks up at the flickering stars. How does the author describe the stars? How does this description help you picture them?
• 6. The author uses a metaphor on page 196 to describe the morning sky. What is the metaphor?
7. What happens to the boys as the story ends? What causes their problem?
8. Do you think that Kayak was right when he said that crossing the frozen waterfall was the worst part of the trail? Why do you think as you do?
9. How is the boys' courage necessary for survival?

Talking About What You've Read

As the story ends, what three problems do the boys face? Think about how Kayak has solved problems in the story. How would you solve any one of their new problems?

Writing About What You've Read

Write a paragraph that explains how you would solve one of the boys' three problems.

• Literary Skills: Literary Language; Personification, simile, metaphor

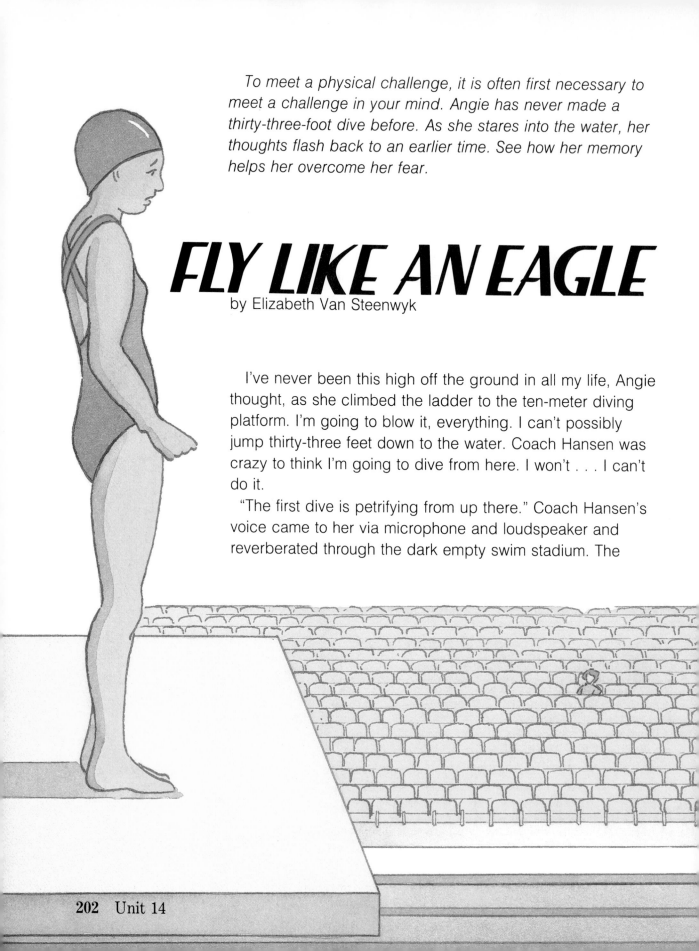

To meet a physical challenge, it is often first necessary to meet a challenge in your mind. Angie has never made a thirty-three-foot dive before. As she stares into the water, her thoughts flash back to an earlier time. See how her memory helps her overcome her fear.

FLY LIKE AN EAGLE

by Elizabeth Van Steenwyk

I've never been this high off the ground in all my life, Angie thought, as she climbed the ladder to the ten-meter diving platform. I'm going to blow it, everything. I can't possibly jump thirty-three feet down to the water. Coach Hansen was crazy to think I'm going to dive from here. I won't . . . I can't do it.

"The first dive is petrifying from up there." Coach Hansen's voice came to her via microphone and loudspeaker and reverberated through the dark empty swim stadium. The coach was seated in her favorite spot, halfway up on the right-hand side—Row M, Seat 56. She always sat there at every practice, to watch and to pronounce sentence, her voice rising sharply into the air like a kite on a windy day.

"You can do it, Angie. I know you can dive from there. It's time for you to move from springboard to platform."

No, I can't do it, Angie thought, and there's no way you're going to psych me into this dive, Coach Hansen.

She stood well back from the edge of the platform, not even wanting to look down. Yet there was an insistent feeling of compulsion which drew her closer to the edge for a short, quick glimpse of the cool blue water below, waiting to swallow her.

"Come on, Angie. Time's wasting and you know you're going to dive."

Angie fluttered her arms and legs, shaking them again and again, as if wanting to be free of them. Then she pulled and tugged at her suit so hard that it seemed to stretch down to her thighs.

"Think your dive through, Angie," Coach Hansen said. "Do it in your mind."

Leave me alone, Angie thought. I've done a front dive in the layout position a million times before on the three-meter, so I know how to do it from down below, but this is different.

"Don't be ashamed to admit you're afraid," Coach Hansen said. "Fear is something we all have."

How would you know? Angie thought. When was the last time you stood up here?

"Let's analyze what it is you're afraid of." Coach Hansen's metallic voice droned on. "Is it fear of landing wrong? I don't think so. You've done that before from the three-meter and from the edge of the pool when you first began to dive. What is it then? Fear of getting the wind knocked out of you?"

Angie looked toward her coach, although she could see nothing in the total void which surrounded the rectangular brightness of the pool. She shook her head negatively.

"Of course not. You're not afraid of that either. Then what is it?" the coached asked. She paused, dramatically Angie thought. Then she said, "I think I know. It's fear of the unknown. Is that what's bothering you?"

Angie nodded, a shiver running uncontrollably through her body as, shakily, she walked back to the farthest edge of the platform and wiped her hands on a towel.

Of course that's it, Hansen, she thought. Is that so hard to understand? I've never done this before, never felt the dive in my body going down from here, never felt the air rush over my skin nor felt gravity at this distance pulling my fingertips. Not from here. I can't dive from here.

"Your fear is perfectly normal," the coach's voice droned on unemotionally. "It's unnatural to want to dive from up there the first time. You need someone you have confidence in to push you."

I don't have any confidence in you, Angie thought. What gave you that idea? I don't think I even like you very much.

"You need someone to know when you're ready to do something you've never done before. I wouldn't let you dive if you weren't ready," Coach Hansen said.

• Why does Angie flutter her arms and legs?

Angie fluttered her arms and legs again, shaking her arms until they felt rubbery, and took a step toward the edge of the platform.

"Confidence will come from the dive itself," Coach Hansen said. "You've learned that with each new one, so now try it."

Angie stood at the edge, then put her toes in space and waited.

"It's just like the springboard," the coach said. "It's the same feeling once you're airborne. You have felt this dive before, Angie."

I wonder if I'm going to throw up, Angie thought. I've never done that from the ten-meter platform either.

• What would be as high as a ten-meter diving platform?

"You may not believe it, but your body will know what to do once you're in the air," Coach Hansen said.

Angie didn't believe it—not for one second. She walked to the rear of the platform, dried her hands again, then she turned and slowly took two steps toward the edge. Her mouth felt so dry she knew she'd have to swallow the entire pool to make it feel wet again. She pulled at her suit and waved her arms.

"Look, Angie, the thing you want most right now is to get this over with, right?"

Angie nodded. She couldn't have spoken, couldn't have uttered a sound.

"It will take you only two or three seconds to be down and out of the water on deck, so don't think, just do it."

Angie flicked her wrists and heard her bones cracking in the stillness. She stood there, shaking inside until she was sure her blood must be frothy.

"What about all your plans for the AAU championship and the Olympics?" Coach Hansen asked.

So she's going to use that old trick on me, is she? Angie thought, anger suddenly inflating her. Throwing the Olympics and the AAU at me like a trainer throws fish to her seals, as if I didn't know what she was doing. Does she think I'm dumb?

Angie walked back on the platform and looked down the steps, longing to use them.

Why did I ever want to do this? she thought miserably. Why couldn't I have played tennis like my sister or golf like Dad or even basketball like my brother? Why did I choose diving?

She remembered how it happened. Micki King, the Olympic gold medallist, had spoken at her Girl Scout district dinner when she was nine. She had listened intently as Micki related her exciting experiences and fantastic feelings about the sport. Right then Angie decided and she enrolled at the Y the next day, showing so much early talent that her folks drove her special places for coaching. Then she had won every medal in sight and now that she was fifteen, everyone was talking Olympics for her in four years. But that was crazy to think about with a coach like Hansen. How could she be ready by then?

"OK, I've had it," the coach said, her voice cold and hard. "Just walk down the steps and go home if you won't do this dive."

She threw the coach a murderous look. No, she thought. No, I won't. You aren't going to make a quitter out of me. She edged closer.

"That's better," the coach said softly. "Don't throw your body to fate now. Think it through, then dive."

Angie slapped a speck of grit from her left foot, dried her hands twice, and threw the towel down.

"You've got a dive inside you," Coach Hansen said. "Your muscles and nerves are programmed for it, and there will come a moment when you know it will happen, Angie. At that moment, dive."

How long had Coach Hansen been coaching her? she thought. At least three years and she'd heard that numerous times before, so maybe it was time to find a new coach, someone who would say something different at least, someone who might say something nice once in a while or be more sympathetic about her fear. Not this woman who treated her like a diving machine and knew only push and shove.

"Just remember to keep your body tightly controlled," the coach said. "If you're limp, that water will tear you apart, so I want you to be as rigid as a nose cone in space."

A nose cone in space. That wasn't bad, Angie thought. She's getting better and maybe if I keep her here long enough she'll write me a poem.

"Now think it through, Angie. You're just about ready, I know you are."

Angie turned to get the towel again, then thought, that's crazy. I keep drying my hands when I'm just going to get them wet in a second or two. That's when she knew she was going to dive.

Now I'm just about ready, she thought, just like the coach said. Angie stood at the edge and felt each muscle respond in anticipation as she thought the dive through from push off to entry.

She'd known it all along, but Coach Hansen had to remind her. There is that moment when you know it's going to happen, that moment when training and reflexes take over. That moment is now.

Angie took a deep breath and pushed off, her body soaring into space. She spread her arms in the classic swan position and felt the air caress her body. For a lazy second Angie hung like a bird she had seen turning cartwheels in the sky. Fly like an eagle, she told herself. Fly. Then she felt her body begin its descent and her mind took total control as she brought her arms over her head and kept her body and legs straight, piercing the water, causing scarcely a ripple. Angie stretched her dive downward before she curved back to the surface in a graceful arc.

"That wasn't bad, Angie," Coach Hansen said, as Angie heaved herself out of the water and toweled herself dry. "But you can do better. Go back up there and try it again."

"Right," she said and grinned, feeling relieved and at ease with herself. By the way, Coach, she thought, as she headed for the ladder, I think you're terrific.

Checking Comprehension and Skills

Thinking About What You've Read

1. How does meeting the challenge of her fear help Angie complete the ten-meter dive?
2. What is Angie actually afraid of?
3. Do you think that Angie really has no confidence in Coach Hansen? Why do you think as you do?
4. Why does Coach Hansen's mention of the Olympics anger Angie? What does this tell you about her?
- 5. What event in Angie's life flashes back to her as she stands on the diving platform?
- 6. How do her thoughts about what happened in the past affect her actions in the present?
7. Why would it be easier for Angie to do the dive a second time?
- 8. How would the story have been different if told from Coach Hansen's point of view?

Talking About What You've Read

At the end of the story, Angie thinks Coach Hansen is terrific. Do you agree? How would you rate Coach Hansen? Does she ask Angie to do what Angie can't do? Why does Coach Hansen keep telling Angie to dive? Is it good for Coach Hansen to have pushed Angie beyond what Angie thinks she can do? Why or why not?

Writing About What You've Read

If you were to describe Coach Hansen's qualifications, what would you say? Write a paragraph explaining your opinion. Use at least three examples from the story.

- Literary Skills: Flashback, Point of view

Use What You Know

Probably none of you has ever had to battle snow and cold to rescue a missing person in the Canadian Arctic. And yet you probably had little trouble understanding what was going on in "Frozen Fire." This was because you could make use of what you already know.

If you live in an area where there is snow, you understand the difficulties that Matthew and Kayak had to face. But even if you have never seen snow, you can probably still understand the action in the story if you remember what you have read, seen, or heard about snow. From articles in newspapers about snowstorms or from pictures on TV—or perhaps from your own experiences—you know how difficult it is to trudge through the snow and how dangerous it is to be out in the freezing cold too long.

It helps to remember what you may already know about the subject of a book before you begin reading it. Here are some questions you might ask yourself before you read.

1. Have I read anything else on this subject?
2. What are some facts I already know about the subject I'll be reading about?
3. Which of these facts seem most important in order to understand this book or article?

You will understand more of what you read if you use what you already know.

On a tiny island off the coast of Maine, young Abbie Burgess is forced to meet a great challenge. The lives of many people depend upon her meeting it successfully. As you read, follow the sequence of events to see what brings about the challenge and how Abbie responds to it.

The Great Storm

by Dorothy Holder Jones and Ruth Sexton Sargent

- What do you know about lighthouses?

In 1853, Samuel Burgess took the job of lighthouse keeper of Matinicus Rock, and he and his family went to live on the Rock, as it was called. Little by little, the family got used to the loneliness of their tiny island, which held only two lighthouse towers connected by a small house in which they lived. Mrs. Burgess was not well, so Abbie, fourteen years old, took on many of the household chores. She also helped her father light the twenty-eight lamps in the two towers every night. Abbie realized the importance of keeping the lamps burning so ships could pass safely through the rocky waters off the coast of Maine. At times, when Mr. Burgess sailed back to Rockland for supplies, Abbie tended all the lamps herself. What follows is based on the true story of how Abbie and her mother and three young sisters weathered one of the worst storms of the 1800s alone. Mr. Burgess had set sail for the mainland on January 19, 1856, thinking the January thaw had begun.

The girls stamped about in their snowshoes for over an hour, pelting one another with snowballs and playing with the hens. It was good to hear her sisters laughing again, Abbie thought, as she finished her morning chores.

While the girls were eating dinner, the kitchen became so dark that Abbie got up to light the kitchen lamp. As she did so, a gust of wind whined down the chimney. This was followed by a blast that set the shutters slamming furiously against the house.

Abbie ran to the window. The clear sky had deepened to an ominous dark gray. Gulls screamed wildly as if bewitched by the wind. From the way the flag on the pole was blowing, she knew the wind had veered to the northeast. A storm was on its way.

Esther and Mahala looked worried. The girls' mother called out from the parlor, "Abigail, your father's caught in this storm!"

"You're right, Mother. But he should be halfway to Rockland by now. And it may be the storm will blow right out to sea."

Esther and Mahala rushed in to them. "What'll we do, Abbie?" Esther asked.

"We'll do exactly what Father would if he were here. We'll batten things down," Abbie said. She directed Lydia and Esther to latch all the shutters. Mahala was sent to bring in the flag.

Outside, Abbie closed up the sheds and moved the hen coop to a more protected spot. After these chores were done, the girls and their mother sat around the fire.

"Now Father can't bring back the supplies until the storm's over," Lydia said. "And that might not be for several days!"

"We won't dwell on that," Abbie told her. "We'll take each day as it comes. I'd better light the lighthouse lamps early today. It's getting so dark."

With each hour, the wind grew more frenzied. Soon it was battering the Rock unmercifully. Huge waves, called breakers, flung themselves at the ledges.

Abbie lost count of the hours she spent minding the twenty-eight lighthouse lamps. In between, she kept her sisters and mother warm and fed and tried to calm their fears. She marveled at their courage in view of their serious situation.

At night, Mahala slept with Mrs. Burgess in the room beneath the first tower. Lydia and Esther spread their blankets by the fire. Abbie, exhausted from her labors, was glad to have the comfort of the couch.

For a week, there was no relief from the hurricane winds. It was as though the elements had gone mad and were venting all their fury upon the Rock. On the eighth morning, Abbie was awakened by a loud boom. She sat up, every nerve taut. A breaker had slammed against the house!

She hurried up to the towers and was relieved to find the lamps still glowing. The sky was so dark, she let the lamps burn on, even though the lamp oil was scarce. In the light the towers cast, she could see gray billows heaving offshore. Each one rose higher than the one before it, and each one splashed farther on the Rock.

When Abbie returned to the kitchen, she found Lydia helping Esther make a batch of pancakes. Mahala was using towels to mop up water that was coming in from under the kitchen door. They all turned to Abbie.

"The storm is worse," Lydia said seriously.

Mahala shouted, "Are we going to be washed away?"

"Not likely," Abbie said, trying to smile. "After we eat, things won't seem so gloomy."

The morning passed swiftly and without incident. But just as they began to eat dinner, a breaker crashed on the roof with the boom of a cannon. They clung to each other in terror, as if waiting for the end. Time passed, and there was only a terrible, deafening roar.

When things quieted down some, Abbie sprang to her feet. "Mother, the coop is bound to be flooded. I must get my hens before they drown."

Her mother grabbed her. "Abigail, don't you dare go outside! You'll be swept right out to sea!"

"But I can't bear to part with my hens. If I go before another breaker comes, there's a chance."

She grabbed a basket, and when the sea fell back a little, she ran down the steps. The water came up to her knees, but she pushed on until she came to the coop. She opened the door and the hens tumbled out. She scooped two into the basket, while the others flapped about frantically. Two white feathery forms were sinking into the water, but she pulled them out and dropped them into the basket. She couldn't find the fifth hen. There was no time left to search—another breaker was rumbling toward her.

She began to sing her favorite song, and its words gave her the courage to complete her task.

Back in the first tower, she snuggled close to her sleeping sisters and closed her eyes. She thought about her father, wondering if she would ever see him again.

She slept lightly, waking at intervals to check the lamps, then dropping off to sleep again. All of a sudden, she felt someone shaking her. She sat up and saw Lydia holding the lamp from the kitchen table. At once, Abbie realized the storm had worsened. Lydia screamed into her ear. "The kitchen's flooding, Abbie! Mother needs help. You must come!"

Abbie got to her feet, stiff and cold, and followed Lydia down into the kitchen. She found their mother on her hands and knees mopping up the floor. Saltwater poured into the room.

Abbie pulled her mother up and sat her on the couch. "You're too weak to do that, Mother. And it won't do any good now. Come—you and Lydia must go to the tower with me. It's dry and warm up there."

Putting her mother's arm across her shoulders, Abbie supported her weight as they climbed the stairs. No

heavy work she'd done with her father compared to the work of that climb. With her last bit of energy, she arranged the bedding.

"Mercy," her mother said. "I wish your father were here. I'm too sick to help you, and you don't have the strength."

Abbie patted her shoulder. "I can take care of things, Mother. You sleep now."

Abbie slept for a little while, then awoke to attend to the lamps. Wearing the heavy coat and boots, she went down to the kitchen. The water had gone out. She entered the parlor. It was flooded now, but she could walk through it. The lamps in the second tower flickered as she entered, but blazed right up again.

The wind had an eerie, high-pitched whine as Abbie stepped out on the catwalk to scrape the windows. She chipped at the icy windows until her hands began to ache despite her thick gloves. The water still churned below.

At the first light of dawn, she snuffed out the lamps, eager to save the precious oil. The ocean's fury was still blasting the Rock, but Abbie discovered it was easier to bear in daylight.

In the kitchen, Abbie managed to build a fire in the stove and put on a pot of cornmeal mush. In between the breakers, she swept water out the kitchen door. Then she built a fire in the fireplace. When the room was fairly warm, she brought the others down.

Once their stomachs were filled, everyone cheered up a little. However, they had little to be cheerful about. The house had withstood the storm so far, but its furnishings were soaked. Their food supply was dangerously low, and there was no relief in sight.

Abbie flew the flag at half-mast. She hoped that some ship, plowing through the rough waters, might think it was a signal of distress and send some supplies to them. But they saw no ships.

In the days that followed, Mrs. Burgess rested, trying to regain her strength. Abbie was in full charge of the household and the lighthouse lamps. Lydia helped do the cooking, being careful not to waste anything. Esther and Mahala kept the kitchen clean and warm. Abbie took care of the lamps, being careful not to waste the valuable oil.

Abbie encouraged them all to carry on with their sewing and drawing. She helped the younger girls with their schoolwork and read to them every night. The busier everyone was, the less they noticed their hunger. They had already cut down on everyone's food in order to stretch what little they had.

Throughout the days, Abbie thought of her father. He'll come today, for sure, she'd tell herself each morning. He must come today. I'm so tired, and there's so little to eat.

The storm continued to rage for two weeks. The ocean never broke over the Rock again, but angry breakers pounded steadily, spraying the windows of the house. Abbie lost sleep and rest, but she kept the lamps burning.

In mid-February, the ocean pulled back. Abbie opened the shutters, and for the first time in weeks, daylight flooded in.

A few evenings later, when she was up in the towers checking the lamps, Abbie noticed a tiny light offshore. She wasted no time getting down to the landing site. Her mother and sisters soon caught up with her, and they all waited on the ledge.

A deep voice called out, "Ahoy there!"

"It's Father!" Abbie called joyously.

"Father! Father!" the girls shouted as they scampered down the steps. Abbie caught the end of the rope he tossed and she hauled in the boat. As soon as he touched shore, they rushed to him, all chattering at once.

He turned to Mrs. Burgess and the girls, and his voice choked. "I knew I'd find you all well and safe. Everyone

in Rockland feared for your lives, but I told them this house would endure. And I knew you'd keep the lights burning, Abbie. They certainly welcomed me."

"Oh, Father, it's so good to have you home!" was all she could say.

That evening the family gathered at the fire, enjoying the fresh milk and fruit Mr. Burgess had brought. Abbie put away the other supplies, her spirits light again. Her father was home. Their pantry was full. Her mother had perked up a great deal already. Best of all, the stone house had weathered the storm.

According to the accounts her father brought from Rockland, it was one of the worst storms anyone could remember. It had caused terrible damage to the shore at Rockland, and there'd been word of many disasters on the high seas.

After a while, Abbie sat down at the kitchen table and began a letter to a friend back at Rockland. She explained some of the events of the past weeks, then added: "Though I was at times greatly exhausted by my labors, not once did the lights fail. I was able to perform all my accustomed duties as well as those of my father."

Checking Comprehension and Skills

Thinking About What You've Read

1. What great challenge is Abbie forced to meet?
2. Why do many lives depend on her successfully meeting that challenge?
3. Name three signs that show that a storm is coming.
4. How does Abbie's rescue of the hens show that she understands the pattern of the ocean waves?
5. What is the single most important decision that saves Abbie's life and the lives of her family?
6. What feelings about herself does Abbie's letter to her friend express?
- 7. List the events in the order in which they occur.
   a. Abbie moves her mother and sisters to the tower.
   b. Mr. Burgess goes to the mainland for supplies.
   c. Mr. Burgess takes the job as lighthouse keeper.
   d. A nor'easter storm strikes the island.
- 8. How would the story have been different if Mr. Burgess hadn't gone to the mainland when he did?
9. Would you want to be a member of a lighthouse keeper's family? Why or why not?

Talking About What You've Read

Fully automatic lighthouses are replacing most older lighthouses. These new lighthouses operate without keepers. Think about the differences between manually and automatically operated lighthouses. What are some advantages of each? What are the disadvantages of each?

Writing About What You've Read

If you were out at sea, would you rather receive your light signals from a manually or an automatically operated lighthouse? Write a paragraph in which you tell why. Use the advantages you have discussed to support your argument.

- Comprehension Skill: Sequence

VELVET SHOES

by Elinor Wylie

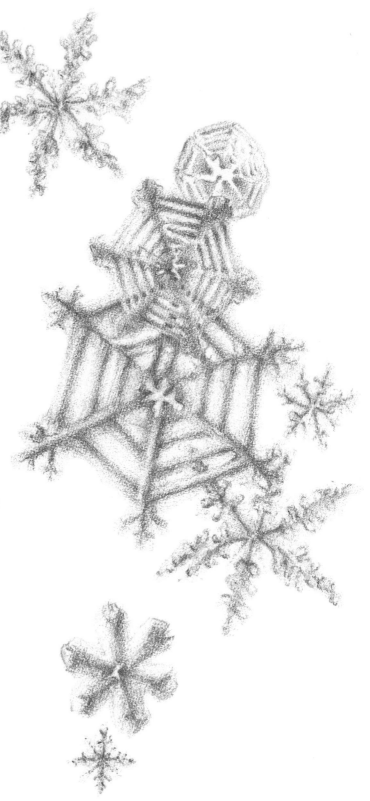

Let us walk in the white snow
   In a soundless space;
With footsteps quiet and slow,
   At a tranquil pace,
   Under veils of white lace.

I shall go shod in silk,
   And you in wool,
White as a white cow's milk,
   More beautiful
   Than the breast of a gull.

We shall walk through the still town
   In a windless peace;
We shall step upon white down,
   Upon silver fleece,
   Upon softer than these.

We shall walk in velvet shoes:
   Wherever we go
Silence will fall like dews
   On white silence below.
   We shall walk in the snow.

LOOKING BACK

Thinking About the Section

Each of the characters in this section meets a challenge that requires great courage. What challenges do Matthew and Kayak, Angie, and Abbie face? What important character traits are required in order to meet the challenge? What fear does each character overcome? Copy the chart below onto a sheet of paper. Answer the questions to fill in the chart.

	What challenge is faced?	What fear is overcome?	What is an important character trait?
Matthew and Kayak			
Angie			
Abbie			

Writing About the Section

Suppose you were Abbie or Matthew or Angie. Write an explanatory paragraph that gives advice to someone who must overcome a similar fear. Use the information on the chart above as well as other information you have learned about the character from the story.

6

Other Lands

Come on a journey to other lands. Bring your curiosity. See what new sights and sounds you will discover. All kinds of experiences will be possible. Other lands can be magical and fascinating. They can offer adventure. They can sometimes be the settings for harsh experiences. Wherever you go, other lands offer new things to see and do and learn.

In this section, you will be able to visit an unusual region in Mexico, to travel through the Australian desert, and to live, for a time, on the Siberian steppe.

Reading a Textbook

Suppose you need to buy a notebook and some pencils in a small department store. You could walk up and down the aisles looking for school and office supplies. Or you could look for signs that tell you what is in the different sections of the store. When you spot the one that says *stationery*, you move in that direction. Knowing where the stationery department is in the store helps you find what you're looking for more efficiently.

A textbook, like a department store, has different kinds of information arranged in an orderly way. When studying the information in a social studies book or

A **chapter** or a **lesson number** tells you where you are in the book.

A **title** tells you the topic of a lesson or a chapter.

Introductory material gives you an idea of what the topic will be about.

A **caption** identifies what the picture shows and often gives you information about it.

A **subhead** is like a title for the paragraphs that follow. It tells you what those paragraphs are about.

Italic type and **dark type** calls your attention to new, important words to learn. New words are underlined in some textbooks.

A **marginal note** may give you special information about the paragraphs next to it or special instructions.

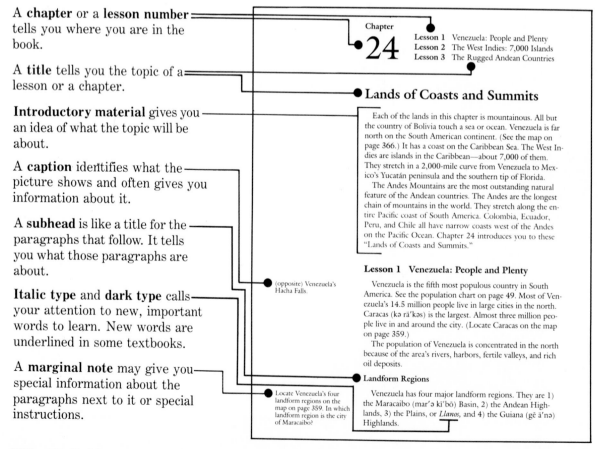

Chapter

24

Lesson 1 Venezuela: People and Plenty
Lesson 2 The West Indies: 7,000 Islands
Lesson 3 The Rugged Andean Countries

Lands of Coasts and Summits

Each of the lands in this chapter is mountainous. All but the country of Bolivia touch a sea or ocean. Venezuela is far north on the South American continent. (See the map on page 366.) It has a coast on the Caribbean Sea. The West Indies are islands in the Caribbean—about 7,000 of them. They stretch in a 2,000-mile curve from Venezuela to Mexico's Yucatán peninsula and the southern tip of Florida.

The Andes Mountains are the most outstanding natural feature of the Andean countries. The Andes are the longest chain of mountains in the world. They stretch along the entire Pacific coast of South America. Colombia, Ecuador, Peru, and Chile all have narrow coasts west of the Andes on the Pacific Ocean. Chapter 24 introduces you to these "Lands of Coasts and Summits."

Lesson 1 Venezuela: People and Plenty

Venezuela is the fifth most populous country in South America. See the population chart on page 49. Most of Venezuela's 14.5 million people live in large cities in the north. Caracas (kə rä′kəs) is the largest. Almost three million people live in and around the city. (Locate Caracas on the map on page 359.)

The population of Venezuela is concentrated in the north because of the area's rivers, harbors, fertile valleys, and rich oil deposits.

Landform Regions

Venezuela has four major landform regions. They are 1) the Maracaibo (mar′ə kï′bō) Basin, 2) the Andean Highlands, 3) the Plains, or *Llanos*, and 4) the Guiana (gē ä′nə) Highlands.

(opposite) Venezuela's Hacha Falls.

Locate Venezuela's four landform regions on the map on page 359. In which landform region is the city of Maracaibo?

some other textbook, use the standard textbook features to help you learn the material efficiently.

The textbook pages shown below and at the left are from a social studies book. The author has organized the information in the lesson by using such textbook features as chapter and lesson numbers, titles, captions, subheads, italic type, dark type, marginal notes, pictures, graphic aids (maps and charts), labels, and map keys. Review questions at the end of a lesson are another feature usually found in textbooks. Finally, textbooks may contain "special" features—facts or stories or other information that usually adds human interest to the text. Special features in this book give you information about someone you should know.

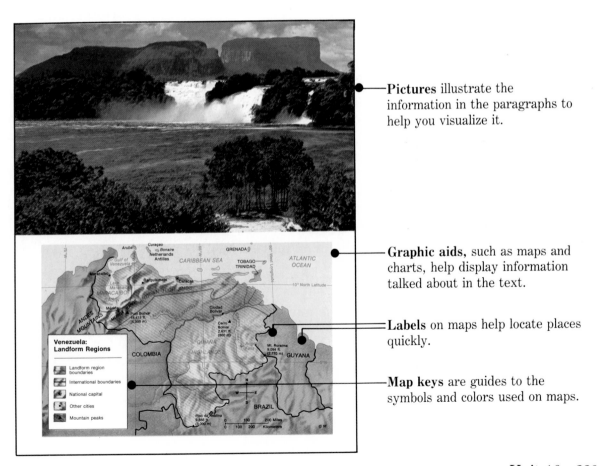

Pictures illustrate the information in the paragraphs to help you visualize it.

Graphic aids, such as maps and charts, help display information talked about in the text.

Labels on maps help locate places quickly.

Map keys are guides to the symbols and colors used on maps.

Using Your Study Skills

The first part of Lesson 1 of Chapter 24 and the map that goes with it are shown again on the opposite page. Make use of the textbook features on the page to help you preview the lesson to see what it is about.

The title tells you the lesson's topic—the people and plenty (resources) of Venezuela. The subhead tells you the paragraphs that follow give information about people and resources in Venezuela's landform regions. The map's title tells you it shows the landform regions of Venezuela.

Now read the first two paragraphs to find out about the population, or people. As you read, you'll be referred to two graphic aids—a chart and a map, shown below, that is located on page 49 of the social studies textbook. These textbook features display some of the information talked about in the text.

1. What is the population of Venezuela?

Is the information needed to answer that question given in the text, on the chart, or in both places? It's given in both places. The third sentence of the first paragraph mentions Venezuela's 14.5 million people. The last country listed on the chart is Venezuela, and its population is given as 14,540,000.

2. Where is most of Venezuela's population?

Did you find the answer—in the north—in the text, on the chart, or on the map? It's found only in the second paragraph of the text.

Read the last paragraph to find out what the landform regions are. Locate each on the map. Notice Venezuela is shaded in a different color.

3. Which landform region is the largest in area?

South America: Countries and Dependency	Populations
Argentina	27,860,000
Bolivia	5,150,000
Brazil	123,000,000
Chile	11,100,000
Colombia	26,400,000
Ecuador	7,814,000
French Guiana (Fr.)	62,000
Guyana	824,000
Paraguay	3,000,000
Peru	17,300,000
Suriname	375,000
Uruguay	2,900,000
Venezuela	14,540,000
total	*240,325,000*

Reproduced from textbook page 49.

Lesson 1 Venezuela: People and Plenty

(opposite) Venezuela's Hacha Falls.

Venezuela is the fifth most populous country in South America. See the population chart on page 49. Most of Venezuela's 14.5 million people live in large cities in the north. Caracas (kə rä'kəs) is the largest. Almost three million people live in and around the city. (Locate Caracas on the map on page 359.)

The population of Venezuela is concentrated in the north because of the area's rivers, harbors, fertile valleys, and rich oil deposits.

Landform Regions

Locate Venezuela's four landform regions on the map on page 359. In which landform region is the city of Maracaibo?

Venezuela has four major landform regions. They are 1) the Maracaibo (mar'ə kī'bō) Basin, 2) the Andean Highlands, 3) the Plains, or *Llanos,* and 4) the Guiana (gē ä'nə) Highlands.

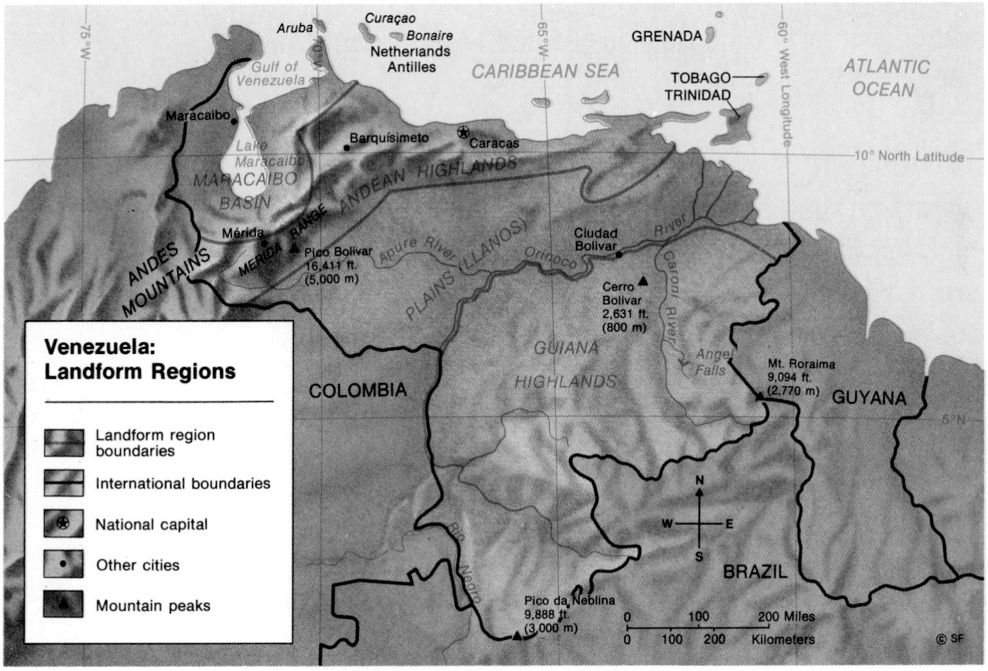

Venezuela: Landform Regions
Landform region boundaries
International boundaries
National capital
Other cities
Mountain peaks
Aruba
Curaçao
Bonaire
Netherlands Antilles
GRENADA
CARIBBEAN SEA
TOBAGO
TRINIDAD
ATLANTIC OCEAN
Gulf of Venezuela
Maracaibo
Lake Maracaibo
MARACAIBO BASIN
Barquisimeto
Caracas
ANDEAN HIGHLANDS
Mérida
MERIDA RANGE
ANDES MOUNTAINS
Pico Bolivar 16,411 ft. (5,000 m)
Apure River
PLAINS (LLANOS)
Orinoco River
Ciudad Bolivar
Caroni River
Cerro Bolivar 2,631 ft. (800 m)
GUIANA HIGHLANDS
Angel Falls
Mt. Roraima 9,094 ft. (2,770 m)
GUYANA
COLOMBIA
BRAZIL
Rio Negro
Pico da Neblina 9,888 ft. (3,000 m)
75° W
70° W
65° W
60° West Longitude
10° North Latitude
5° N
N
S
E
W
0 100 200 Miles
0 100 200 Kilometers
© SF

Practicing Textbook Reading

The rest of Lesson 1 is shown on the opposite page. The headings in dark type tell you that you will read now about each of the four major landform regions of Venezuela. The graph at the bottom of the page compares the average temperatures of three cities, each in a different region. It also shows the elevation of each of those cities. As you read, look for other comparisons among the four regions.

1. Using the information given on the graph, compare the elevations and average temperatures among the three cities. What relationship does the chart show between a city's elevation and its temperature?
2. Which of the landform regions has a large agricultural industry?
3. Is the population of the Guiana Highlands likely to increase or decrease in coming years? Explain.
4. What two natural wonders are found in the highlands regions?
5. Based on what you've read about Venezuela in Lesson 1, what kinds of information do you think Lesson 2 will tell you about the West Indies?

Tips for Reading On Your Own

- Preview your textbook reading assignment by first looking at the textbook features in the lesson.
- If there are review questions at the end of the lesson, think about them before you read the lesson. This will help you set purposes for reading.
- Read your assignment slowly and carefully.
- Look for answers to the review questions as you read.
- Use your reading skills to help you understand what you are reading.
- If you cannot answer all of the review questions, reread the lesson to find the information you need.

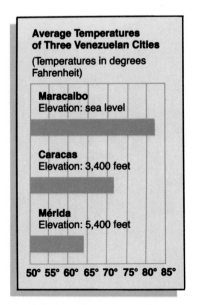

Average Temperatures of Three Venezuelan Cities

(Temperatures in degrees Fahrenheit)

Maracaibo
Elevation: sea level

Caracas
Elevation: 3,400 feet

Mérida
Elevation: 5,400 feet

50° 55° 60° 65° 70° 75° 80° 85°

The Maracaibo Basin. This region includes Lake Maracaibo and the lowlands around it. The lake is the largest in South America. It is smaller, though, than the smallest of North America's Great Lakes—Lake Ontario. Almost all of the basin is circled by mountains. The mountain barrier and the area's low latitude make the basin humid and hot. Thick forests grow around Lake Maracaibo.

The most important resource of the Maracaibo Basin is oil. Forests of oil derricks cover long stretches of the lake's shores. Many stand in the lake itself. Oil was discovered in the region in 1918. Since then, Venezuela has become one of the world's leading producers of oil. The United States imports much of its oil from Venezuela.

The Andean Highlands. East of the Maracaibo Basin is the Andean Highlands Region. This is a land of towering mountain ranges and deep river valleys. Venezuela's highest mountain peak, Pico Bolivar (pē′kō bō lē′vär), is within this region. It is over 16,000 feet above sea level.

Both the Highlands and the Maracaibo Basin are in the low latitudes. Look at the map on page 359. What is the latitude of Maracaibo, a city in the Maracaibo Basin? What is the latitude of Caracas, a city in the Andean Highlands? Though both of these cities have similar latitudes, their climates are very different. See the chart on this page. Which of the three cities listed has the warmest average annual temperature? Which has the coldest? Why do these cities have such different annual temperatures?

The Plains Region. This area is between the Andean Highlands and the Guiana Highlands. Large cattle ranches cover most of this grassland region. Farmers raise rice, sugar cane, cacao, and coconuts. The longest river in Venezuela, the Orinoco (ōr′ə nō′kō), brings water to the plains. Yet most of the land is dry and needs irrigation for farming.

The Guiana Highlands. This mountainous region is southwest of the plains. It is made up of high, forest-covered plateaus cut deeply by swift-flowing rivers. The world's highest waterfall, Angel Falls, is in the Guiana Highlands. It falls 3,212 feet. Few people live in the region because of the thick forests and mountainous terrain. Large deposits of iron ore have been found on the northern rim of the highlands. Mining is bringing more people to this rugged land.

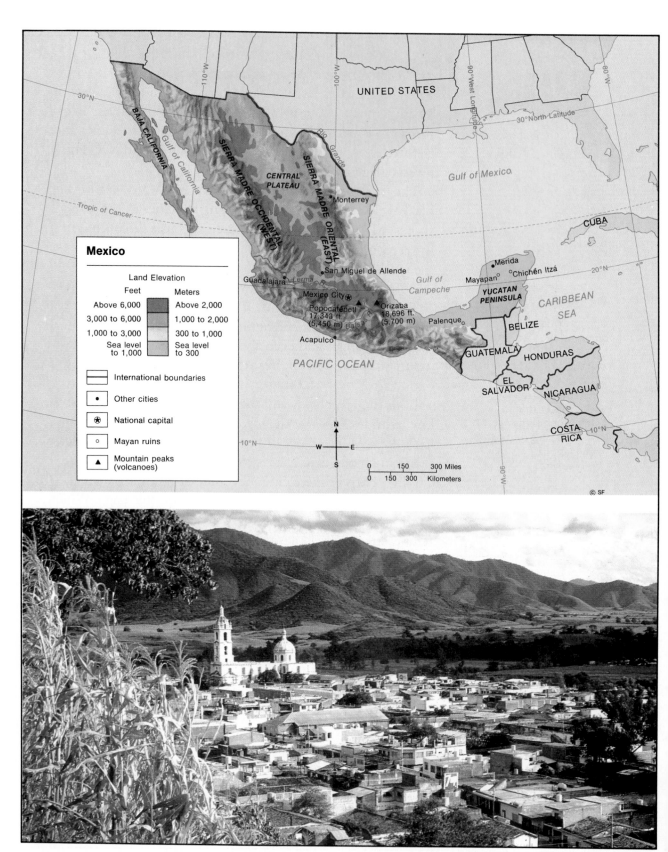

Mexico

Land Elevation

Feet	Meters
Above 6,000	Above 2,000
3,000 to 6,000	1,000 to 2,000
1,000 to 3,000	300 to 1,000
Sea level to 1,000	Sea level to 300

International boundaries

• Other cities

⊛ National capital

○ Mayan ruins

▲ Mountain peaks (volcanoes)

What is so special about the cold lands of Mexico that they draw people from all over the world? Find out, using the textbook features in this social studies textbook selection.

Chapter

20

Lesson 1 San Miguel de Allende
Lesson 2 Market Day
in Mountainside Villages
Lesson 3 Mexico City
Lesson 4 A Strong National Government

Life in Mexico's Cold Lands

The highlands of Mexico are called *tierras frias* (cold lands). (See the map on this page.) But the cold there is nothing like what we feel in the northern United States during winter. Frost in the tierras frias is rare. Snow is found only on the highest mountain peaks. Standing water will freeze only on the very coldest nights of the year. Even during January and February people in the Mexican highlands can wear short sleeves during the day and keep warm by wearing a sweater at night.

In this chapter you will learn about some of the people, cities, and villages of Mexico's tierras frias. You will also read about Mexico's national government. It is located in Mexico City, the largest city in the Western Hemisphere.

Lesson 1 San Miguel de Allende

In the mountains north of Mexico City is a village called San Miguel de Allende. If you recall from Chapter 1, this is the home of María Carrasco. The village looks like a picture in a storybook. Narrow cobblestone streets wind out of the center of town and twist up hills on the outskirts. Lining the streets are houses and churches. Some of them are 300 years old. San Miguel de Allende has such lovely Spanish architecture, that the government of Mexico has made it a national landmark town. That means it is against the law to tear down an existing building and put up a new building in its place.

A visitor can easily find the center of San Miguel by walking toward the tower of a tall church. Spread in front of that church is a tree-shaded plaza. The plaza is a popular gathering place for old and young alike.

María Carrasco
(mä rē ä kä räs'kō
San Miguel de
Allende
(sän mē gel' dā
ä yen'dā)
tierras frias
(tyer'äs frē'äs)

San Miguel de Allende

There are four small colleges in San Miguel. People come from other parts of Mexico and all over the world to study art, literature, and modern languages. Retired people from the United States and Canada also come to San Miguel to live. They enjoy the pleasant climate. Even though San Miguel is in the tierras frias, the winters are not nearly as cold as in the United States or Canada. A fire in the fireplace and an extra blanket at night are all one needs to keep comfortable during a San Miguel winter.

Many writers and artists also live in San Miguel. They like the town because it is such a quiet place to work.

At least, it is quiet most of the time.

Conchero dancers in front of the Parochia.

San Miguel Day is one of the many fiestas celebrated in San Miguel. It is in honor of St. Michael, whom the city is named after. The fiesta starts in the plaza at four in the morning. Hundreds of people crowd into the tiny plaza. The foreign community joins the Mexicans. No one could sleep through this fiesta even if they wanted to. At four in the morning the noisemaking begins. The people in the plaza try to "wake up" St. Michael. Fireworks whiz, crackle, and bang. A dozen bands play a dozen different tunes all at the same time. Children blow cardboard horns and rattle noisemakers. Everyone screams, shouts, and hollers. The people *must* make a lot of noise. After all, they are trying to wake up St. Michael, and he has been dead for several hundred years.

Daylight brings what is called the Running of the Bulls. Big fighting bulls are brought to town in trucks. The bulls are released to run in the streets. Crowds of young people dare the bulls to charge them. The bulls lower their horns and charge. The crowds break up and scatter like a rack of billiard balls.

When the bulls are rounded up the fiesta does not end. A huge parade winds through the streets. Leading the parade are skilled horsemen. They are followed by Indian dancers. Also in the parade are bands, schoolchildren, and floats that carry statues of St. Michael.

At nightfall, the fiesta still goes on. Small bands called *mariachis* (mä rē ä′chēz) rove through the plaza playing brassy music. Choruses of college students sing old Mexican songs. Then the fireworks begin. Rockets that drive pinwheels leave a trail of sparks looking like a circle of fire. Other rockets zoom into the night sky, explode, and rain down to earth like falling stars.

After the fireworks, the fiesta still does not end. The singing, dancing, and band-playing goes on and on into the night.

But finally the fiesta is over. The townspeople go back to their jobs. The students return to school. The writers and artists go back to their typewriters and canvases. Once more San Miguel de Allende becomes a quiet place to work.

At least until the next fiesta.

Dancers performing at the San Miguel festival. The headdresses were fashioned to look like the colorful tail of the quetzal bird, the sacred bird of the Aztecs.

Checking Up

1. How can a visitor find the center of the town of San Miguel de Allende?

2. What celebration in your home town most resembles San Miguel Day?

3. Discuss the statement: San Miguel is a blending of "old" and "new."

SOMEONE YOU SHOULD KNOW

Benito Juarez (ben ē′tō hwär′es) was a Zapotec (zä pə tek′) Indian born in southern Mexico in 1806. He grew up on a farm and could not read or write until age twelve. It was then that a rich man took an interest in Juarez and sent him to school. Juarez never stopped learning.

Juarez became a lawyer, a judge, and in 1858 became president of Mexico.

During the 1850s, Mexico was ruled by rich landowners. Revolutions raged all over the country. When Juarez became president, he vowed to reduce the power of the landowners and give the land back to the poor farmers.

For a while, Juarez made much progress. He reduced the power of the army and returned much farmland back to the poor people of the nation.

But then France invaded Mexico. Juarez was forced to flee his nation. But he was a Mexican citizen in the strongest sense of the word. He vowed to return and bring democracy to his beloved country.

In 1867, Juarez once again became president of Mexico. He hoped to build a huge school system to educate the people of his country. He knew that democracy would only work if the people were educated. Juarez had never forgottten how education had changed his life.

Despite his determination, Juarez never lived to see his dreams for his country come true. He died in 1872. For many years Mexico was run by one dictator after the other. Juarez's public school system was not realized for many years.

But Juarez's ideas about democracy lived on. Today, many of them are a part of Mexico's constitution.

Benito Juarez, as painted by Diego Rivera, one of Mexico's most famous artists.

Markets such as this one can be found in many parts of rural Mexico.

Lesson 2   Market Day in Mountainside Villages

Scattered in the valleys of the Sierra Madre are many small Mexican villages. Life in these **rural areas** is much the same today as it was hundreds of years ago. A rural area is a sparsely populated area outside of a city and its suburbs. While much of Mexico is a modern country, it seems that time has forgotten the mountainside villages.

Some villagers want to move to the big **urban areas**. An urban area refers to a city and its suburbs. Urban areas are generally densely populated. Some villagers believe life in the villages is boring. Other villagers choose to hold onto their old way of life. The mountain air is pure. A family can grow its own flowers and vegetables. And at least once a week village life is certainly not boring. That one day is market day.

On market day people from the surrounding farms all journey into the village. Often whole families walk miles over mountain trails. Sunday is market day in most villages, but some villages hold market day on Tuesday or Thursday. Whatever day they hold it, market day is the liveliest and most important day of the week for the people who live on the mountainside.

A Mayan market at San Cristobal de Las Casas, Mexico.

Every small Mexican village has a market. It is not like a supermarket where people push carts through aisles. A village market is far different and a lot more fun than any supermarket.

The market is open every day. It might be housed in a building or it might be in the open air. It has stands where people sell goods. On market day people come from miles around to sell goods. The vendors spill over from the main market and onto the surrounding streets.

Cars are not permitted near the main market on market day. People spread sheets and blankets on the street and sell goods from them. Most of the vendors are women.

Customers carry on lively conversations with vendors. Bargaining is common in Mexican markets. A seller *expects* a buyer to argue over the price of goods. Often a seller is shocked when a stranger accepts the first price. Sometimes vendors in the market **barter** their goods. Bartering is the direct exchange of goods of equal value without using money.

Close to the main market the sounds, smells, and sights all seem to swim together. Some women sell red ripe tomatoes, potatoes fresh from the ground, lettuce, beets, and spinach. Other women sell juicy watermelons, pineapples, grapes, and papaya. In sunny Mexico these fruits grow abundantly.

Some of the vendors specialize in herbs. Herbs are plants that many people value as medicine. They are dried twigs, roots, leaves, and pieces of bark. Herbs are usually sold in bottles. Signs over each bottle indicate what the herbs are good for. One says, "To stop smoking." Another says, "For toothache pain." Still another says, "To improve memory." A marketplace joke is told about an old man who bought some herbs to improve his memory. "How did the herbs work?" his friend asked a week later. "I don't know," said the old man. "I forgot to take them."

At the main market people sell live turkeys, piglets, and clucking chickens. Some people sell toys. They have traveled to the cities to bring back dolls that cry and roosters that crow. Children from remote farms gaze at these toys with eyes that look as large as flashlights.

In back of the market are outdoor restaurants where people sit at picnic tables. The food there is simple: rice, beans, tortillas, and stews. Most of the food is not spicy hot. But Mexicans will always serve a little dish of chili peppers alongside the main dish.

Clothes are also sold on market day. Hanging on walls are handmade ponchos (sleeveless jackets). Ponchos are both handsome and warm. Customers sort through piles of shirts and pants. Much of the inexpensive clothing comes from the United States. Sellers take trucks to the United States where they buy surplus clothing cheaply. One T-shirt that is on sale says, I SURVIVED THE CHICAGO BLIZZARD OF '79.

When market day is over people go back to their quiet life on the farms. But they can always look forward to the next market day.

A market at Guanajuato, Mexico.

Checking Up

1. Of what importance is market day to the people of the mountainside villages?

2. Describe what would happen to the vendors if a modern shopping center were built in their village. (Assume that the shopping center would sell a greater variety of goods at lower prices than the vendors.)

Checking Comprehension and Skills

1. Why are people from other lands drawn to the highlands of Mexico? Give three reasons.
• 2. What does the term *tierras frias* mean?
3. Where in Mexico is the village of San Miguel de Allende located?
• 4. Look at the picture on page 243. What information does the caption give?
5. If you could attend the fiesta of San Miguel, what part of it would you enjoy the most? Why?
6. What important person is featured in the section Someone You Should Know? Why is this person important?
• 7. Turn to Checking Up on page 247. Why is it important to read and answer the questions?
8. How is the price of goods determined in the markets of the mountainside village?
9. How does shopping in a mountainside village of Mexico differ from shopping in your community?

Talking About What You've Read

Think about all of the pleasant attractions of San Miguel de Allende. What sights and activities are there to see and do? What would you most like to see and do if you could visit there? What suggestions would you make to someone going there?

Writing About What You've Read

Pretend that you have taken a trip to San Miguel. You would like others to know what an interesting place this is. Write a short travel advertisement that would make others want to visit Mexico's *tierras frias*. What photograph from this selection would you include in your ad? Why?

• Study Skills: Reading a textbook

Guacamole

In the United States, this avocado (av'ə kä'dō) mixture is usually served as a dip. But in Mexico, it serves many other uses. Guacamole (guä'kə mō'lē) makes a good topping for tacos (tä'kōs) or tostadas (tôs tä'däs) and makes a refreshing salad all by itself.

There are many ways to make this popular food, and all of them are delicious. The essential ingredients are avocados and lime or lemon juice. Without the fruit juice, the avocados would quickly turn brown. Be sure to add it.

How many chilies you use depends on how hot you want your guacamole to taste. Taste it before adding too many. Instead of chilies, you can use a dash of chili powder or hot pepper sauce if you want a little heat.

Ingredients
  2 large (or 4 small) ripe avocados
  1 small tomato, chopped
  ½ small onion, chopped
  1 to 3 canned green chilies, chopped
  1 tablespoon lime or lemon juice
  ¾ teaspoon salt
  pepper to taste

1. Cut avocados in half lengthwise. Pry out the pits with the point of a knife. Peel and cut the avocados into small pieces. (If avocados are very ripe, you can scoop the flesh out of the shell with a spoon.)
2. Mash avocados with a fork and blend in other ingredients. For a very smooth mixture, combine the ingredients in a blender.
3. Serve with tortilla (tôr tē'yə) chips or raw vegetables.

Makes about 2 cups.

For a native Australian, traveling 1,700 miles through the changeable Australian wilderness is almost like traveling through other lands. Robyn Davidson made such a perilous journey in 1977. Follow the route of her trip on the map as you read this remarkable account from her diary.

ALONE

by Robyn Davidson

Three years ago, at the age of twenty-five, I planned an expedition alone from Alice Springs to the Indian Ocean, a distance of about 1,700 miles (see maps on pages 252–253). The very first requirement was buying camels.

For nearly a century, from the 1860s until recent times, camels were commonly used in the outback.[1] The animals, imported from Afghanistan and India, proved highly successful until cars and trucks began to replace them in the 1920s.

Camels are still trained in Alice Springs for tourist jaunts and for occasional sale to Australia's zoos. Sallay Mahomet (sal′ā ma hom′ it) an Australian-born Afghan[2] and a veteran handler, agreed to teach me the art of camel training.

I worked with Sallay nearly three months, for camels are not the easiest of beasts to train. To begin with, they can kill or injure you with a well-placed kick, and their bite is as painful as a horse's. Patiently Sallay taught me to understand camel behavior. Camels are similar to dogs; a well-trained one answers best to its accustomed handler. For an expedition such as mine, it was essential that I do the training.

Through part-time jobs, loans from friends, and finally with support from

---

1. outback: the sparsely settled, flat, arid inland region of Australia.

2. Afghan: a native or an inhabitant of Afghanistan.

Robyn Davidson leading her camels with Diggety dog in the Australian wilderness

the National Geographic Society, I acquired the necessary equipment and four good camels: Dookie, Bub, Zeleika, and Zeleika's calf, Goliath. Training and preparations took more than a year, but finally, in early April of 1977, I was ready.

On April 8, 1977, Sallay and my father—who had come from Brisbane to see me off—trucked me, the camels, and my dog, Diggity, to Glen Helen Tourist Camp, eighty miles west of Alice Springs. From there I journeyed to nearby Redbank Gorge, pausing long enough to say good-bye to my closest friends and helpers from Alice, who had all gathered there. Then I was off for Australia's west coast, alone except for the intermittent company of photographer Rick Smolan.

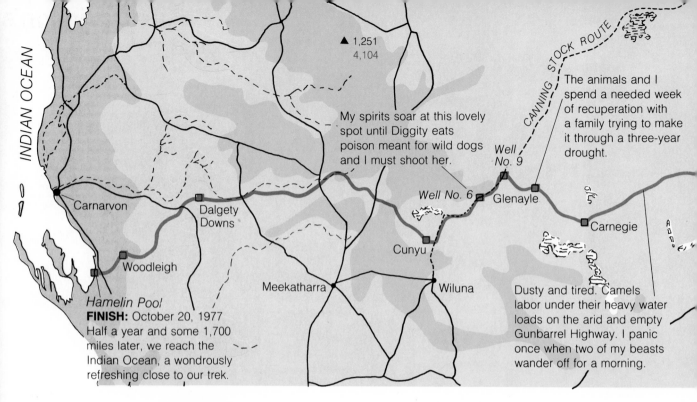

▲ 1,251
4,104

CANNING STOCK ROUTE

The animals and I spend a needed week of recuperation with a family trying to make it through a three-year drought.

My spirits soar at this lovely spot until Diggity eats poison meant for wild dogs and I must shoot her.

Well No. 9

Well No. 6

Glenayle

Carnegie

Carnarvon

Dalgety Downs

Cunyu

Wiluna

Woodleigh

Meekatharra

Hamelin Pool
FINISH: October 20, 1977
Half a year and some 1,700 miles later, we reach the Indian Ocean, a wondrously refreshing close to our trek.

Dusty and tired. Camels labor under their heavy water loads on the arid and empty Gunbarrel Highway. I panic once when two of my beasts wander off for a morning.

AUSTRALIA

Brisbane

Perth

Canberra

DAY 1   That first full day on the trail was both exhilarating and terrifying. My initial stop was to be the Aborigine[3] settlement of Areyonga, via an old abandoned track that wandered through dry, stony creek beds and gullies and often simply disappeared. A dozen times during the day I was struck by the chilling thought, "Am I lost?" It was to become an altogether too familiar question.

3. Aborigine: (ab′ə rij′ə ne) any of the first or earliest known inhabitants of a country or area.

At sundown I camped beside the track and estimated my progress: twenty miles. Not bad for the first day's trek, and only about 1,680 left to go. After hobbling the camels to graze, I built a brushwood fire and cooked a dinner of tinned stew. The blaze was welcome, for nighttime temperatures in the desert can drop to below freezing during Australia's autumn and winter seasons.

Finally I slid into my sleeping bag under an extra blanket or two and spent most of the night alternately dozing and wondering if I would ever see my camels again. But the occasional sound of their bells was reassuring, and at last I drifted off.

The next morning settled one worry; the camels seemed more scared than I

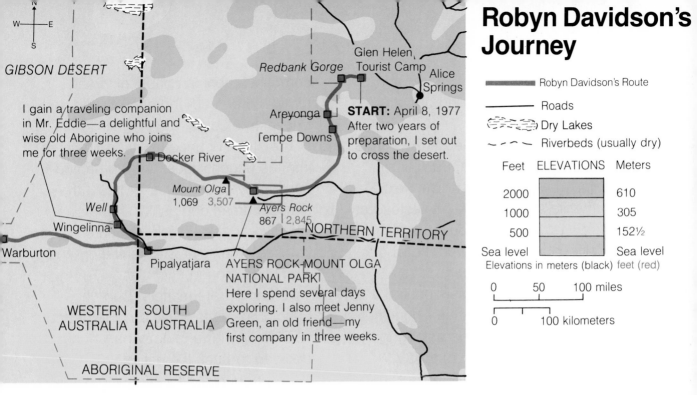

Robyn Davidson's Journey

Robyn Davidson's Route
Roads
Dry Lakes
Riverbeds (usually dry)

Feet	ELEVATIONS	Meters
2000		610
1000		305
500		152½
Sea level		Sea level

Elevations in meters (black) feet (red)

0   50   100 miles

0   100 kilometers

GIBSON DESERT

I gain a traveling companion in Mr. Eddie—a delightful and wise old Aborigine who joins me for three weeks.

Docker River

Well

Wingelinna

Warburton

Pipalyatjara

Redbank Gorge

Glen Helen Tourist Camp

Alice Springs

Areyonga

Tempe Downs

Mount Olga
1,069 3,507

Ayers Rock
867 2,845

START: April 8, 1977 After two years of preparation, I set out to cross the desert.

NORTHERN TERRITORY

AYERS ROCK-MOUNT OLGA NATIONAL PARK
Here I spend several days exploring. I also meet Jenny Green, an old friend—my first company in three weeks.

WESTERN AUSTRALIA | SOUTH AUSTRALIA

ABORIGINAL RESERVE

---

was. I awoke to find them huddled as close as possible around the swag[4] and Diggity snoring happily beneath the blankets.

DAY 4   In the afternoon we reached Areyonga, all slightly the worse for wear. My feet were blistered and my muscles were cramped. Diggity, too, was footsore and had to ride for a spell on Dookie's back, an indignity the dog could scarcely bear.

Zeleika was a complete mess. Her hindquarters were weak, her nose was infected, and she had a huge lump in a vein leading to her udder.

Bub was still uncertain about the whole thing. During those first days he

had shied in terror not only at rabbits but even at rocks and leaves. He obviously wished he were home safe and sound.

Dookie was the only one without grumbles; he was having a great time. He continually smiled to himself, regarded everything around him with satisfaction, and stepped high when he walked. I suspect he has always wanted to travel.

After four days of total solitude, Areyonga came as a shock, though a pleasant one. A mile outside the settlement we were greeted by a welcoming throng of Aborigine children, shouting, giggling, and begging for rides. Seemingly hundreds of small hands reached out to pat Diggity when she was allowed down

---

4. swag: a bundle containing personal belongings.

from exile atop Dookie's back, and there was endless tickling of camel legs.

For three days I rested at Areyonga, worrying about Zeleika, Bub, and Goliath. I wondered what the next thirty-mile stretch to the homestead at Tempe Downs would do to us all. Dookie, of course, viewed the whole thing with lofty unconcern.

Sick or well, the camels proved a key to communication with the Aborigines. The people of Areyonga belong to the Pitjandjara (pit'jand jar a) tribe, who used camels for walkabout[5] until cars and trucks finally replaced the animals. Yet many fond memories and stories of camels survive.

DAY 8   A few Aborigines accompanied us out of Areyonga for the first ten miles toward Tempe Downs. Bidding me good-bye, my companions warned that the route over the mountains was an old one, unused for many years. I promised to call from Tempe Downs over the "flying doctor" radio, the emergency medical network that links Australia's outback settlements.

My friends didn't exaggerate. After fifteen miles the mountain track occasionally began to peter out, and I spent hours sweating over maps and compass. I took a couple of wrong turns into a dead-end canyon and had to backtrack out.

The strain of uncertainty carries over into the unconscious, and I dreamed continually of being lost. Without the almost human companionship of Diggity and the camels, I'm sure I'd be in those mountains still, muttering and stumbling around in circles.

To complicate matters, Bub chose the mountains to throw an unforgettable fit. Shortly after a midday pause, he decided to buck the entire 500 pounds of assorted swag, tucker,[6] and water drums off his back. As each article crashed to the ground, the more terrified Bub became and the harder he bucked. Finally he stood petrified, the dislodged saddle hanging under his belly and the items from the pack scattered for miles.

Despite the setbacks, we made it to Tempe Downs in three days and marked our hundredth mile from the starting point at Glen Helen. After a radio call to my friends at Areyonga, I filled my drinking-water bag with rainwater and set off for Ayers Rock, 150 miles to the southwest.

We were entering sandhill country, an expanse of great motionless waves of reddish sand stretching mile after square mile ahead of us. Flies by the

---

5. walkabout: a period of wandering as a nomad, often undertaken by Aborigines.

6. tucker: food.

zillions engulfed us in dense clouds, covering every exposed square centimeter of human, dog, or camel flesh. Although they didn't bite, they crawled under eyelids, into ears and nostrils, and when they finally gave up at night, clouds of mosquitoes took over.

The country itself was exquisite. Huge stands of desert oak that lined the valleys among the hills sighed, whispered, and sang me to sleep at night. There were varieties of flowers, plants bearing strange seedpods, and other plants adorned with what looked like feathers.

DAY 21   After 250 miles of travel from Glen Helen, we reached Ayers Rock. Among the mass of tourists who fly or drive in to see the great natural wonder, I found Jenny Green, my friend from Alice Springs, who had come to meet me. We talked—or rather, I talked—for four straight days.

The next 140 miles, to the settlement of Docker River at the eastern edge of the Gibson Desert, went smoothly until the weather dealt us an almost fatal blow. So far I had not encountered rain and had wondered how the camels would take to the bright orange plastic raincoats I had designed and made to cover their packs.

Heavy clouds began to bustle over the horizon. Down it came. It rained cats and dogs. It rained elephants and whales, and it hailed! Within an hour the track was a running river and we were all drenched, though the camels soon grew accustomed to the flapping of their orange raincoats.

Robyn Davidson and her camels at Ayers Rock

Camels have feet like bald tires. They simply cannot cope with mud, and leading them over precariously slippery patches is painful and exhausting to both driver and animal. In the midst of the storm Dookie, my best boy, my wonder camel, who was last in line, suddenly sat down with a thud and snapped his noseline.

I went back to him and tried to get him up. He refused. I shouted at him and the poor beast groaned to his feet. To my horror I saw that he was limping. It looked as if the trip was over.

Robyn comforting the injured Dookie

We made it to Docker River in painful stages. Each night in camp along the way I cut shrubbery for Dookie and brought it to him. I massaged his shoulder, I cuddled him, kissed him, shed tears, and begged him to get better. To no avail. The thought of perhaps having to shoot my best camel gnawed away at me. Slowly, painfully, miserably, we limped into Docker River.

In the end it took Dookie a month to recover from what probably was a torn muscle in his shoulder.

DAY 75   This was a memorable day, for it brought the gift of Mr. Eddie! He is a Pitjandjara man, and he arrived at my camp that evening with several carloads of Aborigines from the settlements of Wingelinna (win'jə lēn'a) and Pipalyatjara (pip' al yat'jar ə). I served them all billies[7] of tea, and as we chatted, he caught my notice: a dwarfish man, little taller than five feet, with a straight back, a beautiful face, wonderfully expressive hands, and makeshift shoes on his feet.

My guests spent the night, and the next morning they decided that one of them should accompany me to Pipalyatjara, two-days' walk ahead. I kept a polite silence and simply started off—to be joined by the little man.

_____
7. billies: tin pots used as teakettles by bushpeople.

I turned then, and we looked at each other. There was such humor, depth, life, and knowledge in those eyes that somehow we started laughing. We laughed for five minutes, then he pointed to himself and said, "Eddie." I pointed to myself and said, "Robyn," which I think he mistook for "rabbit" since he pronounces that word "rarbin."

No matter. All day and the next we communicated in pantomime and in broken Pitjandjara or English, falling into helpless laughter at each other's antics. I don't think I ever felt so good in my life. And so we came to Pipalyatjara.

DAY 80   This morning we set off together, and after a mile or two, I began to wonder if we would ever reach Warburton. But Mr. Eddie seemed to flow with time rather than measure it, and eventually I relaxed and began to enjoy my surroundings. It was not the least of lessons he was to teach me.

DAY 94   We parted in Warburton, Mr. Eddie and I. I still think of our three weeks together on the trail as the heart of my entire journey.

The most dangerous part of the journey now lay ahead of me, the Gunbarrel Highway. We would travel 350 miles of the Gunbarrel's total

Gibson Desert

900-mile length, taking us across the forbidding Gibson Desert. The camels could not carry enough water to make it all the way, and so my friend, Glendle Schrader, from Pipalyatjara would drive a truck with additional water from Warburton to the western part of the Gunbarrel. From Pipalyatjara the round trip comes to 800 hazardous miles, whether on foot or by motor. Such is the quality of friends.

Diggity was superb, a perfect and loving friend. She was a ball of muscle, covering fifty miles a day scampering back and forth. She had an unfailing sense of direction, always led me back to camp after an evening stroll, and excelled at chasing away creatures like centipedes and snakes.

The country was harsh, though lovely in its way. Sandhills stretched over some of the route, interspersed here and there with great stands of lacy but impenetrable mulga[8] bush. Golden tufts of spinifex grass turned portions of the trail into a giant pincushion that continually jabbed at our feet. The camels strained under loads consisting largely of water, and noselines frequently snapped. Progress was achingly slow.

Yet there were some moments along the Gunbarrel that I will never forget. One morning before sunrise—gray silk sky, Venus aloft—I saw a single crow, carving up wind currents above the hills.

DAY 112   Two weeks and 220 miles into the Gunbarrel, I had a wham-bammer of a day. It began like most others, except there were clouds. Rain, I thought as the first light slithered under my eyelids and into the

_____
8. mulga: a low plant found in drier parts of Australia.

folds of the blankets. But the clouds vanished, and then I realized something was missing: the sound of familiar camel bells!

Zeleika and Bub were gone, and Dookie, it developed, was only around because he had a great hole in his foot and couldn't walk. Where were Zeleika and Bub? How far had they gone? What about Dookie?

Then I recalled what a very wise friend in Alice once said to me, "When things go wrong on the track, rather than panic, boil the billy, sit down, and think clearly."

So I boiled the billy, sat down with Diggity, and went over the salient points:
- You are a hundred miles from anything.
- You have lost two camels.
- One of the other camels has a hole in his foot so big you could sleep in it.
- You have only enough water to last for six days.
- My hip is sore from walking.
- This is an awful place to spend the rest of your life.

So, having tidied all that up, I panicked. Fortunately, it didn't last, and after four hours I finally managed to get Zeleika and Bub back, doctored Dookie's foot as best I could, and set off once more along the Gunbarrel. The water situation was saved shortly afterward by the arrival of Glendle and his truck.

When he caught up with us, he was so exhausted from the trip he could barely speak. We unloaded two of three forty-gallon water drums from the truck, then filled my own drums from them with gallons to spare.

Next morning Glendle headed back toward Pipalyatjara. When he had become only a dust on the horizon behind us, the silence and solitude closed in again. I was not in the best of shape. My left hip, sore from endless slogging over sandhills, was barely usable. My skin was as dry as dog biscuits, my lips were cracked.

Had it all been worth it? I still thought so.

DAY 118   At the cattle station called Carnegie, at the end of the Gunbarrel, I received another blow: The station was little used because of severe drought, and I could not resupply with food. There was nothing to do but trek northwest seventy-five miles to the station at Glenayle and hope for the best. Food ran so low that I once shared Diggity's dog biscuits—not exactly a banquet, but if they could keep her going, they could do the same for me.

By great luck I met two men traveling by car to Carnegie, and they gave me some tucker. One of them kindly made a leather boot for Dookie's sore foot. It didn't last long, and so I made another

one that lasted even less time. All I could think of was Glenayle and escape from the drought. We straggled in at last, a miserable sight. I hadn't washed, my face and clothes were covered with red dust, I was exhausted, and I looked like a scarecrow. As I entered the Glenayle homestead, the first thing I saw was a lovely, middle-aged lady watering her flower garden. As I approached her, she smiled and without a lift of the eyebrows said, "How nice to see you. Won't you come in for a cup of tea?"

And so I met the Ward family— Eileen, her husband, and their sons. They would not hear of my pushing on for at least a week and insisted that I stay with them. What warm, generous, and utterly charming people. I can never repay their kindness.

Soon afterward we began packing up to leave Glenayle. The camels seemed pleased to get into their traveling kit again, and so I didn't tell them what lay ahead of us: The Canning Stock Route.

The Canning is an Australian legend. It runs nearly 1,000 miles, linking the small towns of Halls Creek and Wiluna and, far north of our route, crossing the Great Sandy Desert, one of Australia's worst.

DAY 129   We left Glenayle after a week and headed for the Canning at

Well Number 6

mountains soared above the desert. Have you ever heard mountains roar and beckon? These did, like a giant lion—a phantom sound. From the pit of my stomach I longed to journey to those mountains. I had found the heart of the world.

On the third night Diggity took a dingo bait. I had to shoot her. Before dawn I left that place I had thought so beautiful.

DAY 137   My only thought now was to push on to the end of my route. The country passed unnoticed beneath my feet, and I recall little of that time. I think I reached Cunyu on August 27. Behind me lay nearly 1,300 miles—five months of travel. Ahead lay only 450 more miles.

DAY 180   A month after leaving Cunyu we arrived at Dalgety Downs cattle station, only 156 miles from the sea.

David and Margot Steadman, homesteaders at Dalgety, took us in and proceeded to spoil all of us. The camels were fed barley, oats, and lollies,[9] an undreamed-of diet. They were praised, patted, stroked, and talked to.

On that final stretch of 156 miles we rode in style for about thirty of them. At Woodleigh, thirty-six miles from the

Well Number 9. This was dingo country, and I was terrified that Diggity would pick up one of the poisoned baits set out to exterminate the wild dogs. I put a muzzle on her, but she was so disconsolate that I took it off.

The area was rougher than anything we had crossed before, and at Well Number 6 I called a halt. The setting was lovely, an infinitely extended bowl of pastel blue haze carpeting the desert, with crescent-shaped hills floating in the bowl and fire-colored sand dunes lapping at their feet. In the far distance five violet, magical

9. lollies: pieces of hard candy.

coast, two kindly homesteaders, David and Jan Thomson, offered to transport the camels and me on their flatbed truck to a point only a couple of hours' walk from the beach.

I accepted, but the camels had reservations. After the long journey, however, their trust in me was complete, and they finally climbed aboard.

DAY 195   Six miles short of our goal we unloaded and set out on the final leg. Oh, how my spirits soared! Two hours later I saw it, glinting on the far side of the dunes—the Indian Ocean, end of trail.

An anticlimax? Never. We rode down to the beach toward sunset and stood thunderstruck at the beauty of the sea. The camels simply couldn't comprehend so much water. They would stare at it, walk a few paces, then turn and stare again.

We stayed one glorious week, then it was time to go. I had decided to leave all four camels in the care of David and Jan Thomson, who loved them dearly

Robyn Davidson and her camels at the Indian Ocean

and who would give them a perfect home at Woodleigh after I returned to my home on Australia's east coast, where I could not keep them. On October 27 David and Jan showed up in the truck. We turned from the beach for the last time. Many times since the trek I have been asked why I made it, and I answer that the trip speaks for itself. But for those who persist I would add these few thoughts. I love the desert and its incomparable sense of space. I enjoy being with Aborigines and learning from them. I like the freedom inherent in being on my own, and I like the growth and learning processes that develop from taking chances.

And obviously, camels are the best means of getting across deserts. Obvious. Self-explanatory. Simple. What's all the fuss about?

Meet the Photographer

While he was shooting an assignment for a magazine in Australia, Rick Smolan was invited to a dinner party by some young people he'd met in Alice Springs. The woman giving the party turned out to be Robyn Davidson. He asked her why she had camels in her backyard, and she told him that she was planning to walk 1,700 miles, across half of Australia.

Later, Rick Smolan was asked by the sponsors of Robyn Davidson's trip if he would be interested in being the photographer. "That was the start of the most interesting year in my life," says Smolan.

"Taking pictures out there was hard at first because it all looked ugly—dry weeds, rocks, flat landscape. Slowly Robyn taught me to see. To notice how the vegetation changed suddenly, indicated there was water underground. The light at dawn and at night was incredible. The sky would shimmer for hours after sunset—lots of shooting stars.

"As the trip progressed, the pictures got better, more to do with how Robyn was affected by the environment. Sometimes I wouldn't photograph for days at a time. As the trip went on, I stopped being an observer and felt that in my own way I was also part of the camel trip.

"Robyn and I are still friends although we don't see each other too much anymore. She's a pretty special person—but she'd say I was prejudiced. (I am.)"

Rick Smolan received the 1985 Innovation in Photography Award presented by the American Society of Magazine Photographers at the Metropolitan Museum of Art in New York City.

Checking Comprehension and Skills

Thinking About What You've Read

1. Why was Davidson's journey through the Australian wilderness like a journey through other lands?
2. What kinds of animals did Davidson take with her?
3. What are two problems that arise from using camels for the trip?
4. What kind of help does Mr. Eddie provide Robyn Davidson? What does she learn from him?
5. How does the diary show that people do not have to speak the same language to communicate?
6. What do you think was the most difficult part of Davidson's trip? Explain your answer.
7. If you had made the trip, at what point would you have thought most seriously about giving up? Why?
• 8. Look at the big map on pages 252 and 253. Locate Ayers Rock. What is its elevation? In what part of Australia is it located?
• 9. Using the map, how many miles is the distance between Wingelinna and Warburton? How many kilometers is that?

Talking About What You've Read

Think about Robyn Davidson's experiences. Which of them did you find the most exciting and adventurous? What else would you like to know about them? If you could talk to Robyn Davidson, what questions would you ask her about her journey?

Writing About What You've Read

Pretend that you traveled with Robyn Davidson on her journey across the Australian wilderness. Write a diary entry for one week of the trip. In your diary, record your thoughts about the wilderness, the animals, the people, and Robyn Davidson.

• Study Skills: Maps

Taking Notes

Suppose Robyn Davidson were going to give a speech about her journey. She might read her diary and take notes about important parts she wanted to include. One way to remember what *you* read is to take notes.

There are two important points to remember about taking notes. First, keep your purpose in mind. For example, are you looking for the main idea in an article? Or are you looking for specific answers to questions? What you decide to write depends on your purpose for reading.

Second, remember that notes can include phrases as well as sentences. The important thing to remember is to try to state *in your own words* the ideas that meet your purpose. Once in a while, you may have to use the exact words of the author. In such cases, add quotation marks around them so you'll know these are the author's words.

Look back at page 256. These are the notes Robyn Davidson might have written for her speech about Day 75 of her journey.

Mr. Eddie arrived
Pitjandjara man
brought Aborigines
spoke little English
hard to communicate but fun trying
accompanied me to Pipalyatjara

If you want to practice taking notes, look back at page 259 and take notes on Day 118 of Davidson's journey.

WILDERNESS RIVERS

by Elizabeth Coatsworth

There are rivers
That I know,
Born of ice
And melting snow,
White with rapids,
Swift to roar,
With no farms
Along their shore,
With no cattle
Come to drink
At a staid
And welcoming brink,
With no millwheel
Ever turning
In that cold,
Relentless churning.

Only deer
And bear and mink
At those shallows
Come to drink;
Only paddles
Swift and light
Flick that current
In their flight.
I have felt
My heart beat high,
Watching
With exultant eye
Those pure rivers
Which have known
No will, no purpose
But their own.

It is difficult for people who are forced to leave their homes to live in other lands. It is far worse to move to the remote land of Siberia. This selection, from Esther Rudomin Hautzig's autobiography, will help you understand why.

The
ENDLESS STEPPE

by Esther Hautzig

Ten-year-old Esther Rudomin lived in Vilna in the northeastern part of Poland. In June 1941, her simple, happy life was shattered. The Russians, who briefly occupied Vilna just before World War II, arrested the Rudomin family and shipped them to a labor camp on a steppe in Siberia. A steppe is a wide, flat grassland without trees. Once there, they were no longer free to come and go as they pleased. Instead, they were forced to work in a gypsum mine and to obey the commands of the mine's director. All the pleasures of their lives in Vilna faded. Then one day something happened to change Esther's life again, though only for a brief time.

The first few weeks of life at the gypsum mine had passed. We settled into a monotony that seemed as vast and endless as the steppe itself. Torn from sleep by the morning whistle, in the beginning I didn't know where I was, what we were all doing sleeping on a floor with strangers. But soon that too passed. I would slip from sleep to wakefulness, barely noticing the difference. We did what we were told. We worked. We munched bread and cheese. Once in a while, a special treat, we had a bowl of soup with bits of meat in it. We slept. We barely talked.

The fever, or whatever it was I had had, flared up again, and I spent a few days alone in the room. Someplace Father had found a straw mattress, and I lay on that—for one day. The next day, when I was in a feverish doze, it was unceremoniously yanked out from under me. Popravka, our warden, had not learned to love us.

A few nights later, he came in and told us to assemble for a meeting. What now?

We gathered in front of the little building where the director of the mine had his office and waited. The air was very hot and still. The sky was darkening too quickly. Way off in the distance, there was a flash of light. The crowd stirred. Before long we would be in for it.

There are those who find a Siberian electrical storm very beautiful and exciting. And I imagine it is if one is not scared to death of it. I was, and so were most of the grown-ups in our midst, it seemed to me. In *our* Siberia, a summer storm was not a summer storm—it was a

judgment that would punish master and slave alike. The lightning would fork out like a malevolent claw in a frenzy to ground itself on the treeless steppe. The fear was that where there was not a tree in sight, nor a hill, it would ground itself in you if you were outdoors, and quite possibly if you were indoors too. There were times when the huge sky was streaked with lightning wherever you looked.

This sky could be highly dramatic even when there was no storm brewing. At night, I would stand at the window by the hour watching meteors race through the enormous blackness. And there were also those dancing, shifting, awesomely beautiful columns of light, the northern lights.

When the mine director walked out, I hoped he would say his say quickly, before the storm struck. He did. To my ten-year-old ears, what he had to say was so unexpectedly exciting that I almost forgot the approaching storm. Every Sunday, six people would be allowed to go to the village. Permission would be granted by him but had to be requested well in advance.

Back in our corner of the room, I hastened to assure my parents, before they might have other ideas, that unless I were allowed to go to the village immediately, I would die—immediately. My poor mother, who was having one of her headaches and whose blistered feet had become so ulcerated that she had to work barefoot, muttered glumly that I was just like my father, always the optimist. Hadn't I learned by now that it was not all that easy to die? My grandmother thought that was a dreadful thing to say to a child—as I did—at which moment the storm broke outside, just in time to interrupt the one that was brewing inside.

Father said that I could have his place. Since Mother said that she could not possibly go with her bad feet, Grandmother hastily offered to go as my chaperone. My father suggested that Rubtsovsk (rupt'sofsk') was not worth her trudging twelve kilometers each way on a hot dusty road. Grandmother, who had flitted about so gaily in Vilna from dinner party to dinner party, to charity bazaars, theater, and opera, ignored the insinuation that she too was starving for amusement: "What do I care about hot dusty roads? After all, what are grandmothers for?"

We received permission to go in two weeks. When we heard that Rubtsovsk had a market, a *baracholka* (ba'ra hol'ka), where one could exchange goods for rubles and which was open on Sunday, it was agreed that Grandmother and I should do some trading. Rubles meant food—potatoes perhaps; anything but the usual bread and brinza cheese. We spent every night deciding which of our few belongings we were ready to sell. One of Mother's lace-trimmed French silk slips went in and out of a bag a dozen times. "I really don't need this for dynamiting gypsum," she said.

"Nor do I need this," Father said, holding up a custom-made silk shirt, "for driving a wagon."

Grandmother wasn't so sure they wouldn't need them. She herself was most reluctant to part with a black silk umbrella with a slender silver handle. "If only we didn't have such nice things . . ." she murmured.

"And what should I part with?" I asked.

"Nothing. You are a growing child," they chorused.

Indeed I was. In those two months—summer being growing time—my skirts already had become almost an inch shorter.

I thought that Sunday would never come. When it did, Grandmother and I set off down the dusty road before anyone else. Along with our wares—the slip, the shirt, and the umbrella, after all—we had wrapped some bread in one of my father's handkerchiefs. The bread was to be our lunch.

It was shortly after six o'clock, the air was still cool and fresh, a hawk was soaring overhead, and, feeling oddly disloyal, I thought the steppe was just a tiny bit beautiful that morning.

I glanced back over my shoulder. No one was coming after us to order us to return to the mine. But I quickened my pace and urged Grandmother to hurry. "Nonsense!" she said. "We will drop dead if we walk too fast." But she too looked back over her shoulder.

When the mine was out of sight, when there was nothing but Grandmother and me and the steppe, nothing else, not even a hawk in the sky, I didn't shout—I wouldn't dare because of the way sound carried—I didn't sing very loud, but I sang, and my funny little voice sounded strange to me. And I felt light, as if I could do a giant leap over the steppe.

"Grandmother, do you know what?"

"What?"

"We are doing something we *want* to do. All by ourselves. We are fr-r-r-eeeee. . . ."

"Shh!" Grandmother looked around. "Not so loud."

She was dressed in her best dress, a rumpled blue silk that was also beginning to fade, and her little hat. In spite of her tininess, Grandmother had always been the *grande dame.*[1] Walking down the dusty road that day, she still was.

We walked for about three hours across the uninhabited steppe without meeting one other person. Before long, I had tied my sweater around my waist—my pleated school skirt and blouse had become my uniform— and Grandmother had opened her umbrella.

We saw a bump in the distance. This turned out to be the first of the widely scattered huts. That meant that before too long we would be in Rubtsovsk.

The village had appeared on the horizon like a mirage always receding from us. We finally did reach it and it was real. Wonderfully real to my starved eyes.

Rubtsovsk, at that time, had an unused church with its onion top, a bank, a library, a pharmacy, a school—even a movie house and a park with a bandstand. But all I saw that day was a square alive with people. Only vaguely did I see a rather mean cluster of wooden buildings and huts.

---

1. grande dame (grän däm′): a woman, especially an older one, of great dignity or many accomplishments.

We squeezed our way through the crowd—the men in peaked caps, here and there an old military cap, women in babushkas, friendly faces sometimes scarred from frostbite, friendly voices. And some Kazakhs,[2] Asia at last! Colorful costumes, the women with their long pigtails encased in cloth and leather pouches. And, sad to see, men, women, and children all with rotting teeth. But Kazakhs!

Trading was going on all around us. There were the stalls around the square with produce from the collective farms—and the small farmers too. There were the buildings with signs proclaiming them to be state-operated stores. One made purchases there only if one had been issued ration books, which we had not been. In one corner, sunflower seeds were being roasted over an open fire. The smell was ravishing. "Come on, Grandmother." I nudged her. "Let's begin to trade."

We made our way to the *baracholka* (bä′rä hôl′kä). Wooden horses were set up all over the interior of the square. Piles of stuff were heaped onto blankets or onto the bare stones: old boots, jackets, babushkas, books, pots, pans—anything and everything.

We found a place to stand. To my surprise, without feeling the least bit self-conscious, I immediately held up my mother's slip, the lacy pink silk blowing in the breeze. In a second, we were surrounded: Where were we from? Where did we live? What did Grandmother do? How old

2. Kazakhs (kə zäks′): a people looking much like Chinese who live in central Asia in the Soviet Union.

was I? They were exceedlingly friendly and frankly inquisitive, these native Siberians. We answered the questions as fast as we could, with Grandmother doing most of the talking, since she knew Russian well and I hardly spoke it. We coaxed our potential customers to note the beauty of the lace, the fact that there were 16, *sixteen,* ribs in the umbrella. How much? Forty rubles. *Forty* rubles? There was a roar of laughter. All right, thirty-eight rubles . . . I caught Grandmother's eye. We smiled at each other.

We were born traders, and we were having a marvelous time. It was, in fact, the happiest time I had had in a long, long time. The guns, the bombs of World War II were thousands of miles away, and at the market place the labor camp seemed far away too. All around me children were giggling over nothing. Girls were showing off their dolls—what if they were made of rags?—and boys were wrestling. These children were just like the children in Vilna. Hunger, fatigue, sorrow, and fright were forgotten. Haggling was a wonderfully engrossing game. Rough hands that had scrounged the earth for potatoes, and been frostbitten more than once, fingered the silk, sometimes as if it were sinful for anything to be that silky, more often to test it for durability. If an egg was around fifteen rubles, how much should a silk slip with *hand-drawn* lace be? Hand drawn, mule drawn, what difference if you couldn't eat it? We all joined in the laughter. I don't remember who brought Father's shirt and Grandmother's umbrella. But the slip was finally bought by a young woman with lots of orange rouge

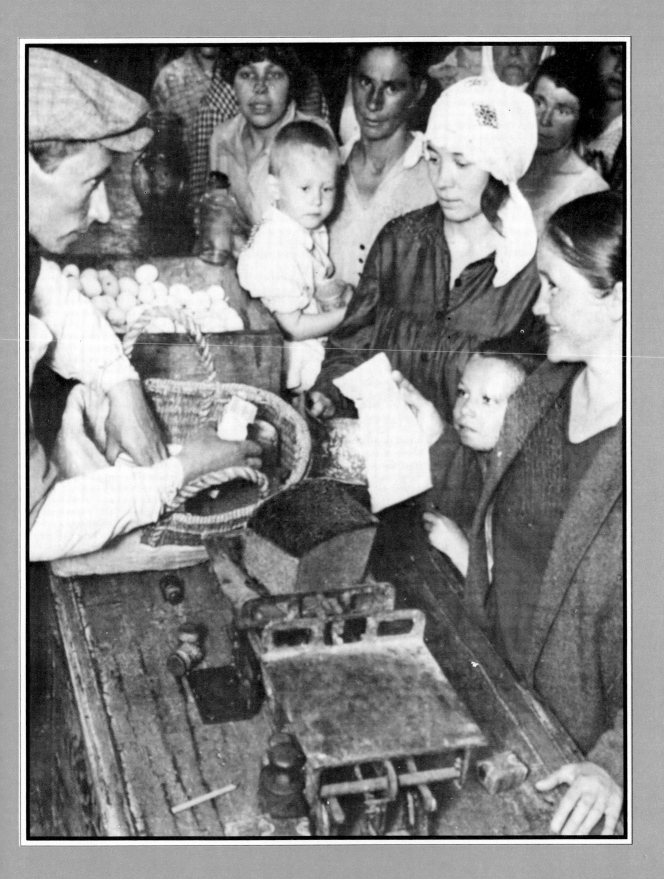

on her cheeks. She was so plump I wondered how she was going to squeeze into it, but that, I decided, was her worry, not mine.

Feeling very proud of ourselves with our newly acquired rubles, we now became the customers. What to buy? We went to the stall where the produce was—watermelons, cucumbers, potatoes, milk, flour, *white* bread—a great luxury—and meat. Everything was incredibly expensive. We walked back and forth from stall to stall, unable to make a decision. I stood perfectly still in front of the roasting sunflower seeds, ostentatiously breathing in and out. Grandmother counted the rubles we had. "Come," she said, "what are grandmothers for?" The first purchase was a small glassful of sunflower seeds. I slit the shell between my teeth and extracted the tiny nut. I nursed it as if it were a piece of precious candy. It could not have tasted better. Siberians love sunflower seeds. I think ninety percent of them bore a little notch in a front tooth to prove it.

After much deliberation and more bargaining, we bought a piece of meat and a bag of flour. There was a communal outdoor stove at the schoolhouse. We could boil the meat on it. After mixing the flour with water, we could bake little flat breads.

By that time, the sun had begun to set. Grandmother said we must start our long hike home. But I could tell that she was as reluctant to leave this carnival as I was. So, it seemed, was everyone else. The stalls were empty of their produce. It was all like some kind of game:

Everyone had everyone else's belongings, wrapped in blankets, coats, babushkas, old flour sacks. But having come together in this vast, lonely steppe, having joked and gossiped and even sung songs, no one wanted to leave.

However, as we began our long trudge back, we were very happy, thinking only of the *baracholka,* not of the mine. Grandmother and I had this in common. We were "very" people—either very sad or very gay, with nothing in between. Oh, if we could only live in the village and go to the *baracholka* every Sunday, Siberia would be bearable. I started to tick off the things I had to sell— three dresses, one blouse, a coat . . . Grandmother laughed. "Stop before you go naked in exchange for a glassful of sunflower seeds."

No matter, I thought, whether I had something to sell or not. I hoped that one day we would be allowed to live in the village within sight and sound of the Sunday *baracholka.*

After her release from Russia, Esther spent nearly a year in Lodz, Poland. She, her mother, and her grandmother had been reunited with her father, who had been in the army and after his release had gone to Poland earlier. Then the family went to Sweden. Soon after, Esther sailed alone for the United States to live with her mother's brother and his family. Her parents joined her later, while her grandmother went to live in Israel.

Meet the Author

When Esther Hautzig lived with her aunt and uncle and their children in Brooklyn, New York, she didn't know any English. But the children helped her. They did this by speaking slowly and very loudly.

The writing of *The Endless Steppe,* which was a National Book Award Honor Book and an American Library Association Notable Book, came about because of a suggestion by the late Adlai E. Stevenson. In 1959 Governor Stevenson went on a trip to the Soviet Union and wrote a series of newspaper articles about it. One article was about Rubtsovsk. Esther Hautzig wrote him a three-page, single-spaced, typed letter, telling him about her experiences there. Governor Stevenson wrote to her, suggesting that she write a book about her life in Rubtsovsk.

You have read how the author and her grandmother traded the family's precious possessions at the fair in Rubtsovsk. Even today Hautzig likes fairs. She says, "I have a terrible weakness for flea markets in this country and often come home loaded down with stuff I never use—much to everyone's disgust with me! If I had the nerve, I'd set up a yard sale at the corner near my apartment house and have my own private baracholka. I guess I'm a horse trader at heart."

Between the years 1942 and 1944, children in a concentration camp drew and painted and wrote poetry. The poem and drawing are done by two of these children.

Birdsong

Anonymous

He doesn't know the world at all
Who stays in his nest and doesn't go out.
He doesn't know what birds know best
Nor what I want to sing about,
That the world is full of loveliness.

When dewdrops sparkle in the grass
And earth's aflood with morning light,
A blackbird sings upon a bush
To greet the dawning after night.
Then I know how fine it is to live.

Hey, try to open up your heart
To beauty; go to the woods someday
And weave a wreath of memory there.
Then if the tears obscure your way
You'll know how wonderful it is
   To be alive.

LOOKING BACK

Thinking About the Section

The selections in this section describe other lands that have different kinds of environments: Mexico's *tierras frias*, the Australian desert, and the Siberian steppe. Your information about these places comes from several sources: the descriptions you have read, the photographs you have seen, and the maps you have seen.

Using all of the information you have, compare and contrast these three environments. What is the climate of each area? Is the area flat or mountainous?

Suppose you were going to take a trip to each of these places. Based on what you know, what would you pack in your suitcase for each place? Copy the chart below onto a sheet of paper. Fill in the chart by "packing" your suitcases.

Things to Take to the *Tierras Frias*	Things to Take to the Australian Desert	Things to Take to the Siberian Steppe
shorts	canteen	coat

Writing About the Section

Now select one of these places. Write a narrative paragraph that describes a difficult experience that you had on your trip. Select one of the items you brought with you and tell how it saved the day.

Books to Read

Mrs. Frisby and the Rats of NIMH by Robert C. O'Brien, Atheneum © 1971

Mrs. Frisby the mouse must move before planting begins on Mr. Fitzgibbons's farm. She turns in desperation to an owl for advice, and with the aid of Nicodemus and Justin, two highly intelligent rats recently escaped from NIMH, the owl's plan works. But have all problems been solved?

Cider Days by Mary Stolz, Harper © 1978

Polly wonders what it will be like to spend the winter holidays in Vermont without her best friend. Will she ever find another close friend? Perhaps the newcomer from Mexico will fill that place.

Moonshadow of Cherry Mountain by Doris Buchanan Smith, Four Winds © 1982

The mountain was Moonshadow's, the dog, but suddenly more people arrive. Gradually Moonshadow's territory dwindles. Greg knows that his dog would never harm anyone. Will Cherry Mountain be big enough for all to share?

Sally Ride and the New Astronauts by Karen O'Connor, Watts © 1983

In April 1983, Sally Ride's childhood dream came true—she became the first American woman to orbit in space. Here is a chance to share some of her experiences in space.

7

Coming to America

' *"Give me your tired, your poor, Your huddled masses, yearning to breathe free . . ."* '

With these words, the Statue of Liberty welcomes the people who come to America. For the families who arrived many years ago or last week, from East or West or North or South, the statue is a symbol of freedom, hope, and opportunity for us all.

You'll take a close look at Liberty in this section. You'll also read about some European immigrants who came here many years ago seeking better lives. And you'll meet a group of recent Asian immigrants, who have come seeking freedom and the right to preserve their ancient traditions.

Using and Evaluating Reference Sources

Have you ever played hopscotch? The picture above shows a group of children of long ago playing hopscotch, a game that was brought to America from England. To find out how the game was played in colonial America, you could look for information in an encyclopedia.

An **encyclopedia** is a set of books that contain information about people, places, things, events, and ideas. The articles, called **entries,** are in alphabetical order. Since you want information about the game of hopscotch, *hopscotch* is your key word. You can find the entry in Volume 9, which contains all the entries beginning with H.

A **key word** is the word to look for, and experience using encyclopedias will make it easier for you to decide what key word to look up. Some entries, for example, have more than one word and can be found by looking up the first word: Puerto Rico (Volume 15, P) Mount Everest (Volume 13, M). Names of people are listed by last name first: Bradford, William (Volume 2, B).

Once you have chosen the right volume, you can quickly find the entry you want by using the **guide words.** These are at the top of each set of facing encyclopedia pages and show the first and last entry word on those pages. At the end of some entries you will find the words *See also* or *See.* These are **cross-references.** *See also* refers you to other entries that have more information about the subject. *See* will appear only where there is no article after the entry word and refers you to one or more entries that give information about the subject.

Sometimes you need more information about a subject than is given in an encyclopedia article. When this occurs, the card catalog can be very helpful. Most libraries have a **card catalog,** a set of drawers containing cards that are filed in alphabetical order. In some libraries, the same information is available from a computer. If your library uses a computerized system, ask your librarian how to use it.

For most books in the library, there are usually three kinds of cards in the card catalog—an **author** card, a **title** card, and a **subject** card. The cards for one book are shown on page 288. If you are looking for a book by a particular

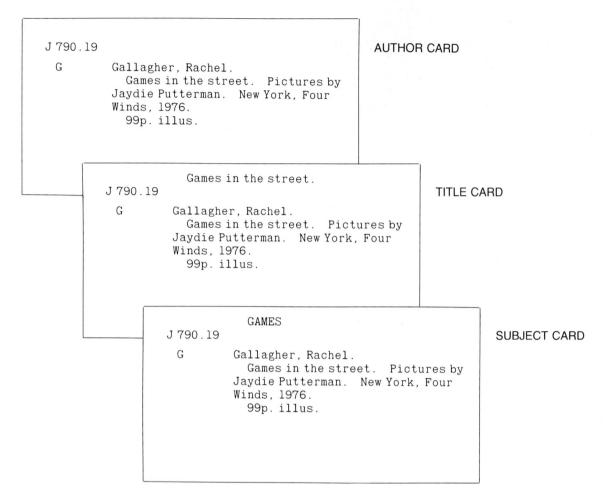

author, look for the card or cards with the author's name on
the top line. Who is the author named on the author card
above?

If you know the title of the book you want, look up its title
card. The title is on the top line of the card. Title cards for
books that begin with *A*, *An*, or *The* are not filed under **A** or
T. They are filed in alphabetical order by the second word in
the title. What is the title of the book on the title card?

If you are not looking for a particular book, but are trying
to find information on a particular subject, you should look
for a subject card for that subject. The top line of a subject
card tells what subject the book is about. What subject is the
book named on the cards about?

Once you have found the right card, how do you go about finding the book you want?

The numbers and letters in the upper left-hand corner of the card catalog also are on the spine of the book. When you find a card for a book you want, write down the call number, the author, and the title. Then follow the signs in the library until you find the shelves with books that have the number you are looking for. Now you are ready to find the book on the shelf and do more research about hopscotch.

Information in reference sources such as an encyclopedia is usually quite reliable. Most, if not all, of the facts found in them are correct. But what about other reference sources? How can you be sure whether or not the information you find in them is accurate?

There are several things you can check to help you determine whether the information you find in a reference book is probably accurate or not. One of these is the **copyright date.** Reference books with the latest dates usually have the latest information on a subject. The copyright date can be found on the cards for that book in a card catalog. It can be found on the copyright page of the book itself. The copyright date of a story or an article can often be found in a footnote on the first page of the story or article.

Checking the author's background can sometimes be helpful too. Sometimes you will find information about the author on the jacket of the book or in a headnote at the beginning of an article. This information can help you decide if the author has a good background for writing an article on a particular subject.

Another way you can check on the accuracy of information you find in some source is to check to see if the information agrees with the facts about the same subject from other sources. If it does, it is likely that the information is correct.

Read the encyclopedia article on page 290 about the early English settlers in America. Think about how you'd find additional information on this topic.

PILGRIMS were the early English settlers of New England. The first group landed at what is now Plymouth, Mass., in 1620. The Pilgrims established Plymouth Colony along Cape Cod Bay.

The early Pilgrims included many *Separatists*. These people once belonged to the body of English Protestants known as *Puritans*. The Puritans wished to adopt reforms that would purify the Church of England, the nation's official church. The Separatists decided that they could not reform the church from within. They separated from the church and set up their own congregations.

In 1606, William Brewster helped form a small Separatist congregation in Scrooby, England. Separatist groups were illegal in England, and in 1607 the Scrooby congregation tried to flee to Amsterdam, Holland, to avoid arrest. They were caught, but most of them left England the next year. In 1609, the congregation settled in the Dutch town of Leiden.

After several years in Holland, some Separatists began to fear that their children would be more Dutch than English. As foreigners, they could not buy land or work in skilled trades. In addition, war had begun in Europe. The new land of America appealed to them. They offered to establish an English colony in America and found a group of English merchants willing to finance their expedition. In September 1620, 41 members of the Leiden congregation sailed for America on the ship *Mayflower*, along with 61 other English people. The group reached what is now Provincetown Harbor on Nov. 21, 1620. They explored the nearby coast and soon chose Plymouth as the site of their colony.

The term *Pilgrim* may have come from William Bradford, the second governor of Plymouth Colony. Bradford wrote that "they knew they were pilgrims" when they left Holland. However, for 200 years these people were known as "Founders" or "Forefathers," rather than "Pilgrims." JOAN R. GUNDERSEN

See also PLYMOUTH COLONY; COLONIAL LIFE IN AMERICA; BRADFORD, WILLIAM; MASSACHUSETTS (picture: A Pilgrim House); MAYFLOWER; MAYFLOWER COMPACT.

From THE WORLD BOOK ENCYCLOPEDIA, vol. 15, pp. 415–416. Copyright © 1985 by World Book, Inc. Reprinted by permission.

1. If you wanted to know about the Pilgrims' voyage to America, which cross-reference would you look up?

Since the article tells you the Pilgrims sailed on the ship *Mayflower*, the most logical cross-reference is *Mayflower*, or possibly *Mayflower Compact*. The other cross-references all seem to be about the life of the Pilgrims after their voyage.

2. You need to find out what happened to the Puritans who were left behind in Holland. What would you look up in the card catalog?

Since you don't have the title of a specific book to look for, your best choice would be to look for a subject card under *Puritans*. Another possibility is to see if the author of the encyclopedia article, Joan R. Gundersen, has written a book about the Puritans.

3. What information about Joan R. Gundersen would help you to evaluate the information in the encyclopedia article?

Practicing Using and Evaluating Reference Sources

Use what you know about using and evaluating reference sources to explain how to find information about the English settlers who established the southern settlement of Williamsburg, Virginia, in 1633.

1. What key word would you look up in the encyclopedia?
2. Aside from *Williamsburg*, what would you look for in the card catalog to find out detailed information?
3. Which author would be better qualified to write about colonial Williamsburg—a science teacher who lives in Williamsburg at the present time, or a history professor who teaches a class called "The Early English Colonies in America"?

Tips for Reading on Your Own

- Use an encyclopedia to find general information about a subject.
- Think of key words to help you decide what to look up in an encyclopedia.
- Use the card catalog to find books about a subject when you need detailed, specific information.
- When using a card catalog, decide whether you need to find the *author* or *title* of a particular book or books on a particular *subject*. Then look for the appropriate card.
- Evaluate the source of information by noting the copyright date, checking the author's background, and comparing facts with other sources.

What is the history of the Statue of Liberty? Why has it become a symbol of freedom for the many people who have come to America? The encyclopedia entry provides factual information about the statue's past and present, and it gives references for related topics as well. See how much information is available from this one source.

STATUE OF LIBERTY

STATUE OF LIBERTY is the large copper statue that stands on Liberty Island (formerly Bedloe's Island) in New York Harbor. Its proper name is *Liberty Enlightening the World.* This statue is one of the largest ever made. France gave the Statue of Liberty to the United States in 1884 as a symbol of friendship and of the liberty that citizens enjoy under a free form of government. The French people donated about $250,000 for the construction of the statue, and the people of the United States gave about $280,000 for the pedestal. A model of it stands on a bridge over the Seine River in Paris.

Description. The statue represents a proud woman, dressed in a loose robe that falls in graceful folds to the top of the pedestal on which the statue stands. The right arm holds a great torch raised high in the air. The left arm grasps a tablet bearing the date of the Declaration of Independence. A crown with huge spikes, like sun rays, rests on the head. At the feet is a broken shackle symbolizing the overthrow of tyranny.

This statue is one of the most celebrated examples of *repoussé* work, which is a process of hammering metal over a mold in order to shape it. The statue is made of more than 300 thin sheets of copper, with a total weight of about 100 short tons (91 metric tons). The outer layer of copper is supported by an iron framework, which resembles that of an oil derrick. The statue stands 151 feet 1 inch (46.05 meters) high and weighs 450,000 pounds (204,000 kilograms). The torch rises 305 feet 1 inch (92.99 meters) above the base of the pedestal. It gleams at night with powerful incandescent and mercury vapor lights as a symbol of liberty lighting the world. Floodlights from the base of the pedestal shine on the statue.

An elevator carries visitors up the pedestal to the foot of the statue. At this point, an observation balcony

Cutaway View of the Statue of Liberty

The Statue of Liberty is one of the largest statues ever made. It is 151 feet 1 inch (46.05 meters) from the sandals to the top of the torch. It stands on a granite and concrete pedestal on Liberty Island. The torch towers 305 feet 1 inch (92.99 meters) above the base of the pedestal. The statue, made of sheets of copper over a framework of iron, weighs 450,000 pounds (204,000 kilograms).

Liberty's Torch shines through leaded glass, illuminated by five mercury vapor lamps.

Liberty's Crown has a 25-window observation platform that can accommodate 30 viewers.

Interior of the Statue has two parallel, spiral stairways. Visitors climb 171 steps from the base of the statue to the crown. The staircase has rest seats at every third turn.

Liberty's Framework is made of iron and is supported by steel columns. It was made by Gustave Eiffel, who built Paris' Eiffel Tower.

Liberty's Base is reached by an elevator which brings visitors from the ground floor up through the pedestal, a distance of about 150 feet (46 meters).

Scale: $\frac{1}{16}''$ = approximately 2'

affords a magnificent view of the harbor and the city. Visitors may climb a steep, narrow, spiral staircase from the pedestal as high as the crown on the statue's head. A ladder inside the arm leads to the torch but this is too narrow and steep for public use.

"The New Colossus," a poem by Emma Lazarus, was inscribed on a tablet in the pedestal in 1903.

History. The French historian Édouard de Laboulaye first suggested a monument to symbolize liberty. His friend Frédéric Auguste Bartholdi designed the statue and chose its site. Bartholdi also spent a great deal of time and energy raising funds in France and the United States to bring the plan to completion. Alexandre Gus-

tave Eiffel, who designed the Eiffel Tower in Paris, built the supporting framework.

The people of France presented the Statue of Liberty to the Minister of the United States in Paris, on July 4, 1884. The statue was shipped to the United States in 214 cases aboard the French ship *Isère* in May 1885. The site chosen for the statue was the center of old Fort Wood, on Bedloe's Island, overlooking the ship channel of New York Harbor. President Grover Cleveland dedicated the monument on Oct. 28, 1886. It was unveiled before representatives of both countries.

The floodlights at the base were added in 1916. The statue became a national monument in 1924. It was repaired and strengthened throughout in 1937. Congress changed the island's name to Liberty Island in 1956. The American Museum of Immigration, built inside the statue's base, opened in 1972. The National Park Service maintains the Statue of Liberty National Monument. In 1984, the park service began a project to repair damage to the Statue of Liberty caused by wear. The repairs were to include strengthening the connections between the arm, the head, and the rest of the statue. The repairs were scheduled to be completed during 1986. THOMAS M. PITKIN

See also BARTHOLDI, FRÉDÉRIC A.; EIFFEL, ALEXANDRE G.; LAZARUS, EMMA; LIBERTY ISLAND; UNITED STATES (color picture).

STATUE OF LIBERTY NATIONAL MONUMENT is on Ellis and Liberty islands in New York harbor. The colossal statue by Frédéric Bartholdi stands on Liberty Island. The people of France presented it to the United States on July 4, 1884. Ellis Island was an immigration station until 1954. It became part of the monument in 1965. See also ELLIS ISLAND; STATUE OF LIBERTY.

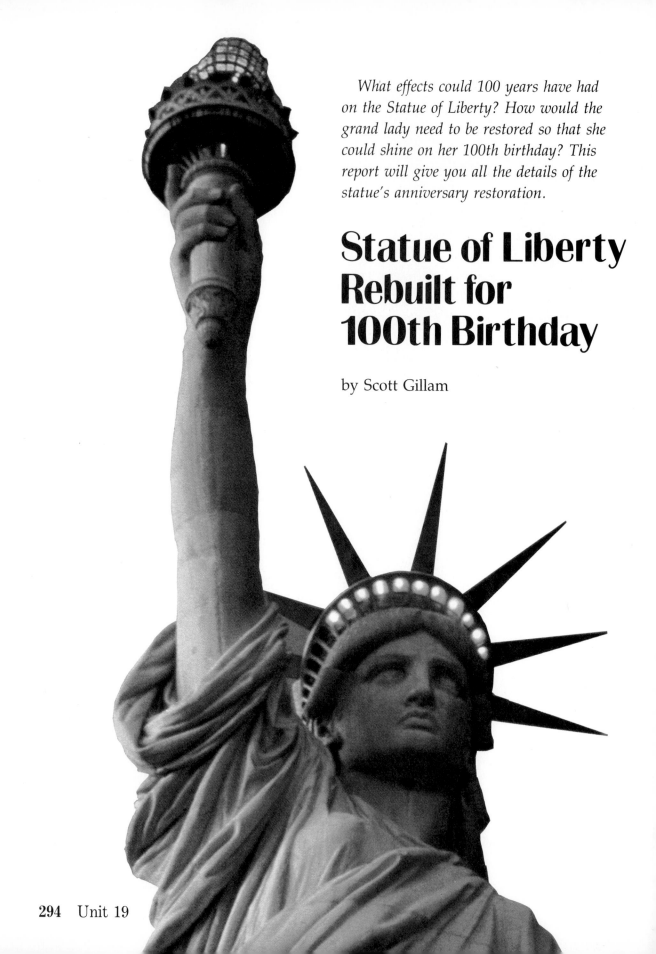

What effects could 100 years have had on the Statue of Liberty? How would the grand lady need to be restored so that she could shine on her 100th birthday? This report will give you all the details of the statue's anniversary restoration.

Statue of Liberty Rebuilt for 100th Birthday

by Scott Gillam

The huge statue seemed to reach up with new power as its cover was taken off. Hundreds of boats with colorful sails bobbed in New York Harbor, competing with one another for the best views of the famous figure with the spiked crown, raised arm, and flaming torch. Fireboats sprayed plumes of water across the sky. Larger ships fired a salute in honor of the grand lady's birthday. Important people made speeches about the ideal of liberty and gave thanks for a country that stands for this ideal. Air Force jets screamed out of the sky and added their booming sounds of welcome. As day turned into night, fireworks lit up the sky.

The day marked the end of the rebuilding of the Statue of Liberty. Once again the majestic arm was raised over the harbor. At night the bright flame again cast its glow across the water. Visitors were able for the first time in several years to enjoy the full effect of a visit to what is perhaps the most famous statue in the world.

Why did the Statue of Liberty need rebuilding? A statue reaching the age of one hundred needs a little extra special care. In the case of the Statue of Liberty, however, more than a little care was needed.

It seems that Miss Liberty was never the sturdy statue that most people had thought she was. Her copper skin is only one-tenth of an inch thick (though it weighs over one hundred tons). She also has a permanent tilt to her neck and shoulder. This problem arose because Liberty's raised arm reaches eighteen inches farther forward than was first planned. Even her head is not quite screwed on correctly. It sits about two feet more to the right than it was supposed to. This position causes one of the seven spikes in her crown to rub against her raised arm. In short, Liberty has had a rather painful life in some ways. (Her posture, by the way, was not corrected when she was rebuilt. It seems that people had become used to her the way she was! She was just given a stronger frame.)

We don't know quite why Liberty had these problems. One reason may be that the workers who put her together had trouble following Gustave Eiffel's instructions. In any case, the result is a figure that had faults even from the beginning of her life in Frédéric Bartholdi's workshop.

Liberty's problems multiplied when she was shipped to the United States. Have you ever tried to take apart a watch or a bicycle and then put it back together again? If so, you know what could happen (and did) when Liberty was taken apart and sent by train to the coast of France. There it was to be shipped to the United States, but first it lay in pieces in a port warehouse all winter. Soon its thin copper sheets began to sag. Then it had to withstand a rough trip by sea to America. Finally, it was rebuilt with great care on Bedloe's Island (later Liberty Island), its final home. Is it any wonder that some of the parts no longer quite fit right? The workers did the best they could. They made new rivet holes when the old ones no longer fit.

To this list of Liberty's original flaws one must add the rough effects of living outdoors for a century. Water, for example, takes a terrible toll on even the strongest metals. It slips into every crack and can act as a wedge to break up the material. Liberty, of course, is made entirely out of metal: iron and steel for the framework and copper for the skin. When water passes between two different metals, electricity can flow between them and damage both metals. This action caused some of the iron pieces inside Miss Liberty to weaken over time. Before rebuilding, workers found that more than one-third of the metal devices that connect the copper skin to the iron ribs had pulled away from each other.

Then there were the problems caused by 1.8 million visitors who traveled to the statue each year. With that many people walking all around there was bound to be some wear and tear. How could Liberty not be damaged when even a visitor's *breath* created carbon dioxide that further weakened her fragile frame? Finally, in 1984, the statue was closed to the public for two years (though the grounds remained open), and the work of rebuilding Liberty began.

First, a huge aluminum scaffolding was built around the entire statue. This allowed workers to clean and repair the skin, which was still in very good shape in most places. Holes were plugged with a special kind of copper. Seams were closed with a special seal. Layers of old paint and tar were stripped or blasted off from the inside of the skin.

Fixing the iron framework inside Liberty was a much harder job. Almost every iron support had rusted from exposure to water, salt, and air. Every metal rib—about 1800 in all—was replaced with stainless steel. The old ribs were removed a few at a time to avoid weakening the statue. Duplicates of these ribs were then made to take the place of the old ones. The result was a solid new framework.

The rebuilding of the torch and the arm presented new difficulties. Yellow glass that was not a part of Bartholdi's plan had been placed in the torch windows to make the light brighter. The work was done by Gutzon

Borglum, the same artist who carved the faces of four presidents out of solid rock on Mount Rushmore. The windows, however, had not been correctly sealed, and so the torch leaked. To correct this problem, the entire upper half of the torch was removed by crane and completely rebuilt. The new torch is made of copper and covered with gold leaf. It has more powerful lamps, and so it appears brighter than before. The lamps at the torch's base shine up and reflect off the gold leaf. The torch no longer has any windows or glass and therefore is leakproof.

The work of building the new torch was carried out in the same way that Liberty's skin was first made. The copper was hammered into a mold. A French firm was chosen to do this work from eight companies that had made bids. Meanwhile, an American team worked to replace the 1800 iron bars in Liberty's main body. All of this work was carried out in a workshop on Liberty Island. Visitors were able to watch the repairs as they were done.

Also removed from Liberty for repairs were the seven spikes that top her crown. Each point is at least 9 feet long and weighs at least 150 pounds. These spikes stand for the seven seas and the seven continents. The spike that rubbed the arm needed special work. All, however, needed to be

cleaned and made stronger. This work, too, could be seen in the Liberty Island workshop.

One improvement to the Statue of Liberty cannot be seen from either inside or outside of the statue but from *under* it. That is the new

Statue of Liberty Restoration

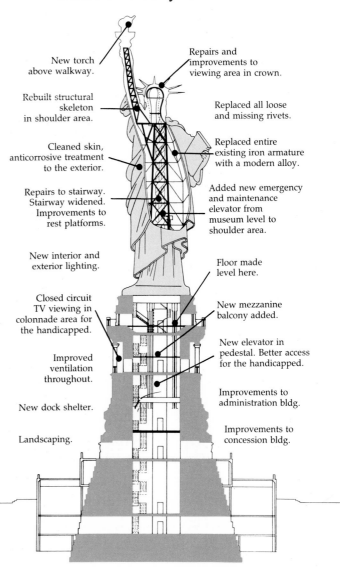

New torch above walkway.

Rebuilt structural skeleton in shoulder area.

Cleaned skin, anticorrosive treatment to the exterior.

Repairs to stairway. Stairway widened. Improvements to rest platforms.

New interior and exterior lighting.

Closed circuit TV viewing in colonnade area for the handicapped.

Improved ventilation throughout.

New dock shelter.

Landscaping.

Repairs and improvements to viewing area in crown.

Replaced all loose and missing rivets.

Replaced entire existing iron armature with a modern alloy.

Added new emergency and maintenance elevator from museum level to shoulder area.

Floor made level here.

New mezzanine balcony added.

New elevator in pedestal. Better access for the handicapped.

Improvements to administration bldg.

Improvements to concession bldg.

water-powered elevator, which is in the base of the statue. It is the highest of its kind in the world. The elevator allows visitors to see the inside of the base on which Liberty rests. Until the new elevator was installed, the huge space inside the pedestal was blocked off by floors and stairs built after the base was first made.

Moving outside the statue onto Liberty Island itself, we see more improvements. The entrance was streamlined and rebuilt to make it easier to get into the area. The mall area was changed, and new landscaping was done. The pier, where ferries and boats dock at Liberty Island, was rebuilt. So were the food stands and the National Park Service building.

Who paid for all these changes and improvements? Support came from individuals and businesses. To take charge of the whole job, President Ronald Reagan formed the Statue of Liberty–Ellis Island Centennial Commission in 1982.

The President appointed Lee A. Iacocca as head of the commission. The choice was fitting. Iacocca was the son of an immigrant father who twice had passed through Ellis Island. He was alone the first time. The second time he returned with his bride. Iacocca based his appeal for money on his own background. "More than 100 million Americans," he stated, "had relatives who first saw America by sailing past the Statue of Liberty on their way to Ellis Island." These relatives included about 17 million people who passed through Ellis Island between 1892 and 1954. They are the forebears of about 40 percent of the people in the United States today.

The operating, nonprofit part of the commission is the Statue of Liberty–Ellis Island Foundation, Inc., headed by William F. May. It had three goals:

1. to rebuild and restore the Statue of Liberty and Ellis Island;
2. to make a lasting memorial to the millions of immigrants who helped build the United States;
3. to plan the 100th birthday parties for the Statue of Liberty in 1986 and Ellis Island in 1992.

To do this work, the foundation raised more then $230 million from many sources. These included

official sponsors;
other businesses and groups;
individuals, including many
    schoolchildren;
the sale of products, including
    T-shirts and clothing, flags
    and banners, postcards,
    pins, key rings, buttons,
    pads, and pencils.

William May reminded people that Ellis Island and the Statue of Liberty

The red-brick main building at Ellis Island on its opening day December 17, 1900. The earlier building on this site was destroyed by fire.

After a short ferryboat ride to Ellis Island from Manhattan, the immigrants walked to the main building to be examined and questioned.

A fireworks display during the four-day gala of the Statue of Liberty's 100th anniversary beginning July 3, 1986.

are "more than monuments to immigration. They celebrate the ethnic heritage of every group of Americans."

Among those whose heritage is marked by the "new" Statue of Liberty are the hundreds of thousands of schoolchildren who gave money to rebuild it. In so doing, these children followed the example of children 100 years earlier who gave money to build the statue's base. Although the French paid for the statue itself, the United States agreed to pay for its pedestal. In 1886 Joseph Pulitzer, the immigrant editor of the *New York World,* organized a fund drive to raise money for that purpose. People of all ages gave. One letter writer said, "Please receive from two little boys one dollar for the pedestal. It is our savings. . . ." The children of the late twentieth century, along with thousands of others, responded in the same way. With enthusiasm like this behind it, the new Statue of Liberty should last at least another hundred years.

Checking Comprehension and Skills

Thinking About What You've Read

1. Why is the Statue of Liberty a symbol of freedom for the many people who have come to America?
- 2. What kinds of information about the Statue of Liberty can you find in an encyclopedia?
   a. a description of the statue
   b. the name of the designer of the statue
   c. how people today feel about the statue
- 3. Would an encyclopedia published in 1980 be a good resource on the renovation of the statue? Why?
4. In which three ways did being outdoors damage the Statue of Liberty?
5. List three renovations, made since 1984, that have improved the Statue of Liberty.
6. Where were most of the improvements for the statue carried out?
- 7. Under what three headings in a card catalog would you look up an article similar to the one you just read?
8. How have schoolchildren helped with the renovations on the statue?
9. If you were going to build a statue to honor America, what subject would you choose? Why?

Talking About What You've Read

The Statue of Liberty is a symbol that has been used to welcome people to America. What other landmarks symbolize America? Name five well-known landmarks, and discuss why each is a symbol of America.

Writing About What You've Read

Choose one of the five landmarks you have named. Write three or four sentences in which you tell how and why it represents America.

- Study Skills: Encyclopedia, Card catalog

Learning About Word Histories

People who have recently come to America might have trouble reading signs in English. But tired and hungry travelers would know which door to enter if they knew their word histories. The history of a word is its etymology. The etymology of a word tells what language the word came from and what the word meant in that language.

Restaurant comes from the French *restaurant* (res′tō ran′) and can be traced back to the Latin *restaurare* (res′tou ra′rā), meaning "restore." If the travelers knew this, they would go into a restaurant to "restore their bodies."

Pharmacy comes from the Latin word *pharmacia* and can be traced back to Greek *pharmakon* (fär mä kōn′), meaning "drug" or "medicine." If the travelers knew this, they would know to go to the pharmacy if they needed medicine.

Words that are derived from the same word and are spelled alike belong to the same *word family*. *Studio* comes from the Latin *studium* (stü′dē ům), which means "to study." The words *student*, *study*, and *studious* also come from *studium* and all have to do with studying.

Reading Word Histories

Read each of the following words, its history, what it means today, and how it is used today. Notice that some meanings have changed over time while others have not.

maze   The word comes from the Middle English word *masen* (mā′zən), which means "to confuse." It can also be traced back to the Norwegian words *mas* (mäs′), which means "exhausting labor, whim, idle chatter," and *masa* (mä′sä), which means "to pester, to be busy, to chatter." Originally the word *maze* seemed to mean "to be lost in thought." Today, a *maze* is "a network of paths through which it is hard to find one's way." It can also mean "confusion." *I couldn't find the hoe in the maze of things in the tool shed.*

indomitable   The word comes from the Latin *in*, meaning "not," and *domitare* (dō′mē tȧ′rā), which means "to subdue or tame." The word today means "not able to be discouraged, beaten, or conquered." *After five straight wins, the team felt they were indomitable.*

contagious   The word comes from the Latin *cum* (kùm), meaning "with," and *tag*, a form of *tangere* (tän′jā rā), which means "to touch." *Contagious* today means "spreading by contact." *Colds are quite contagious.*

physical   This word comes from the Greek *physikē* (fe si kē′), meaning "natural, physical" and from the Latin *physica* (fē zē′kä), meaning "natural science." The meaning today is related to the Old French *fisique*, or "science of medicine." Today a *physician* is a doctor of medicine. *The physician set my broken arm.* The words *physican* and *physicist* belong to the same word family as *physical*.

Tips for Understanding and Appreciating Language
- Learning about a word's etymology, or history, helps you appreciate language.
- Many words come from languages other than English.
- The meanings of some words have changed over time.
- Glossaries and dictionaries are sources for etymologies.

Many immigrants recall the stories of how they came to America. What is the value of preserving these stories? Pay special attention to two personal accounts in this article, and summarize the most important memories in each one.

IMMIGRANTS OF YESTERYEAR

by Russell Freedman

In the years around the turn of the century, immigration to America reached an all-time high. Between 1880 and 1920, 23 million immigrants arrived in the United States. They came mainly from the countries of Europe, especially from impoverished towns and villages in southern and eastern Europe. The one thing they had in common was a fervent belief that in America, life would be better.

Most of these immigrants were poor. Somehow they managed to scrape together enough money to pay for their passage to America. Many immigrant families arrived penniless. Others had to make the journey in stages. Often the father came first, found work, and sent for his family later.

Immigrants usually crossed the Atlantic as steerage passengers. Reached by steep, slippery stairs, the steerage lay deep down in the hold of the ship. It was for passengers paying the lowest fare.

Men, women, and children were packed into dark, smelly compartments. They slept in narrow bunks stacked three high. They had no showers, no lounges, and no dining rooms. Food served from huge pots was dished into dinner pails given by the steamship line. Because steerage life was crowded and uncomfortable, passengers spent as much time as they could up on deck.

(opposite page)
The great inspection hall at Ellis Island

(left)
The eye examination

Those who failed to get past both doctors had to take a more thorough medical exam. The others moved on to the registration clerk, who questioned them with the help of an interpreter: What is your name? Your nationality? Your occupation? Can you read and write? Have you ever been in prison? How much money do you have with you? Where are you going?

Some immigrants were so upset that they could not answer. They were allowed to sit and rest and try again.

About one immigrant out of every five or six was held for additional examinations and questioning.

The writer Angelo Pellegrini has remembered his own family's detention at Ellis Island:

We lived there for three days—Mother and we five children, the youngest of whom was three years old. Because of the rigorous physical examination that we had

Waiting for the ferry
to Manhattan, 1912

to submit to, particularly of the eyes, there was this terrible anxiety that one of us might be rejected. And if one of us was, what would the rest of the family do? My sister was indeed momentarily rejected; she had been so ill and had cried so much that her eyes were absolutely bloodshot, and Mother was told, "Well, we can't let her in." But fortunately, Mother was an indomitable spirit and finally made them understand that if her child had a few hours' rest and a little bite to eat she would be all right. In the end we did get through.

Most immigrants passed through Ellis Island in about one day. Carrying all their worldly possessions, they left the examination hall and waited on the dock for the ferry that would take them to Manhattan, a mile away. Some of them

New arrivals

still faced long journeys overland before they reached their final destination. Others would head directly for the teeming immigrant neighborhoods of New York City.

Immigrants still come to America. Since World War II, more than eight million immigrants have entered the country. Although this is a small number compared to the mass migrations at the turn of the century, the United States continues to admit more immigrants than any other nation.

Many of today's immigrants come from countries within the Western Hemisphere and from Asia and Africa as well as Europe. After they move to the United States, they face many of the same problems and hardships that have always confronted newcomers. And they come here for the same reason that immigrants have always come: to seek a better life for themselves and their children.

Checking Comprehension and Skills

Thinking About What You've Read

1. What is the value of preserving the stories of immigrants?
2. What belief about America did turn-of-the-century immigrants share?
3. How might the conditions in which the steerage passengers lived have affected the examinations they had to take later?
- 4. State two main ideas that you would include in a summary of Edward Corsi's memory of his journey to America.
5. Was it fair that the immigrants who arrived at Ellis Island were examined by doctors? Why or why not?
6. Why were some immigrants too upset to answer the questions of registration clerks?
- 7. Summarize in two or three sentences Angelo Pelligrini's memory of his family's stay on Ellis Island.
8. Name two things that today's immigrants have in common with earlier immigrants.
9. If you moved to another country, what would you want to find out first? second? third?

Talking About What You've Read

America can be a wondrous place to newcomers. Imagine what it must be like to set foot finally in the place you dreamed of coming to for so long. What would you want to do after you leave Ellis Island? Where would you go? What places or things would you want to see? Why? How would you spend your first day here?

Writing About What You've Read

Imagine that you have just arrived in America. You are writing a letter to a friend in your old country. You have told about your journey and Ellis Island. Now write a paragraph telling your friend what you did on your first day in your new country.

- Comprehension Skill: Summarize

Some Test-taking Tips

Fortunately, the exams you have to take are not like those faced by the immigrants at Ellis Island. But if taking a test may sometimes upset you, you'll find that tests are easier to take when you have done your homework and have read the directions and questions carefully.

A common type of test is the multiple choice.

Circle the letter for the correct answer.
1. Which statue is a symbol of freedom?
   a. Statue of Freedom   **c.** Sitting Lincoln
   b. Washington Monument   **d.** none of the above

After reading the directions and the questions carefully, you should also read all the choices before selecting your answer. Finally, you should eliminate wrong choices. The answer to the sample item should be *Statue of Liberty*. These words, however, do not appear in choices **a, b,** or **c.** Therefore, the correct answer is *none of the above*. Answer *none of the above* only when you are certain that the other choices are wrong.

Another type of test is the matching test.

In front of each word in the first column, write the letter of the word in the second column that means almost the same thing.

__c__ **1.** liberty   **a.** sickness

_____ **2.** disease   **b.** wealthy
                             ~~c~~. freedom
_____ **3.** impoverished   **d.** poor

Read the first word and all the choices. When you find the right choice, put a slash through it. Then you won't have as many choices to consider when you go on to the second word. If you repeat this procedure for each word, you will be able to complete matching the items quickly and accurately.

A new group of immigrants has come to America, among them the Royal Laotian Dance Troupe and their families. Why have they come to America? As you read this article, note related topics that you could look up for further information in an index or a Readers' Guide to Periodicals.

New Americans

by Brent Ashabranner

In its June 6, 1980, issue, *The Tennessean,* a Nashville newspaper, carried announcements of two musical events. One, entitled "Gobble It Up," began, "Country music goes wild with an all-star roster of musicmakers tomorrow and Sunday at the first Wild Turkey Jamboree of Country Music in Columbia. . . ." The other story carried the title "Far Eastern Delights" and the first paragraph read, "The Royal Laotian Classical Dance Troupe brings pageantry and 600 years of history to the stage in a benefit performance tomorrow night in Goodletsville. . . ."

A visitor to Nashville, which bills itself as the Country Music Capital of the U.S.A., might understandably have been puzzled at seeing those news items side by side. Laotian classical dancing in the home of the Grand Ole Opry? Classical Asian music in the land of country music? To which many Nashville citizens might have responded, "And why not? Good music of every kind has a place here."

As if to make this point, the Royal Laotian Classical Dance Troupe was invited to dance at Nashville's Centennial Park as part of the city's Century III Celebration of the Arts.

Classical Laotian dances tell the story of the beginning of the ancient Laotian kingdom, the "land of a million elephants." The dancers are dressed in beautiful costumes, headdresses, and masks. They act out the stories through their movements and gestures. They dance to the music of traditional Laotian string and percussion instruments.

There are many kinds of dancing in Laos. But these classical dances, created over 600 years ago, have always been reserved for the royal Laotian court. They were to be seen only by the king and his guests. For centuries the royal dancers and their families lived in the king's palace. They were a part of his household. The dancer's art was passed down from generation to generation.

This tradition ended in 1975 when the Communists came to rule in Laos. They dethroned the king. And they ordered all cultural activities such as classical dancing to stop. The story of how the Royal Laotian Classical Dance Troupe came to Nashville begins at that point.

The leader of the dance troupe in 1975 was a young man named Eckeo Kounlavong (ek′ā ō gün la′vong). His father and grandfather had been leaders of the royal dancers. He received his formal dance training as a teenager. Then he became a part of the troupe. When his father died, Kounlavong took his place as leader of the royal dancers.

Then almost overnight his life fell apart. With the dethronement of the king, it became clear that all persons close to him were marked for arrest. Kounlavong talked the danger over with the other dancers. He then made his decision quickly and quietly. One night he and his mother simply disappeared from the palace.

The royal capital of Luang Prabang (lü äng′ prä bäng′) is in a lush mountain province of Laos. The journey to the border was difficult. Kounlavong knew that at any second he and his mother might be caught and put in jail.

He had some money, and he bribed government workers and soldiers with it. His mother had jewelry and that went for bribes also.

At last they reached the great Mekong (mā'köng) River that forms the border between Laos and Thailand. On a moonless night Kounlavong slipped into the river. His mother, who could not swim, was tied by a rope to his side. Kounlavong is not a big man but his body is lean and strong, a professional dancer's body. For what seemed like hours he swam, using the river's current to help them. At last they reached the far shore and were in Thailand.

For the next three years Kounlavong and his mother lived at the Nong Khai (nong'kī) Refugee Camp in Thailand. In the first months following their arrival, a few other dancers from the royal troupe escaped from Laos and made their way to the Nong Khai camp. Kounlavong discovered that there were other Laotian dancers in the camp, though they were not classical dancers.

Slowly an idea formed in Kounlavong's mind. Why not get together the Royal Laotian Classical Dance Troupe here in the refugee camp? If it wasn't done here while there were still some dancers around, a lovely part of Laotian culture would be lost forever. Besides, rebuilding the dance troupe would be a way to fight the terrible boredom of life in the refugee camp.

The other dancers liked the idea. And so Kounlavong and the former members of the king's troupe trained the other dancers in the classical forms. Slowly they used every piece of cloth they could put their hands on. The dancers and their families made the musical instruments, costumes, and masks that the dances needed. Performances by the Royal Laotian Classical Dance Troupe became one of the very few bright spots in Nong Khai camp life.

Then came disaster. Fire swept through the camp. It destroyed everything—every tent, every building, every

Eckeo Kounlavong,
leader of the
Laotian Classical
Dance Troupe, with
one of his masks

poor possession of the refugees—and every costume,
musical instrument, and mask of the dance troupe. It was
a blow that might have brought an end to the troupe if it
had not been for an American worker at the camp. On his
own, he raised money for new dance equipment. These
were to be made, under Kounlavong's supervision, by
Thai artisans and costumers.

Over time the members of the dance troupe decided
that they wanted to go together to their country of
resettlement, wherever that might be, whenever it might
be. They discussed the possibility with refugee
resettlement officials. It seemed out of the question,
utterly hopeless. There were 70 dancers, 48 families, 260
people altogether. Still, they hoped for the impossible.

Rumors are a cruel fact of life in refugee camps. Every
day brought new ones. They were going to be sent back

A Laotian refugee worker on a Nashville assembly line

to Laos. They were all going to Australia next week. They were never going to be let go from the refugee camp. They were going to be split into small groups and sent to many different countries. Hopes rose and fell, fears flamed and died, on rumors that were never true.

Then came news that was too good to be true. Even the most hopeful were afraid to believe it. The whole dance troupe and their families were going to the United States. They were going to live in a big city called Nashville. They could take all of their costumes, musical instruments, and masks with them. No, they said, it could not be true; but this time it was.

The dream of the Laotian refugee dancers came true because of a great amount of work on the part of many people. U.S. government refugee officials had to believe in the idea and take on the mountain of paperwork it involved. Sponsors, housing, and jobs were found. English-language training was planned, and much more. Many groups agreed to sponsor a number of the Laotians. Persons who sponsor refugees agree to help them get settled, answer their questions, help with their problems, and stay in touch with them during the long period of adjustment. Sponsorship is entirely a volunteer service.

Today the Laotian dancers and their families are well settled in Nashville. Other Laotian refugees are coming because of the successful group already in the city. Over eighty Laotians work in the telephone plant of a large organization. The Laotians are good workers. They work hard. They can also piece things together quickly, which may be traced to their dancing training.

Kounlavong, a man whose only job once was to dance for a king, is now a machine operator in a cloth factory. He has taken this change with dignity.

It has not been easy to learn a new job, a new language, a new way to live in a strange city. Still, the dance troupe has stayed together. They practice on weekends, and they give special performances in Nashville and other cities nearby. They dance when the Laotians celebrate their new year and on religious occasions. They are preserving a rich part of Laotian culture and are sharing it with America.

The Royal Laotian Classical Dance Troupe is probably the most dramatic example of how Asians today are making a musical contribution in America. It is by no means the only example. Korean-American musicians perform at the yearly folk festival on the Mall in Washington, D.C. A Cambodian dance group in Silver Spring, Maryland, gives regular performances. At the famous Juilliard School of Music in New York City, about 15 percent of the enrollment is Asian.

In an article in *The New York Times Magazine* about

how new Asian immigrants are making their mark on America, Robert Lindsey wrote:

"From Sejii Ozawa (sā′jē ō zä′wä), the conductor of the Boston Symphony Orchestra, who came from Japan, to Yo-Yo Ma, the amazing Chinese cellist, to Myung Whun Chung (mə yung′wun chung), who grew up in Korea, came to this country to study at Juilliard and went on to become one of this country's most exciting young conductors and pianists, Asians have already become a major part of the classical-music world in America."

A Korean folk dancer performs in Washington, D.C.

Index

READERS' GUIDE TO PERIODICAL LITERATURE
March 1984–February 1985

Dance

Companies
See also
Performance

American ballet theater in
  rehearsal. R. Goldstone. il Time
  33:416 Aug '84
Asian companies in America. S.
  Gordon. il Newsweek 32:37 Je '84
Twentieth century choreographers
  in production. R. Perls. High Fidel
  28:46 Ap '84

Performance
See also
Companies

Cambodian royal ballet in America.
  S. Peterson. il National Observer
  47:382 Ma '84
Chicago ballet at White House.
  F. Jones. Around Wash 27:36
  May 16 '84
Laotian dance company in
  Nashville. S. McCarren. il
  Nation 32:16 S '84

Checking Comprehension and Skills

Thinking About What You've Read

1. Why did the Royal Classical Laotian Dance Troupe come to America?
2. What event caused Kounlavong and his mother to flee Laos? How did they escape?
3. Where did the dance troupe first reassemble and perform?
4. Why do you think Kounlavong and the other Laotian dancers want to preserve their national dances?
5. List three ways that a sponsor helps a new immigrant to settle in this country.
6. List two ways that show that the Laotians have become productive members of their community.
7. How has the Laotian Dance Troupe managed to preserve the art of its country here in the United States?
• 8. If you wanted to learn about other Asian immigrant groups in America, what topics listed in the index on page 322 would you look up?
• 9. Also on page 322 are entries similar to the way they would appear in the *Readers' Guide to Periodical Literature*. Which articles will give more information about the Cambodian dance group in Maryland?

Talking About What You've Read

List three difficulties that Kounlavong and the members of his company faced as they tried to adjust to living in a new land. Think about the qualities that Kounlavong demonstrates that probably made it possible for him to make this adjustment successfully.

Writing About What You've Read

Choose one of the qualities that you think Kounlavong demonstrates and that you believe will help him succeed in this country. Write a paragraph supporting your opinion.

• Study Skills: Index, *Readers' Guide*

DREAMS

by Langston Hughes

Hold fast to dreams
For if dreams die
Life is a broken-winged bird
That cannot fly.

Hold fast to dreams
For when dreams go
Life is a barren field
Frozen with snow.

Meet the Poet

Langston Hughes was elected class poet by his eighth-grade classmates. He was pleased with the honor. But it didn't occur to him at the time that he would have to write a poem. The poem would be read on the stage on graduation day.

Hughes wasn't afraid of standing up in front of an audience. But he was worried that his poem wouldn't be good enough. He wanted his family, classmates, and teachers to be proud of him.

Hughes went to work on his poem, reading other poems to get inspiration. The poem was the longest he ever wrote—16 verses. In the first eight verses he wrote that the school had the finest teachers, and in the last eight verses he wrote that the class was the greatest ever to be graduated. The audience applauded loudly. Hughes's first poem was a great success. It was the first of hundreds of poems.

LOOKING BACK

Thinking About the Section

   People who come to America are usually impressed with the Statue of Liberty, both for what it symbolizes and for its great beauty.

   Turn-of-the-century immigrants looked at it from the ground up. What must the statue have looked like to immigrants standing at the foot of its pedestal? What did they see? How would they have described it? What emotions might they have been feeling?

   Modern-day immigrants might have the opportunity to see Liberty from a plane, which gives a totally different view. How would they describe the statue from this air-born position? How would they describe what they see and what they might be feeling?

   Copy the chart below on a sheet of paper and fill it in according to the directions.

	List the parts of the statue immigrants would see in the order they would see them.	How does each part look?	What feeling might an immigrant be feeling?
from the ground in the 1800s			
from the air today			

Writing About the Section

   Select one view of the statue. Using the information you have gathered, write a paragraph describing what you would see if you were looking at the statue from that view. Pay attention to the order in which you would see the parts, and end the paragraph with a sentence that describes your feelings about this American symbol.

8

Communication

Clear communication requires more than just understanding words. Tone of voice, gesture, and body language are part of communication too. Getting your message across depends not only on deciding what to say (and what not to say), but also on how to say it.

The characters in this section all have problems communicating. Creatures from outer space learn the importance of using words correctly. The players on a softball team recognize the strong message hidden in a tone of voice. And another group of characters discovers that, sometimes, not using words can cause the most serious problems of all.

Recognizing Types of Fiction

Do you have a favorite type of fiction? Each of the pictures above illustrates characters communicating in a fictional story. Judging from the pictures, however, the stories are quite different. Which story do you think you'd most like to read?

Two popular types of fiction are modern realistic fiction and science fiction. **Modern realistic fiction** tells about things that could really happen in the present.

Science fiction is based on science and often tells about life in the future. Science-fiction stories are a kind of fantasy because they depict events that couldn't happen or haven't happened yet. Science-fiction writers usually have a good understanding of science. For example, a science-fiction story about life on the moon would probably contain accurate information about the moon, not just imagined details. Science fiction can be serious. The author may try to make the story seem very believable, or the author may write a humorous science-fiction story that is not meant to be believable.

Recognizing what type of fiction a story is will help you to know what to expect and will give you a better understanding of what takes place in the story. Think about how you can recognize modern realistic fiction and science fiction as you read the following paragraphs from two different stories in which machines play an important role in communicating.

from **"The Fun They Had"**
by Isaac Asimov

That night, Margie talked about it into her personal tape diary. In the "take" for May 17, 2155, she said, "Today Tommy found a real book."

It was a very old book, printed on paper. Margie remembered her grandfather saying that *his* grandfather had talked about real books printed on paper.

Margie and Tommy turned the old pages. They were yellow and crinkly. It was comical to read words that stood still instead of moving like on a book screen. Then, when they turned back to the page before, the same words were still on it. That was comical, too, because book screens kept moving on to other words.

"This kind of book seems like such a waste," said Tommy. "I guess you just throw it away when you're through reading it. My book screen must have at least a thousand books on it, and it's good for plenty more. I'd never throw it away."

from **"The Blizzard"**
by W. J. Hager

Ramiro's brain flooded with thoughts. His father was unconscious. Could he get help? This road was officially closed, so there probably wouldn't be any cars before morning when the snowplows went to work. He could barely see the trunk of the huge tree they had hit. They had traveled about two miles since their last stop. That meant they were three miles from home.

All at once, he remembered a television program he had seen recently. Because so many people had been stranded in cars during the last snowstorm, the station had broadcast advice for people who might find themselves stranded. The first rule had been, "Stay in the car," so Ramiro gave up the idea of going for help.

1. Is "The Fun They Had" modern realistic fiction or science fiction? How do you know?

To answer question 1, look for details that would describe real life in the present or details that would describe something that couldn't happen or couldn't happen yet and is probably taking place in the future. For example, the date on the diary, Margie's and Tommy's surprise at finding a real book, their amusement at seeing words stand still, and their familiarity with book screens are all important details. These details describe an event that could not happen or could not happen yet, and the event must be taking place in the future. Therefore, "The Fun They Had" must be science fiction.

2. How can you tell that "The Blizzard" is modern realistic fiction?

Practicing Recognizing Types of Literature
Think about the differences between modern realistic fiction and science fiction as you read the following

paragraphs from **"From the Diary of Yeddo Ski-Kredo"** by Caroline D. Henry.

The visitors wore protective suits and helmets. One of them carried a box which seemed to be for testing the atmosphere. After studying it carefully, they took off their helmets. They breathe oxygen as we do. Their heads are about the same size as ours and are large enough to hold brains. Beings who solved the riddle of space travel would, of course, be highly intelligent.

Our language experts will develop a workable language with them. The beginnings of communication are there.

There are some dramatic differences between the visitors and us, but my fears were laid to rest. These beings from space were not ugly, evil giants ready to smash us in an instant. Then I had to remember my mother's warning against rudely laughing at them if they looked strange to us.

Yet, they are odd looking. They are nearly hairless, having only a tuft on top of their heads, and they have only two legs!

1. Are these paragraphs from modern realistic fiction or science fiction?
2. How do you know?

Tips for Recognizing Types of Literature
- Before you begin to read, preview the selection. Try to figure out what type of literature it is. Ask yourself whether it is fiction or nonfiction. Then ask yourself what kind of fiction or nonfiction it is.
- As you read, see if you were right about what kind of selection it is. Does the selection describe an event that could really happen? Does it take place in the present day? It's probably modern realistic fiction. Does the selection use scientific details? Does it describe an event that couldn't happen yet? It's probably science fiction.

Could a book save our planet from a Martian invasion? How on earth could it do so? Aren't books supposed to communicate ideas and make things clear? Well, perhaps if you were a Martian, you might misunderstand the written word. Notice how the fantasy elements in this science-fiction play create a humorous situation set in the future.

The BOOK That SAVED the EARTH

by Claire Boiko

CHARACTERS

HISTORIAN
GREAT AND MIGHTY THINK-TANK
APPRENTICE NOODLE
CAPTAIN OMEGA

LIEUTENANT IOTA
SERGEANT OOP
OFFSTAGE VOICE

SCENE 1

TIME: *The twenty-fifth century*
PLACE: *The Museum of Ancient History:*
Department of the Twentieth Century
on the Planet Earth

BEFORE RISE: *Spotlight shines on* HISTORIAN, *who is sitting at table down right, on which is a movie projector. A sign on an easel beside her reads:* MUSEUM OF ANCIENT HISTORY: DEPARTMENT OF THE TWENTIETH CENTURY. *She stands and bows to audience.*

HISTORIAN: Good afternoon. Welcome to our Museum of Ancient History, and to my department—curiosities of the good old, far-off twentieth century. The twentieth century was often called the Era of the Book. In those days, there were books about everything from anteaters to Zulus. Books taught people how to, and when to, and where to, and why

to. They illustrated, educated, punctuated, and even decorated. But the strangest thing a book ever did was to save the Earth. You haven't heard about the Martian invasion of 2004? Tsk, tsk. What *do* they teach children nowadays? Well, you know, the invasion never really happened, because a single book stopped it. What was the book, you ask? A noble encyclopedia? A tome about rockets and missiles? A secret file from outer space? No, it was none of those. It was—but here, let me turn on the historiscope and show you what happened many centuries ago, in 2004. *(She turns on projector, and points it left. Spotlight on* HISTORIAN *goes out, and comes up down left on* THINK-TANK, *who is seated on a raised box, arms folded. He has a huge, egg-shaped head, and he wears a long robe decorated with stars and circles.* APPRENTICE NOODLE *stands beside him at an elaborate switchboard. A sign on an easel reads:* MARS SPACE

CONTROL. GREAT AND MIGHTY THINK-TANK,
COMMANDER-IN-CHIEF. BOW LOW BEFORE
ENTERING.)

NOODLE *(bowing):* O Great and Mighty Think-Tank, most
powerful and intelligent creature in the whole
universe, what are your orders?

THINK-TANK *(peevishly):* You left out part of my salutation,
Apprentice Noodle. Go over the whole thing again.

NOODLE: It shall be done, sir. *(in a singsong)* O Great and
Mighty Think-Tank, Ruler of Mars and her two
moons, most powerful and intelligent creature in the
whole universe—*(out of breath)* what-are-your-orders?

THINK-TANK: That's better, Noodle. I wish to be placed in
communication with our manned space probe to that
ridiculous little planet we are going to put under our
generous rulership. What do they call it again?

NOODLE: Earth, your Intelligence.

THINK-TANK: Earth—of course. You see how insignificant
the place is? But first, something important. My
mirror. I wish to consult my mirror.

NOODLE: It shall be done, sir. *(He hands* THINK-TANK *a mirror.)*

THINK-TANK: Mirror, mirror, in my hand. Who is the most
fantastically intellectually gifted being in the land?

OFFSTAGE VOICE *(after a pause):* You, sir.

THINK-TANK *(smacking mirror):* Quicker. Answer quicker next
time. I hate a slow mirror. *(He admires himself in the
mirror.)* Ah, there I am. Are we Martians not a
handsome race? So much more attractive than those
ugly Earthlings with their tiny heads. Noodle, you
keep on exercising your mind, and someday you'll
have a balloon brain just like mine.

NOODLE: Oh, I hope so, Mighty Think-Tank. I hope so.

THINK-TANK: Now, contact the space probe. I want to invade
that primitive ball of mud called Earth before lunch.

NOODLE: It shall be done, sir. *(He adjusts levers on switchboard.
Electronic buzzes and beeps are heard as the curtains open.)*

SCENE 2

TIME: *A few seconds later*

PLACE: *Mars Space Control and the Centerville Public Library*

AT RISE: CAPTAIN OMEGA *stands at center, opening and closing card catalog drawers in a confused fashion.* LIEUTENANT IOTA *is up left, counting books in a bookcase.* SERGEANT OOP *is at right, opening and closing a book, turning it upside down, shaking it and then riffling the pages and shaking his head.*

NOODLE *(adjusting knobs):* I have a close sighting of the space crew, sir. (THINK-TANK *puts on a pair of enormous goggles and turns toward the stage to watch.*) They seem to have entered some sort of Earth structure.

THINK-TANK: Excellent. Make voice contact.

NOODLE *(speaking into a microphone):* Mars Space Control calling the crew of Probe One. Mars Space Control calling the crew of Probe One. Come in, Captain Omega, and give us your location.

CAPTAIN OMEGA (*speaking into a disk which is on a chain around her neck*): Captain Omega to Mars Space Control. Lieutenant Iota, Sergeant Oop, and I have arrived on Earth without incident. We have taken shelter in this (*indicates room*)—this square place. Have you any idea where we are, Lieutenant Iota?

IOTA: I can't figure it out, Captain. (*holding up a book*) I've counted two thousand of these peculiar items. This place must be some sort of storage barn. What do you think, Sergeant Oop?

OOP: I haven't a clue. I've been to seven galaxies, but I've never seen anything like this. Maybe they're hats. (*He opens a book and puts it on his head.*) Say, maybe this is a haberdashery!

OMEGA (*bowing low*): Perhaps the Great and Mighty Think-Tank will give us the benefit of his thought on the matter.

THINK-TANK: Elementary, my dear Omega. Hold one of the items up so that I may view it closely. (OMEGA *holds a book on the palm of her hand.*) Yes, yes, I understand now. Since Earth creatures are always eating, the place in which you find yourselves is undoubtedly a crude refreshment stand.

OMEGA (*to* IOTA *and* OOP): He says we're in a refreshment stand.

OOP: Well, the Earthlings certainly have a strange diet.

THINK-TANK: That item in your hand is called a sandwich.

OMEGA (*nodding*): A sandwich.

IOTA (*nodding*): A sandwich.

OOP (*taking book from his head*): A sandwich?

THINK-TANK: Sandwiches are the main staple of Earth diet. Look at it closely. (OMEGA *squints at book.*) There are two slices of what is called bread, and between them is some sort of filling.

OMEGA: That is correct, sir.

THINK-TANK: To confirm my opinion, I order you to eat it.

OMEGA *(gulping):* Eat it?

THINK-TANK: Do you doubt the Mighty Think-Tank?

OMEGA: Oh, no, no. But poor Lieutenant Iota has not had her breakfast. Lieutenant Iota, I order you to eat this— this sandwich.

IOTA *(dubiously):* Eat it? Oh, Captain! It's a very great honor to be the first Martian to eat a sandwich, I'm sure, but—but how can I be so impolite as to eat before my Sergeant? *(handing* OOP *the book and saying brightly)* Sergeant Oop, I order you to eat the sandwich immediately.

OOP *(making a face):* Who, Lieutenant? Me, Lieutenant?

IOTA and OMEGA *(saluting):* For the glory of Mars, Oop!

OOP: Yes, of course! *(unhappily)* Immediately. *(He opens his mouth wide.* OMEGA *and* IOTA *watch him breathlessly. He bites down on a corner of the book, and pantomimes chewing and swallowing, while making terrible faces.)*

OMEGA: Well, Oop?

IOTA: Well, Oop? *(*OOP *coughs.* OMEGA *and* IOTA *pound him on the back.)*

THINK-TANK: Was it not delicious, Sergeant Oop?

OOP *(saluting):* That is correct, sir. It was *not* delicious. I don't know how the Earthlings can get those sandwiches down without water. They're dry as Martian dust.

NOODLE: Sir, sir. Great and Mighty Think-Tank. I beg your pardon, but an insignificant bit of data floated into my mind about those sandwiches.

THINK-TANK: It can't be worth much, but go ahead. Give us your trifling bit of data.

NOODLE: Well, sir, I have seen surveyor films of those sandwiches. I noticed that the Earthlings did not *eat* them. They used them as some sort of communication device.

THINK-TANK *(haughtily):* Naturally. That was my next point. These are actually communication sandwiches. Think-Tank is never wrong. Who is never wrong?

ALL *(saluting):* Great and Mighty Think-Tank is never wrong.

THINK-TANK: Therefore, I order you to listen to them.

OMEGA: Listen to them?

IOTA and **OOP** *(to each other, puzzled):* Listen to them?

THINK-TANK: Do you have marbles in your ears? I said, listen to them. *(Martians bow very low.)*

OMEGA: It shall be done, sir. *(They each take two books from the case, and hold them to their ears, listening intently.)*

IOTA *(whispering to* OMEGA*):* Do you hear anything?

OMEGA *(whispering back):* Nothing. Do you hear anything, Oop?

OOP *(loudly):* Not a thing! *(*OMEGA *and* IOTA *jump in fright.)*

OMEGA and **IOTA:** Sh-h-h! *(They listen intently again.)*

THINK-TANK: Well? Well? Report to me. What do you hear?

OMEGA: Nothing, sir. Perhaps we are not on the correct frequency.

IOTA: Nothing, sir. Perhaps the Earthlings have sharper ears than we do.

OOP: I don't hear a thing. Maybe these sandwiches don't make sounds.

THINK-TANK: What? Does somebody suggest the Mighty Think-Tank has made a mistake?

OMEGA: Oh, no, sir; no, sir. We'll keep listening.

NOODLE: Please excuse me, your Brilliance, but a cloudy piece of information is twirling around in my head.

THINK-TANK: Well, twirl it out, Noodle, and I will clarify it for you.

NOODLE: I seem to recall that the Earthlings did not *listen* to the sandwiches; they opened them and watched them.

THINK-TANK: Yes, that is quite correct, I will clarify that for you, Captain Omega. Those sandwiches are not for ear communication, they are for eye communication. Now, Captain Omega, take that large, colorful sandwich over there. It appears to be important. Tell me what you observe. (OMEGA *picks up a very large*

volume of Mother Goose, *holding it so that the audience can see the title.* IOTA *looks over her left shoulder, and* OOP *peers over her right shoulder.)*

OMEGA: It appears to contain pictures of Earthlings.

IOTA: There seems to be some sort of code.

THINK-TANK *(sharply interested):* Code? I told you this was important. Describe the code.

OOP: It's little lines and squiggles and dots—thousands of them alongside the pictures.

THINK-TANK: Perhaps the Earthlings are not as primitive as we have thought. We must break the code.

NOODLE: Forgive me, your Cleverness, but did not the chemical department give our space people vitamins to increase their intelligence?

THINK-TANK: Stop! A thought of magnificent brilliance has come to me. Space people, our chemical department has given you vitamins to increase your intelligence. Take them immediately and then watch the sandwich. The meaning of the code will slowly unfold before you.

OMEGA: It shall be done, sir. Remove vitamins. *(Crew takes vitamins from boxes on their belts.)* Present vitamins. *(They hold vitamins out in front of them, stiffly.)* Swallow vitamins. *(They pop the vitamins into their mouths and gulp simultaneously. They open their eyes wide, their heads shake, and they put their hands to their foreheads.)* The cotangent of a given angle in a right triangle is equal to the adjacent side divided by the hypotenuse.

IOTA: *Habeas corpus ad faciendum et recipiendum!*[1]

OOP: There is change of pressure along a radius in curvilinear motion.

THINK-TANK: Excellent. Now, decipher that code.

ALL: It shall be done, sir. *(They frown over the book, turning pages.)*

OMEGA *(brightly):* Aha!

---

1. Habeas corpus ad faciendum et recipiendum (hā bē′əs kôrpəs äd fä chē en′düm et rā chē pē en′düm).

IOTA (brightly): Oho!

OOP (bursting into laughter): Ha, ha, ha.

THINK-TANK: What does it say? Tell me this instant. Transcribe, Omega.

OMEGA: Yes, sir. (She reads with great seriousness.)

Mistress Mary, quite contrary,
How does your garden grow?
With cockle shells and silver bells
And pretty maids all in a row.

OOP: Ha, ha, ha. Imagine that. Pretty maids growing in a garden.

THINK-TANK (alarmed): Stop! This is no time for levity. Don't you realize the seriousness of this discovery? The Earthlings have discovered how to combine agriculture and mining. They can actually *grow* crops of rare metals such as silver. And cockle shells. They can grow high explosives, too. Noodle, contact our invasion fleet.

NOODLE: They are ready to go down and take over Earth, sir.

THINK-TANK: Tell them to hold. Tell them new information has come to us about Earth. Iota, transcribe.

IOTA: Yes, sir. (She reads very gravely.)

Hey diddle diddle! The cat and the fiddle,
The cow jumped over the moon,
The little dog laughed to see such sport,
And the dish ran away with the spoon.

OOP (laughing): The dish ran away with the spoon!

THINK-TANK: Cease laughter. Desist. This is more and more alarming. The Earthlings have reached a high level of civilization. Didn't you hear? They have taught their domesticated animals musical culture and space techniques. Even their dogs have a sense of humor. Why, at this very moment, they may be launching an interplanetary attack of millions of *cows!* Notify the invasion fleet. No invasion today. Oop, transcribe the next code.

OOP: Yes, sir. *(reading)*

Humpty Dumpty sat on the wall,
Humpty Dumpty had a great fall;
All the King's horses and all the King's men,
Cannot put Humpty Dumpty together again.
Oh, look, sir. Here's a picture of Humpty Dumpty.
Why, sir, he looks like—he looks like—*(turns large picture of Humpty Dumpty toward* THINK-TANK *and the audience)*

THINK-TANK (*screaming and holding his head*): It's me! It's my Great and Mighty Balloon Brain. The Earthlings have seen me, and they're after me. "Had a great fall!"— That means they plan to capture Mars Central Control and me! It's an invasion of Mars! Noodle, prepare a space capsule for me. I must escape without delay. Space people, you must leave Earth at once, but be sure to remove all traces of your visit. The Earthlings must not know that I know. (OMEGA, IOTA, *and* OOP *rush about, putting books back on shelves.*)

NOODLE: Where shall we go, sir?

THINK-TANK: A hundred million miles away from Mars. Order the invasion fleet to evacuate the entire planet of Mars. We are heading for Alpha Centauri, a hundred million miles away. (OMEGA, IOTA, *and* OOP *run off right as* NOODLE *helps* THINK-TANK *off left and the curtain closes. Spotlight shines on* HISTORIAN *down right.*)

HISTORIAN (*chuckling*): And that's how one dusty old book of nursery rhymes saved the world from a Martian invasion. As you all know, in the twenty-fifth century, five hundred years after all this happened, we Earthlings resumed contact with Mars, and we even became very chummy with the Martians. By that time, Great and Mighty Think-Tank had been replaced by a very clever Martian—the Wise and Wonderful Noodle! Oh, yes, we taught the Martians the difference between sandwiches and books. We taught them how to read, too, and we established a model library in their capital city of Marsopolis. But as you might expect, there is still one book that the Martians can never bring themselves to read. You've guessed it—*Mother Goose!* (*She bows and exits right. Curtain.*)

THE END

Checking Comprehension and Skills

Thinking About What You've Read
1. What book saves Earth from a Martian invasion? How does it do so?
2. Give two examples that show that Think-Tank is self-centered.
3. Why is Think-Tank proud of having a huge, egg-shaped head?
4. What three incorrect guesses are made by Think-Tank about the purpose of the books found on Earth?
5. Give two other examples that show that Think-Tank is not as smart as he thinks he is.
6. How does Noodle avoid offending Think-Tank while at the same time correcting his mistakes?
• 7. What are two characteristics of science fiction? Find an example of each of these in the play.
8. Pretend you are Noodle. How would you handle Think-Tank's mistakes?

Talking About What You've Read
   Think-Tank is mistaken about what the nursery rhymes mean. His explanations are alarming for Martians and humorous for Earthlings. Think of other nursery rhymes. What explanation of each might Think-Tank give?

Writing About What You've Read
   Pretend you are Think-Tank. You have just heard three nursery rhymes. Write an explanation of each rhyme. Remember to explain each in terms of what it might mean to a Martian like Think-Tank.

• Literary Skills: Science fiction

Tom Swift was the young hero of several adventure books written around 1900. Whenever Tom spoke, he never simply "said" anything. He said it "thoughtfully," "quickly," or "excitedly." The following sentences are called "Tom Swifties" because they are like the sentences Tom spoke in his books.

Tom Swifties

"There's a sale on light bulbs,"
Tom said brightly.

"I'm the new custodian,"
Tom said sweepingly.

"I lost my crutches,"
Tom said lamely.

"I'm waiting for the doctor,"
Tom said patiently.

"I forgot to buy the peaches, plums, grapes, apricots, and bananas,"
Tom said fruitlessly.

"I did *not* invent the airplane,"
Tom said righteously.

*The importance of honest communication is a lesson that
M. C. Higgins and a mysterious young woman learn the hard
way. As you read, notice how the setting of this story adds
drama to the events that take place.*

M. C. Higgins, the Great

by Virginia Hamilton

*Mayo Cornelius Higgins, who calls himself M. C. Higgins,
the Great, is a great swimmer. He, his two younger brothers,
Harper and Lennie Pool, and their little sister, Macie Pearl,
often swim in a lake near their home. One day a young
woman, who has been living in a tent nearby, joins them at
the lake. She sees M. C. swim through an underwater tunnel
and learns that he's the only person who can do this. She
wants to swim through the tunnel, too. M. C. reluctantly
agrees to lead her through, and his brothers and sister go
along to watch.*

The lake lay as serene and peaceful as when they had left it. Way down at the other end was a ridge. In between the ridge and the rocky end where now he and the girl crouched was the tent, like an intruder in the sun. All around them were pines, undergrowth, greens and browns closing in the magical shimmer of the lake.

He and the girl hung onto rocks just above the waterline. The children were clinging a foot above them.

"The tunnel's right down there," M. C. told her. "About eight to ten feet down. Maybe twelve feet long and that's a couple of body lengths." He paused, looking out over the lake. "Now I lead," he told her. "I lead and we hold together like this." With his right hand, he took hold of her left arm, forcing her to balance herself with her back against the rocks. "Hold on to my arm just above the wrist."

"Like this?" She grabbed his arm with fingers stronger than he'd expected. So close to her, he felt shy but calm.

"We jump here, we get more power," he told her. "We get down faster but it has to be done just right."

"How?" she said.

M. C. didn't know how. He was figuring it all out as he went along, working fast in his head the best way to jump and the quickest way to get through the tunnel.

"Best way is . . . if I jump backward and you jump frontward." He spoke carefully. "See, I hit and go in facing the tunnel. I have your left arm and you are pulled over. You follow in just in back of me. Now. In the tunnel, you have your right arm free and I have my left." They would use their free arms to push them through if they had to, and they could kick with their feet.

"Tunnel sides are moss," he said. "Push off from them when you bump them. It'll feel slimy but it won't hurt."

"Okay," she said.

"Pay no mind to fishes," he went on. "Most times, they're but just a few. They don't do nothing but get out of your way."

She nodded. M. C. could feel her tension through her arm.

"You all ready?" Macie asked from above them.

M. C. looked at the girl. "I'm ready," she said.

"You have to hold out for most of a minute."

"I can do it," she said.

"If you lose air, just stay calm," M. C. said. "I can get us out."

"I said I can do it!"

Her anger cut through him again, making him ashamed, he didn't know why.

"Macie, you count it off," he said grimly.

"She always gets me to do something," Harper said.

"He told *me,* now shut," Macie said.

"Stay out of the water. Wait for us at the pool. Now," M. C. said.

"Ready!" Macie yelled. "Get yourself set. . . ."

The girl grew rigid.

"You have to stay calm," M. C. told her. He held her arm as tightly as he could without hurting her. Her fingers dug into his wrist.

"Watch your nails!" he warned. They both sucked in air.

"Go, y'all!"

They leaped out and plunged. They hit the water at the same time but M. C. went under first because he was heavier. The girl turned facing him before her head went under. That was good, but pulling her after him slowed M. C. It seemed to take forever to get down to the tunnel level. Water closed in on them. Sounds became muffled and then no sound at all. They were alone as never before. And there was nothing for M. C. to do but get it over with.

M. C. liked nothing better than being in the deep, with sunlight breaking into rays of green and gold. Water was a pressure of delicious weight as he passed through it, down and down. It was as if feeling no longer belonged to him. The water possessed it and touched along every inch of him.

He pulled out of his downward fall at the sight of the gaping tunnel opening. He no longer felt the girl next to him. He knew she was there with him by the impression she made on the deep. And he would remember her presence, her imprint, on this day for weeks.

Bending her wrist forward, he stretched her arm out straight as he kicked hard into the tunnel. Here the water was cooler and cast a gray shimmer that was ghostly. Pressure grew like a ball and chain hanging on his right shoulder. It was the girl like a dead weight.

Kick with your feet!

With a powerful scissoring of his legs, he tried to swim midway between the ceiling and bottom of the tunnel.

Push off with your hand!

Her dead pressure dragged him down. His knees banged hard against the bottom. His back hit the tunnel side as he realized she was struggling to get away. Fractions of seconds were lost as he tried twisting her arm to pull her body into line. Fishes slid over his skin, tickling and sending shivers to his toes. They must have touched the girl. For he had no moment to brace himself as she shot up on her back toward the ceiling.

Won't make it.

Horror, outrage stunned him. He had taken for granted the

one thing he should have asked her. For the want of a
question, the tunnel would be a grave for both of them.

She kicked futilely against the tunnel side and rose above
him, twisting his arm straight up.

Yank, like Macie will pull down on a balloon.

If he could get the girl turned over, they might have a
chance. But his breath seemed to be gone.

Not a grave, it's a tunnel.

In his lungs, emptiness was pain. But the will not to fail was
there in his burning chest, in his free arm pushing hard
against the deep. His legs were still loose and working. Then
a sudden surge of strength, like a second wind.

Be M. C. Higgins, the Great.

He yanked the balloon down—he mustn't break the string.
At the same time he propelled himself forward, knowing she
would follow as she turned over.

An awful pounding in his head snapped his brain open.
M. C. shot out of the tunnel like a cork from a jug of cider.
And arching his back, he swung mightily with his right arm.

Dark balloon to the light above.

He hadn't the strength to hurl her to the surface. But he was right behind her. Before she could struggle down again, he was there, pulling at her. She opened her mouth in a pitiful attempt to breathe. He pounded her back, hoping to dislodge water. And held her close a split second to calm her. She was rigid.

Girl, don't drown.

Swiftly he caught her ankles and tossed her up over his head. She broke the surface. He was there, feeling sweet air just when he would have to open his mouth or have his lungs collapse.

M. C. fought against dizziness, aware he had his hand on her neck in a bruising clasp to hold her up. He had to let go or break it.

The girl was gagging, trying to breathe. He heard his own breath in a harsh, raw heaving. He was daydreaming a distant cheering. Then he saw the children, feet jumping up and down on the grassy bank. A swirl of rocks before he realized the girl was sinking. He must have let her go. But he had the sense to catch her again around the waist.

Still M. C. Still the leader. He had taken her through the tunnel and they were back in the world together. Still all the blame was his. But he could fix it. Could keep the children from knowing about her.

Moaning cry, coughing, she clung to him.

"No." He knocked her hands away. With just the pressure of his arm and shoulder on her back, he forced her flat out. As though she were dog-paddling, he glided her into the land. The feet jumping on the grassy bank fell back and were still.

Macie stood there on the bank, closest to M. C.'s head.

"She's weak," he said to Macie. "See if you can help pull her some . . . my wind is gone."

Macie clasped the girl's arms. M. C. had her by the waist. Halfway out of the water, she kicked M. C. away. She slithered and kneed her way over the bank. On the grass, she hunched into a ball, and struggling to breathe, closed her eyes.

Dark balloon.

M. C. climbed out and crawled a distance to collapse on his back. He was away from the girl, with the children between them, but he kept his eye on her. They were close together in his mind, where a vision had started. Day after day, they swam the lake. Hour upon hour, they sunned themselves on the shore.

M. C.'s chest wouldn't stop its heave and fall. His mouth watered with stomach bile as the pounding ache spread out across his forehead.

None of them moved. For a long while neither Harper nor Macie asked a single question. Lennie Pool never did say much.

M. C. felt as if every muscle were trying to get out of his skin. He was sick with exhaustion. But light out of the sky bore into him, warming and relaxing him. It was a healing band on his eyelids. As the ache in his forehead moved off, tunnel and water filled his mind. His eyes shot open, blinding the awful memory.

Seeing that M. C. was awake, Macie came over to him. "You did it!" she said happily. "Were you scared?"

He knew he would vomit if he tried to talk. He swallowed hard.

"You sure took your time. Was it any trouble?" Macie went on.

"Just took it easy," he said finally.

The girl brought up pool water she had swallowed. Half an hour later, she sat up shakily on her knees. In a slow, mechanical sweep, she brushed grass from her clothes.

M. C. raised his head. "You all right?" he asked her.

When she stood, the children stood with her. M. C. was on his feet as well, as though he moved only when she moved.

Slowly she seemed to change. He watched her grow stronger, throwing her head back, thrusting out her chin.

"I went all the way through that tunnel," she said, smiling vaguely. "I could have drowned—I can't even swim a lick."

The children gaped at her. Shocked, they turned to M. C.

"And you took her down?" Macie gasped. "You took her clear through . . . you didn't even know!"

The kids began to giggle, jostling one another, with the girl looking solemnly on.

M. C. felt the heat of shame rising in his neck. Only this one secret between them, but the girl wouldn't have it. She made him stand there with the kids laughing at him. He stared at his hands, at the jagged nails which he bit down to the skin.

"I can't stand a lying kid," the girl said.

Worse than a slap in the face, but he said evenly, "I'm not any kid. And I didn't lie."

"You told your sister we took it easy," she said, smirking at him.

"*I* took it easy," he said. "If I hadn't, you wouldn't be here, girl."

The children stared at him soberly now. The girl looked uncertain.

"It's no joke not to tell somebody you can't swim," he said.

"Somebody didn't ask me," she said sullenly.

"Didn't need to ask—you should've told me!"

"I just wanted to see it. I didn't know it was going to be so *long.*"

"So you want to see something and we almost drown?" He was shaking now with the memory of the tunnel. "Ever think of somebody but yourself?"

The girl shrank back. Uncomfortably, they watched her. M. C. hadn't meant to make her appear stupid. But she was quick to apologize.

"I'm sorry," she said simply. "You told me you were some M. C., the Great . . . ."

The look she gave him, as if she knew only he could have saved her, made him feel proud. He had to smile. "You have some good nerve. A lot of real good nerve," he said at last.

Meet the Author

Virginia Hamilton grew up with her four brothers and sisters on a farm in Yellow Springs, Ohio. She was the youngest. Her brothers and sisters treated her with love, and her parents spoiled her. She often went to see cousins, aunts, and uncles who lived on neighboring farms. In looking back on her childhood, Hamilton considers herself fortunate to have been part of such a warm, loving, extended family.

The author remembers her family as being great storytellers. No doubt, they were an influence on her because storytelling became her life's work.

The author's family helped to make the history of Yellow Springs, for they lived there for generations. The town of Yellow Springs played a part in the history of the United States. It was a station on the Underground Railway, and many of the people living there today are descendants of abolitionists and fugitive slaves. The Underground Railway was a source of inspiration to Hamilton for a book called *The House of Dies Drear*. It tells about an old house that was used as a shelter by the people who ran the Underground Railroad. The book was later made into a TV movie.

The author still lives in Yellow Springs on land that was once part of the farm on which she grew up.

Hamilton's book, *M. C. Higgins, the Great,* received the Newbery Award and the National Book Award in 1975. Many of her other books have received awards, too.

Checking Comprehension and Skills

Thinking About What You've Read

1. How does a lack of communication create serious danger for M. C. Higgins and a mysterious young woman?
• 2. How does the setting of the tunnel give M. C. the opportunity to show off?
3. Why is the young woman interested in going through the tunnel?
4. Give two examples that show the young woman is nervous before she plunges into the water.
5. Why does every second count when M. C. and the young woman are under water?
6. M. C. feels that "all the blame was his" for what happened. Do you agree? Explain your answer.
7. Why do you think M. C. thinks of the young woman as a balloon while they are under water?
8. What reason does the young woman give for not telling M. C. that she can't swim?
9. How would the story be different if the young woman knew how to swim?

Talking About What You've Read

Both M. C. and the young woman learn a lesson: You take a serious risk when you are not truthful about your abilities or humble about your limits. What might the younger children learn from this incident? If you were M. C. or the young woman, what would you tell the children to keep them from making a mistake of this kind?

Writing About What You've Read

Write four or five sentences in which either M. C. or the young woman tells the younger children what he or she has learned from this incident. Try to convince the younger children not to make the same kind of mistake.

• Literary Skills: Setting

The Dive

by Cornelia Brownell Gould

One moment, poised above the flashing blue:
The next I'm slipping, sliding through
The water that caresses, yields, resists,
Wrapping my sight in cooling grey-green mists.
Another moment—and I swirl, I rise,
Shaking the water from my blinded eyes,
And strike out strong, glad that I am alive,
To swing back to the grey old pile from which I dive.

The Uses of Paraphrasing

You may be surprised to learn that the people who live on the planet Mavula look just like the Earthlings. You may be even more surprised to learn that the Mavulans tried to invade us a few years ago. They prepared for the invasion by learning our language. They all had read a book written by Professor Wordy. Professor Wordy got carried away with words, and so he wrote reams and reams of words. Fortunately for us, the Mavulans learned our language a little too well.

The first Mavulan to land on our planet stopped a woman in the street and said, "I demand that you cease from your activities and escort me into the presence of your most exalted official." The woman looked at the Mavulan and started to laugh. Now it so happens that Mavulans are terribly afraid of laughter, and so the Mavulan hurried back to his planet and told them that an invasion was hopeless.

If only the Mavulans had learned how to paraphrase Professor Wordy's sentences, they might have been more succesful in their invasion.

When you paraphrase, you put a difficult sentence into simpler words. Paraphrasing helps you when you are reading because you're able to understand pieces of information and ideas better when you can state them in your own words.

The first step in paraphrasing a sentence is to figure out what all the words mean. The next step is to put the sentence into your own words. The last step is to make sure that nothing is missing from the new sentence.

If the Mavulan had been able to paraphrase, he would have told the woman, "Stop what you're doing and take me to your leader!" That might have been a little more effective than what he did say.

What does it feel like to be a winner? a loser? Caine knows. So do his teammates, and they don't hesitate to communicate this to him! See what is revealed about the characters of Caine and some of the other players in a typical schoolyard softball game.

STRIKING OUT

by Michael David Quinn

Jerry Miller says terrible things about me behind my back. I know he does because he says terrible things about me to my face.

"You stink, Caine. You really stink," he says. His folded, muscular arms neatly frame the bright red lettering printed across his chest.

"Batter up!" someone shouts.

"Well, don't just stand there," Miller says. I put on a big show of ignoring him as I shuffle up to home plate, dragging a bat behind me. It makes a thin, wavering path through the footprints of many predecessors.

Miller is right. I do stink. I stink at football, basketball, soccer, tennis, and volleyball even. (Volleyball isn't as bad as the others, because if you miss a volley, you can always blame it on the person behind you.) Every season there is something new for me to stink at. A basket to miss, a ball to fumble, a net to ensnare me—all punctuated by Jerry Miller's anguished cry of "Caine, you stink! You hear me? Stink!" When he's especially upset, he'll spell it out—"S!-T!-I!-N!-K!"—like some kind of cheerleader in reverse, each letter echoing crisply from wall to wall in our modern gymnasium. The other kids say nothing. I think they believe that humiliation helps build your character, or something like that.

My left ear is being pinched by the straps in the batter's helmet, and a fierce sun hangs directly over the pitcher's mound as I lean over the plate and take a couple of great-looking practice swings. It's a shame, really—I'd be such a first-class softball player, if there were no such things as softballs.

I hear the catcher clearing his throat impatiently. The pitcher is smiling at me. It isn't a friendly smile. It's more like the smile you give to a pepperoni pizza. The outfielders have moved in so close, they've practically become the infield. I raise my bat to shoulder level.

From out of the sun, the ball comes racing toward home plate, a bit high and inside. For a moment, I silently hope that a wild pitch will injure me, seriously, so that at least I can walk to first base and receive the heartfelt sympathy of my teammates. I step forward and swing the bat, the momentum pulling me along and—

Suddenly I realize the ball isn't there any more.

"STRIKE ONE!" yells the catcher.

"You stink, Caine!" screams Jerry Miller.

The ball sails back to the pitcher's mound.

Softball is the worst. Most team sports move fast and furiously. The moments of defeat, however embarrassing, pass in an instant. But when you step up to bat in softball, when you lift that bat high into the morning air, every eye follows your movements and evaluates your stance, your grip, your unmistakable attitude of terror. And for those hours that you hover about home plate, *you* are the entire game, you and that cunning softball. Once, twice, three times you swing and once, twice, three times, the resounding thunk! of leather on leather behind you announces your defeat to the world—

"STRIKE TWO!"

"Caine! Wake up! What's the matter with you?"

And back goes the ball to the pitcher's mound.

The outfield isn't even paying attention any more. They're talking among themselves, discussing some upcoming test in Modern European History and whether or not Mr. Taylor marks on the curve. The sun is burning directly into my eyes now. Everything and everyone is surrounded by a bluish-white glow. It makes the perfectly green hills and orderly housing developments of our town look like another planet.

The pitcher slams the softball into his mitt a few times. I think he knows that this annoys me.

Actually, when you think about it, there *are* worse things than softball. In football, you get trampled; in dodgeball, pelted with rubber. Besides, softball is the last unit of the year. After that, you have a whole summer to belly-flop into swimming pools and twist your ankles on overnight hikes, without Jerry Miller's colorful commentary.

Now the pitcher launches the attack, stretching back and whipping the ball past his hip. This time, I'm ready and alert. I respond with a mean and powerful swing of the bat, the kind you see only on commercials for after-shave lotion. A firm, level swing, with a splendid follow-through. Unfortunately, this all happens while the ball is still somewhere between home plate and the pitcher's fingers. The sudden realization transforms my graceful swing into a dizzying lurch that nearly makes me lose my balance.

"OUT!" cries the catcher, while the ball is still in flight. It shoots past his mitt and bangs angrily against the backstop. This satisfies me a bit, but not much. The bat slips from my fingers. It clatters clumsily on the hard ground. I shuffle back to the grass beside the first-base line, feeling like the victim of some terrible practical joke. The sun toasts the back of my neck and yet one more chorus of "Caine, you stink!" beats against my ears. I find

a place to sit, as far away from the rest of my team as possible. I'd cross the state line, if I didn't have algebra next period.

Oh, well. The hour is almost up and we are trailing the other side pretty badly, so at least there's no chance I'll be summoned to the plate again.

It's May, late May. We've been playing softball for the past month. I've made it to first base twice and to second once. Third has been like a foreign country—home plate, like the lost continent of Atlantis. Just my luck, the weather this spring has been unusually beautiful and we've never gotten rained out. We chose up sides at the end of April and by now, team spirit has become strong enough to inspire shoving matches over contested calls.

Choosing up. Sitting here, pulling up the grass and watching my teammates put me to shame, I wonder if choosing up for softball is even worse than *playing* softball. We all lined up by the backstop, like suspects in a bank holdup. Jerry Miller was voted one of the captains, naturally. The other was this kid whose name I always forget, but he is very big. And he likes to do things that he figures baseball players do, like spitting and kicking the dirt a lot.

Anyway, it didn't take Miller and Big Kid too long to pick the first ten players or so, who'd leap forward when their names were called, pounding each other on the back and acting very pleased with themselves. But as the teams grew larger and the crowd of players-to-be started thinning out, choosing up sides became less of a pleasure and more of a responsibility—like picking up the bases at the end of a game. Names were called out more slowly and less enthusiastically. That's when the arguing started. Arguments over who gets the best players are never as loud and intense as arguments over who gets the worst players. ("Forget it, we're not taking him! We had him last semester! You have to take him this time!")

Finally, there were only two of us left standing forlornly against the cold iron mesh of the backstop. I was one. Murch was the other. It has always ended this way, ever since grade school—me and Murch, like a pair of mismatched socks buried in the bottom of a hamper. Murch is all we call him. Like everyone else, he is required to leave his first name in the locker rooms, along with his street clothes. I've never had a phys ed teacher call me David. "You—Caine." That's all, ever.

Murch is the absolute worst athlete in the class—even worse than I am. Today's game is no different. His teammates have exiled Murch to the wilderness of right field—the same place I usually find myself planted. Normally, the softball shows up in right field about once a semester, but today no less than three fly balls have whizzed above, around, or through Murch's stiffly outstretched arms. The previous inning, Big Kid moved Murch to center field, figuring that the players on either side could cover for him. This is, of course, a waste of time. As I know only too well, a gifted athlete's talents may occasionally fail him, but a rotten athlete's rottenness is as constant as the law of gravity.

I begin to fidget, waiting for the gym teacher's whistle or perhaps a particularly long fire drill to put an end to my misery. A high pop to center field plummets to earth

right in front of Murch and bounces between his legs.
With mounting horror, I realize that my team is making an
eleventh-hour rally and that I may be forced to return to
the batter's box. Murch isn't making it any easier for me.

Now, you might think that since Murch and I are both
serious contenders for the Least Valuable Player Award, we
would be natural friends. But it isn't that way at all. In
fact, I think I hate Murch a little. He is too much like me.
Looking at him on the playing field reminds me of just
how ridiculous I must appear. As he stumbles after a line
drive to center or tosses a ball and watches it drop into
a mud puddle, halfway to its destination, Murch is my
painfully faithful reflection. Seeing him strike out and fumble
balls hurts more than anything Jerry Miller ever said.

And then there's the fact that as long as Murch is
slightly worse than I am, I can at least be superior to
somebody. Everyone talks about the pressure to remain
first. Well, it's nothing compared to the pressure to stay
second to last, believe me.

Actually, maybe I envy Murch. Because as awful as he
is, Murch doesn't care. Not a bit. Miller and the others
stopped mocking him ages ago. It just wasn't any fun—
Murch didn't react. For me, each vain swing of the bat is
the loneliest moment of my life. But for Murch, it is simply
another distraction from the only thing that seems to
matter to him—murder mysteries. He reads murder
mysteries the way Jerry Miller reads the sports pages. He
reads them on the bus to school. He reads them walking
through the halls between classes. He hides them in
lunch bags and behind the covers of American history
textbooks. He would probably take Agatha Christie out to
right field with him if the gym teachers weren't looking.

So instead, he simply stands out there, rubbing his nose
with his baseball mitt, his skinny legs sticking out of a
pair of gym shorts that always look too big on him. I don't
know what he thinks about there in the mud and the

dandelions. The perfect murder, perhaps, or the jewel heist of the century.

Oh, no! There's no doubt about it now—we're on our way to a major comeback. I return for my disgraceful performance at bat, and suddenly everyone else becomes our school's answer to Pete Rose. Two more of my teammates have just raced jubilantly across home plate. We picked up our second out just a while ago, when Miller was tagged at first. But he made a lot of noise about "sacrifice plays" and nobody said a word. Reputation is everything—when you're hot, an out is a sacrifice. When you're not, an out is an out.

Except for Miller, they've all made it to home or are somewhere along the way. The opposition is beginning to panic. Murch, as uncomplaining as ever, has been moved back to right field. Big Kid has personally replaced the smiling pitcher, who hasn't been smiling for some time now. A grim silence has spread across the field. The second baseman is exchanging nervous glances with the third baseman. The shortstop keeps looking at his watch, and the player covering first is constantly wiping his forehead, noticing the heat for the first time.

We trail by three runs. Three players precede me in the batting order. An out by any one of them will end the game and make my day that much brighter. But the first one reaches base. So does the second, on an error. Two players on. I'm on deck. Jerry Miller is pacing frantically behind the backstop, the scent of blood driving him mad.

Just one player ahead of me now, a tall, quiet kid named Cook. Cook wears heavy glasses that turn the tip of his nose red, and he uses the word *pizzazz* a lot—in fact, it's become something of a nickname for him.

"Let's go, Pizzazz," shouts Miller.

Strike out, Pizzazz, I say to myself. Pull a muscle. Faint. Anything.

Pizzazz, generally an unspectacular ballplayer, for once

lives up to his name. He drives the ball deep into right field. My team comes to its feet, expecting a home run. But at the last moment, the centerfielder races to his right. He practically tramples Murch as he scoops up the ball on a bounce and shoots it to home, holding everyone to a base.

It is the classic situation: bases loaded, last inning, two away. A triple will make it a tie. A grand slam will put us over the top.

"Who's up? Who's up?" Miller asks, almost growling with excitement.

Then he remembers. "Caine." He shakes his head. "Caine. Oh, no!"

I pick myself up off the ground.

"Caine, you blow this and I'll—"

I wipe my palms on my shorts and reach for a bat.

"You hear me, Caine?"

"Knock it off, Miller," I answer under my breath as I approach the plate.

"I'll get you, Caine, I swear," he cries, shaking the mesh of the backstop. "I'll get you, I'll—"

"SHUT UP, MILLER! JUST SHUT UP!" I shout loudly, real loudly, spinning about and raising the bat like a club.

Miller shuts up. He's startled. Everyone's startled. Even *I'm* startled. A hot, angry glow has filled my body. It feels great. There is an odd moment of silence. I turn to face the pitcher once again, and I discover a soft but determined smile on my face.

Something has changed, and the other side knows it. The outfield doesn't bother moving in. Big Kid scratches his thigh. He takes the softball out of his mitt, almost dropping it. He nods to the catcher.

"Come on, Dave," one of my teammates says quietly.

The first pitch arrives low and on the outside. It's wild. I let it pass.

"Ball One."

"That's looking them over, Caine."

The ball returns to the pitcher.

He pauses.

Somehow we both know that the next pitch is mine.

I watch the wind-up and the release with a feeling I have never had before, a scientific calm and a sense of total security. I am aware of each distinct instant, so much that it all seems to happen in slow motion. The ball glides toward me, spinning in the sunlight. Gradually it swells larger and larger, till it's almost as tremendous as the sun itself. At the same time, my shoulders flex, my whole body brings the bat down and across to meet the oncoming target.

The ball seems about to drift past the corner of my eye when there is a sharp, brilliant *crack!* and a sudden jolt in the smooth part of the bat. And when I see it next, the ball has already started to shrink and disappear into the blue, cloudless sky.

"Run, Caine!" screams Miller, shocking me back to life. A surge of fire rushes into my legs. I scramble to first, dust and breeze dashing against my face, shouts and yells bombarding me from all directions. As I approach the base, I realize that I am still gripping the bat in my left hand.

I toss it away and round first, heading for second. Now I can see the ball at the very peak of its path, high, high, high over right field. I'm well on my way to second when it begins to plunge to earth, nothing between it and the ground but the pathetic figure of Murch. He seems almost confused by the din and the turmoil.

So this is what it feels like to be a winner. This is what that great guy Jerry Miller is willing to kill for. I don't blame him a bit, I think. Second base speeds toward my flying feet.

The ball drops below the horizon and is lost against the landscape. Murch raises his arms, as much to protect

himself from injury as anything else. My left leg reaches out for second base . . . .

There is a far-off thud of leather on leather. The sound brings me to a dead stop.

Murch stands in right field. The softball rests snugly in his mitt.

"Caine, you stink! S!T!I!—"

The rest of Miller's words are lost in an explosion of sound, as Murch's teammates toss their gloves into the air and rush toward their new-found hero, grabbing him, pounding him, shouting his name. Murch seems as unconcerned in victory as he has always seemed in defeat.

My team looks on in disbelief. The gym teacher finally blows his whistle.

Eventually, they all head back to the locker room, thoughts already turning to the next class and the less important realities of the Civil War and the great white whale.

I lean against the backstop. If I wait long enough, maybe they'll all be gone by the time I hit the showers. This is one day I definitely want to shower alone.

There is a sound of movement beside me.

It is Murch. He is standing there, with a bit of an embarrassed grin.

We say nothing.

He shrugs. "Oh, well," he says. "You can't lose them all."

And taking a paperback out of his mitt, he walks off to the locker rooms.

Checking Comprehension and Skills

Thinking About What You've Read

1. How do some of the players communicate to Caine that he is a loser at softball? Find two examples in the story that explain your answer.

2. Why does Caine sometimes think that softball is the worst sport?

3. How is "choosing up sides" worse for Caine than actually playing the game?

• 4. Give two reasons why Caine does not like Murch.

• 5. What does Miller's description of his out as a "sacrifice play" tell you about his character?

6. Suppose you are the coach giving Caine a pep talk. What can you tell him about his personality that might help him?

7. In the story Caine has a brief success. What is the success? Why is it brief?

8. Suppose Caine's trouble was that he couldn't do well on history tests rather than at playing softball. How would the story be different?

Talking About What You've Read

The author has shown how one game can bring out the widely different personalities of the players. How would you describe each of the main characters? What differences in their personalities would you point out? What adjectives would you choose to describe Murch, Caine, and Miller?

Writing About What You've Read

Using the words you have chosen, write two-line sketches of Caine, Murch, and Miller for the class yearbook. Keep in mind that you want to tell the truth, but you don't want to say anything bad. Try to stay true to the story.

• Literary Skills: Character

PEANUTS

by Charles M. Schulz

© 1955 United Feature Syndicate, Inc.

LOOKING BACK

Thinking About the Section

You've just read three selections in which characters try to communicate with one another with varying degrees of success.

The scale below can be used to measure success in communication.

1	2	3	4	5
Least	Less	Moderately	More	Most

The number 1 at the left means least successful in communication. The number 5 at the right means most successful. Draw the scale on a separate sheet of paper. Rank the main characters from each selection. Fill in the name of the character above the number on the scale that shows how successful that character was in communicating.

Writing About the Section

Choose one character from each selection. Write a short paragraph explaining why you think that character communicated successfully or unsuccessfully. Give reasons that will help to persuade someone that your opinion is right. The opening sentence of each paragraph should read:

I think (name of character) was (least, less, moderately, more, most) successful in communicating for these reasons. . . .

The reasons you include should support your opinion. You may make comparisons among the different characters from each selection to help support your opinion. Remember to use your own skills in communication to help you present a convincing case.

9

The Great Outdoors

Breathe the fresh, clean air. Taste the cool spring water. Explore the beauty of the great outdoors.

The wonders of nature seem endless—but are they? In fact, they are not. If we want the riches and the resources of nature to be available to us, we must all work to protect our environment.

In this section, you'll read about people and agencies working to protect our natural resources. You'll meet a boy who learns how to live in the wilderness. And you'll take a road trip with characters who disagree about the pleasures of their natural surroundings.

Using PQ2R

The family in this picture is enjoying a vacation in the great outdoors. They are using a map and following road signs to help them find their way.

Reading a textbook is something like taking a trip. To get the most from your reading or your traveling, you should have an idea of where you are going and how you will get there *before* you set out

Here is a system to help you read material you want to remember. It has four steps: Preview, Question, Read, and Review. It's called **PQ2R**.

1. Preview. To preview, you take a quick look ahead to see what a chapter or a lesson is about. When you preview, you glance at the textbook features—titles, headings, diagrams, pictures, maps, charts, graphs, marginal notes, and any words in dark type. Your purpose is to get a general idea about the content. Preview the science lesson from a textbook, shown on the next four pages. Notice that the lesson title on page 379 and the heading on page 381 are both questions. You can expect the lesson to contain the answers.

2. Question. After you have a general idea about the content, you need to ask yourself questions that you expect the lesson to answer. You can look at the Think About It questions on page 382 to help you. You can also make up some questions of your own. For this lesson you might ask, "What is a flood plain?" and "How does a meander in a river become a lake?"

3. Read. Now read the science lesson on the next four pages. Keep in mind your questions and the ones included in the text. Look for the answers as you read. When you finish reading, you will do step 4 of PQ2R—**Review.**

2 Where Do Rivers Run?

drainage basin, all the land drained by a river and by the small streams that join the river.

Rain or snow that falls on hills, mountains, or fields flows into low places because water runs downhill. Rivers are low places into which the water flows. Rivers carry part of the rainfall into the oceans.

All rivers begin as tiny streams that carry away—or drain—rainfall from the surrounding land. The land drained by a stream is the stream's **drainage basin.** As a stream flows, it is joined by other small streams. Eventually, the stream becomes large enough to be called a river. The drainage basin of a river is all the land drained by the river and the land drained by each small stream that joins the river.

The picture shows the largest drainage basins in the United States. Notice how much land the Mississippi River drains. The Mississippi River is about 4,000 kilometers long. It begins as a narrow stream in Minnesota. It is nearly 1 kilometer wide where it empties into the Gulf of Mexico.

Drainage basins in the United States

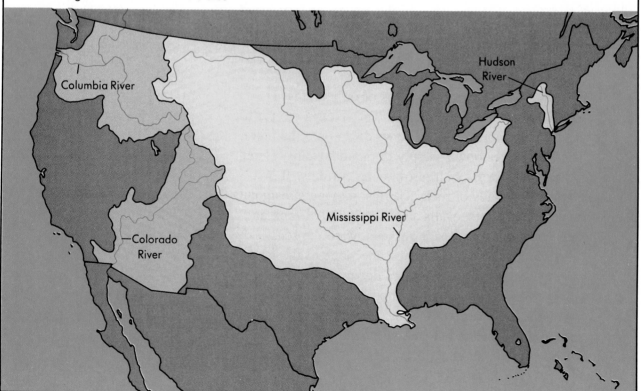

A mountain stream   A fan-shaped mound of earth

Most rivers start in mountains or on land that is higher than the level of the sea. The river in the picture starts in the mountains and flows down onto the plain. The land slopes down sharply in the mountains. Here, the river is narrow with fast-moving currents. It is bordered by walls of rock. The fast-moving stream cuts down through these walls and carries bits of rock and soil, called **sediment,** as it gushes toward the sea.

At the foot of the mountains, the slope of the land is more gentle and the river slows down. When the river slows down, some of the soil and rocks carried from the mountains drop from the water. Sometimes this sediment becomes a fan-shaped mound of earth, such as the one in the picture.

Have You Heard?

Rain and river water carved a large cave in the bluffs — or rock cliffs — at Cave in Rock, Illinois, on the Ohio River. In the 1700s and 1800s, river bandits used this cave as a hideout. From the cave, they could spot boats traveling up and down the river.

sediment (sed′ə mənt), pieces of rock and soil.

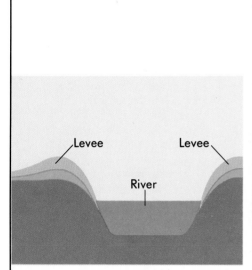

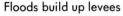

Floods build up levees

Flood plain of a river

How Does a River Change the Land?

A river picks up, carries, and drops sediment as it flows across land. You can feel this sediment squeeze between your toes when you wade through a muddy-bottomed stream.

The photograph shows a **flood plain**—or wide, flat area—that borders a river. During a flood, a river rises above its banks and covers the land. A thin layer of sediment settles out of the water and coats the flooded land. The river sediment contains minerals that enrich the soil. In spite of yearly floods, pioneers in this country settled on fertile flood plains first.

Levees are wall-like hills along a river's banks. During floods, levees build up where sediment drops at a river's banks as shown in the drawing. After repeated floods, some levees are high enough to protect people against rising flood water. When a river is rising rapidly, people often build artificial levees by putting sandbags along a river's banks.

flood plain, the flat land that borders a river and is covered by water and sediment when the river floods.

levee (lev'ē), wall-like structure made of sediment that builds up along a river's banks, or similar structure that is built on river banks by people.

The photograph on the previous page also shows curves—or **meanders**—in a river. During floods, a meander might disappear. Notice in the drawings how a river can cut across the narrowest part of a meander and take a shorter, straighter route. As a result the meander disappears. Sometimes, however, a thin, curved lake is left in the old meander.

A river ends at its mouth, where it empties into a lake or an ocean. River water slows down here and drops some of its sediment. The river sediment can build up in the large body of water and create new land at the river's mouth. This new land is a **delta.** The city of New Orleans is built on the Mississippi River delta.

A river builds up and wears down the land. A river often changes its course.

Have You Heard?

Some historic towns are located in out-of-the-way places. For instance, the first capital of Illinois, Kaskaskia, lies at the bottom of the Mississippi River! The town was once on the banks of the river. In the flood of 1881, the river cut off a large meander and took a shorter path. This change put the town under water. People built a new Kaskaskia on higher ground—an island in the Mississippi River.

A meander in a river

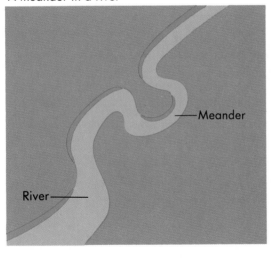

Lake formed from the meander

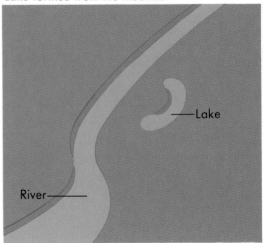

Think About It

1. What is the drainage basin of a river?
2. Explain how rain on the land reaches oceans.
3. **Challenge** If a message placed in a bottle were dropped into the Mississippi River in St. Louis, Missouri, where might the bottle later be found?

meander (mē an′dər), a loop in a river.

delta, new land that builds up at the mouth of a river in a body of water.

4. Review. After you read, see if you can answer your own questions as well as the ones under Think About It. You might need to reread parts of the text and skim to find facts that answer the questions. (Some of the questions you had may not have been answered. In such cases, you may want to check another reference source.) Another way to review is to make a list of the main points in the article. Put them in your own words. This is a good way to study for a test.

Practicing PQ2R

Now answer the questions below about the textbook selection you just read using the PQ2R system.

1. What is a flood plain? Which three textbook features give you information about what a flood plain is?
2. How does a meander in a river become a lake?
3. Name the three largest drainage basins in the United States. Where in the text can you find information about these basins?
4. What three purposes do the marginal notes serve in this chapter?

Tips for Reading on Your Own

- Preview your textbook reading assignments by looking at the parts of the lesson.
- Use the textbook features such as title, subheads, and review questions to help you form questions. These will help you set a purpose for your reading.
- As you read the entire assignment carefully, look for answers to your questions and any other questions asked in the text.
- Review the main points of the assignment. Make sure you know the answers to the questions.

Many people are helping to solve environmental problems of the great outdoors. To find out what has been done and what you can do, use PQ2R as you read this textbook lesson.

9-2 Working to Solve Environmental Problems

- Who are some of the people working to solve environmental problems?
- What are some things being done to help solve air, water, land, and noise problems?

Environmental problems are not new. But many problems are worse now than ever before. Why?

One reason is the increased population. More people live on the earth today than at any time in the past. More people means more pollutants are added to the air, water, and land. More people means more noise is made. And more people means natural resources are used up faster.

In addition, certain advances in technology have made some environmental problems worse. For example, modern technology involves the production of many chemical wastes. Some chemical wastes are dangerous pollutants. Completely safe ways to dispose of these wastes have not yet been developed.

Today's environmental problems are very serious. But many of them can be solved. It is important to try to solve them because a healthy environment can greatly benefit physical, mental, and social health. Who is working to help solve environmental problems?

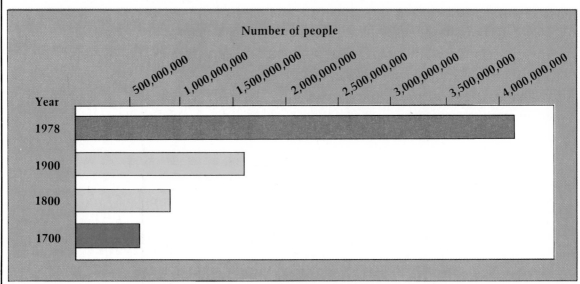

The chart shows you how much the world's population has increased in the past three hundred years.

People Who Help the Environment

Many people work to help the environment. Some of these people work for the government. Others work for voluntary agencies and certain industries. With the help of these and other people, solutions to some environmental problems are being found.

Government Workers Several agencies of the federal government are responsible for helping the environment. Among these agencies are the National Park Service and the Environmental Protection Agency (EPA).

People who work for the National Park Service help preserve national parks and other places that are naturally beautiful or have unusual natural features. People who work for the Environmental Protection Agency decide, among other things, how much of certain materials can be safely added to the environment.

In addition to the work of these agencies, the federal government passes laws to protect the environment. Each state and local government must help enforce these laws. But state and local governments can establish other agencies and pass even stricter laws, if they wish.

The adults you see work for the National Park Service.

The smoke coming from the smokestacks of this factory meets EPA air pollution limits.

Others Who Help Government workers are not the only ones who work to solve environmental problems. People working for voluntary agencies and industries help as well.

People in the Boy Scouts of America, Girl Scouts of America, National Wildlife Federation, and Sierra Club are among those who help. These groups work to educate the public about the environment. Many of them also work for stricter laws to protect the environment.

People in the paper, glass, aluminum, and automobile industries are among those in industry working to help solve environmental problems. People in these industries work to reduce pollution caused by industries and to conserve natural resources used by the industries.

What Is Being Done to Solve Environmental Problems?

What are people in government, voluntary agencies, and industry actually doing to help the environment? What are they doing now to solve air, water, land, and noise problems?

Solving Air Problems Scientists working for the Environmental Protection Agency decide how much of each air pollutant is safe for people to breathe. Then the EPA sets and helps enforce limits for each pollutant. These limits apply to such things as automobile exhaust and smoke from factory smokestacks.

To meet the EPA limits, people in industry must find ways to reduce the amount of pollutants they add to the air. For example, new devices have been added to many automobiles to reduce air pollution.

People in many state and local governments have passed and are enforcing air pollution laws. Burning of leaves is prohibited in many areas, for example. And many places require that the incinerators used to burn solid wastes have antipollution devices on the smokestacks.

In addition to what people in government and industry do, people in voluntary agencies study air pollution. They teach others about the possible effects of air pollution. They also work for stricter laws.

Solving Water Problems People in government also work to solve water problems. For example, the EPA sets limits on water pollutants. By law, materials known to be harmful are not supposed to be dumped into

This person works for a local public health department. He makes sure the community's water supply is safe. Other jobs done by local public health department workers include checking air pollution levels and inspecting food stores and restaurants.

lakes, streams, and rivers. Industries also are supposed to reduce thermal pollution by cooling the water they use before returning it to the environment.

Most communities have sewage treatment plants. These plants treat sewage that comes from homes and other sources. At these plants, screens remove large wastes from the water. Certain chemicals are added to make the water cleaner. And the water is filtered through sand and gravel to remove dirt and other small wastes. After treatment, the water is returned to the water supply.

To meet government limits, drinking water supplies must be tested and treated, if necessary. Most communities have water treatment plants. Water is piped to the plants from the water supply. At the plant, workers operate equipment that removes impurities and kills pathogens in the water. The water then can be sent to homes and other places for drinking.

Many communities also are working to conserve water supplies. For example, washing cars and watering lawns is limited in some areas. What is being done to conserve water in your community?

People in voluntary agencies work to make people aware of water problems. These agencies also work to conserve water and protect drinking water supplies.

Solving Land Problems People in government work to help solve land problems too. For example, recent laws control the disposal of chemical wastes more strictly. When, where,

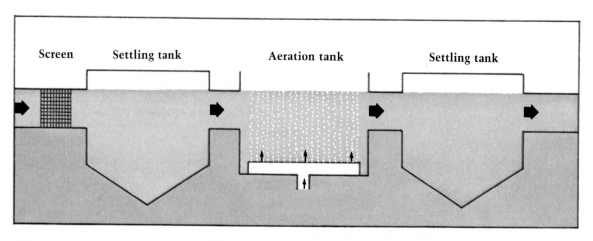

After sewage enters a treatment plant, it passes through a large screen. This screen removes large solid wastes from the water. The water then passes into a large settling tank where smaller solid wastes rise to the top or sink to the bottom of the tank. The cleaner water between the two layers of wastes is drained off through an aeration tank, where oxygen is added. Chlorine is added at the end of the treatment.

and how chemicals are disposed of must be recorded. The disposal sites will be watched by the EPA for any problems that may develop. Other laws control where and how solid wastes are disposed of.

To help solve the waste disposal problem and to conserve fuel, scientists are finding ways to use garbage to provide energy. In some communities, for example, garbage is burned in large incinerators that give off steam. This steam is used to provide some of the electricity the community needs.

People in voluntary agencies work to make others aware of land problems. These agencies encourage governments to pass laws to conserve natural resources and help solve other land problems.

Many industries now encourage *recycling*. Recycling is the changing of something so it can be used again. Recycling reduces solid waste and helps conserve natural resources. Aluminum, glass, and paper are some materials collected at recycling centers. Later, industries reuse these materials.

Solving Noise Problems People working for the federal government have set decibel limits for certain kinds of noise. For example, areas where people work cannot be too

noisy. If high levels of noise have to exist, the workers must be protected. How are the workers in the picture being protected from noise?

Many communities also have set decibel limits. In these communities, car horns may be used only in emergencies. Motorcycles and other vehicles must have mufflers to limit noise.

People working for certain industries are developing quieter products, such as quieter household appliances. Even quieter airplane engines, jack hammers, and garbage trucks are being made and used.

People in voluntary agencies also are working to solve noise problems. For example, people in these agencies are working to make others more aware of how to protect their hearing.

The work of people in government, voluntary agencies, and industry is important in helping the environment. But their work is not enough. The environment needs everyone's help—including yours.

What Do You Remember?

1. Why are many environmental problems worse now than ever before?
2. How are people in government working to help the environment?
3. How are people in voluntary agencies working to help solve environmental problems?
4. How are people in industry working to help solve environmental problems?

Checking Comprehension and Skills

Thinking About What You've Read

1. According to this selection, why is it important to take care of the great outdoors?
2. Which government agency is responsible for enforcing environmental laws?
3. Give two examples that show how voluntary agencies and industry work to solve environmental problems.
4. Explain why some communities limit the washing of cars and the watering of lawns.
5. Name two ways in which garbage can be useful.
6. Do you consider loud radios an example of noise problems? Explain your answer.
7. Which of the environmental problems mentioned in this selection affects you most strongly? How does it do so?
• 8. List at least three subheads that you noticed when you previewed this selection.
• 9. State two questions that you expected to be answered in this selection based on your preview of it. Were the questions answered?

Talking About What You've Read

How well do you think your community is solving the environmental problems discussed in this selection? Be prepared to discuss specific examples of actions that have been taken and need to be taken.

Writing About What You've Read

Write a short letter to your local newspaper. State an environmental problem you think is not being solved in your community. Propose a series of steps that can be taken to help solve the problem.

• Study Skills: PQ2R

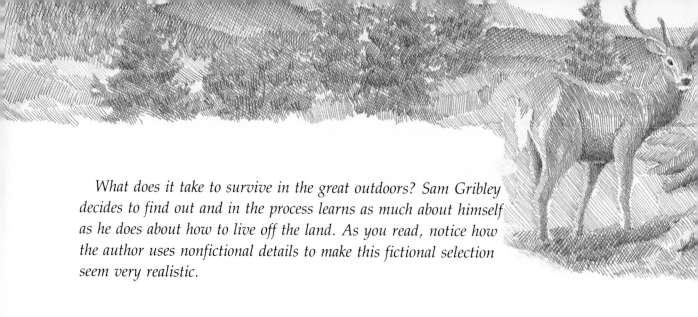

What does it take to survive in the great outdoors? Sam Gribley decides to find out and in the process learns as much about himself as he does about how to live off the land. As you read, notice how the author uses nonfictional details to make this fictional selection seem very realistic.

MY SIDE of the MOUNTAIN

by Jean Craighead George

Fourteen-year-old Sam Gribley left New York City for the Catskill Mountains to prove to himself that he could survive in the wilderness. He had a few things from home, such as flint and steel to start a fire. But otherwise he would live off the land. Sam arrived on the mountain that his great-grandfather once farmed and began exploring a forest of giant hemlock trees, looking for a place to live.

Never, never have I seen such trees. They were giants— old, old giants. They must have begun when the world began.

I started walking around them. I couldn't hear myself step, so dense and damp were the needles. Great boulders covered with ferns and moss stood among them. They looked like pebbles beneath those trees.

Standing before the biggest and the oldest and the most kinglike of them all, I suddenly had an idea.

I knew enough about the Catskill Mountains to know that when the summer came, they were covered with people. Although Great-grandfather's farm was somewhat remote,

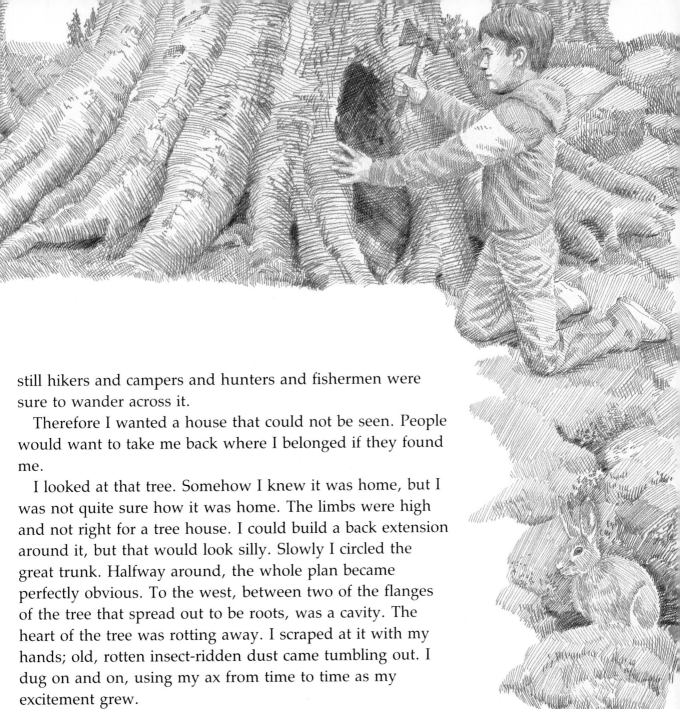

still hikers and campers and hunters and fishermen were sure to wander across it.

Therefore I wanted a house that could not be seen. People would want to take me back where I belonged if they found me.

I looked at that tree. Somehow I knew it was home, but I was not quite sure how it was home. The limbs were high and not right for a tree house. I could build a back extension around it, but that would look silly. Slowly I circled the great trunk. Halfway around, the whole plan became perfectly obvious. To the west, between two of the flanges of the tree that spread out to be roots, was a cavity. The heart of the tree was rotting away. I scraped at it with my hands; old, rotten insect-ridden dust came tumbling out. I dug on and on, using my ax from time to time as my excitement grew.

With much of the old rot out, I could crawl in the tree and sit cross-legged. Inside I felt as cozy as a turtle in its shell. I chopped and chopped until I was hungry and exhausted. I was now in the hard good wood, and chopping it out was work. I was afraid December would come before I got a hole big enough to lie in. So I sat down to think.

• Put the description of how Sam felt into your own words.

You know, those first days, I just never planned right. I had the beginnings of a home, but not a bite to eat, and I had worked so hard that I could hardly move forward to find that bite. Furthermore it was discouraging to feed that body of mine. It was never satisfied, and gathering food for it took time and got it hungrier. Trying to get a place to rest it took time and got it more tired, and I really felt I was going in circles and wondered how primitive people ever had enough time and energy to stop hunting food and start thinking about fire and tools.

I left the tree and went across the meadow looking for food. I plunged into the woods beyond, and there I discovered the gorge and the white cascade splashing down the black rocks into the pool below.

I was hot and dirty. I scrambled down the rocks and slipped into the pool. It was so cold I yelled. But when I came out on the bank and put on my two pairs of trousers and three sweaters, which I thought was a better way to carry clothes than in a pack, I tingled and burned and felt coltish. I leapt up the bank, slipped, and my face went down in a patch of dogtooth violets.

• Paraphrase Sam's description of the violets.

You would know them anywhere after a few looks at them at the Botanical Gardens and in colored flower books. They are little yellow lilies on long slender stems with oval leaves dappled with gray. But that's not all. They have wonderfully tasty bulbs. I was filling my pockets before I got up from my fall.

"I'll have a salad type lunch," I said as I moved up the steep sides of the ravine. I discovered that as late as it was in the season, the spring beauties were still blooming in the cool pockets of the woods. They are all right raw, that is, if you are as hungry as I was. They taste a little like lima beans. I ate these as I went on hunting food, feeling better and better, until I worked my way back to the meadow where the dandelions were blooming. Funny I hadn't noticed them earlier. Their greens are good, and so are the roots—a little strong and milky, but you get used to that.

A crow flew into the aspen grove without saying a word. The little I knew of crows from following them in Central Park, they always have something to say. But this bird was sneaking, obviously trying to be quiet. Birds are good food. Crow is certainly not the best, but I did not know that then, and I launched out to see where it was going. I had a vague plan to try to noose it. This is the kind of thing I wasted time on in those days when time was so important. However, this venture turned out all right, because I did not have to noose that bird.

I stepped into the woods, looked around, could not see the crow, but noticed a big stick nest in a scrabbly pine. I started to climb the tree. Off flew the crow. What made me keep on climbing in face of such discouragement, I don't know, but I did, and that noon I had crow eggs and wild salad for lunch.

At lunch I also solved the problem of carving out my tree. After a struggle I made a fire. Then I sewed a big skunk cabbage leaf into a cup with grass strands. I had read that you can boil water in a leaf, and ever since then I had been very anxious to see if this were true. It seems impossible, but it works. I boiled the eggs in a leaf. The water keeps the leaf wet, and although the top dries up and burns down to the water level, that's as far as the burning goes. I was pleased to see it work.

• In your own words, tell what happens when you boil water in a leaf.

Then here's what happened. Naturally, all this took a lot of time, and I hadn't gotten very far on my tree, so I was fretting and stamping out the fire when I stopped with my foot in the air.

The fire! Indians made dugout canoes with fire. They burned them out, an easier and much faster way of getting results. I would try fire in the tree. If I was very careful, perhaps it would work. I ran into the hemlock forest with a burning stick and got a fire going inside the tree.

Thinking that I ought to have a bucket of water in case things got out of hand, I looked desperately around me. The water was far across the meadow and down the ravine. This would never do. I began to think the whole inspiration of a home in the tree was no good. I really did have to live near water for cooking and drinking and comfort. I looked sadly at the magnificent hemlock and was about to put the fire out and desert it when I said something to myself. It must have come out of some book: "Hemlocks usually grow around mountain streams and springs."

I swirled on my heel. Nothing but boulders around me. But the air was damp, somewhere—I said—and darted around the rocks, peering and looking and sniffing and going down into pockets and dales. No water. I was coming back, circling wide, when I almost fell in it. Two sentinel boulders, dripping wet, decorated with flowers, ferns, moss, weeds—everything that loved water—guarded a bathtub-sized spring.

"You pretty thing," I said, flopped on my stomach, and pushed my face into it to drink. I opened my eyes. The water was like glass, and in it were little insects with oars. They rowed away from me. Beetles skittered like bullets on the surface, or carried a silver bubble of air with them to the bottom. Ha, then I saw a crayfish.

I jumped up, overturned rocks, and found many crayfish. At first I hesitated to grab them because they can pinch. I gritted my teeth, thought about how much more it hurts to be hungry, and came down upon them. I did get pinched, but I had my dinner. And that was the first time I had planned ahead! Any planning that I did in those early days was such a surprise to me and so successful that I was delighted with even a small plan. I wrapped the crayfish in leaves, stuffed them in my pockets, and went back to the burning tree.

Bucket of water, I thought. Bucket of water? Where was I going to get a bucket? How did I think, even if I found water, I could get it back to the tree? That's how citified I was in those days. I had never lived without a bucket before—scrub buckets, water buckets—and so when a water problem came up, I just thought I could run to the kitchen and get a bucket.

"Well, dirt is as good as water," I said as I ran back to my tree. "I can smother the fire with dirt."

Days passed working, burning, cutting, gathering food, and each day I cut another notch on an aspen pole that I had stuck in the ground for a calendar.

Five notches into June, my house was done. I could stand in it, lie down in it, and there was room left over for a stump to sit on. On warm evenings I would lie on my stomach and look out the door, listen to the cicadas and crickets, and hope it would storm so that I could crawl into my tree and be dry. I had gotten soaked during a couple of May downpours, and now that my house was done, I wanted the chance to sit in my hemlock and watch a cloudburst wet everything but me. This opportunity didn't come for a long time. It was dry.

One morning I was at the edge of the meadow. I had cut down a small ash tree and was chopping it into lengths of about eighteen inches each. This was the beginning of my bed that I was planning to work on after supper every night.

With the golden summer upon me, food was much easier to get, and I actually had several hours of free time after supper in which to do other things. I had been eating frogs' legs, turtles, and best of all, an occasional rabbit. My snares and traps were set now. Furthermore, I had a good supply of cattail roots I had dug in the marsh.

If you ever eat cattails, be sure to cook them well, otherwise the fibers are tough and they take more chewing to get the starchy food from them than they are worth. However, they taste just like potatoes after you've been eating them a couple of weeks, and to my way of thinking are very good.

Well, anyway, that summer morning when I was gathering material for a bed, I heard a cry in the sky. I looked up. Swinging down the valley on long pointed wings was a large bird. I was struck by the ease and swiftness of its flight. This bird, I was sure, was the peregrine falcon, the king's hunting bird.

"I will get one. I will train it to hunt for me," I said to myself.

I went straight to town to the library where Miss Turner, the librarian, had helped me look up the location of Great-grandfather's farm when I first arrived.

Miss Turner was glad to see me. I told her I wanted some books on hawks and falcons, and she located a few, although there was not much to be had on the subject. We worked all afternoon, and I learned enough. I departed when the library closed. Miss Turner whispered to me as I left, "Sam, you need a haircut."

I hadn't seen myself in so long that this had not occurred to me. "I don't have any scissors."

She thought a minute, got out her library scissors, and sat me down on the back steps. She did a fine job, and I looked like any other boy who had played hard all day, and who,

• In your own words, tell how to cook cattails.

with a little soap and water after supper, would be going off to bed in a regular house.

I didn't get back to my tree that night. The May apples were ripe, and I stuffed on those as I went through the woods. They taste like a very sweet banana, are earthy and a little slippery. But I liked them.

At the stream I caught a trout. Everybody thinks a trout is hard to catch because of all the fancy gear and flies and lines sold for trout fishing, but, honestly, they are easier to catch than any other fish. They have big mouths and snatch and swallow whole anything they see when they are hungry. With my wooden hook in its mouth, the trout was mine. The trouble is that trout are not hungry when most people have time to fish. I knew they were hungry that evening because the creek was swirling, and minnows and everything else were jumping out of the water. When you see that, go fish. You'll get them.

I made a fire on a flat boulder in the stream, and cooked the trout. I did this so I could watch the sky. I wanted to see the falcon again. I also put the trout head on the hook and dropped it in the pool. A snapping turtle would view a trout head with relish.

I waited for the falcon patiently. I didn't have to go anywhere. After an hour or so, I was rewarded. A slender speck came from the valley and glided up the stream. It was still far away when it folded its wings and bombed the earth. I watched. It arose, clumsy and big—carrying food—and winged back to the valley.

I sprinted down the stream and made myself a lean-to near some cliffs where I thought the bird had disappeared. Having learned that day that duck hawks prefer to nest on cliffs, I settled for this site.

Early the next morning, I got up and dug the tubers of the arrow-leaf that grew along the stream bank. I baked these and boiled mussels for breakfast, then I curled up behind a willow and watched the cliff.

The hawks came in from behind me and circled the stream. They had apparently been out hunting before I had gotten up, as they were returning with food. This was exciting news. They were feeding young, and I was somewhere near the nest.

I watched one of them swing in to the cliff and disappear. A few minutes later it winged out empty-footed. I marked the spot mentally and said, "Ha!"

After splashing across the stream in the shallows, I stood at the bottom of the cliff and wondered how on earth I was going to climb the sheer wall.

I wanted a falcon so badly, however, that I dug in with my toes and hands and started up. The first part was easy; it was not too steep. When I thought I was stuck, I found a little ledge and shinnied up to it.

I was high, and when I looked down, the stream spun. I decided not to look down any more. I edged up to another ledge, and lay down on it to catch my breath. I was shaking from exertion and I was tired.

I looked up to see how much higher I had to go when my hand touched something moist. I pulled it back and saw that it was white—bird droppings. Then I saw them. Almost where my hand had been sat three fuzzy whitish-gray birds. Their wide-open mouths gave them a startled look.

"Oh, hello, hello," I said. "You are cute."

When I spoke, all three blinked at once. All three heads turned and followed my hand as I swung it up and toward them. All three watched my hand with opened mouths. They were marvelous. I chuckled. But I couldn't reach them.

I wormed forward, and *wham!*—something hit my shoulder. It pained. I turned my head to see the big female. She had bit me. She winged out, banked, and started back for another strike.

Now I was scared, for I was sure she would cut me wide open. With sudden nerve, I stood up, stepped forward, and picked up the biggest of the nestlings. The females are bigger than the males. They are the "falcons." They are the pride of kings. I tucked her in my sweater and leaned against the cliff, facing the bulletlike dive of the falcon. I threw out my foot as she struck, and the sole of my tennis shoe took the blow.

The female was now gathering speed for another attack, and when I say speed, I mean fifty to sixty miles an hour. I could see myself battered and torn, lying in the valley below, and I said to myself, "Sam Gribley, you had better get down from here like a rabbit."

I jumped to the ledge below, found it was really quite wide, slid on the seat of my pants to the next ledge, and stopped. The hawk apparently couldn't count. She did not know I had a youngster, for she checked her nest, saw the open mouths, and then she forgot me.

I scrambled to the river bed somehow, being very careful not to hurt the hot fuzzy body that was against my own. However, Frightful, as I called her right then and there because of the difficulties we had had in getting together, did not think so gently of me. She dug her talons into my skin to brace herself during the bumpy ride to the ground.

I stumbled to the stream, placed her in a nest of buttercups, and dropped beside her. I fell asleep.

When I awoke my eyes opened on two gray eyes in a white stubbly head. Small pinfeathers were sticking out of the stubbly down, like feathers in an Indian quiver. The big blue beak curled down in a snarl and up in a smile.

"Oh, Frightful," I said, "you are a raving beauty."

Frightful fluffed her nubby feathers and shook. I picked her up in the cup of my hands and held her under my chin. I stuck my nose in the deep warm fuzz. It smelled dusty and sweet.

I liked that bird. Oh, how I liked that bird from that smelly minute. It was so pleasant to feel the beating life and see the funny little awkward movements of a young thing.

The legs pushed out between my fingers, I gathered them up, together with the thrashing wings, and tucked the bird in one piece under my chin. I rocked.

"Frightful," I said. "You will enjoy what we are going to do."

I washed my bleeding shoulder in the creek, tucked the torn threads of my sweater back into the hole they had come out of, and set out for my tree.

I circled the meadow and went over to the gorge. On the way I checked a trap. It was a deadfall. A figure four under a big rock. The rock was down. The food was rabbit.

I picked a comfortable place just below the rim of the gorge where I could pop up every now and then and watch my tree. Here I dressed down the rabbit and fed Frightful some of the more savory bites from a young falcon's point of view: the liver, the heart, the brain. She ate in gulps. As I watched her swallow I sensed a great pleasure. It is hard to explain my feelings at that moment. It seemed marvelous to see life pump through that strange little body of feathers, wordless noises, milk eyes—much as life pumped through me.

The food put the bird to sleep. I watched her eyelids close from the bottom up, and her head quiver. The fuzzy body rocked, the tail spread to steady it, and the little duck hawk almost sighed as it sank into the leaves, sleeping.

Meet the Author

It is fitting that Jean Craighead George has written so many books about the world of nature. Her father, an entomologist, used to take her and her twin brothers, now wild life ecologists, on nature hikes. They searched for birds, insects, and flowers in the wild areas along the Potomac River outside of Washington, D.C., where the author was born. In the summers the family went to their old family home in Pennsylvania. There, George went with her father and brothers on camping trips. She fished and swam in the swift mountain streams, climbed to the tops of cliffs to look for falcons, and searched the forest floors for wild life.

Her childhood home was always filled with pets, as her own home is today. The author says she lives with every animal she writes about, except bears and mountain lions. George's house is surrounded by woods, and sometimes, in winter, a deer wanders up to her windows.

Some of George's most popular books are *My Side of the Mountain* and *Coyote in Manhattan*. Her *Julie of the Wolves* won the Newbery Medal.

Checking Comprehension and Skills

Thinking About What You've Read

1. Give two examples of how Sam's knowledge of nature helps him survive in the great outdoors.
2. Give one example of how Sam's failure to plan ahead causes him hardship during his first days in the wild.
3. As Sam gains experience, he begins to plan ahead. Give two examples of how Sam plans ahead as he learns to live in the wilderness.
4. In what kind of wilderness environment do you think you would survive best? Explain your answer.
5. How does Sam capture the falcon?
6. How might Frightful help Sam?
• 7. Name three nonfictional details provided by the illustrations for the story that help make it seem realistic.
• 8. Name three nonfictional details about nature that make the selection seem realistic.

Talking About What You've Read

Although this selection is fiction, it contains facts and information about nature. What are some facts that you learned about nature from reading this story? Think specifically about facts that you did not know before reading. Did any of these surprise you? Why?

Writing About What You've Read

Make a list of five facts that you learned from reading about Sam's experiences in the wild. Write two sentences telling which fact surprised you most and why.

• Comprehension Skill: Fiction and nonfiction

Encounter
by Lilian Moore

We both stood
heart-stopping
still,

I in the doorway
the deer
near
the old apple tree,

he
muscle wary
straining
to hear

I holding breath
to say
do not fear.

In the silence
between us
my thought said
stay!

Did it snap
like a twig?
He rose on a curve
and fled.

Reading for Different Reasons

When making a trail through the woods, you move more slowly than if you are traveling a well-worn path. In the same way, when you read something new or difficult, you tend to read more slowly. You may have to reread some parts for complete understanding. On the other hand, if you are reading about a topic you already know something about, you can probably read faster.

Your speed also depends on your purpose for reading. For example, suppose you are reading a newspaper to find out a specific fact, such as the date of a concert. You need not read every word. Instead, **skim,** or glance over, each page, looking for the place where a date is mentioned. See if it is the date you are looking for. If not, continue skimming until you find it. Suppose you want to find out the details about the latest developments in the space shuttle program. In this case, you must read every word carefully. You may even decide to reread certain sections and take notes.

1. Turn to page 239, "Life in Mexico's Cold Lands." What kind of reading should you do to find the answer to "How old are some of the houses in San Miguel de Allende?"
2. Find out on page 239 why the cold in the highlands of Mexico is nothing like what we feel in the northern United States during winter. What kind of reading should you do now to get the information?

Remember that how you read depends on how familiar you are with the topic, your purpose for reading, and how easy or difficult the material is that you are reading.

The call of the open road doesn't always turn out to be as exciting as it sounds. In this classic tale, the great outdoors seems to offer Toad the possibility of adventure, but Rat and Mole are not so sure.

The Wind in the Willows

by Kenneth Grahame

"Ratty," said the Mole suddenly, one bright summer morning. "If you please, I want to ask you a favor. Won't you take me to call on Mr. Toad? I've heard so much about him. I do so want to make his acquaintance."

"Why, certainly," said the good-natured Rat. "Get the boat out, and we'll paddle up there at once. It's never the wrong time to call on Toad. Early or late he's always the same fellow. Always good-tempered, always glad to see you, always sorry when you go!"

"He must be a very nice animal," observed the Mole, as he got into the boat and took the sculls, while the Rat settled himself comfortably in the stern.

"He is indeed the best of animals," replied Rat. "So simple, so good-natured, and so affectionate. Perhaps he's not very clever—we can't all be geniuses; and it may be that he is both boastful and conceited. But he has got some great qualities, has Toady."

Rounding a bend in the river, they came in sight of a handsome, dignified old house of mellowed red brick, with well-kept lawns reaching down to the water's edge.

"There's Toad Hall," said the Rat. "That creek on the left, where the notice board says, 'Private. No landing allowed,' leads to his boathouse, where we'll leave the boat. The stables are over there to the right. That's the banqueting hall you're looking at now—very old, that is. Toad is rather rich, you know, and this is really one of the nicest houses in these parts, though we never admit as much to Toad."

They glided up the creek. The Mole shipped his sculls as they passed into the shadow of a large boathouse. Here they saw many handsome boats slung from the crossbeams or hauled up on a slip but none in the water. And the place had an unused and a deserted air.

The Rat looked around him. "I understand," said he. "Boating is played out. He is tired of it, and done with it. I wonder what new fad he has taken up now. Come along and let's look him up. We shall hear all about it quite soon enough."

They disembarked, and strolled across the gay flower-decked lawns in search of Toad, whom they presently happened upon resting in a wicker garden chair, with a preoccupied expression of face and a large map spread out on his knees.

"Hooray!" he cried, jumping up on seeing them. "This is splendid!" He shook the paws of both of them warmly, never waiting for an introduction to the Mole. "How *kind* of you!" he went on, dancing round them. "I was just going to send a

boat down the river for you, Ratty, with strict orders that you were to be fetched up here at once, whatever you were doing. I want you badly—both of you. Now what will you take? Come inside and have something! You don't know how lucky it is, your turning up just now!"

"Let's sit quiet a bit, Toady!" said the Rat, throwing himself into an easy chair, while the Mole took another by the side of him and made some civil remark about Toad's "delightful residence."

"Finest house on the whole river," cried Toad boisterously. "Or anywhere else, for that matter," he could not help adding.

Here the Rat nudged the Mole. Unfortunately the Toad saw him do it, and turned very red. There was a moment's painful silence. Then Toad burst out laughing. "All right, Ratty," he said. "It's only my way, you know. And it's not such a very bad house, is it? You know you rather like it yourself. Now, look here. Let's be sensible. You are the very animals I wanted. You've got to help me. It's most important!"

"It's about your rowing, I suppose," said the Rat, with an innocent air. "You're getting on fairly well, though you splash a good bit still. With a great deal of patience, and any quantity of coaching, you may—"

"O, pooh! boating!" interrupted the Toad, in great disgust. "Silly boyish amusement. I've given that up *long* ago. Sheer waste of time, that's what it is. It makes me downright sorry to see you fellows, who ought to know better, spending all your energies in that aimless manner. No, I've discovered the real thing, the only genuine occupation for a lifetime. I

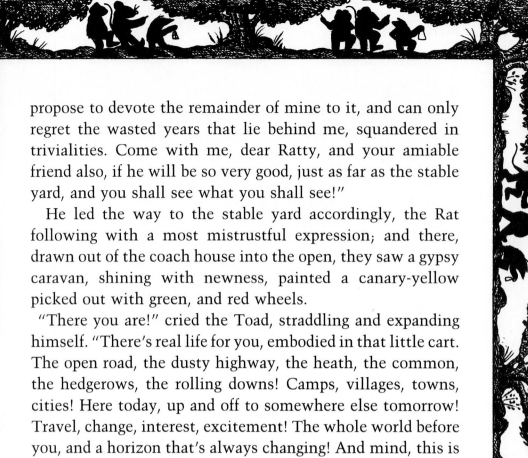

propose to devote the remainder of mine to it, and can only regret the wasted years that lie behind me, squandered in trivialities. Come with me, dear Ratty, and your amiable friend also, if he will be so very good, just as far as the stable yard, and you shall see what you shall see!"

He led the way to the stable yard accordingly, the Rat following with a most mistrustful expression; and there, drawn out of the coach house into the open, they saw a gypsy caravan, shining with newness, painted a canary-yellow picked out with green, and red wheels.

"There you are!" cried the Toad, straddling and expanding himself. "There's real life for you, embodied in that little cart. The open road, the dusty highway, the heath, the common, the hedgerows, the rolling downs! Camps, villages, towns, cities! Here today, up and off to somewhere else tomorrow! Travel, change, interest, excitement! The whole world before you, and a horizon that's always changing! And mind, this is the very finest cart of its sort that was ever built, without any exception. Come inside and look at the arrangements. Planned 'em all myself, I did!"

The Mole was tremendously interested and excited, and followed him eagerly up the steps and into the interior of the caravan. The Rat only snorted and thrust his hands deep into his pockets, remaining where he was.

It was indeed very compact and comfortable. Little sleeping bunks—a little table that folded up against the wall—a cooking stove, lockers, bookshelves, a bird cage—with a bird in it—and pots, pans, jugs and kettles of every size and variety.

"All complete!" said the Toad triumphantly, pulling open a locker. "You see—biscuits, potted lobster, sardines—everything you can possibly want. Soda water here—letter paper there—bacon, jam, cards, and dominoes—you'll find," he continued, as they descended the steps again. "You'll find that nothing whatever has been forgotten, when we make our start this afternoon."

"I beg your pardon," said the Rat slowly, as he chewed a straw, "but did I overhear you say something about *we*, and *start*, and *this afternoon*?"

"Now, you dear good old Ratty," said Toad imploringly, "don't begin talking in that stiff and sniffy sort of way, because you know you've *got* to come. I can't possibly manage without you, so please consider it settled, and don't argue—it's the one thing I can't stand. You surely don't mean to stick to your dull fusty old river all your life, and just live in a hole in a bank, and *boat*? I want to show you the world! I'm going to make an *animal* of you, my boy!"

"I don't care," said the Rat doggedly. "I'm not coming, and that's flat. And I *am* going to stick to my old river, *and* live in a hole, *and* boat, as I've always done. And what's more, Mole's going to stick to me and do as I do. Aren't you, Mole?"

"Of course I am," said the Mole loyally. "I'll always stick to you, Rat, and what you say is to be—has got to be. All the same, it sounds as if it might have been—well, rather fun, you know!" he added wistfully.

Poor Mole! The Life Adventurous was so new a thing to him, and so thrilling; and this fresh aspect of it was so

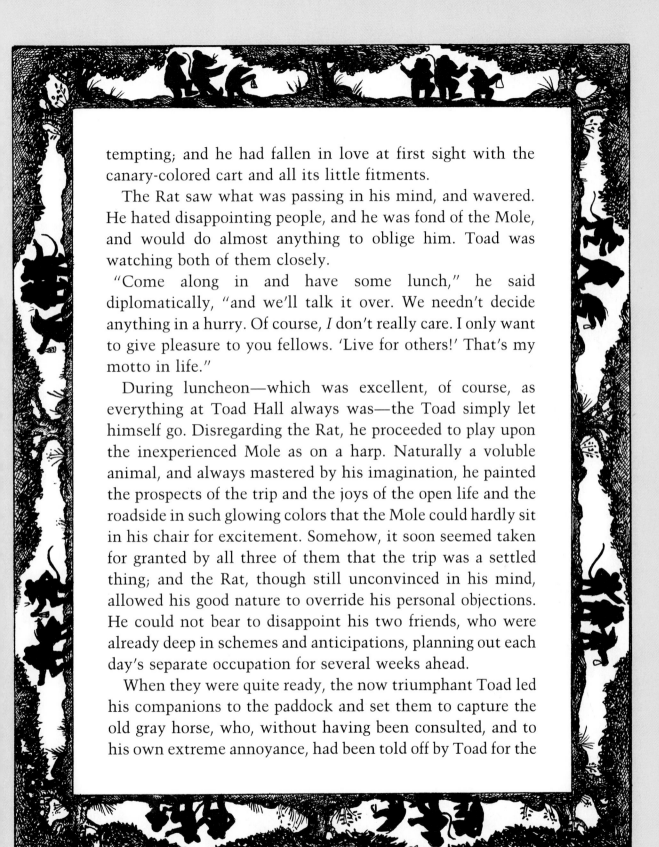

tempting; and he had fallen in love at first sight with the canary-colored cart and all its little fitments.

The Rat saw what was passing in his mind, and wavered. He hated disappointing people, and he was fond of the Mole, and would do almost anything to oblige him. Toad was watching both of them closely.

"Come along in and have some lunch," he said diplomatically, "and we'll talk it over. We needn't decide anything in a hurry. Of course, *I* don't really care. I only want to give pleasure to you fellows. 'Live for others!' That's my motto in life."

During luncheon—which was excellent, of course, as everything at Toad Hall always was—the Toad simply let himself go. Disregarding the Rat, he proceeded to play upon the inexperienced Mole as on a harp. Naturally a voluble animal, and always mastered by his imagination, he painted the prospects of the trip and the joys of the open life and the roadside in such glowing colors that the Mole could hardly sit in his chair for excitement. Somehow, it soon seemed taken for granted by all three of them that the trip was a settled thing; and the Rat, though still unconvinced in his mind, allowed his good nature to override his personal objections. He could not bear to disappoint his two friends, who were already deep in schemes and anticipations, planning out each day's separate occupation for several weeks ahead.

When they were quite ready, the now triumphant Toad led his companions to the paddock and set them to capture the old gray horse, who, without having been consulted, and to his own extreme annoyance, had been told off by Toad for the dustiest job in this dusty expedition. He frankly preferred the paddock, and took a deal of catching. Meantime Toad packed the lockers still tighter with necessaries, and hung nose bags, nets of onions, bundles of hay, and baskets from the bottom of the cart. At last the horse was caught and harnessed, and they set off, all talking at once, each animal either trudging by the side of the cart or sitting on the shaft, as the humor took him. It was a golden afternoon. The smell of dust they kicked up was rich and satisfying; out of thick orchards on either side the road, birds called and whistled to them cheerily; good-natured wayfarers passing them gave them "Good day," or stopped to say nice things about their beautiful cart; and rabbits, sitting at their front doors in the hedgerows, held up their forepaws, and said, "O my! O my! O my!"

Late in the evening, tired and happy and miles from home, they drew up on a remote common far from habitations, turned the horse loose to graze, and ate their simple supper sitting on the grass by the side of the cart. Toad talked big about all he was going to do in the days to come, while stars grew fuller and larger all around them, and a yellow moon, appearing suddenly and silently from nowhere in particular, came to keep them company and listen to their talk. At last they turned into their little bunks in the cart; and Toad, kicking out his legs, sleepily said, "Well, good night, you fellows! This is the real life for a gentleman! Talk about your old river!"

"I *don't* talk about my river," replied the patient Rat. "You *know* I don't, Toad. But I *think* about it," he added pathetically, in a lower tone. "I think about it—all the time!"

The Mole reached out from under his blanket, felt for the Rat's paw in the darkness, and gave it a squeeze. "I'll do whatever you like, Ratty," he whispered. "Shall we run away tomorrow morning, quite early—*very* early—and go back to our dear old hole on the river?"

"No, no, we'll see it out," whispered back the Rat. "Thanks awfully, but I ought to stick by Toad till this trip is ended. It wouldn't be safe for him to be left to himself. It won't take very long. His fads never do. Good night!"

The end was indeed nearer than even the Rat suspected.

After so much open air and excitement, the Toad slept very soundly, and no amount of shaking could rouse him out of bed next morning. So the Mole and Rat turned to, quietly and manfully, and while the Rat saw to the horse, and lit a fire, and cleaned last night's cups and platters, and got things ready for breakfast, the Mole trudged off to the nearest village, a long way off, for milk and eggs and various necessaries the Toad had, of course, forgotten to provide. The hard work had all been done, and the two animals were resting, thoroughly exhausted, by the time Toad appeared on the scene, fresh and gay, remarking what a pleasant easy life it was they were all leading now, after the cares and worries and fatigues of housekeeping at home.

They had a pleasant ramble that day over grassy downs and along narrow by-lanes, and camped, as before, on a common, only this time the two guests took care that Toad should do his fair share of work. In consequence, when the time came for starting next morning, Toad was by no means so rapturous about the simplicity of the primitive life, and indeed attempted to resume his place in his bunk, whence he was hauled by force. Their way lay, as before, across country by narrow lanes, and it was not till the afternoon that they came out on the high road, their first high road; and there disaster, fleet and unforeseen, sprang out on them—disaster momentous indeed to their expedition, but simply overwhelming in its effect on the after-career of Toad.

They were strolling along the high road easily, the Mole by the horse's head, talking to him, since the horse had complained that he was being frightfully left out of it. Nobody considered him in the least; the Toad and the Water Rat walking behind the cart talking together—at least Toad was talking, and Rat was saying at intervals, "Yes, precisely; and what did *you* say to *him*?"—and thinking all the time of something very different, when far behind them they heard a faint warning hum, like the drone of a distant bee. Glancing back, they saw a small cloud of dust, with a dark center of energy, advancing on them at incredible speed, while from out the dust a faint "Poop-poop!" wailed like an uneasy animal in pain. Hardly regarding it, they turned to resume their conversation, when in an instant (as it seemed) the peaceful scene was changed, and with a blast of wind and a whirl of sound that made them jump for the nearest ditch, it was on them! The "poop-poop" rang with a brazen shout in their ears. They had a moment's glimpse of an interior of glittering plate glass and rich morocco; and the magnificent motorcar, immense, breath-snatching, passionate, with its pilot tense and hugging his wheel, possessed all earth and air for the fraction of a second, flung an enveloping cloud of dust that blinded and enwrapped them utterly, and then dwindled to a speck in the far distance, changed back into a droning bee once more.

The old grey horse, dreaming, as he plodded along, of his quiet paddock, in a new raw situation such as this simply abandoned himself to his natural emotions. Rearing, plunging, backing steadily, in spite of all the Mole's efforts at his head, and all the Mole's lively language directed at his better feelings, he drove the cart backwards towards the deep ditch at the side of the road. It wavered an instant. Then there was a heart-rending crash—and the canary-colored cart, their pride and their joy, lay on its side in the ditch, an irredeemable wreck.

The Rat danced up and down in the road, simply transported with passion. "You villains!" he shouted, shaking both fists. "You scoundrels, you highwaymen, you—you—road hogs! I'll have the law on you! I'll report you! I'll take you through all the Courts!" His homesickness had quite slipped away from him, and for the moment he was the skipper of the canary-colored vessel driven on a shoal by the reckless jockeying of rival mariners, and he was trying to recollect all the fine and biting things he used to say to masters of steam-launches when their wash, as they drove too near the bank, used to flood his parlor carpet at home.

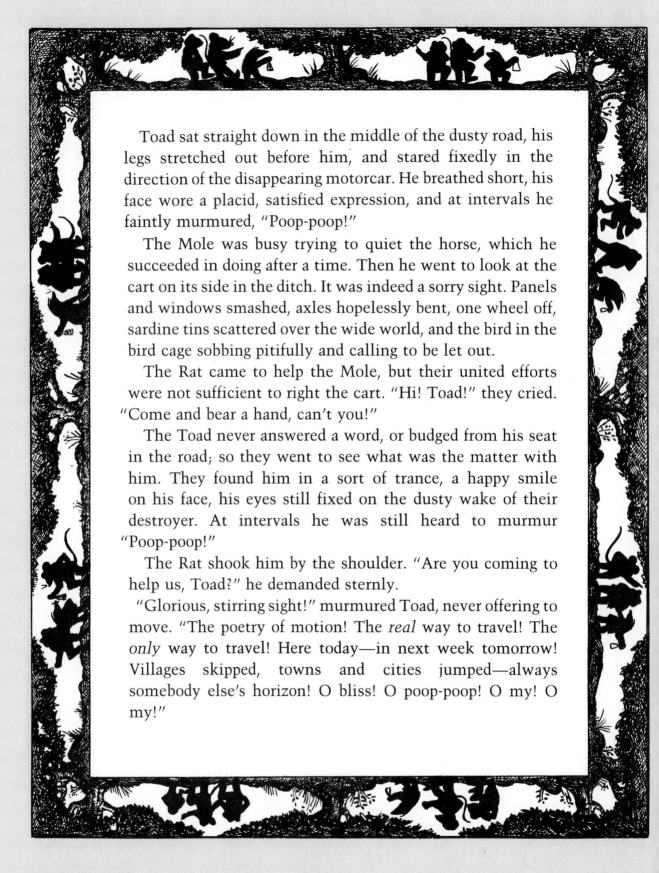

Toad sat straight down in the middle of the dusty road, his legs stretched out before him, and stared fixedly in the direction of the disappearing motorcar. He breathed short, his face wore a placid, satisfied expression, and at intervals he faintly murmured, "Poop-poop!"

The Mole was busy trying to quiet the horse, which he succeeded in doing after a time. Then he went to look at the cart on its side in the ditch. It was indeed a sorry sight. Panels and windows smashed, axles hopelessly bent, one wheel off, sardine tins scattered over the wide world, and the bird in the bird cage sobbing pitifully and calling to be let out.

The Rat came to help the Mole, but their united efforts were not sufficient to right the cart. "Hi! Toad!" they cried. "Come and bear a hand, can't you!"

The Toad never answered a word, or budged from his seat in the road; so they went to see what was the matter with him. They found him in a sort of trance, a happy smile on his face, his eyes still fixed on the dusty wake of their destroyer. At intervals he was still heard to murmur "Poop-poop!"

The Rat shook him by the shoulder. "Are you coming to help us, Toad?" he demanded sternly.

"Glorious, stirring sight!" murmured Toad, never offering to move. "The poetry of motion! The *real* way to travel! The *only* way to travel! Here today—in next week tomorrow! Villages skipped, towns and cities jumped—always somebody else's horizon! O bliss! O poop-poop! O my! O my!"

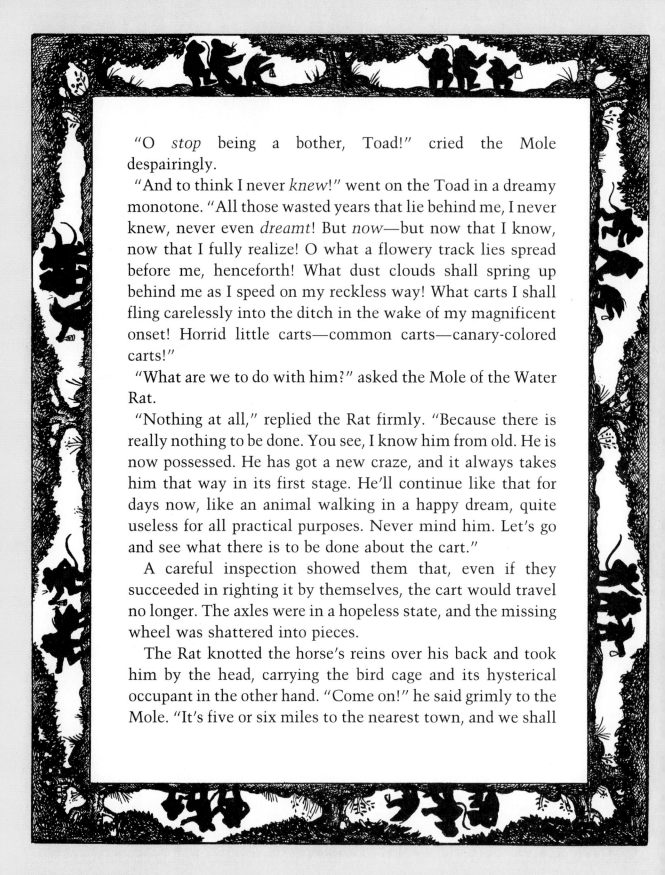

"O *stop* being a bother, Toad!" cried the Mole despairingly.

"And to think I never *knew*!" went on the Toad in a dreamy monotone. "All those wasted years that lie behind me, I never knew, never even *dreamt*! But *now*—but now that I know, now that I fully realize! O what a flowery track lies spread before me, henceforth! What dust clouds shall spring up behind me as I speed on my reckless way! What carts I shall fling carelessly into the ditch in the wake of my magnificent onset! Horrid little carts—common carts—canary-colored carts!"

"What are we to do with him?" asked the Mole of the Water Rat.

"Nothing at all," replied the Rat firmly. "Because there is really nothing to be done. You see, I know him from old. He is now possessed. He has got a new craze, and it always takes him that way in its first stage. He'll continue like that for days now, like an animal walking in a happy dream, quite useless for all practical purposes. Never mind him. Let's go and see what there is to be done about the cart."

A careful inspection showed them that, even if they succeeded in righting it by themselves, the cart would travel no longer. The axles were in a hopeless state, and the missing wheel was shattered into pieces.

The Rat knotted the horse's reins over his back and took him by the head, carrying the bird cage and its hysterical occupant in the other hand. "Come on!" he said grimly to the Mole. "It's five or six miles to the nearest town, and we shall

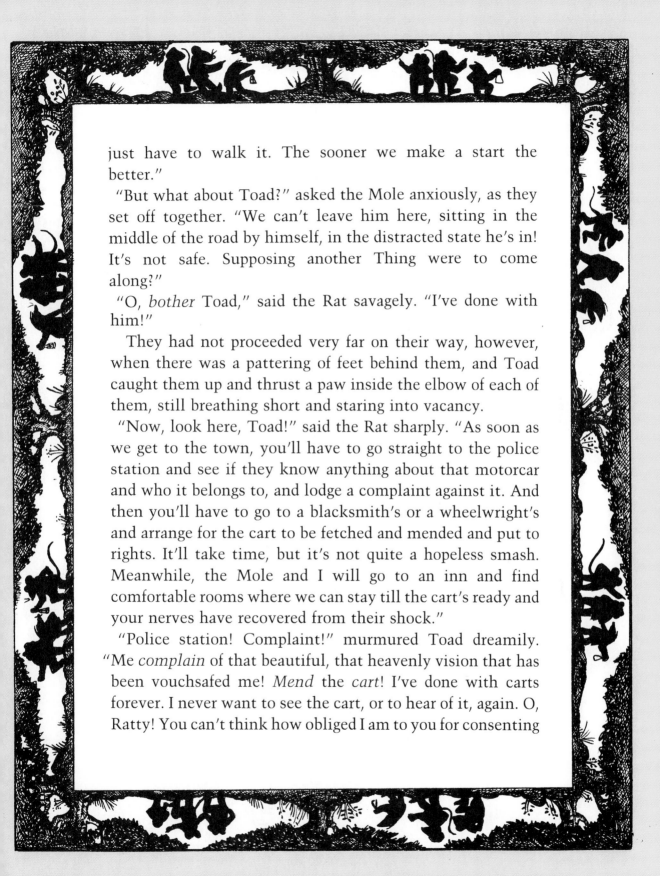

just have to walk it. The sooner we make a start the better."

"But what about Toad?" asked the Mole anxiously, as they set off together. "We can't leave him here, sitting in the middle of the road by himself, in the distracted state he's in! It's not safe. Supposing another Thing were to come along?"

"O, *bother* Toad," said the Rat savagely. "I've done with him!"

They had not proceeded very far on their way, however, when there was a pattering of feet behind them, and Toad caught them up and thrust a paw inside the elbow of each of them, still breathing short and staring into vacancy.

"Now, look here, Toad!" said the Rat sharply. "As soon as we get to the town, you'll have to go straight to the police station and see if they know anything about that motorcar and who it belongs to, and lodge a complaint against it. And then you'll have to go to a blacksmith's or a wheelwright's and arrange for the cart to be fetched and mended and put to rights. It'll take time, but it's not quite a hopeless smash. Meanwhile, the Mole and I will go to an inn and find comfortable rooms where we can stay till the cart's ready and your nerves have recovered from their shock."

"Police station! Complaint!" murmured Toad dreamily. "Me *complain* of that beautiful, that heavenly vision that has been vouchsafed me! *Mend* the *cart*! I've done with carts forever. I never want to see the cart, or to hear of it, again. O, Ratty! You can't think how obliged I am to you for consenting to come on this trip! I wouldn't have gone without you, and then I might never have seen that—that swan, that sunbeam, that thunderbolt! I might never have heard that entrancing sound, or smelt that bewitching smell! I owe it all to you, my best of friends!"

The Rat turned from him in despair. "You see what it is?" he said to the Mole, addressing him across Toad's head. "He's quite hopeless. I give it up—when we get to the town, we'll go to the railway station, and with luck we may pick up a train there that'll get us back to River Bank tonight. And if ever you catch me going a-pleasuring with this provoking animal again—" He snorted, and during the rest of that weary trudge addressed his remarks exclusively to Mole.

On reaching the town they went straight to the station and deposited Toad in the second class waiting room, giving a porter twopence to keep a strict eye on him. They then left the horse at an inn stable, and gave what directions they could about the cart and its contents. Eventually, a slow train having landed them at a station not very far from Toad Hall, they escorted the spellbound, sleepwalking Toad to his door, put him inside it, and instructed his housekeeper to feed him and have him put to bed. Then they got out their boat from the boathouse, sculled down the river home, and at a very late hour sat down to supper in their own cozy riverside parlor, to the Rat's great joy and contentment.

The following evening the Mole, who had risen late and taken things very easy all day, was sitting on the bank fishing,

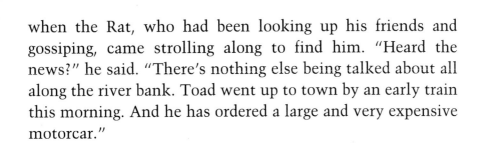

when the Rat, who had been looking up his friends and gossiping, came strolling along to find him. "Heard the news?" he said. "There's nothing else being talked about all along the river bank. Toad went up to town by an early train this morning. And he has ordered a large and very expensive motorcar."

Meet the Author

When Kenneth Grahame, the Scottish author of *The Wind in the Willows*, left London to live in the country, someone said that though he seemed no longer interested in his London friends, "he knew the name of every horse, cow, and pig in the neighborhood." This fondness for animals may have been one reason why Mr. Grahame chose to write about them in his delightful fantasy. Another reason was that he wanted to entertain his young son. The author began the story as a series of letters to his son, Alastair, who was called Mouse.

After reading about the adventures of Rat, Mole, and Toad, you can see why this threesome has had such a wide following for more than three quarters of a century.

LOOKING BACK

Thinking About the Section

In this section, you have read an article about serious environmental problems and the work that is being done to solve them. You have also read two stories in which the setting is the great outdoors.

Sam Gribley and Rat, characters in the two stories, live in problem-free environments: Sam lives in a mountainous wilderness; Rat lives on a quiet river bank. What kinds of things might each of them do to keep their environments problem free? Copy the chart below onto a sheet of paper, and complete the boxes.

Great Outdoors	Problems	Causes	Prevention
Mountains	1. forest fires 2. _____ 3. _____	1. _____ 2. _____ 3. _____	1. _____ 2. _____ 3. _____
River bank	1. garbage in water 2. _____ 3. _____	1. _____ 2. _____ 3. _____	1. _____ 2. _____ 3. _____

Writing About the Section

Choose either Sam Gribley or Rat. Think about the characteristics of his environment that he enjoys most. Write a descriptive paragraph that either Sam or Rat might write to describe how a visitor to his environment should act in order to keep it free of waste, noise, and pollution.

Books to Read

Hello, My Name Is Scrambled Eggs by Jamie Gilson, Lothrop © 1985

Harvey Trumble is about to tackle an important assignment. His mission is to help newcomer Tuan Nguyen from Vietnam become an American. The method Harvey uses is unusual and his results are, well, scrambled!

Anastasia on Her Own by Lois Lowry, Houghton © 1985

Anastasia has great faith in the Krupnik Family Nonsexist Housekeeping Schedule until her mother goes on a ten-day business trip. Little by little the schedule crumbles as Anastasia is hit with unexpected complications creating hilarious predicaments for Anastasia, her brother Sam, and her father, a professor of English.

Monkey Puzzle and Other Poems by Myra Cohn Livingston, Atheneum © 1984

What is a monkey puzzle? Can you describe a horse chestnut? What's a jacaranda? The answers to these questions and more are in *Monkey Puzzle and Other Poems*.

The Sign of the Beaver by Elizabeth George Speare, Houghton © 1983

Matt, a thirteen-year-old boy, was left alone to guard his family's wilderness home. Only after meeting a Native American boy does Matt begin to learn new ways to survive in the forest. He also begins to understand the way of life of the Native Americans and their problems in adapting to the changing frontier in the eighteenth century.

10

Words, Words, Words

Words are part of just about everything you do in a day. Whether you hear them or speak them, write them or read them, think them or sing them, words are our main means of communicating. Do you choose your words with care? What problems can arise if you don't? How can you make words work for you?

In this section, you will see how some students skillfully use words to defend different opinions on the same subject. You'll read about characters who create lots of confusion with the word games they play. And you'll meet a club president who uses his words effectively enough to convince the members to start a business for kids.

Biased Writing

**Picasso Sculpture
Greeted with
Jeers and Cheers**

Picasso Work Is a Big Letdown

Unveiling Reveals Picasso's Genius

When you read a newspaper headline, do you ever ask yourself, "Is this headline giving just the facts, or is it presenting an unfair report?" Read the newspaper headlines above and ask yourself that question about each.

Pablo Picasso is thought by many to be the greatest artist of the twentieth century. He was asked to do a sculpture to be set up in a plaza at a new government center in downtown

Chicago. When the five-story statue, shown in the picture on page 428, was dedicated, there was a lot of talk about it.

The three headlines, also on page 428, each report the event. The words in each headline have been chosen carefully to present the event in a particular way.

The first one reports the fact that there were mixed reactions to the sculpture. But it does not show strong feeling for or against the sculpture. It is an example of balanced writing. **Balanced writing** presents all sides of an issue.

The other two headlines do not present balanced writing. They are both examples of biased writing. **Biased writing** is writing that shows strong feeling for or against something or someone or that favors one side too much. It presents just one point of view or one side of an argument. The second headline shows strong feeling against the sculpture. The third one, on the other hand, shows strong feeling for the sculpture. In addition to presenting only one point of view, these two headlines use loaded words. **Loaded words** are words that not only describe but also try to slant a reader's view of something. *Letdown* and *Genius* are examples of loaded words. Biased writing often contains loaded words.

Biased writing may be present in many other forms of writing besides newspaper headlines. To be a biased text, the whole text must consistently reflect the writer's bias. A text that only quotes or cites biased views can still be balanced if it presents the different views equally.

Recognizing the difference between balanced writing and biased writing will help you think critically about what you read so that you will know when you are reading an objective account or report and when you are reading an account that is slanted in one direction.

On page 430 are parts of some newspaper articles and some letters to the editor about the unveiling of the Picasso sculpture. Decide if each is a balanced or biased account. Watch for examples of loaded words.

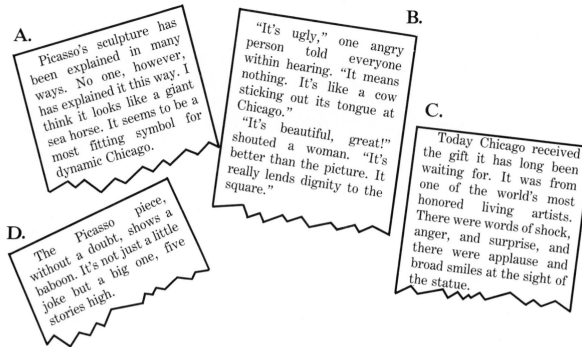

A. Picasso's sculpture has been explained in many ways. No one, however, has explained it this way. I think it looks like a giant sea horse. It seems to be a most fitting symbol for dynamic Chicago.

B. "It's ugly," one angry person told everyone within hearing. "It means nothing. It's like a cow sticking out its tongue at Chicago."
"It's beautiful, great!" shouted a woman. "It's better than the picture. It really lends dignity to the square."

C. Today Chicago received the gift it has long been waiting for. It was from one of the world's most honored living artists. There were words of shock, anger, and surprise, and there were applause and broad smiles at the sight of the statue.

D. The Picasso piece, without a doubt, shows a baboon. It's not just a little joke but a big one, five stories high.

1. Which items are examples of balanced writing? How do you know?

To answer question 1, ask yourself, "Which newspaper items present both sides of the issue?" Items B and C report that the statue received favorable and unfavorable reactions. Both are examples of balanced writing. Item C reports "words of shock, anger, and surprise," as well as "applause and broad smiles" as reactions. Item B actually quotes one negative and one positive reaction: "It's ugly," and "It's beautiful, great!"

2. Which one is an example of biased writing against the sculpture? How can you tell it's biased?

To answer question 2, ask yourself, "Which newspaper item presents only a negative reaction to the sculpture?" Item D is the only one that reports a completely negative view and makes no reference to any positive views.

3. What examples of loaded words can you find in the articles and letters?

Practicing the Skill

Each letter to the editor talks about the same issue—full-day kindergarten. Each writer, however, expresses a different view of the subject. As you read, decide whether each letter presents a balanced view or a biased view.

A.

Dear Editor:
Though extending the kindergarten schedule may make the lives of parents a bit easier, it creates serious problems for the children and teachers involved. No five-year-old should be forced to endure such a long and tiring schedule. No teacher can be expected to remain energetic for such a long day. This decision can only result in burnout for both the kids and their caretakers.
Sincerely,

B.

Dear Editor:
Everyone agrees that something must be done to provide quality care for children of working parents. The recent decision of the school board to extend the kindergarten program to a full-day schedule is one solution—a good one for many people. Parents, however, should be given a choice of daycare arrangements, including on-site care at local places of business.
Sincerely,

C.

Dear Editor:
Thanks to the school board's decision to lengthen the kindergarten day, both parents and children can relax. Parents will know that their children are being well cared for—in a creative learning environment. And children will be allowed to remain in a familiar setting for the entire school day. After all, schools are designed for kids, and teachers are trained to provide the right kind of care.
Sincerely,

1. Which letter is an example of balanced writing? How do you know?
2. Which letter is an example of biased writing? How can you tell it is biased?
3. What examples of loaded words can you find in the letters?

Tips for Reading on Your Own

• To check for bias, look for loaded words—words that not only describe one point of view but also try to slant a reader's view of something. If these words are present, the writing may be biased.
• See whether the author presents only one point of view or presents both sides of an issue. Biased writing presents only one side. Balanced writing presents both sides.

Television can seem like nothing but pictures, words, words, and more words. How would you feel about turning off your TV set for a week? Some students got the chance to answer that question. As you read their letters, decide whether each is an example of balanced or biased writing. Is each biased letter in favor of or against the issue?

Letters to the Editor

November 10. . . .
From the Editor's Desk

TV Turn Off Not Enough

- The average student in elementary school watches from six to seven hours of TV a day. (That's about 2,100 to 2,500 hours, or two to three months a year!)
- TV viewing is linked to an increase in violent behavior.
- Students' learning skills, especially listening skills, are not as good as they once were.
- TV presents stereotyped characters.
- TV sells junk food and junk products.

These are some of the facts that led the school board to decide to name one week next month TV Turn Off Week. All student council members at the board meeting supported the TV Turn Off Week.

I agree that TV Turn Off Week is a good idea. Students who take part in the TV Turn Off and keep their TVs off for a week may learn a valuable lesson—that they can live without TV. But we students have to learn more than that. When the TVs go back on, we have to learn to make critical decisions about what we watch. That's why I say TV Turn Off Week is not enough. Not tuning in isn't the whole answer. We also must learn how to tune in intelligently.

The school board, addressing most of their comments to parents, discussed ways to monitor and control our TV viewing. I think we should control our own habits. How would you feel about turning off your set for a week? We want to know where *you* stand.

Write to us. Below is a questionnaire which you could use as a guide to form your comments. To get more views about turning TV off for a week, you may also want to use the questionnaire to poll your family and friends.

Then place your letters in the box in front of Room 321. All letters should be signed. Be sure to include your class number. We will publish your letters in the November 24 issue of the *Tubman Public School Tribune.* Let your voice be heard.

Harriet Tubman Public School Tribune Questionnaire
TV—TURN IT ON OR OFF?

Please write your comments on a separate piece of paper.

1. How many hours a day do you think students should watch television? Why?

2. What other activities, besides watching television, do you think students should take part in? Why?

3. Which of the following two statements do you agree with? Explain why.
   • There should be a TV Turn Off Week.
   • There should not be a TV Turn Off Week. Instead, students should cut down on the number of hours they spend watching TV.

November 24. . . .
From the Editor's Desk

Two weeks ago, we asked readers to send in letters about TV Turn Off Week—which is just two weeks away. We received so many letters, and so most of this issue is made up of them. Some of you also sent in drawings that show how you feel about turning off TV. Those drawings also appear in this issue.

TV Turn Off/On?

In one way, I think TV Turn Off Week is a good idea. This will give me more time to practice my part in the school play and to do more research for the report I'm writing. As it is now, I sometimes become so interested in a program that I leave my work for the last minute.

Then again, maybe a TV Turn Off Week isn't such a good idea. My grades are good. (Of course, they could be better.) I like to watch TV and will really miss it if I have to do without it for a whole week. I wouldn't want to miss a crucial football game. And every Wednesday night I watch a detective show that's really exciting.

If the student council has decided that a TV Turn Off Week is a good idea, I'm willing to give it a try.

Lee McCarthy
Class 6–1

TV, I SHOULD HAVE TURNED YOU OFF WHEN I HAD THE CHANCE.

Alan Madison
Class 6–3

WILL WE LOOK LIKE THIS AFTER A WHILE?

Ed Higgins
Class 6–2

Old-Fashioned Fun

During a thunderstorm last summer, our TV went dead. Lightning damaged our set right in the middle of a *Star Light* mission. For a moment, we thought it was a *Star Light* special effect. That lightning almost ruined my week along with the TV. (A week is how long it took to repair it.) But, on the second TVless night, my grandmother, who lives with us, fortunately got tired of our complaints. She told us one of her "When I was a little girl" stories. The point of her story—as I'm sure you can guess—was that we can have fun without TV just as she did when she was our age. Then she went through a list of ways that we could occupy our time.

After listening to her choices, I decided to go along with the suggestion that we play a game of checkers. Well, we dusted off the checkerboard and spent two hours trying to outjump one another. It was fun, and so was listening to mysteries on the radio, reading *The Odyssey* aloud, and putting together a really gigantic puzzle. Our TV is back now, but every now and then we still have a No-TV Night.

I know that it is hard to manage without TV. The rewards are great, though. I've had many chances to talk with my family. That's hard to do while watching a *Star Light* mission. I think people should try to do without TV for a week. They may learn that they can live without TV, just as I did.

Lisa Huttula
Class 5–6

Just Switch Channels

I object strenuously to a TV Turn Off Week. Instead of turning off all TV, we should turn off only the shows that aren't worthwhile. I don't want to miss seeing things like a space shuttle launch, a football play-off, or a cartoon special. Sure, I could do without seeing some reruns, but I wouldn't like missing my favorite game show. I think instead of turning off TV, we should just switch channels.

Rhea Clark
Class 6–1

Council Wasting its Time

The student council shouldn't be wasting time discussing whether we students should or should not watch TV. One week without TV won't change anyone's viewing habits— good or bad. I know that I could live for one week without TV, but why should I? How will that change my viewing habits? The student council will have to do a better job of convincing me that this idea is a good one.

Diana Snyder
Class 6–2

SOME OF THIS STUFF IS PERFECTLY GOOD. WHY WOULD ANYONE THROW IT AWAY?

Kim Warwick   Class 6–2

Don't Blame TV

Why hold a TV Turn Off Week? Just because some of us spend too much time watching it is no reason to have everyone shut it off. Besides, TV is just about the most useful invention—next to the computer—that has ever come along.

But TV is always being blamed for all kinds of problems. I know plenty of us who spend hours on the telephone, but no one wants to hold a Telephone Turn Off Week (except maybe parents).

Do you know how much better off and smarter we are because of TV? My younger brother, whom we adopted from Korea when he was four, learned a lot of English from watching TV. After only one week here, he could count to ten in both English and Spanish from watching children's shows.

My mother learned to repair leaky faucets by watching a show that teaches you how to fix the plumbing in your home. Why, that show probably saved the city gallons of water. Just imagine if that show were on during a TV Turn Off Week!

And my dad is up early to view TV. He's learning conversational Spanish at the same time that he makes our breakfast. Sometimes he confuses us by telling us to eat our *huevos* instead of eggs, but he hopes to get a promotion if he learns a second language.

I learned more about computers by watching a science show that stars kids our age. Mr. Katz taught me most of what I know about computers, but next to Mr. Katz, TV is the best teacher there is.

Bob Blank
Class 6–1

Computer Monitor Best Use for TV

I'm for a TV Turn Off Week but only if the turn off is for TV programs. I used to have a TV that I never watched. Then I got a personal computer. Now my TV is a computer monitor, which is just about the only thing a TV is good for. I'll be using my TV during TV Turn Off Week but only when I'm running software or doing some programming.

Judy Bennett
Class 5–3

TV or Not TV

In my family we are split down the middle about TV Turn Off Week. My mother doesn't like the idea; my father does.

Mom says that we three already have good TV habits. She says we watch worthwhile programs and we talk about what we watch. She says we are intelligent viewers.

My father says that though we are intelligent viewers, we should turn off the TV so that we could spend the time on other activities. He says we may discover a talent for cooking or writing or painting.

It's up to me, my folks say, to decide because mine is the tie-breaking vote in our family. I agree with both my parents, and so I'm going to try a compromise. I think we should watch TV three of seven days during TV Turn Off Week, and on the other four days we should do other things.

Andrew Hamlet
Class 5–3

Admits TV Mania Problem

I think TV Turn Off Week is a good start toward solving the problem of TV mania. One week without TV may be enough to change bad viewing habits.

I am a TV buff. As soon as I wake up, I turn on the TV, sometimes I even go to sleep to TV.

I watch exercise shows, even though I don't exercise. I once watched a show that taught typing, even though I don't own a typewriter.

My father is sympathetic to my problem. He said that when his family got their first TV, he and his brothers used to sit and watch *all* the commercials.

Anyway, my father has talked to me, and we've decided that one week without TV is a good beginning. If I can survive that week, I'll try to cut down on the amount of time that I watch TV from then on.

If there are any other TV buffs out there, try one week of no TV, too. It's going to be hard for me, but I am looking forward to building model planes. Maybe you, too, can look forward to enjoying a hobby.

Paul Buckley
Class 6–4

Checking Comprehension and Skills

Thinking About What You've Read

1. How would you feel about turning off your TV set for a week? Explain your answer.
2. What does the editor of the paper mean when she writes, "We also must learn how to tune in intelligently"? (page 433)
• 3. Select two biased letters, one in favor of and one against TV Turn Off Week. Explain why each letter is biased.
• 4. Name two students who present balanced views. Tell why these letters are examples of balanced writing.
5. Name two kinds of TV shows shown in the cartoon on page 436 that you think are "perfectly good." Tell why.
6. What is the main idea of Lisa Huttula's letter? (page 435) State it in a sentence.
7. How well do you think Paul Buckley (page 438) will be able to carry out his plan for watching TV? Why?
8. How entertaining are board games, radio mysteries, and puzzles compared to your favorite TV program? Explain.
9. Do you think that TV has value? State three reasons to support your bias.

Talking About What You've Read

How would you manage without TV for a week? Would you want to? If you "tuned out," what activities would you carry out in the time you usually spend watching TV? Why might you want to keep your TV plugged in and turned on? Do you think that both sides of this issue have merit?

Writing About What You've Read

Select one of three possible positions: a bias in favor of TV Turn Off Week, a bias against it, or a balanced argument presenting both sides of the issue. Write a five- or six-line letter to the editor in which you express your views.

• Comprehension Skill: Biased writing

The City of Dictionopolis is a city of words, words, words. Be very careful when you visit there or before you know it, you may find yourself swallowing your pride or digesting the facts. As you read this modern fantasy, decide what the author's purpose was in writing it.

THE PHANTOM TOLLBOOTH

by Norton Juster

The boy Milo and his watchdog Tock arrive in the city of Dictionopolis in the Kingdom of Wisdom in time for the royal banquet. Dictionopolis is the city where all the words in the world grow on trees, and it is ruled by Azaz, the unabridged king.

Preparations for the banquet have been made, and Milo and Tock are to be escorted by the king's cabinet: The Duke of Definition, The Minister of Meaning, The Count of Connotation, The Earl of Essence, and the Undersecretary of Understanding.

"The Royal Banquet is about to begin," said the king's cabinet members. "Come with us."

They seemed very agitated and out of breath as Milo walked along with them.

"But what about my car?" he asked.

"Don't need it," replied the duke.

"No use for it," said the minister.

"Superfluous," advised the count.

"Unnecessary," stated the earl.

"Uncalled for," cried the undersecretary. "We'll take our vehicle."

"Conveyance."

"Rig."

"Char-a-banc."

"Chariot."

"Buggy."

"Coach."

"Brougham."

"Shandrydan," they repeated quickly in order, and pointed to a small wooden wagon.

"Oh dear, all those words," thought Milo as he climbed into the wagon with Tock and the cabinet members. "How are you going to make it move? It doesn't have a—"

"Be very quiet," advised the duke, "for it goes without saying."

And, sure enough, as soon as they were all quite still, it began to move quickly through the streets, and in a very short time they arrived at the royal palace.

"Right this way."

"Follow us."

"Come along."

"Step lively."

"Here we go," they shouted, hopping from the wagon and bounding up the broad marble stairway. Milo and Tock followed close behind. It was a strange-looking palace, and if he didn't know better he would have said that it looked exactly like an enormous book, standing on end, with its front door in the lower part of the binding just where they usually place the publisher's name.

Once inside, they hurried down a long hallway, which glittered with crystal chandeliers and echoed with their footsteps. The walls and ceiling were covered with mirrors, whose reflections danced dizzily along with them, and the footmen bowed coldly.

"We must be terribly late," gasped the earl nervously as they reached the tall doors of the banquet hall.

It was a vast room, full of people loudly talking and arguing. The long table was carefully set with gold plates and linen napkins. An attendant stood behind each chair, and at the center, raised slightly above the others, was a throne covered in crimson cloth. Directly behind, on the wall, was the royal coat of arms, flanked by the flags of Dictionopolis.

Milo noticed many of the people he had seen in the marketplace.

Everyone seemed quite grumpy about having to wait for lunch and they were relieved to see the tardy guests arrive.

"Certainly glad you finally made it, old man," said the Humbug, a large beetlelike insect cordially pumping Milo's hand. "As guest of honor you must choose the menu of course."

"Oh, my," he thought, not knowing what to say.

"Be quick about it," suggested the Spelling Bee, an enormous bee. "I'm famished—f-a-m-i-s-h-e-d."

As Milo tried to think, there was an ear-shattering blast of trumpets, entirely off key, and a page announced to the startled guests:

"KING AZAZ THE UNABRIDGED."

The king strode through the door and over to the table and settled his great bulk onto the throne, calling irritably, "Places, everyone. Take your places."

He was the largest man Milo had ever seen, with a great stomach, large piercing eyes, a gray beard that reached to his waist, and a silver signet ring on the little finger of his left hand. He also wore a small crown and a robe with the letters of the alphabet beautifully embroidered all over it.

"What have we here?" he said, staring down at Tock and Milo as everyone else took his place.

"If you please," said Milo, "my name is Milo and this is Tock. Thank you very much for inviting us to your banquet, and I think your palace is beautiful."

"Exquisite," corrected the duke.

"Lovely," counseled the minister.

"Handsome," recommended the count.

"Pretty," hinted the earl.

"Charming," submitted the undersecretary.

"SILENCE," suggested the king. "Now, young man, what can you do to entertain us? Sing songs? Tell stories? Compose sonnets? Juggle plates? Do tumbling tricks? Which is it?"

"I can't do any of those things," admitted Milo.

"What an ordinary little boy," commented the king. "Why, my cabinet members can do all sorts of things. The duke here can make mountains out of molehills. The minister splits hairs. The count makes hay while the sun shines. The earl leaves no stone unturned. And the undersecretary," he finished ominously, "hangs by a thread. Can't you do anything at all?"

"I can count to a thousand," offered Milo.

"A-A-R-G-H, numbers! Never mention numbers here. Only use them when we absolutely have to," growled Azaz disgustedly. "Now, why don't you and Tock come up here and sit next to me, and we'll have some dinner?"

"Are you ready with the menu?" reminded the Humbug.

"Well," said Milo, remembering that his mother had always told him to eat lightly when he was a guest, "why don't we have a light meal?"

"A light meal it shall be," roared the bug, waving his arms.

The waiters rushed in carrying large serving platters and set them on the table in front of the king. When he lifted the covers, shafts of brilliant-colored light leaped from the plates and bounced around the ceiling, the walls, across the floor, and out the windows.

"Not a very substantial meal," said the Humbug, rubbing his eyes, "but quite an attractive one. Perhaps you can suggest something a little more filling."

The king clapped his hands, the platters were removed, and, without thinking, Milo quickly suggested, "Well, in that case, I think we ought to have a square meal of—"

"A square meal it is," shouted the Humbug again. The king clapped his hands once more and the waiters reappeared carrying plates heaped high with steaming squares of all sizes and colors.

"Ugh," said the Spelling Bee, tasting one, "these are awful."

No one else seemed to like them very much either, and the Humbug got one caught in his throat and almost choked.

"Time for the speeches," announced the king as the plates were again removed and everyone looked glum. "You first," he commanded, pointing to Milo.

"Your Majesty, ladies and gentlemen," started Milo timidly, "I would like to take this opportunity to say that in all the—"

"That's quite enough," snapped the king. "Mustn't talk all day."

"But I'd just begun," objected Milo.

"NEXT!" bellowed the king.

"Roast turkey, mashed potatoes, vanilla ice cream," recited the Humbug, bouncing up and down quickly.

"What a strange speech," thought Milo, for he'd heard

many in the past and knew that they were supposed to be long and dull.

"Hamburgers, corn on the cob, chocolate pudding—p-u-d-d-i-n-g," said the Spelling Bee in his turn.

"Frankfurters, sour pickles, strawberry jam," shouted Officer Shrift, a police officer two feet tall and almost twice as wide, from his chair. Since he was taller sitting than standing, he didn't bother to get up.

And so down the line it went, with each guest rising briefly, making a short speech, and then resuming his place. When everyone had finished, the king rose.

"Pâté de foie gras, soupe à l'oignon, faisan sous cloche, salade endive, fromages et fruits et demi-tasse,"[1] he said carefully and clapped his hands again.

The waiters reappeared immediately, carrying heavy, hot trays, which they set on the table. Each one contained the exact words spoken by the various guests, and they all began eating immediately with great gusto.

"Dig in," said the king, poking Milo with his elbow and looking disapprovingly at his plate. "I can't say that I think much of your choice."

"I didn't know that I was going to have to eat my words," objected Milo.

"Of course, of course, everyone here does," the king grunted. "You should have made a tastier speech."

Milo looked around at everyone busily stuffing himself and then back at his own unappetizing plate. It certainly didn't look worth eating, and he was so very hungry.

"Here, try some somersault," suggested the duke. "It improves the flavor."

---

1. Pâté de foie gras (pä tä′ də fwä grä′), soupe à l'oignon (süp′ ä lôn yôn′), faisan sous cloche (fā zän′ sü klush), salade endive (sä läd′ on dēv′), fromages et fruits et demi-tasse (frō mäzh′ ā frwē ā de mē täs′): French for chopped meat paste, onion soup, pheasant under glass, endive salad, cheese and fruit, and a small cup of coffee.

"Have a rigmarole," offered the count, passing the breadbasket.

"Or a ragamuffin," seconded the minister.

"Perhaps you'd care for a synonym bun," suggested the duke.

"Why not wait for your just desserts?" mumbled the earl indistinctly, his mouth full of food.

"How many times must I tell you not to bite off more than you can chew?" snapped the undersecretary, patting the distressed earl on the back.

"In one ear and out the other," scolded the duke, attempting to stuff one of his words through the earl's head.

"If it isn't one thing, it's another," chided the minister.

"Out of the frying pan into the fire," shouted the count, burning himself badly.

"Well, you don't have to bite my head off," screamed the terrified earl, and flew at the others in a rage.

The five of them scuffled wildly under the table.

"STOP THAT AT ONCE," thundered Azaz, "or I'll banish the lot of you!"

"Sorry."

"Excuse me."

"Forgive us."

"Pardon."

"Regrets," they apologized in turn, and sat down glaring at each other.

The rest of the meal was finished in silence until the king, wiping the gravy stains from his vest, called for dessert. Milo, who had not eaten anything, looked up eagerly.

"We're having a special treat today," said the king as the delicious smells of homemade pastry filled the banquet hall. "By royal command the pastry chefs have worked all night in the half bakery to make sure that—"

"The half bakery?" questioned Milo.

"Of course, the half bakery," snapped the king. "Where do you think half-baked ideas come from? Now, please don't

interrupt. By royal command the pastry chefs have worked all night to—"

"What's a half-baked idea?" asked Milo again.

"Will you be quiet?" growled Azaz angrily; but, before he could begin again, three large servings carts were wheeled into the hall and everyone jumped up to help himself.

"They're very tasty," explained the Humbug, "but they don't always agree with you. Here's one that's very good." He handed it to Milo and, through the icing and nuts, Milo saw that it said "THE EARTH IS FLAT."

"People swallowed that one for years," commented the Spelling Bee, "but it's not very popular these days—d-a-y-s." He picked up a long one that stated "THE MOON IS MADE OF GREEN CHEESE" and hungrily bit off the part that said "CHEESE." "Now *there's* a half-baked idea," he said, smiling.

Milo looked at the great assortment of cakes, which were being eaten almost as quickly as anyone could read them. The count was munching contentedly on "IT NEVER RAINS BUT IT POURS" and the king was busy slicing one that stated "NIGHT AIR IS BAD AIR."

"I wouldn't eat too many of those if I were you," advised Tock. "They may look good, but you can get terribly sick of them."

"Don't worry," Milo replied; "I'll just wrap one up for later," and he folded his napkin around "EVERYTHING HAPPENS FOR THE BEST."

Meet the Author

Norton Juster began to write stories by accident. He always liked to write but never seriously considered being a professional writer until one day he felt he needed some relaxation from his work as an architect. He had been working very hard on a project that was quite difficult, and so he started to write a short story just for fun. The story grew and grew, and *The Phantom Tollbooth* was the result. From then on, Juster continued with his writing as well as with his work as an architect. Today he also teaches at a college in western Massachusetts.

The author lives with his wife, who is a book designer, on an old farm in western Massachusetts. He likes living in a rural community even though he was raised in a big city.

The Phantom Tollbooth has won a number of prizes and was even made into a full-length cartoon feature. Some of Juster's other books are *The Dot and the Line, Alberic the Wise,* and, most recently, *Otter Nonsense.*

Checking Comprehension and Skills

Thinking About What You've Read

1. Why is it necessary to choose your words with care in the City of Dictionopolis?
2. Why do you think the cabinet members use so many words to refer to the wooden wagon?
3. Why is it fitting that the palace look like a book?
4. How does King Azaz feel about numbers? How do you know?
5. What two meanings of the words *light* and *square* are being confused on pages 444 and 445?
6. What words does Milo have to eat?
7. Give three examples from the selection of phrases that have meanings different from their ordinary meanings.
8. Name two "half-baked ideas" *not* from the selection that you are tired of hearing. Explain their meanings.
• 9. Do you think the author's main purpose in writing this story was to inform, entertain, or persuade? Explain why you think as you do.

Talking About What You've Read

The residents of Dictionopolis always use and understand words literally. One reason why this story is amusing is that the author uses idioms in a literal way. What are five idioms used in the story? What is amusing about the way each one is used?

Writing About What You've Read

Make a list of three idioms that you have heard and that are not used in the story. Write down the literal and the idiomatic meanings of each one. Select one of these idioms and draw a picture to illustrate the literal meaning of it.

• Comprehension Skill: Author's purpose

The Flotz

by Jack Prelutsky

I am the Flotz, I gobble dots,
indeed, I gobble lots and lots,
every dot I ever see
is bound to be a bite for me.
I often munch on myriads
of sweet, abundant periods,
I nibble hyphens, and with ease
chew succulent apostrophes.

From time to time, I turn my gaze
to little dotted "i's" and "j's,"
and if I chance upon a dash,
I soon dispatch it with panache.
I chomp on commas half the day,
quotation marks are rarer prey,
a semicolon's quite a treat,
while polka dots are joys to eat.

When I confront a dotted line,
my tongue flicks out, those dots are mine,
Morse code becomes a feast, and yes,
I've snacked upon an S.O.S.
For I'm the Flotz, who gobbles dots,
I gobble them in pails and pots,
and you'll not like my brief embrace
if you have freckles on your face.

451

Zany Brainies

Each group of words or letters below is printed so that it stands for a familiar phrase. For example, the first one means "mind over matter." Now see if you can find out the meanings of the others! Check your answers at the bottom of the page.

Example:	MIND	(mind over matter)
	MATTER	

1. HE   ART

2.

```
      O            R   O
   G     I       A       U
      G     N       D   N
```

3.

```
   C      C      C        C
      C      C      C
```

4. EGSG   GEGS   GGES   SGGE   SEGG

5.

```
          R
      C     A
        U
      Y   Z
```

6.   iiiiiii
          U

Using a Telephone Directory

Locating names in a telephone directory, either a white residence directory or a yellow business directory, should be as simple as locating words in a dictionary. Read the names and their spellings carefully and remember these tips:

- Guide words show the first and the last surname (family name) on the page: KELLER—KELLY.
- Names are listed alphabetically by surname. Skim the list of names until you reach the correct alphabetical listing.
- If there is more than one listing of the same surname, look for the first name or initial, which is listed in alphabetical order: for example, Kelly Agnes; Kelly Brian.
- Businesses are listed by full name even if a business begins with a first name. For example, *Rita Lot Bookstore* is listed under *R*, not *L* for *Lot*.
- Business names beginning with numbers are listed the way each number is spelled out. For example, *222 Shoes* is listed as if it were spelled out "Two two two."
- A business name beginning with initials is found at the beginning of the section listing the first capital letter in the initials. *U.S. Auto School* is found near the beginning of the *U* section.

Match each name with the correct set of guide words.

1. S & R Video Rentals
2. Shelley Silverstein Travel Agency
3. 711 Photo Service
4. Smithy J A
5. Smith Laura

a. SMITHE—SNELLING
b. SETZER—SEWALL
c. S & A CORPORATION— S & W CLAIMS
d. SHEAFFER—SHERIDAN
e. SMITH C—SMITH R

Morgan has a brilliant idea about how to make money for his club. In order to persuade the club members that his idea will work, he must choose his words with care. Notice how Morgan uses statements of facts to support his statements of opinion.

by Jill Ross Klevin

The Turtle Club of Calabasas, California, is a secret club for the kids who live on Turtle Street: Morgan, P. J. (for Priscilla Jane), Mikey, and Fergy—all twelve years old. There's also Morgan's little brother, Sanford, the club's unofficial mascot. The club was founded so the kids could do fun things like go to Disneyland— except it's hard to do that without money, and how do you get money when you're too young to have a job?

The Turtles hold a meeting to discuss becoming businesspersons.

"Anybody's allowed to go into a business, even someone who's twelve."

Fergy sat down on the floor next to Mikey and blinked at Morgan. "We can't get jobs because we're not old enough to get working papers, right?"

"Right!" they all chorused.

"But that doesn't mean we can't get money."

"What's that, a riddle?" P. J. muttered sarcastically.

Fergy shook his head. "No, a fact of life. Okay, it's true you have to be sixteen or over to get working papers, but you don't have to be any particular age to go into your own business. Anybody's allowed to go into a business, even someone who's twelve."

"What kind of business could four inexperienced kids go into?" Morgan asked.

"I don't know," Fergy replied. "I haven't gotten that far yet."

"There's got to be some business we could go into. Come on, Morgan. Think!" P. J. demanded.

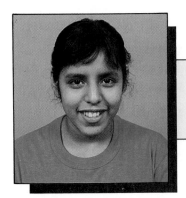

"There's got to be some business we could go into."

Morgan told the others about the most successful businessperson he knew—his dad.

Morgan told the others about the most successful businessperson he knew—his dad. His dad was always talking business. Business, business, business, that's all he ever thought about. He owned not one but three stores already, and he was thinking about opening a fourth. They all had the same name: Pierpont's Party Supply Store. And they all made money.

Morgan's dad had started from the bottom and worked his way up from there. He said that if you wanted to be a success in your own business, you had to keep in mind the basic, fundamental principle behind all American big business—*supply* and *demand.* That meant you had to dream up an idea for a product or service the public really needed—even if it didn't know it yet—make it available, then convince the public that it couldn't live without it.

What product or service could four inexperienced kids make available to the public that somebody else hadn't already made available?

That was a toughie! Right down there on Ventura Boulevard was every conceivable kind of business under the sun except one: a business run exclusively by and especially for kids.

That was it, the perfect business for them to go into: a business just for kids. At least they knew something about kids. Not like some other business, about which they knew nothing. Let's see, what kind of kids' business could it be?

> *". . . a business just for kids would probably stand a pretty good chance of making it in a place where kids make up half the population."*

That depended on what kids in this area needed and wanted but didn't already have.

Did Morgan know any kids? Normal ones?

Sanford was a kid, a kid who collected all kinds of junk. If it was junk, and it cost money, he nagged their parents into buying it for him. Of course once he got it he didn't want it anymore and started nagging for something else. And what happened to all that junk he lost interest in? It got stashed away in a carton in the back of their closet, that's what.

A light bulb went on inside Morgan's head. What if, instead of getting stashed away, their old junk could be recycled instead?

"You know," he said as casually as he could under the circumstances, "I was reading the other day. Kids make up fifty percent of the population in this area."

"How fascinating!" P. J. exclaimed. "But just what does that handy-dandy bit of information have to do with us?"

"Oh, nothing much; only, in my opinion, a business just for kids would probably stand a pretty good chance of making it in a place where kids make up half the population."

Morgan explained his idea. Fergy's eyes narrowed, and he said, "You mean you want us to go into the junk-recycling business?"

"More like the junk-trading business. Don't you get it, you guys? A trading company where kids could come and bring

". . . we'll also be helping the environment by conserving natural resources."

in all their old junk and trade it for other junk brought in by other kids. I'm talking about a big-time operation here. We could all wind up tycoons!"

P. J. lifted her skinny shoulders in a shrug. "Sounds more like a public service to me."

"That too," Morgan exclaimed. "It's very ecological. While we're providing a unique service to our customers, we'll also be helping the environment by conserving natural resources."

"It's not a bad idea, I guess," P. J. said half-heartedly.

"I think it's good!" Mikey put in but he always said what he thought Morgan wanted him to, so his opinion didn't really count.

Morgan looked at Fergy. "Well?"

Fergy didn't say anything. Not for a couple of minutes, a couple of very long minutes. Then after giving it his careful consideration, he uttered one single word: *"Wow!"*

Morgan grinned delightedly. That one word said it all.

"Wow!"

"*Where do we get the inventory from?*"

"*Fergy liked it.* That must mean it's good," Mikey said to Morgan.

"I don't need him to tell me that. I know it already," he said.

"I don't get it," P. J. interjected. "Just how would this thing work?"

"It's not terribly complicated, P. J.," Morgan replied. "Not like elementary algebra or plane geometry or something like that. I'll explain. Let's say a kid comes into our trading company with something he wants to trade."

"Like what, Morgan?" Sanford piped up.

"Um, let's say it's a kite, okay?"

"A new one or an old, beat-up one, Morgan?"

"Stow it, Sanford. Don't be a pest. Say this kid brings in this kite. We look it over. We put a value on it. We tell him it's worth that amount and he can trade it for anything we have worth the same amount."

"Anything we have *where?*" P. J. asked.

Morgan frowned. "Good question! In our inventory, that's where."

"Where do we get the inventory from?" Mikey asked.

"Out of the air," P. J. mumbled.

"Out of our garages is more like it," Fergy added. "Mine's so full of junk, it looks like the Pasadena Flea Market on alternate Sundays. My dad would probably pay us to take it away—if he had any money, that is."

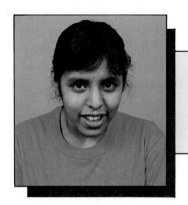

"What if this kid with the kite didn't want to trade it in for something worth the same amount?"

"Wait a sec. I have a question," P. J. put in. "What if this kid with the kite didn't want to trade it in for something worth the same amount? What if he wanted to trade it for something worth more?"

"He could pay us the difference in cash," Morgan replied. "We have nothing against money."

"But what if he wanted to trade it for something worth less, Mr. Smarty?"

Morgan hesitated for a minute. They couldn't go around giving their customers money. They wouldn't be in business long if they did that. "We'll give them credit," he concluded, feeling pretty proud of himself for solving that one.

"Then," Morgan went on, "our customers will pay us a certain percentage for providing this service to them. That amount will be our commission. Don't you get it, Mikey?" he added when he saw that Mikey was still confused.

Morgan decided to try a different approach. "Look, Mikey, pretend we're open for business, okay? A kid comes in, the one with the kite. Remember him? Riiiight! He wants to trade his kite for something else. We look the kite over. We decide what it's worth—a dollar. We say to the kid, 'Okay, your kite's worth a dollar. That means you can trade it in for anything we have in our inventory worth a dollar.'"

"Inventory?" Mikey interjected.

"Yeah, inventory. Remember, we said it would come out of our garages?" Morgan explained very patiently. "To start off

with, we'll provide the inventory. Once the business gets going, and our customers bring in stuff to trade, that will be our inventory. Okay, let's say the kid looks through all our inventory and can't find anything he wants worth one dollar. We tell him he can trade his kite for something worth more if he wants to, or something worth less. If he decides to trade it for something worth more, he pays us the difference in cash. If it's worth a dollar fifty, he gives us back fifty cents, right? Right! If he decides to trade for something worth less, we don't give him the difference in cash. We give him a credit and tell him he can come back and use it up another time."

"What's a credit?" Sanford asked.

"A little piece of paper saying that we owe him a certain amount," Morgan explained to him. "You know, like the credit slips Mom gets when she returns something at the

"What's a credit?"

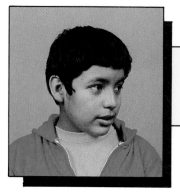

"Ten percent isn't enough of a commission for us to charge our customers."

department store? Okay, do we all get it so far? Good! Now moving right along here, we go on to the question of how much commission we ought to charge for our unique and original service. Say we decide it ought to be ten percent. That means that on a kite for one dollar we get ten cents just for providing the service."

"Ten percent isn't enough of a commission for us to charge our customers," Fergy said. "We'll never make any money charging ten percent. We have to charge more, say, twenty or twenty-five percent."

Morgan chewed his lip thoughtfully. Twenty-five percent sounded pretty exorbitant. Maybe their customers would think they were trying to cheat them it they charged that much.

"They'll just think we're smart businessmen," Fergy said when Morgan pointed that out to him.

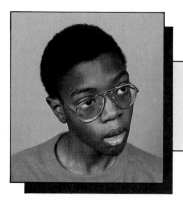

"I still say ten percent is enough."

*"What's inventory, Morgan?
Tell me again."*

"Businesspersons," P. J. said.

"Ex-cuse *me, Ms.* Alberoy," Fergy said, and doffed an imaginary hat in her direction. P. J. put her nose in the air and turned her back on him to show how little he or his ideas meant to her.

"I still say ten percent is enough," Morgan said, eager to get back to the business at hand.

"And I say it ought to be twenty-five," Fergy argued. "Who's the financial wizard anyway, me or you?"

"You, I guess," Morgan said, not all that convinced.

Mikey crept over closer to him and asked, "What's *inventory,* Morgan? Tell me again. I forgot."

"All the stuff we'll have on hand to trade for the stuff our customers bring in," Morgan replied.

Finally Morgan made the official announcement to end the meeting so they could all go home and start rounding up some inventory for their new business.

During their first week of business, the club members earned $300. After Morgan's mother, a reporter for The Herald, *wrote an article called "Local Kids Turn Old Junk into Big Business," their business became even more successful. The club members were even asked to appear on a TV news show.*

Checking Comprehension and Skills

Thinking About What You've Read

1. What carefully chosen words by Morgan convince the other Turtles that Morgan's money-making plan will work?
2. What traits does Morgan consider necessary to be a good businessperson like his father?
• 3. Name two of Morgan's reasons for saying that a company trading kids' toys is the Turtles' best business bet. Is each reason a fact or an opinion?
4. How would Morgan's plan work? Explain two possible kinds of trades.
5. How well do you think Morgan's plan would work in your community? Explain.
6. What do you think was the author's main purpose in writing this selection?
• 7. What statement of fact on page 457 supports Morgan's opinion that a kids' trading company would be a success?

Talking About What You've Read

Suppose you had to sell the idea of the Turtle Street Trading Co. to customers. How would you describe the company to make it sound attractive? What facts and opinions would you state that would make it sound like a good place to trade?

Writing About What You've Read

Write a five-line advertisement describing the Turtle Street Trading Co. The ad will be posted on a community bulletin board. Use facts as well as opinions to advertise the company. Choose your words carefully.

• Comprehension Skill: Fact and opinion

LOOKING BACK

Thinking About the Section

In this section you have learned about the power of words. The authors have used loaded words to show a bias, idioms to entertain, and objective words to present statements of fact.

The following is a list of words and phrases that have been taken from the selections you have read. Decide if each word or phrase on the list is loaded, objective, or idiomatic.

splitting hairs	an official announcement
50% of the population	eating your words
crucial	mania
goes without saying	three out of four members
strenuously object	

Copy this chart onto a sheet of paper. Fill it in by writing the words and phrases in the proper categories.

Loaded	Objective	Idiomatic

What other words or phrases can you think of that will fit into these categories? Write these on your chart, too.

Writing About the Section

Using as many examples as possible from your chart, write a business letter in which you do one of the following:

1. Ask the president of a local TV network to reprogram the network to make it more educational.
2. Tell the King of Dictionopolis why people should not always have to eat their words.
3. Ask Morgan's father to support the Turtles' business venture.

What other words or phrases will fit into these categories? Be sure your phrases are appropriate to the person you are writing to. For example, if you are writing to the King of Dictionopolis, you might want to use idioms.

11

Exploring the Universe

Seek, probe, discover. Come explore the universe. There are distant moons and stars, and planets—a whole world in outer space. There are treasures hidden in the earth and under the sea. There are the powerful forces of nature just waiting for you to figure out why and how they happen.

You'll read about explorers and explorations in this section. You'll get to know what astronauts experience as they travel through outer space. You will meet a man who chases tornados. And you'll read about some interesting farms and foods that may be in your future.

Outlining

Whether you are a scientist exploring some parts of the universe or a shopper exploring a new shopping mall, it is important to have a plan. Have you ever tried to find a particular store or a kind of store in a shopping mall? Did you spend a lot of time wandering around until you found what you were looking for? Or did you think to look at the mall's directory and floor plan, which is usually located near the main entrance? It is a plan that shows how the mall is organized. The directory shows clearly where each store is.

In a similar way, a plan can help you see how an article is organized so that you can understand it. An **outline** is a plan that shows how an article is organized. It shows the important points of an article and how those points are related one to another.

Below and on the next two pages is an article about a scientist's study of a particular kind of gorilla—the mountain gorilla.

Dr. Dian Fossey became the world's leading expert on the mountain gorilla—an endangered species of the ape family. Dr. Fossey spent more than thirteen years living among these gentle apes in the mountains and rain forests of Rwanda (rü än′də), a nation in central Africa.

For Dr. Fossey, getting used to the wilderness was not difficult. Getting close to the gorillas proved to be more of a challenge.

She had to let the gorillas get to know her. To do this, she had to let them know she meant them no harm.

Dr. Dian Fossey
with gorillas

One way of doing this was to pretend that she was one of them. When she approached them, she didn't walk upright. She crawled. She also pretended to munch on leaves and vines—the diet of the gorillas.

Her other ploy required much patience; she simply had to wait.

"It didn't happen overnight," she once recalled. After two years of waiting and watching, the gorillas accepted her.

Then it was her turn to get to know them. Each day, Dr. Fossey studied both their physical appearance and social habits. She took notes and photos to record the way they looked, and she made tapes to record the gorillas' sounds for fright, contentment, and anger.

To learn their habits, she observed what they ate and how they cared for their young.

Dr. Fossey learned a lot about the mountain gorillas. She learned about their lifestyles and about dangers facing the apes.

In studying their lifestyles, she found that gorillas travel in groups. (A group of gorillas is called a band.) A band is made up of as many as twenty members. This is their family unit. The family leader is a large male called the silverback because his back hair becomes white as he ages.

The gorillas spend about half their day resting. In nice weather they sunbathe. As they rest, they make a noise that sounds like a cross between a cat's purr and a stomach growl. "That means they are happy and content," Dr. Fossey noted.

The mountain gorillas spend much of their day lazily munching on ferns, leaves, plant shoots, stems, and fruit. They never eat other animals. At night they sleep in nests made from grasses, bark, and leaves.

Band of mountain gorillas

Even though they seem to lead peaceful lives, the mountain gorillas face grave dangers. One of the most serious dangers comes from poachers, illegal hunters who set wire traps to capture them.

Besides poachers, the mountain gorillas face another danger. They are running out of room to roam and graze. The area in which they live is very small—only 25 miles long, and from 6 to 12 miles wide. As people move into the gorillas' lands, the animals are pushed into even smaller areas. Their food supplies are being destroyed to make way for farms and homes.

1. What is the article about?

The article is about Dian Fossey's study of the mountain gorilla. The subject of the article is often used as the title of the outline.

2. What main points does the article make?

The article makes two main points: how Dr. Fossey and the gorillas got to know each other and what Dr. Fossey learned about the gorillas. If you had difficulty recognizing this, look at the article again. The second paragraph through the sixth paragraph present the first main point. Most of the remaining paragraphs present the second main point. In an outline, these main points are called **main topics.** Here is how you might begin to make an outline of this article.

Dian Fossey's Study of the Mountain Gorilla
I. How Dr. Fossey and the gorillas got to know each other
II. What Dr. Fossey learned about the gorillas

Important points about each main topic should be put into the outline.

3. What important points does the article give about how Dr. Fossey and the gorillas got to know each other?

The article tells you these important points about the first main topics: how Dr. Fossey let the gorillas get to know her and how Dr. Fossey got to know the gorillas. The third, fourth, and fifth paragraphs tell about the first point. The sixth paragraph tells about the second point. In an outline, important points that tell or explain something about a main topic are called **subtopics.** Here is how to show these subtopics in an outline.

Dian Fossey's Study of the Mountain Gorillas
I. How Dr. Fossey and the gorillas got to know each other
  A. How Dr. Fossey let the gorillas get to know her
  B. How Dr. Fossey got to know the gorillas
II. What Dr. Fossey learned about the gorillas

4. What are some facts that tell about how Dr. Fossey let the gorillas get to know her?

To answer that question, look for the facts in the article that tell about the main topic. In an outline, the facts that tell more about a subtopic are called **details.** Here is how the outline looks when the details are added.

Dian Fossey's Study of the Mountain Gorillas
I. How Dr. Fossey and the gorillas got to know each other
  A. How Dr. Fossey let the gorillas get to know her
    1. By pretending she was one of them
    2. By being patient with them for two years
  B. How Dr. Fossey got to know the gorillas
II. What Dr. Fossey learned about the gorillas

Look at the partly completed outline above. Notice how Roman numerals, capital letters, and Arabic numerals—all followed by periods—are lined up in an outline. Also notice that the first word of the main topic, subtopics, and details begin with a capital letter.

Practicing Outlining

On a separate sheet of paper, outline the second part of the article, using as your main topic: II. What Dr. Fossey learned about the gorillas. Answering the questions below will help you complete this portion of your outline.

1. What two main kinds of information did Dr. Fossey learn about the mountain gorillas? (The answers will be the subtopics of your outline.)
2. Name four facts about how the gorillas live. (The answers will be the details in your outline.)
3. Name two sources of danger the gorillas face. (The answers will be the details in your outline.)

Tips for Outlining on Your Own

- Before you begin to outline, read the article to see what it is about and how it is organized. As you outline, reread the article when necessary.
- Decide the topic of the article, and use it as the title of the outline.
- Find the main points of the article, and write them as main topics in the outline.
- Decide the important points about the main topics, and write them as subtopics.
- Find the example or facts that tell more about the subtopics, and write them as details.
- Make sure you have used Roman numerals, capital letters, and Arabic numerals correctly.

How is life in an orbiting space capsule different from life on earth? As astronauts continue to explore the universe, they must adjust to some very unusual conditions. As you read this article, decide what ideas and details you would include in an outline.

LIFE ON A SPACE SHUTTLE

by Bruce Meberg

Travelers in Space

The chances that you may one day take a trip into space are getting better all the time. As it becomes easier to live in a space capsule, more and more people who are *not* trained astronauts will be able to travel in space. At first, the National Aeronautics and Space Administration (NASA) would only choose as astronauts trained pilots to carry out the early space programs. These were the Mercury and Gemini programs. For the Apollo and Skylab flights, doctors and scientists were added to the list of those able to take part in space flights.

A space shuttle crew may number up to seven people. The commander, the pilot, and the mission specialist are NASA astronauts. Other people in the crew are called *payload specialists.* They may or may not be NASA astronauts. Payload specialists are people who are already trained in special scientific or medical skills. They are taken along on spaceflights to carry out the scientific and medical experiments of a mission. What special skills of your chosen career might be useful on a space shuttle mission? This is where your chance to travel in space might be.

Today, choosing candidates for space travel is still hard to do but the Space Shuttle Program has made some of its requirements easier to meet. Now, ordinary people are sometimes able to take part in a space flight. Through NASA's Space Flight Participant Program politicians and other civilians have had their chance. One day, you, too, may be able to travel into outer space.

As the dream of space flight becomes real for more and more people, you may wonder, "What

Aboard a space shuttle, objects and travelers must be anchored with straps and other devices to keep from floating about. Rhea Seddon, one of the first women NASA astronauts, is shown at the left having dinner.

might a space flight be like? How is life in a space capsule different from life on Earth?"

Conditions of Space Travel
Microgravity

Space travel includes some very strange conditions. One that is very different from any earthly condition is the almost complete absence of gravity in outer space. This condition is called *zero* or *microgravity.* In microgravity, things act differently than they do in gravity as we know it on Earth. In microgravity people and things float around above the ground, and there is no sense of up or down.

Some parts of the body, such as the inner ear, must get used to microgravity. On Earth, a person's sense of balance is helped by fluids in the inner ear. These fluids depend upon gravity. In microgravity, the inner ear might send different messages to the brain. The wrong messages can cause a sickness known as space sickness. It is a lot like the motion sickness that some people feel when they travel on moving boats and planes and even in cars. Symptoms include dizziness, drowsiness, and vomiting.

Routine Life in Space

Microgravity also changes every part of the daily routine in space. Even a little thing like spilling food can cause problems. Since spilled particles will float around the cabin, these bits can dirty the cabin and clog equipment. But the problem is solved easily because a space traveler can chase floating food bits and swallow them.

Eating a meal in space has changed greatly since the early flights. The freeze-dried foods (frozen, with the water removed) in tube-shaped plastics bags that were used in the Mercury flights are long gone. Today's space travelers can choose from many kinds of foods and drinks. Tasty, healthy foods that come in small, lightweight containers are now available. Some choices are turkey with gravy, tuna, and ham, as well as snacks.

Although the choice of foods to eat in space is like our choice on Earth, in other ways, cooking, eating, and storing food are very different in space. Salt and pepper come in liquid form so they won't float around the cabin. Foods can be heated, but there is no refrigerator to keep things cold. Liquids MUST be sipped through straws. Trays must be tied down to keep them from floating away.

To sleep, space travelers can get into sleeping bags. A traveler can sleep without straps. Space travelers can also sleep in the air. But if they do, they have to tie themselves to the wall so they won't float around the cabin, bumping into things all "night." (Night, too, is different in space. The shuttle travels around the earth once every 90 minutes or so. That means that there are 16 periods of light and dark every 24 hours.)

It is very important to keep the shuttle clean. Certain germs will multiply in such closed weightless conditions. The dining, bath, and sleeping areas must be cleaned often to keep these germs from polluting the air.

Most shuttle flights last about a week. To keep from overloading the shuttle, supplies must be limited. Necessities, like water, must be used very carefully. Clothes and dishes

Sample of Space-Shuttle Food and Beverage List

*Foods		Beverages
Applesauce (T)	Green beans and broccoli (R)	Apple drink
Apricots, dried (IM)	Ham (I) (T)	Cocoa
Asparagus (R)	Macaroni w/cheese (R)	Grape drink
Bananas (FD)	Meatballs (T)	Grapefruit drink
Beef (I) (T)	Peaches (T)	Instant breakfast
Bread (I) (NF)	Peanut butter	Lemonade
Broccoli (R)	Pears (T)	Orange drink
Breakfast roll (I) (NF)	Peas (R)	Orange-pineapple drink
Cauliflower w/cheese (R)	Pineapple, crushed (T)	Strawberry drink
Cereal, cornflakes (R)	Pudding (T)	Tea
Cereal, granola (R)	Rice (R)	Tropical punch
Cheddar cheese spread (T)	Salmon (T)	
Chicken and noodles (R)	Shrimp cocktail (R)	**Condiments**
Chicken and rice (R)	Soup, cream of mushroom (R)	Barbecue sauces
Crackers, graham (NF)	Spaghetti w/meatless sauce	Catsup
Eggs, scrambled (R)	(R)	Hot pepper sauce
Food bar, almond crunch	Strawberries (R)	Mayonnaise
(NF)	Tomatoes, stewed (T)	Mustard
Food bar, granola (NF)	Tuna (T)	Pepper and salt
Fruit cocktail (T)	Turkey (T)	
Green beans (R)	Vegetables (R)	

*Abbreviations in parentheses indicate type of food: T = thermostabilized, I = irradiated, IM = intermediate moisture, FD = freeze-dried, R = rehydratable, and NF = natural form.

don't get washed; instead, they are stored, after use, in airtight bags. Food trays and utensils are cleaned with a strong cleaning fluid instead of water.

Showers can cause water drops to float around. After wetting themselves with a water gun and sponging themselves clean, space travelers use a vacuum hose to dry themselves and to collect floating drops of water.

Shuttle Flights

So what would a shuttle flight be like?

Goals

In general, some goals of shuttle flights are these:

1. to send satellites into space
2. to repair or deploy satellites
3. to bring satellites back to earth to be readied for reuse.
4. to carry out scientific experiments

Flight of Mission-51 D

Let's take a look at Mission-51 D.

Mission 51-D began on April 12, 1985, and lasted for seven days. Its main goals were to carry out a number of scientific experiments and to send out a communications satellite. The mission specialist on this flight was Rhea Seddon, a doctor turned astronaut.

As Seddon describes it, liftoff is like an explosion. The rocket engines are loud and very powerful, and the whole spaceship vibrates. Because you are moving ahead against gravity, your body feels much heavier than normal. You are traveling in space and gravity is gone. You feel weightless.

Seddon prepared for the flight by practicing in NASA flight simulators.

On the inside, these look just like real spaceships. The simulators make it possible for the astronauts to go through most of the situations and movements they will experience during a flight. But, as Seddon said, nothing can duplicate those first few seconds of a real takeoff.

Experiments in Medicine

Seddon was the only medical person in the crew. She was in charge of an experiment known as the American Flight Echocardiogram.

The simulator reproduces the conditions of space flight and helps an astronaut become familiar with the instruments of the space shuttle orbiter.

In this experiment, scientists study the shape of the heart. Research on the heart and other muscles is very important, since scientists need to know the effects of space travel on the human body. In microgravity, muscles don't always have to work hard. As a result, they can lose some of their strength. This can be dangerous if space travelers stay in space for a long time. The return to earth can place too much strain on unused muscles causing them to pull or even tear. Bones are also under study because in space they lose some of their calcium and can become brittle. Exercise is very important to keep bones and muscles in shape.

Experiments in Physics

The crew of Mission 51-D also experimented with science study toys to see how they would work in space. Some of the toys were a gyroscope, a yo-yo, jacks, a paddle ball, magnetic marbles, and a paper airplane. Seddon played jacks by tossing the ball against the wall and grabbing the jacks out of the air. The crew discovered that paper airplanes just hang in microgravity. A light push will start one moving in a slow glide.

The crew also learned about the other scientific toys. Magnetic marbles form a ring when put together. The north pole of one marble attracts the south pole of the next.

The gyroscope shows that spinning objects are stable. Once the gyro starts spinning, its spin axis stays pointed in the same direction even if you try to knock it off balance. This is the same principle that keeps the earth and a satellite spinning in a stable manner. These experiments help scientists understand how the laws of physics work in outer space.

Problems

As with any complicated flight some problems were bound to come up. On Mission 51-D, the communications satellite was successfully released. However, it didn't go into proper orbit. In Houston, Texas, Mission Control reviewed the situation and worked out a plan to save the launch. If a lever on the outside of the spinning satellite could be moved, there was a chance that the satellite would go into its proper orbit.

The crew of Mission 51-D quickly made a yard-long flyswatter out of some spare parts. This was attached to the end of the shuttle's remote manipulator system (RMS), a sixty-foot-long robot arm. The pilot of the shuttle brought the craft to within thirty feet of the satellite. Seddon, working the controls of the robot arm, tried to flip the satellite's starter switch. On her third try, she was successful. The shuttle moved back and waited for the satellite motor to fire. It never did. The problem was more complicated than anyone had thought. Its solution would have to wait for yet another shuttle flight.

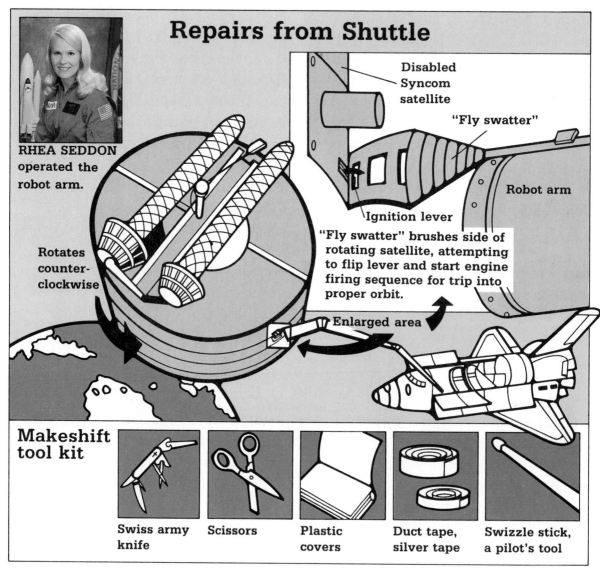

Repairs from Shuttle

RHEA SEDDON operated the robot arm.

Rotates counter-clockwise

Disabled Syncom satellite

"Fly swatter"

Robot arm

Ignition lever

"Fly swatter" brushes side of rotating satellite, attempting to flip lever and start engine firing sequence for trip into proper orbit.

Enlarged area

Makeshift tool kit

Swiss army knife

Scissors

Plastic covers

Duct tape, silver tape

Swizzle stick, a pilot's tool

These are the makeshift tools which Rhea Seddon used to flip on the ignition lever of the communications satellite on Mission 51-D.

The Rewards of Space Travel

Though not all of the goals of Mission 51-D were met, the flight was rewarding. One of the most pleasing aspects of space travel is just looking out the window. Seeing the earth go by from about 150 miles up is, for many astronauts, one of the greatest sights they will ever see. Seddon says that by the end of her mission "there were a lot of nose prints on the window."

With just one long look, a space traveler can see sights such as the Mediterranean Sea, southern Europe, much of the Middle East, and the entire coast of northern Africa! At night city lights from all over the world can be seen. They remind the space traveler that there are people below going about their everyday lives while the traveler is speeding by overhead. In just seven days the space flight ends, and the journey becomes just a memory . . . until next time!

Meet a Reader

Tonya Knight likes to read stories and articles about outer space, but she doesn't think she would like to fly on a rocket ship. She admits she is afraid of heights and prefers to keep her feet firmly planted on the ground.

Tonya lives in Mississippi. She is in the sixth grade and she enjoys her schoolwork, especially social studies. Her great interest in social studies is reflected in her personal reading—books about history and historical figures. She particularly likes to read about the Civil War and World War I.

Tonya also likes poetry and has read many poems by her favorite poet, Emily Dickinson. Art books are another interest. She enjoys looking at books with reproductions of famous paintings in them. The beautiful paintings inspire her to paint and draw on her own.

Besides reading, Tonya is active in sports. She swims and plays basketball, kickball, and soccer.

Checking Comprehension and Skills

Thinking About What You've Read

1. State two conditions of life in a space capsule to which astronauts exploring the universe must adjust.
2. How does microgravity change daily routine? Give two examples.
3. Explain how microgravity causes space sickness.
• 4. Look at the outline on the next page. Some of the outline is already filled in. Copy the outline onto a sheet of paper, and then complete the outline.
5. What are two adjectives that describe Rhea Seddon's character? Give one detail from the article to support each adjective.
6. Determine whether this sentence is a statement of fact or opinion and tell how you know. "People, who are not trained as astronauts, have participated in space shuttle flights."
7. Which of your hobbies, interests, or general experience might make you a candidate for a space shuttle flight? Why?

Talking About What You've Read

Think about the condition of microgravity. How would it affect such activities as reading a book, playing checkers, or exercising? Would microgravity make these activities easier or more difficult to carry out? Why? What special problems would a lack of gravity cause in each case?

Writing About What You've Read

Select one of the three activities, or any other one you can think of, and write a paragraph describing how microgravity affects your ability to carry out the activity. How would you solve these problems?

• Study Skills: Outlining

Life on a Space Shuttle

I. Travelers in space
   A. Commander
   B. Pilot
   C. _____
   D. _____
II. Conditions of space travel
   A. _____
      1. Almost complete absence of gravity in outer space
      2. Some of its effects
   B. _____
III. _____
   A. Goals of shuttle flights
   B. Flight of Mission 51-D
      1. Purposes
      2. The mission specialist
   C. Experiments in medicine
      1. _____
      2. _____
   D. Experiments in physics
      1. _____
      2. _____
      3. _____
      4. _____
   E. Problems
      1. A difficult launch
      2. Efforts to solve the problem
IV. _____

Using Common Word Parts

A scientist who is checking several computer printouts at a volcano study center, says to her assistant, "The rumblings are much like those that occurred before the eruption of Mount St. Helens. Its strength is building fast. People must be moved out of the area. Get me the mayor on the phone."

Many times when we relate information about something that is happening to a pattern, we can predict what might happen next. The scientist who is studying the volcano doesn't have to wait for it to erupt. She can predict that it will erupt because her information fits the pattern of other eruptions.

Patterns are found in many things—even in words, and recognizing patterns in words can help you with your reading. Often when reading you come upon words that you haven't seen before. To figure them out, look for familiar patterns, or word parts such as prefixes and suffixes. Other patterns in words may not be as familiar or as easy to spot, but once you recognize them, they can be useful to you.

For example, you may not know the word *consequential.* You can see, however, that it begins like *continent*, ends like *facial,* and has middle parts that remind you of *sequence* and *question.* Seeing this pattern can help you say the word. Then you can use the context to get a good sense of what the word means.

The scientist knew the increased rumblings of the volcano were *consequential* and required action.

Sometimes you will not be able to think of a familiar word for every part of an unknown word. Using just the parts that are familiar to you can still be helpful. For example, use

just one part of each of these words to help you read the underlined words in the following sentences.

photograph   computed

1. The seismograph reported the earth's tremors.
2. These tremors could not be disputed by the scientists.

In the first sentence, recognizing the word part *graph* as in *photograph* makes the word simpler to read. In the second sentence, *puted* looks familiar. From the context you can see what these words mean.

Practicing Using Common Word Parts

Use parts of the words in the box to figure out how to say the underlined words in the sentences. Then use the context of the sentences to see what the words mean.

appreciate	volcanic	prevention
ap · pre · ci · ate	vol · can · ic	pre · ven · tion

1. The scientist made a prediction based on a pattern of similar events.
2. She was able to associate the current situation with similar events that had occurred.
3. There will be a dynamic eruption of the nearby volcano.
4. Although serious, the eruption would not compare to the titanic event at Mount St. Helens.
5. The event was discussed at the scientists' convention.
6. If a local eruption occurred, the value of the land in the area would depreciate.
7. The handmade ceramic vase was broken by accident.
8. "Why do I humiliate myself by being so clumsy?" he said.

Tips for Reading on Your Own

• When you see an unfamilar word, look for familiar word parts to help you say the word.
• Then look for context clues that will help you figure out what the word means.

Why would anyone want to "chase" a tornado? A tornado's potential force, as the chart in this article indicates, can cause danger, destruction, even death. But to storm chasers, the risk is worth the knowledge they gain as they explore the universe in their own unique ways.

Storm Chasers

by Marion Long

David Hoadley started his car. He was getting set to drive into the teeth of a tornado. He looked at the clouds, then he looked west across the plains of Oklahoma. "That's our storm," he said, pointing to the black and rolling clouds far away.

Of course, most of the time tornadoes "chase" people. But David Hoadley chases tornadoes. To photograph and gather facts, he and the twenty or so other serious storm chasers in the country are rained on, hailed on, struck by lightning, and all but blown away. It is not so much a hobby or a career as it is something they must do.

Storm chasers know the damage their special storms do to other people. But the chasers try to make it safer for the rest of us to live in the shadow of the tall clouds. While chasing storms, the chasers call in warnings before damaging weather takes place. Some call to report strange sounds, lightning, or clouds shaped like funnels. Meteorologists often track storms as part of their work. It helps them to understand better what makes very bad storms happen and to find out about them earlier. Someday their findings may help them control the storms. But the storm chasers' most important contribution has been the hundreds of picture slides sent to the National Weather Service. These are used to help train storm spotters— people in local programs who drive to special places to look for early signs of very bad weather. Radar tracking often does not tell everything, and many times the telephone calls from the local spotters are the ones that save lives.

Most of the storm chasers in the

Storm chasers, fifteen minutes after a tornado, view churning clouds.

Twister-tracking gear spread about. David Hoadley prepares for the chase. The INFLOW plates refer to storm-fueling winds.

United States work with either the National Severe Storm Laboratory in Norman, Oklahoma, or with the Institute for Disaster Research at Texas Tech University in Lubbock. The scientists in Oklahoma and Texas keep looking at the local radar scans and the other latest facts to pinpoint the chase for their people in the field. But not David Hoadley.

Hoadley chases storms on his own. He uses only the information given to anyone who walks into a U.S. Weather Service station. And while the chasers at the Severe Storm Lab or at Texas Tech can chase storms anytime, for

Hoadley, tornado season is his yearly three-week vacation. Most of the year he works as a budget analyst[1] for the Environmental Protection Agency. But in May he heads for the Great Plains. He watches the stretch of land from Texas to Iowa known as Tornado Alley—states most often hit by tornadoes yearly. Usually he travels alone, but once he allowed this reporter to go with him.

---

1. budget analyst. A person who examines in detail how money will be received and spent for various purposes in a given time. Governments, companies, schools, etc. make budgets.

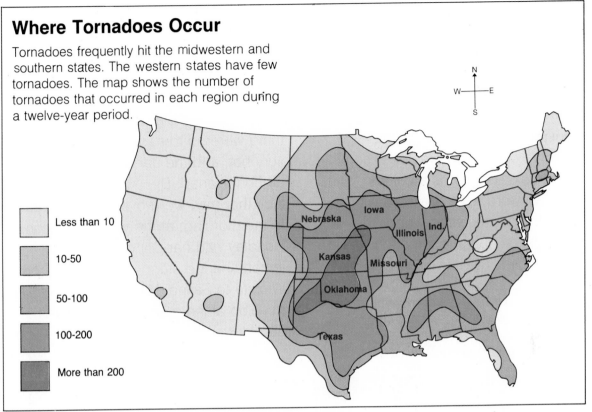

Where Tornadoes Occur

Tornadoes frequently hit the midwestern and southern states. The western states have few tornadoes. The map shows the number of tornadoes that occurred in each region during a twelve-year period.

Less than 10

10-50

50-100

100-200

More than 200

From THE WORLD ENCYCLOPEDIA, Vol. 19, p. 269
Copyright © 1986 by World Book, Inc. Adapted by permission.

On May 8, Hoadley packed my bag into the back of his car. A day later, we arrived bright and early at the Norman, Oklahoma, weather station, where the staff greeted him warmly. They look forward to his visit every year.

Hoadley could hardly wait to get down to business—pinpointing the day's chase. He has found that after closely analyzing surface data, he can regularly forecast storm-watch areas that are smaller than those forecast by the National Weather Service. And he is able to make these predictions up to nine hours before the beginning of severe weather. Last year, he was correct 71% of the time. Today, the data seemed to show many chasing choices. Long, dynamic storm systems with changing patterns were building quickly. The next step was to get ahead of the storm, on its southwest side.

We headed toward the west Texas panhandle,[2] Hoadley's choice. He explained to me that scientists aren't exactly sure of how tornadoes are born, but they know what weather conditions come before them. All it takes is an area of warm air filled with

---

2. panhandle. A narrow strip of land projecting like a handle.

moisture and an area of cold, heavy air above it, preventing its efforts to rise.

At some spot in the layer, warm air escapes and the cold air moves down. The rising warm air gives the falling cold air a high-speed spin. As the atmosphere struggles to adjust, a vortex[3] of currents is created. The air begins spinning, forms a column, and falls downward. Low pressure within the vortex causes water vapor to condense, so that the tornado can be

seen. That low pressure also causes a pull upward. Chickens have had all of their feathers pulled. Cars, houses, and bridges have been picked up and moved. So have people.

Here, on the plains of western Texas, there were no tornadoes in sight. It was very hot, and the car was not air-conditioned. Because we had no luck that day, we drove on to Kansas. In the morning, at the weather station, Hoadley had happily drawn a big lemon-shaped storm-watch circle from Wichita to Salina. Most tornadoes develop along a boundary between cool dry air from the north and

---

3. vortex. A whirling mass or movement of air that sucks everything near it toward its center.

 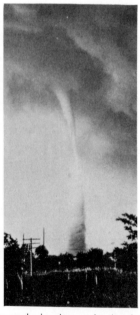 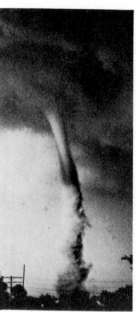 

The Development of a Tornado is shown in the four pictures above. First, a dense, dark cloud forms (at left). The second picture shows rotating air at the bottom of the cloud forming into a narrow cloud called a *funnel*. The funnel then extends toward the earth's surface. If the funnel touches the surface, it raises a huge dust cloud (far right) and destroys almost everything in its path. (From THE WORLD ENCYCLOPEDIA, vol. 9, p. 260. Copyright © 1986 by World Book, Inc. Reprinted by permission.)

warm, humid air from the Gulf of Mexico. It was 38 degrees in Cook, Nebraska, and it would reach the 70s in Kansas. We sat in the car on a deserted road, looking at stormy clouds that were ragged with turning. (On a normal weather day, the bottoms of fluffy, cumulus clouds are flat.) We listened to the eerie wind in the power lines.

Because we had no luck in Kansas, we drove south to the weather station in Hobart, Oklahoma. We found that this was what was called a high-risk day for storm activity—a very rare occurrence.

In the car, Hoadley was lost in thought and very happy. He let out a yell and began to shoot pictures of huge, hard, well-defined clouds. As we drove, conditions changed amazingly fast. Even in the short time between picture stops, the sky was being rearranged.

A twenty-foot curtain of dust blew thick across the highway. "There go the tumbleweeds,"[4] shouted Hoadley. Bunches of them went rolling across the road before the wind.

Then, suddenly, all was sunlight and chirping birds. Hoadley got out of the car and pointed his arm west. The storm was picking up again. Now the clouds were moving very quickly. The trees were defying the strong gusting winds that rocked the car.

"This is the kind of storm that takes seventy-ton boxcars and lifts them off the tracks," Hoadley said. He followed this observation with a few short instructions about how to survive in a ditch if we had to leave the car. The tops of the clouds were rounding and getting tighter. It was nearly sunset. It became almost calm again for a minute. Hoadley was relaxed enough to begin talking about the kinds of birds you hear at sunset. Then a huge blue tornado dropped out of the sky. Like a snake, it whipped through space, slithering along for miles. But it was duller and heavier than a snake. It was like a wavy pillar of smoke. As the seconds went by, it seemed to grow in size until it was huge and black. The tornado picked at the fields and sucked huge pieces up, spinning them in the darkness. The winds were moaning, almost howling. We had made the good forecast and had found the storm.

Then there was stillness on the plains. The whole world seemed to glow. There was great fear associated with the thing. As it pushed toward us, it seemed to wind like a smoky veil.

But the path of a tornado is no place for sitting and thinking. Hoadley suddenly threw up his hands in panic.

---

4. tumbleweed. Plant growing in the western United States that breaks off from its roots and is blown by the wind.

A camera lens banged to the ground. He put the car into motion. "If you can't see the cloud and ground in the camera's viewfinder," said Hoadley, "or if you can hear the roar of the funnel, then you're too close." He looked back to see the tornado across the field behind, and he continued to drive away from the storm.

This tornado was later classified as the largest one that day, about 500 yards wide. It cut a path for seventeen miles behind where we first saw it touch down.

Hoadley told me about the beginning of his obsession with storms. As a youth, he had gone to see a movie. When he entered the theater it wasn't even raining. Once inside, young Hoadley could hear heavy thunder in the distance. Suddenly his father appeared and whispered, "There's a better show outside in the street."

When Hoadley came out of the theater, he found the city transformed. Water rushed down the streets. Large trees lay flat on the ground, their huge roots pushed skyward. Houses were unroofed. Electricity was out. Hoadley could hardly believe what he saw!

Hoadley became interested in forecasting these storms. The Weather Service had developed a forecasting system for tornadoes, but it was not foolproof. Many were the afternoons when young Hoadley would sit right in the middle of the forecast area, munching his lunch and staring out into the clear blue sky.

Later in the evening, he would hear about how his storm had popped up states away. When this had happened often, he decided to try to plot his own storm maps. Gradually, he began to see the same things repeated. For years he chased over the Dakotas and western Minnesota in the family car and drove nearly 70,000 miles before he saw his first tornado. For Hoadley, this was more than enough payment for years of effort. "The science is still young," says Hoadley, "and each chaser must draw upon science, experience, and hunch." There is no textbook for storm chasers.

Hoadley continued, "In the middle of a huge storm, with its wind and lightning and thunder, its greatness and power, I experience a great happiness." For Hoadley, zeroing in on tornadoes is the highest possible experience.

Just a few minutes old, a tornado looms in this rare picture of both the funnel and its entire cloud.

The TORRO tornado intensity scale

TORRO force	Tornado description	Characteristic damage
FC	Funnel cloud incipient tornado	No damage except to top of tallest towers. Some agitation in tree tops. Possible whistling or rushing sound.
0	Light	Light litter, hay, growing plants, spiral from ground. Temporary structures, like marquees, seriously affected. Damage to unsound roofs. Twigs snapped off.
1	Mild	Planks, corrugated iron, garden furniture levitated. Damage to sheds and outbuildings. Dislodged tiles and chimney pots. Haystacks disarranged, and small trees uprooted.
2	Moderate	Mobile homes displaced or damaged. Considerable roof damage. Big branches of trees torn off and tornado track traceable through crops and hedgerows.
3	Strong	Mobile homes overturned or badly damaged. Outbuildings torn from supports or foundations. Roofs stripped of tiles or thatch, serious damage to windows and doors. Strong trees uprooted or snapped.
4	Severe	Mobile homes destroyed. Entire roofs torn off, but walls left standing. Well-rooted trees torn up or twisted apart.
5	Intense	Vehicles over one ton lifted clear off ground. Small weak buildings in exposed areas collapse. Trees carried through the air.
6	Moderately devastating	Vehicles over one ton lifted and carried along in air. Some heavier roofs torn off public buildings, and many less strong buildings collapse. Every tree across tornado track in open country damaged or uprooted.
7	Strongly devastating	Steel-framed industrial buildings buckled. Railway locomotives turned over.
8	Severely devastating	Frame house leveled and most other houses collapse in part or in whole. Cars hurled some distance.
9	Intensely devastating	Railway locomotives hurled some distance. Many steel structures badly damaged.
10	Super tornadoes	Entire frame and wooden houses hurled from foundations. Steel-reinforced concrete buildings severely damaged.

G. T. Meaden, Tornado and Storm Research Organisation, Trowbridge, Wiltshire, England.

Checking Comprehension and Skills

Thinking About What You've Read

1. What knowledge do storm chasers gather as they explore the universe in their unique ways? Why is the information worth the risks they take?
2. When and where does David Hoadley spend his annual three-week vacation? Why?
3. List two ways that Hoadley's work tracking storms is different from that of other storm chasers.
4. Describe the weather conditions that signal tornadoes.
5. Using the map on page 489, what states make up Tornado Alley?
6. How do you think you would have felt watching the tornado with Hoadley and the reporter? Why?
7. Review the reporter's description of the tornado on page 491. Give one example of literary language that you find in the description and label it.
• 8. According to the chart on page 494, at what TORRO force would a tornado destroy a mobile home?
• 9. Using the chart on page 494, compare the damage done by super tornadoes to that of severe tornadoes.

Talking About What You've Read

David Hoadley could certainly be called a memorable character. Why? What will you remember about him? Which of his activities impressed you most? Why?

Writing About What You've Read

Suppose the U.S. Weather Service were going to print a pamphlet about the nation's most successful storm chasers. Write a paragraph in which you describe David Hoadley. Include what you think is most memorable or unusual about him.

• Study Skills: Charts

Wind-Wolves

by William D. Sargent

Do you hear the cry as the pack goes by,
The wind-wolves hunting across the sky?
Hear them tongue it, keen and clear,
Hot on the flanks of the flying deer!

Across the forest, mere, and plain,
Their hunting howl goes up again!
All night they'll follow the ghostly trail,
All night we'll hear their phantom wail,

For tonight the wind-wolf pack holds sway
From Pegasus Square to the Milky Way,
And the frightened bands of cloud-deer flee
In scattered groups of two and three.

Solving Word Problems in Mathematics

Understanding a math problem is similar to launching a rocket. Both take place in stages. The firing of a rocket can happen only after a series of steps are followed. In the same way, you must follow a series of steps in solving math problems.

1. **Read** the entire problem. What facts are given? What question is asked?
2. **Plan** how to solve the problem. What operations are suggested? Decide what steps need to be taken.
3. **Solve** the problem. Answer the question.
4. **Check** your answer. Reread the problem. Ask yourself, "Does my answer make sense?"

Study the way these tips were used for a math problem.

Read   Suppose that the distance to the moon is 230,000 miles. How long would it take a rocket to travel to the moon, stay 24 hours, and return if the average speed each way is 15,000 miles per hour?

Plan   Distance to moon = 230,000 mi
Average speed   =   15,000 mph

Solve   15.33 hours to moon
15.33 hours to return
24.00 hours on moon
54.66 hours total

Check   Reread the problem and decide whether the answer makes sense. Then make sure that your figures are correct.

Growing foods in outer space or under water is no longer a fantasy. In fact, the picture above is of an experimental model of a drum in which astronauts may someday grow food. Food experts are exploring the universe with a definite goal in mind. What is it? As you read, look for the main idea of this article.

FAR OUT FARMS

by Lisa Hsia

The world's population is growing fast. Today there are 4½ billion people in the world. By the time you become thirty, there will be 6½ billion. These people will take up much of the earth's food-growing space. Therefore, new places and ways have to be found to grow enough healthful food to feed the world's increasing population.

Perhaps the food in your future will be grown with the help of computers or strange potions. Greenhouses might help future farmers grow food in deserts, under the sea, or even in space. Some foods might not resemble anything you eat today. Food may never be the same again.

Food from Down Under

Imagine a farm with rows and rows of plants. They stretch as far as the eye can see. A farmer drives a mechanical harvester through the field gathering the crop. It sounds like a pretty normal scene—until you learn that the farm is underwater!

Of course, farmers aren't driving harvesters on the ocean floor right now. But farming is already going on in the sea. Someday, when people settle on dry land now used for growing food, underwater farms could come in handy.

Today's underwater farming, called aquaculture, is not a big business. People are growing sea plants such as kelp and algae in small, offshore water fields in California and Japan. Some people eat the high-protein plants. Kelp is even used as an ingredient in some ice creams. Some day there could be huge farms on the sea floor. They could grow hundreds of thousands of acres of plants for food and fuel.

There's another kind of underwater farming being done now that isn't farming plants. It's farming fish! Salmon ranchers grow fish in pens that float in the sea. Some shellfish, such as clams, grow from ropes dangling into the water from floats. Lobsters are also raised in underwater cages.

"Aquaculture accounts for 11 percent of the fish eaten in the United States," says Peter Cook, an aquaculture expert. Therefore, there's a good chance that some of the fish you eat already comes from a fish farm.

Space Food

Imagine that it's the year 2020. You are an astronaut assigned to Space Station Delta orbiting Earth. It's dinner time, and you're starving. You float over to the agri-center, a room full of plants. Ahead of you, in a spinning plastic drum, leaves of spinach are growing from a "field" of plastic. You push a button to stop the drum and pick your salad for dinner.

Fish farms are sprouting. These lobsters must be raised in separate boxes underwater. If put together, they would fight.

This far-out scene might come true in the future. Today when astronauts blast into space, they take their food with them. But the cost of sending up that food is huge—about $1,000 per pound. In the future, people may be spending more time in space—even living in orbit above Earth. Finding a way for these space residents to grow their own food would save lots of money and provide fresher, tastier meals for them, too.

The spinning space drum is an idea already being tested at Arizona's Environmental Research Laboratory (ERL). Scientists there experiment with new ways to grow food. Plants grow through holes in the plastic sides of the drum toward a light in its center. The drum spins about 50 times a minute. The spinning motion creates a force like gravity. On Earth, gravity "tells" plant roots to grow down. In space, the force would help roots know which way to grow, also— outward away from the drum. All this work may one day make a space garden a not-so-far-out possibility.

High-rise Food

When people in cities ran out of room to spread out, they built upward and made skyscrapers. When future farmers need more space, they might use the same idea. Taller plants can produce more food in the same space.

Another space saver is to grow several plants in one spot. In the Environmental Research Lab, melons grow dangling over a pool of water. On the water, heads of lettuce grow floating on pieces of white plastic. Fish are being raised in the water. Still, not every project is foolproof. "One kind of fish we tried to raise was eating the lettuce," says a plant specialist.

New Foods

Have you ever heard of a honeylope? How about a buffalo gourd? Probably not. But you may be eating these tasty morsels in the future.

Winged beans are just one of the new food crops being discovered in remote areas. Some people already eat these foods. In the future, many more may be part of your diet.

Plant engineers, scientists who develop new kinds of plants, have come up with new plants like the honeylope—part cantaloupe and part honeydew melon.

Plant engineers are also tinkering with cells of plants in laboratory dishes. They are creating plants that resist disease, or can grow in harsh climates, or have other special qualities.

Tomatoes are being grown now with tougher skins and less juice. They don't taste as good as old-fashioned tomatoes. Also, they may not be as healthful. But the point is that they are hard enough to be picked by machines without getting smashed.

Some scientists think that our best hope for future food is not newfangled foods. They think the answer is to use foods we've got right here on Earth—but have never used. Today there are still many unknown plants. About 80,000 could be eaten. But people use only about 3,000. People don't eat the rest because they may not be used to them. You probably don't use more than 30 to 40.

Some scientists are now taking a closer look at plants that have been ignored or considered poisonous in the past. One day you may sit down to your favorite dish—a buffalo gourd, marama bean, and winged bean salad. Now that's food for thought!

At the foot of a stone wall built by her Inca ancestors, a Peruvian villager offers to barter her freshly harvested fruit for other fruits and vegetables.

Some "new" foods on American grocery shelves are actually old in other parts of the world. As farmers explore the universe of neighboring environments, they, too, are seeking to achieve a goal. What might that be? As you read, find the main idea of this article.

GIFT OF THE INCAS

by Noel Vietmeyer

Francisco Pizarro and his conquistadors invaded Peru in 1531. They were looking for gold and silver and found it. But along with treasure, they brought back to the Old World something else. It was an Inca crop, not previously known outside the Andes, called the potato.

The potato became a mainstay of the world's diet. Other unusual cereals, root crops, legumes, and fruits ignored by the invaders are now getting a second look. Like the potato, these ancient foods could become an important part of the modern world's food supply.

Almost all these foods seem strange to our eyes. Thanks to scientists and growers, however, they may even become household words.

Cereals

Cereals formed a large part of the Inca diet. Some of these are grown to this day, yet they have been ignored by most of the world.

Quinoa (kē nō′ə): This plant thrives in poor soils even at an altitude of 15,000 feet. There the dry, cold climate keeps other grains from growing.

Quinoa seeds range from white to red or brown and are shaped like sesame seeds. When cooked, they have a light taste and the feel of wild rice. They are prepared like rice or are used to thicken soups. Some kinds can also be puffed like puffed wheat. With up to 50 percent more protein than rice, wheat, or corn, quinoa seeds are an adequate substitute for meat in a vegetarian diet.

In 1982 this old Inca crop was successfully cultivated outside South America for the first time. A farmer in Boulder, Colorado, organized home gardeners and farmers in eleven different mountain areas of Colorado to grow 48 varieties of quinoa in experimental plantings. Now a marketing company is being set up to distribute the seed nationwide.

Amaranth (am′ə ranth): Like quinoa, amaranth is a wide-leaved plant that produces cereallike seeds.

Its leaves can be eaten like spinach. Its mild-tasting white seeds are barely bigger than poppy seeds. These grow in great numbers—sometimes more than 20,000 to a plant. When heated, the seeds pop and taste like nutty popcorn.

Amaranth seeds are high in protein. That sparked the interest of the National Research Council in Washington, D.C., and other organizations. Two million dollars has been spent on amaranth research, and now this Inca and Aztec crop is making a comeback. Already the plant has caught the imagination of some North American farmers. One miller in Texas is selling amaranth flour. A California producer is marketing a "sprouted amaranth" breakfast cereal.

Root Crops

Along with cereals, root crops provided the main part of the Inca diet. The following root crops have also been largely ignored by the rest of the world.

"Other" potatoes: Many of these potatoes, both the farmed and wild kinds, have a bitter taste but turn sweet after freezing and drying. Some are all black inside. Others are golden yellow. Some can withstand the greatest cold. Others have notable flavors (such as a nutty taste). Most provide more nutrition than our white potato.

Oca (ō′kə): For the Incas, oca was second in importance only to the

Cereals

Root Crops

potato. It is cooked like potatoes: boiled, baked, or fried. The white tubers have a high sugar content and a pleasant, slightly acid taste.

Arracacha (är ä kä'chä): The late David Fairchild, dean of American plant explorers before World War II, considered arracacha "much superior to carrots." Many people of the Andes agree with him. In many places, farmers grow this distant relative of the carrot instead of the potato. Arracacha roots are boiled or fried as a table vegetable or added to stews. They have a crisp texture; white, yellow, or purple flesh; and a delicate flavor that combines the tastes of celery, cabbage, and roasted chestnuts.

Recently the crop has gained popularity in the big cities of southern Brazil. There the climate is not very different from parts of the southern United States. It seems likely that North Americans, too, might soon be

enjoying these forgotten "superior" carrots of the Inca.

Legumes

The Incas also produced at least two unique legumes. (Legumes include nutritious foods such as peas, beans, soybeans, and peanuts.)

Tarwi (tär'wē): This plant is related to the Texas bluebonnet and other wild flowers of the Americas. Its seeds are as rich or richer in protein than peas, beans, soybeans, and peanuts—the world's leading protein crops. They also contain as much vegetable oil as soybeans.

Tarwi's seeds are bitter. The Incas soaked them in running water for a day or two to wash out the bitterness. Recently engineers in Peru and Chile developed machines that clean them more quickly. Now they may become readily available to all.

Nuñas (nü'nyäs): Nuñas is a

Legumes

Fruits

wonderful kind of bean. The Incas counted on beans for much of their nourishment. At high altitudes, water boils at too low a temperature to cook most beans in a reasonable time. To solve this, Inca farmers raised nuñas. They are bean counterparts of popcorn. Dropped into hot oil, they pop out of the seed coat. The resulting food has a soft consistency. Its taste is something like roasted peanuts.

A researcher in Cali, Colombia, is studying the cultivation of nuñas. He has gathered varieties at high altitudes in the Andes and has started growing them. If his efforts succeed, "popping beans" could be a new nutritious food.

Fruits

Tree tomatoes, gooseberries, passionfruits, and tennis-ball-size "melons" called pepino were Inca foods. Today some of these fruits are showing up in our stores.

Cherimoya (cher ē moi′yə): Of all the Inca fruits, only the cherimoya is grown in North America. This fruit, prized by the Incas, is being grown in southern California. With its banana and pineapple flavor, it is thought by many to be the aristocrat of fruit. From December through May, you may find it in many markets and gourmet food stores.

A leading cherimoya grower in Carpinteria, California, began with seeds from a valley in Peru. Now he has thirty acres of orchard that he harvests weekly during the season, and his fruits are marketed nationwide.

In Spain and Chile, there are thousands of acres of cherimoya groves. The fruit is well known and much beloved. The United States, at last, is catching up and catching on to another nearly forgotten food of a remarkable, vanquished people.

Checking Comprehension and Skills

Thinking About What You've Read

1. What is the goal of food experts who are exploring the universe?
- 2. Find the sentence on page 498 that tells the main idea of the article, "Far Out Farms."
3. Name two ways in which food grown in space would be better for space travel than food grown on earth. Why?
4. Why are plant scientists at the Environmental Research Lab in Arizona developing taller plants?
- 5. State the main idea, found on page 502, of the article, "Gift of the Incas."
- 6. Give two examples of ancient foods that could help meet the world's growing need for nutritious food. Tell how each could be used.
7. Make a chart showing "new" foods. List each of four kinds in column 1. In column 2, list one or more examples of each kind.
8. What "new" food do you think you would like best? Give two reasons for your choice.
9. What do the experiments discussed in both articles have in common?

Talking About What You've Read

How would you persuade people to eat the "new" foods you have read about? Describe the foods mentioned in a way that will make them sound "good enough to eat."

Writing About What You've Read

Write a short dinner menu for the New Foods Restaurant. Your menu should list at least one appetizer, two main courses (meat or fish, vegetable, grain or root), and one dessert. For each "new" food, write a brief descriptive phrase or sentence.

- Comprehension Skill: Main idea—nonfiction

Thinking About the Section

In this section, you have read about several ways in which people are exploring the universe. The purpose of their activities is to try to improve the quality of life—that is, to make it safer, or healthier, to provide better places to live, and so on. Think about these activities again. Decide in what ways each one tries to improve the quality of life. Then copy the chart below onto a sheet of paper. Fill in the spaces by determining the benefits of each activity.

Exploring Outer Space	Exploring Weather Systems	Exploring New Sources of Food

Writing About the Section

Using information from the selections and from the chart, write a report on the following topic: How Exploration Helps Improve the Quality of Life. To help you organize your information, use the headings on the chart as the subtopics of your report. The information on the chart gives the details that you need to include to explain the subtopics. You may include any other information on this topic that you may know from other reading you have done.

12

Changes

Change takes many forms. Changes occur in nature—day turns into night, winter becomes spring. Changes happen in life—people can change their minds, their goals, their plans. Sometimes changes are unexpected; other times changes are carefully planned.

Several kinds of change are described in this section. A photographer changes her attitude as she learns about the elephants she is studying. Two myths, from different parts of the world, explain the change of season from winter to spring. A boy strives to tame a wild horse, and learns some difficult lessons about life from the changes that occur.

Making Generalizations

The top photo shows some live lobsters just caught. The bottom photo also shows a live lobster. No, it is not a trick photo. Once in about every 30 million births a change— or a mutation—occurs in lobsters. It results in a royal blue lobster. Other mutations produce tangerine red-, yellow-, and white-shelled lobsters. These mutations, like the royal blue lobster, are very rare. As you can see in the top photo, live lobsters are usually dark green or brown.

Once in a while, there is a surprising variation in the color of a lobster. Nevertheless, you can still make the general statement—or generalization—that *most* lobsters have dark green or brown shells. A **generalization** is a broad statement or a conclusion that is true for *most*—but not all—examples. A generalization is reached after thinking about a number of facts and what they have in common. Often a generalization is signaled by a clue word such as *most* or *usually*, as shown in the following examples. *Most* major league football players played football in high school or college. Schools *usually* close for two days at Thanksgiving. Other clue words that can signal a generalization are *many*, *some*, *few*, *sometimes*, *seldom*, *always*, *generally*, and *in general*.

A generalization that is supported by facts and by knowledge is called a **valid generalization.** A generalization that is not supported by facts and knowledge is a **faulty generalization.** Often a faulty generalization can be made valid by changing the clue word. "All lobsters have dark green or brown shells" is a faulty generalization. We know from the first passage on this page that some lobsters' shells are not dark green or brown. Changing *All* to *Most* makes the statement a valid generalization.

Being able to make valid generalizations based on your reading will help you to follow and judge an author's arguments. It will also help you to understand the meaning of facts in an article or a graph.

As you read the following article about other mutations, think about what you already know about changes in the plant and animal world and about the facts the author presents.

Mutation is a natural process. It happens to all kinds of living things. Normally, mutation produces tiny changes. If the changes help that kind of plant or animal to survive, they get passed on from generation to generation over a long time.

For example, most moths in one area of England used to be white. Then one gene of a moth mutated or changed. This moth produced offspring which were black. At first, there were only a few black moths. But when factories began to fill the air with black soot and smoke, the white moths were easy to spot by their enemies. So most of them got gobbled up. By and by, almost all the English moths left in this area were black.

Later, however, people cleaned up the air by controlling the smoke that factories put out, and the black moths became more visible to their enemies than the white ones. Many black moths were eaten up, and more white ones were left to reproduce. Today, most of the moths in that area of England are white again.

1. Which generalization can you make based on the information in the article (and your own knowledge)? Cite facts from the article to support the generalization.
   a. Usually more white moths survive than black moths.
   b. Moths that match their surroundings often live longer than moths that do not match.

To answer, look in the article for facts that could support each generalization. Ask yourself what facts the article contains to support generalization **a.** The passage describes one instance in which white moths lived longer than black moths and one in which black moths lived longer. The article does not provide any facts to support the survival of either group over the other on the basis of color. Thus the text does not support generalization **a**—it's a faulty generalization. In contrast, the text does support generalization **b.** The article describes how changing colors to match their surroundings helped both groups to survive.

2. Complete the following sentence by writing a generalization of your own based on the information in the article.

Sometimes mutations in nature can _____.

One generalization you could make after reading the article is that sometimes mutations in nature can be influenced by changes in the environment. You could cite the following facts from the article to support this generalization: The white moths were eaten up because they were easy to spot in the sooty, dark environment. Most of the moths that survived were black. When the air was cleaned up, the black moths were easy to see. Then more white ones were left to reproduce.

3. Based on the facts in the article, explain why the following generalization is valid or faulty: Air pollution always causes moths to change color.

Practicing Making Generalizations

Read the following article about how scientists can copy useful mutations. Think about what generalization you can make based on the facts in the article.

Scientists can sometimes speed up the natural process of mutation for animals and plants. They can create or copy useful mutations in their labs. Here's how it works.

All plants and animals are made up of cells. Each cell has thousands of genes. Genes contain the basic information that tells the cells how to grow. Genes tell a giraffe to be a giraffe and not a lemon. But sometimes a gene changes or mutates. It might cause a tomato to look like a square block instead of a round ball.

In fact, a few years ago, scientists found a tomato plant that was producing square-shaped tomatoes. These tomatoes didn't bruise as easily when they were picked by machines. And it would be easier to pack them in boxes to ship to tomato-canning factories.

So scientists wanted to produce more of these square tomatoes. They crossed one of the square tomatoes with a normal-shaped one. The first young tomatoes they got still looked round. But they had a hidden mutated gene for squareness. Then, by breeding these baby tomatoes with each other or their square parent, researchers created many more square-shaped tomatoes.

Of course, square tomatoes aren't sold in your market, but they may be hiding in your catsup.

1. Which generalization can you make based on the information in the article? Cite facts.
   a. Usually scientists can change the shapes of fruit.
   b. Sometimes square tomatoes are preferable to round ones.
   c. All kinds of fruit should be square.

2. Complete the sentence by writing a generalization of your own based on the information in the article. Cite facts.

   Sometimes scientists can create mutations that _____.

Tips for Finding and Making Generalizations
- Look for broad statements or conclusions that apply to many examples. These are generalizations.
- Look for clue words that signal generalizations: *most, many, usually, sometimes, few, seldom, all,* and *generally.*
- If a broad statement does not contain a clue word but a clue word could be added to the statement without changing its meaning, the statement is probably a generalization.
- To make a generalization, think about a number of specific examples and decide what they have in common.
- Decide whether the facts in the article support the generalization. If they do, the generalization is valid. If they do not, the generalization is faulty.
- Use your knowledge and reasoning as well as the facts in a selection to decide whether a generalization is valid or faulty.

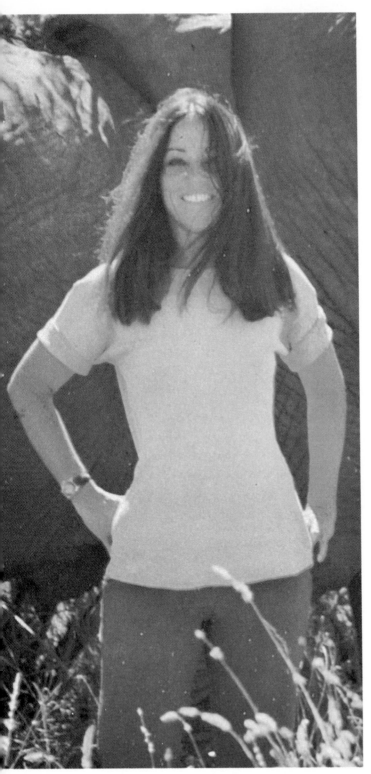

Imagine coming face to face with an elephant! Oria Douglas-Hamilton works to change her fear of elephants into a comfortable, confident ability to live and work among them. As you read, see what generalizations you can make about the elephants.

AMONG the ELEPHANTS

by Iain and Oria Douglas-Hamilton

Oria Douglas-Hamilton, a photographer, was born in Kenya, a country on the east coast of Africa. She grew up among the Masai (mä sī′) and at an early age was taught to hunt by a Masai warrior. She and her husband, Iain, a zoologist, moved to Lake Manyara (mən yär′ə) in Tanzania (tan′zə nē′ə) to study the elephants of East Africa in their natural habitat. This article tells how Oria Douglas-Hamilton began her work photographing the elephants.

I wanted to build a photographic story of individual elephants. First I would have to learn how to accept them and be accepted by them. I would have to recognize these elephants so that I could get to know which were the "goodies," the "heavies," and the "baddies." I wondered if this would be possible. If it were, then I could stay and work with the "goodies" on my own. This was my one chance to do something new and to get to know elephants really well.

It was quite simple, Iain explained. The "goodies" just lived their everyday lives, and anyone was safe with them. The "heavies" were certain big females and a couple of temperamental bulls. Their ferocious manner would make most people take flight, unless the people knew how to approach the elephants and knew what sort of things they disliked. No one could approach the "baddies." They would charge anyone coming within sight. I would just have to find out who was who.

Iain seemed to know exactly how far he could go with these elephants, but sometimes even he was surprised. I feared meeting any "baddies." Every time we drove through the south of the park and I heard an elephant trumpet, I was sure our jeep was a death trap unless we got out of there fast. But after following Boadicea (bō ad′ə sē′ə), one of the park elephants, and

her kinship group[1] for long periods together with Iain, I got to know her and other members of her family well. Each had its own personality. With more knowledge about elephants, I lost my fear of them.

Virgo and Right Hook were the first to help me lose my fear. Whenever we drove near the family, Virgo would come right up to us, flip her trunk back and forth, and stand at trunk's length from Iain.

At that time the trees were in fruit. Mhoja (mə hō′jə), a park ranger, and Iain gathered sacks full of various kinds of pods, hard fruit gardenia, and sweet dates to see which the elephants preferred. These were then spread out near the car. We were able to watch with fascination how fast Virgo could eat them and which fruits she chose first. If Right Hook or others were nearby, she could put three gardenias, which are bigger than tennis balls, into her mouth and keep another two in her trunk. She used a wrap-around hold, like a cupped

---

1. kinship group: African elephants live in herds made up of a number of families, each with several adults and their young. Female elephants are called cows, males are called bulls. Bulls mate with several cows and never stay with one cow and her young. Most herds are led by an old cow called a matriarch (mā′trē ärk).

hand over one's arm. Some pods were no bigger than dried-up beans. These were picked up one by one and blown into her mouth. Most elephants went through the same choosing and eating patterns. They chose the fruits they loved.

Whenever we met Virgo and had an odd gardenia fruit in the car, we gave it to her. This was certainly the beginning and the most exciting part of our making friends. We began to know her character really well and she trusted us.

Right Hook, Virgo's closest companion, became just as friendly in spite of the fact that we hardly ever gave her fruit after our experiments to find out about elephant eating patterns were over. She was quite different from Virgo, far less curious and less observant. Virgo made me feel as if she were watching us and, therefore, responded much more to our movements.

Iain decided the best places for my elephant-identification lessons were by the big pool and along the riverbed. He gave me his family-unit photo files from which I could pick out other well-known matriarchs of the elephant society, besides Boadicea. I hoped to become a sharp observer.

At first Iain or Mhoja accompanied me to the river to show me how to approach elephants on foot. Sometimes the wind blew up from the lake. This let us creep along the rocks until we were only a few feet away from them. But often the wind was tricky in the valley, suddenly changing direction. A knotted handkerchief, with ash in it, was the best wind indicator. It helped me to dominate my fear by forewarning me when the herd was likely to be driven away by my scent.

Mhoja built me a small hide[2] under a tamarind tree. It offered a patch of shade on the edge of the river. Here I could sit alone for as many hours as I wished. The hide was built of branches to make it look like a neighboring bush. Bald, egg-shaped rocks stuck out of the grass for me to sit on. In front of the hide, the river ran over a flat and sandy area. Here, if there was enough water, the elephants would often stop to drink or just stand around like people in a piazza. They murmured and leaned on one another as they watched their babies play with other youngsters.

The elephant I first recognized was a matriarch who arrived at an unhurried pace. She stopped a few

---

2. hide: an enclosure for observing animals without being seen.

feet away from my fragile shelter. Only my eyes moved. They went from the elephant to the photograph file and back to the elephant as I tried to identify her ears. She had crossed tusks and must therefore be one of three matriarchs—Sarah, Anita, or Anitoid. Only her ears could tell me which. Anita had a big notch in her right ear. Anitoid had a similar notch but with square instead of rounded edges. This elephant had a string of tiny holes on each ear. She was Sarah, with a family of twelve.

Sarah stood about ten feet high, on legs like pillars with cushioned feet. Each forefoot was adorned by five smooth hooflike nails and four on each hind foot. These thick nails gave the leading edge of her foot a hard and shiny appearance like well-polished shoe caps. Using the edge of the inner toenails, she scratched the side of her leg with great delicacy. Then as if the sole of her foot were itchy, she rubbed it over a rock. I caught a glimpse of the hard pad with its crisscross cracks. Iain told me these were different in every elephant, enabling skilled trackers to follow one particular elephant through the footprints of a herd. Sarah drank rhythmically, lifting her trunk from the water into her mouth and then letting it drop back into the water.

Next to her was another female who was eating the grass at the edge of the river. With her trunk she pulled one tussock at a time. Then she gave a forward kick with her foot, the toenails of which cut through the fibers as cleanly and efficiently as cutting hay with a scythe. Then she popped the little bunch of grass into her mouth. The roots were left in the ground so no earth got into her mouth.

Suddenly the wind changed. A whiff of my scent reached Sarah's trunk. She wheeled, and, within seconds, loomed up in front of me. She trumpeted and kicked up sand, shaking her head. Then she looked down as if she were aiming through the crossed tips of her tusks, searching for the intruder. I did not move. This giant animal was powerful, confident, and coordinated in her movements. There was a certain completeness about her. Then, quietly, looking like a grand woman who had been offended, Sarah moved away. She led her family past me toward the bush. The fifty-two thickly padded feet made hardly a sound.

Iain had warned me never to get overconfident, for one of these elephants could turn out to be a "baddie" I might not recognize in time. Then no hand-clapping or waving of my arms would keep her from carrying out her threat. For such an emergency I had a special rapid-exit path made behind the hide. From there I could hop over the rocks where she would not have a chance of catching up.

To get good photographs I had to figure out what the elephants were going to do seconds before it happened. The easiest thing in the world is to take an elephant's portrait when it is standing still. But for every good action picture or to catch the expression I wanted, hundreds of reject pictures piled up. In the end, I learned to sit for hours in the car or in my hide, with my camera at the ready, never getting bored, observing, waiting. I began to understand what they were doing, and why. This was my reward.

The first time I saw Boadicea at Ndala (eng däl'ə), not a single elephant or any other animal had been to the river during the whole of that day. I went back to camp for a drink. Then suddenly the whole riverbed was covered with snorting, rumbling elephants. None of us heard them come. There must have been about one hundred, including Boadicea's kinship group and several other families. They were strolling up on either side of the river. Instantly I picked out Leonora, Slender Tusks

with her son N'Dume (eng dü'mā) at her heels, and Jezebel with her family closely grouped around her. Boadicea was heading for the top pool. Virgo and Right Hook were walking together. There were some big bulls mingling with the families, and a lot of younger ones straggled behind. Overcome with excitement, I picked up my cameras and the ash bag and rushed down to my hide. I bent as I ran to keep myself hidden. The wind was blowing upstream toward the house, which was ideal.

I found myself in the middle of an elephant world, many of whose personalities I knew. It was like feeling the excitement of sitting in a theater just before the curtain goes up, watching the people arriving, recognizing some, and listening to the musicians tuning their instruments. I knew that all sorts of things were going to happen.

The families drifted slowly upstream until they reached the clear water. There were young bulls who dared not come too close to the females. They stood at the water holes where the river stopped flowing. At this season the water was only inches deep, and not all the elephants could use the top pool. I noticed for the first time how they began digging holes along the river's edge. The well diggers were usually bulls or old cows. Using their feet as shovels to loosen the earth, they kicked the sand backwards and forwards, until a wide hole was formed. At times they would dig down three feet or more with their trunks and feet, their toenails acting like a spade. They would push the sand with the side of a foot on to the curved end of the trunk, which they used like a cupped hand to throw the sand to one side. When the sand got damp and the water began to seep into the hole, they used the tips of their trunks, like fingers, to dig a deep, narrow, clean hole. From these holes, the elephants could drink clear water undisturbed by others. Wild elephants drink up to forty gallons of water daily. It was amazing how professional they were at their digging job. Within about a quarter of an hour, little wells had been dug all over the place, some only a few feet apart.

I could see how each family was organized within the hierarchy that Iain had told me so much about. Not

Family units mingle peaceably.

only was there competition between a mother and her young, but also between families.

On one side, Jezebel, the matriarch of her family, was drinking rhythmically from her well. Others were standing nearby sucking up trunkfuls at a time and then waiting for the water to seep back. Boadicea's family, having already drunk at the top pool, walked down to where Jezebel was drinking. With hardly a movement of her head, Boadicea took over from Jezebel and so did her family. Even though Jezebel's family had dug these holes, they just moved further up without a sign of annoyance and drank right from the river. Boadicea really was a queen whom all respected.

Elephant families walking up and down sometimes stopped to greet each other with their trunk to mouth gesture, while young babies walked up to a big bull and one by one greeted him. In return the bull put his trunk to each little mouth or touched the babies on their heads in the way in which Masai elders greet their children. A small cluster of elephants stood a little way from Boadicea waiting patiently for her to leave the water holes. Their trunks were slung over their tusks, or were just hanging like a length of hose from a fire engine. None showed any sign of aggression, except when the young bulls ventured too near. The only ones who never seemed to be able to get any water out of the holes were the smallest calves. They spent most of their time pushing, pulling, or walking around their mothers. The older calves either drank elsewhere or started digging holes themselves.

When Boadicea and her family had had their fill, they quietly ambled off to the flat piece of sand, where they threw trunkfuls of dust over themselves.

Covered in a rough loose-skinned armor the color of stones, rich in ivory, Boadicea's polished tusks stood out like weapons. I could imagine this great elephant preparing for battle. At one end hung a whiskered tail, sought after by humans for its few hairs to twist into a bracelet. At the other end hung that masterpiece of the elephant—the trunk. It must be great to have a body of that size and also to have a trunk to do all the work the body needs to keep it always full and clean. Partly lip and partly nose, with two fingers on the tip, it is used as a worker's arm and hand. It has double hoses for sucking in and spraying out water or dust, and can test the wind. It can push down trees or pick off the smallest leaf. It can be as gentle and as loving as the most tender arms, to greet and tickle, to scratch and rub, to smell and caress, always twisting, moving, rolling. At the same time, it can change into an efficient weapon. When it detects the smell of an enemy, it rears back above the head like a serpent preparing to strike.

I was relieved that Boadicea was not near my hide as I was sure she would have smelled me, chased me away, and emptied the whole riverbed of elephants at one signal. But when Right Hook and Virgo walked past me I wanted to go "psst" to attract Virgo's attention. We were daily becoming more friendly with her. I felt that soon we would be able to walk alongside her.

To get to know elephants' personalities, and to be able to sit quite confidently a few feet from them and not feel afraid, was one of the most exciting things about the whole study and our work.

A mother and her first calf

Checking Comprehension and Skills

Thinking About What You've Read

1. What change occurred in Oria Douglas-Hamilton's attitude toward the elephants?
2. What kind of work was Oria Douglas-Hamilton doing among the elephants?
• 3. Into what general categories did the Douglas-Hamiltons separate the elephants? Describe each.
4. How did Mhoja and Iain help Oria understand the elephants' behavior? Give three examples.
• 5. What is one generalization that you can make about the elephants' behavior? What facts support your answer?
6. What routine did Oria Douglas-Hamilton follow in order to get good photographs of the elephants?
7. How did her knowledge of the elephants help Oria Douglas-Hamilton overcome her fear? Give two examples.
8. What fact that you learned about elephants from reading this article was of great interest to you? Why?

Talking About What You've Read

Suppose you were going to interview Oria Douglas-Hamilton. What questions would you want to ask her about her experiences while living in the wild? What would you want to know about the elephants she studied? How do you think she would answer your questions?

Writing About What You've Read

Write five questions that you would like to ask Oria Douglas-Hamilton in an interview. Then write the answers that you would expect her to give.

• Comprehension Skill: Making generalizations

Our seasons continually change—from summer to fall . . . to winter . . . to spring . . . and back to summer again. Today we know why this happens. The ancient Greeks had an explanation of the change in seasons, too. Compare their explanation, given in this myth, with what we know today about why the seasons change.

Persephone and Demeter

A Greek Myth Retold by Ingri and Edgar Parin d'Aulaire

Thousands of years ago in the land of Greece people told each other stories about gods and goddesses. In many ways these Greek gods and goddesses were like people, but they were thought to have superhuman powers. They were taller, better-looking, stronger, and perfect in every way.

Zeus[1] was the most important of all the gods and goddesses. He headed a family of twelve major gods and goddesses. These were called the Olympians because they lived on top of Mount Olympus. No mortal, or human being, was able to go there, but the gods and goddesses often descended to Earth—sometimes in their own forms and sometimes disguised as humans or animals. Many of the stories about the gods and goddesses tell about such trips to Earth, where these immortals mingled with ordinary people.

Zeus had two brothers, one of whom was Hades.[2] He was ruler of the realm that bore his name. The Greeks believed that the dull, drab kingdom of Hades was located beneath the secret places of the Earth. Sooner or later all mortals went to Hades, from which there was no escape. Cerberus,[3] the three-headed, dragon-tailed dog with gnashing teeth, stood at the gates of the underworld.

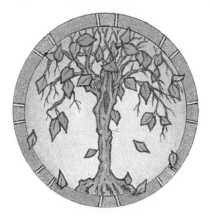

1. Zeus (züs).
2. Hades (hā′dēz′).
3. Cerberus (ser′ber əs).

Persephone[4] grew up on Olympus, and her laughter rang through the brilliant halls. She was the daughter of Demeter,[5] goddess of the harvest, and her mother loved her so dearly she could not bear to have her out of her sight. When Demeter sat on her golden throne, her daughter was always on her lap; when she went down to Earth to look after her trees and fields, she took Persephone. Wherever Persephone danced on her light feet, flowers sprang up. She was so lovely and full of grace that even Hades, who saw so little, noticed her and fell in love with her. He wanted her for his queen, but he knew that her mother would never consent to part with her, so he decided to carry her off.

One day as Persephone ran about in the meadow gathering flowers, she wandered away from her mother and the attendants. Suddenly, the ground split open. Up from the yawning crevice came a dark chariot drawn by black horses. At the reins stood grim Hades. He seized the frightened girl, turned his horses, and plunged back into the ground. A herd of pigs rooting in the meadow tumbled into the opening. Persephone's cries for help died out as the ground closed again as suddenly as it had opened. Up in the field, a little swineherd stood and cried over the pigs he had lost. Demeter rushed wildly about in the meadow, looking in vain for her daughter, who had vanished without a trace.

With the frightened girl in his arms, Hades raced his snorting horses down away from the sunlit world. Down and down they raced on the dark path to his grim underground palace. He led weeping Persephone in, seated her beside him on a throne of black marble, and decked her with gold and precious stones. But the jewels brought her no joy. She wanted no cold stones. She longed for warm sunshine and flowers and her golden-haired mother.

---

4. Persephone (pər sef′ə nē).
5. Demeter (di mē′tər).

Around the palace of Hades there was a garden where whispering poplars and weeping willows grew. They had no flowers and bore no fruit. No birds sang in their branches. There was only one tree in all of Hades that bore fruit. That was a little pomegranate tree. The gardener of the underworld offered the tempting pomegranates to the queen, but Persephone would not touch the food of the dead.

Wordlessly she walked through the garden at silent Hades' side. Slowly her heart turned to ice.

Above, on Earth, Demeter ran about searching for her lost daughter. All nature grieved with her. Flowers wilted, trees lost their leaves, and the fields grew barren and cold. In vain did the plow cut through the icy ground. Nothing could sprout and nothing could grow while the goddess of the harvest wept. People and animals starved. The gods begged Demeter again to bless the earth. But she would not let anything grow until she found her daughter.

Bent with grief, Demeter returned to the meadow where Persephone had vanished and asked the sun if he had seen what had happened, but he said, no, dark clouds had hidden his face that day. She wandered around the meadow and after a while she met a youth whose name was Triptolemus.[6] He told her that his brother, a swineherd, had seen his pigs disappear into the ground and had heard the frightened screams of a girl.

Demeter now understood that Hades had kidnapped her daughter, and her grief turned to anger. She called Zeus and said that she would never again make the earth green if he did not command Hades to return Persephone. Zeus could not let the world perish, and he sent Hermes[7] down to Hades, bidding him to let Persephone go. Even Hades had to obey the orders of Zeus, and sadly he said farewell to his queen.

---

6. Triptolemus (trip tol′ə məs).
7. Hermes (her′mēz): a god, the messenger for Zeus and the other gods.

Joyfully, Persephone leaped to her feet, but as she was leaving with Hermes, a hooting laugh came from the garden. There stood the gardener of Hades, grinning. He pointed to a pomegranate from which a few of the kernels were missing. Persephone, lost in thought, had eaten the seeds, he said.

Then dark Hades smiled. He watched Hermes lead Persephone up to the bright world above. He knew that she must return to him, for she had tasted the food of the dead.

When Persephone again appeared on Earth, Demeter sprang to her feet with a cry of joy and rushed to greet her daughter. No longer was she a sad woman, but a radiant goddess. Again she blessed her fields, and the flowers bloomed anew and the grain ripened.

"Dear child," she said, "never again shall we be parted. Together we shall make all nature bloom." But joy soon was changed to sadness, for Persephone had to admit that she had tasted the food of the dead and must return to Hades. However, Zeus decided that mother and daughter should not be parted forever. He ruled that Persephone had to return to Hades and spend one month in the underworld for each seed she had eaten.

Every year, when Persephone left her, Demeter grieved, nothing grew, and there was winter on Earth. But as soon as her daughter's light footsteps were heard, the whole earth burst into bloom. Spring had come. As long as mother and daughter were together, the earth was warm and bore fruit.

Demeter was a kind goddess. She did not want humankind to starve during the cold months of winter when Persephone was away. She lent her chariot, laden with grain, to Triptolemus, the youth who had helped her to find her lost daughter. She told him to scatter her golden grain over the world and teach people how to sow it in spring and reap it in fall and store it away for the long months when again the earth was barren and cold.

The Chippewa,[1] a large Native American tribe, also explained the change of seasons. As you read their myth, compare the explanation with that of the ancient Greeks.

Ice Man and the Messenger of Springtime

A Chippewa Myth Retold by Dee Brown

Ice Man was sitting in his birch-bark wigwam by the side of a frozen stream. His fire was almost out. He had grown very old and melancholy, and his hair was long and white. He was lonely, and day after day he heard nothing but the howling of winter storms sweeping snow across the land.

One day as his fire was dying to its last orange ember, Ice Man saw a young man approaching his wigwam. The boy's cheeks were red, his eyes shone with pleasure, and he was smiling. He walked with a light and quick step. Around his forehead was a wreath of sweetgrass, and he carried a bunch of flowers in one hand.

"Come in, come in," Ice Man greeted him. "I am happy to see you. Tell me why you come here."

"I am a messenger," replied the young man.

"Ah, then I will tell you of my powers," said Ice Man. "Of the wonders I can perform. Then you shall do the same." From his medicine bundle, the old man drew out a wonderfully carved pipe and filled it with aromatic leaves. He lighted it with one of the last coals from his dying fire, blew smoke to the four directions, and then handed the pipe to the young stranger.

After the pipe ceremony was concluded, Ice Man said, "When I blow my breath, the streams stand still and the water becomes hard and clear as crystal."

1. Chippewa (chip'ə wä, chip'ə wā, chip'ə wə).

"When I breathe," replied the young man, "flowers spring up all over the land."

"When I shake my long white hair," Ice Man declared, "snow covers the earth. At my command, leaves turn brown and fall from the trees, and my breath blows them away. The water birds rise from the lakes and fly to distant lands. The animals hide themselves from my breath, and the very ground turns hard as flint."

The young man smiled. "When I shake my hair," he said, "warm showers of soft rain fall upon the earth. The plants lift themselves with delight. My breath unlocks the frozen streams. With my voice I call back the birds, and wherever I walk in the forests their music fills the air." As he spoke, the sun rose higher in the sky and a gentle warmth came over the place. Ice Man sat silent, listening to a robin and a bluebird singing on top of his wigwam. Outside, the streams began to trickle, and the fragrance of flowers drifted on the soft spring breeze.

The young man looked at Ice Man and saw tears flooding from his eyes. As the sun warmed the wigwam, the old man became smaller and smaller and gradually melted completely away. Nothing remained of his fire. In its place was a small white flower with a pink border, the wild portulaca. People would call it Spring Beauty because it is among the first plants to signal the end of winter and the beginning of springtime.

Meet a Reader

Suzanne Turk enjoys myths because they are beautiful fantasy tales. She also finds the lessons to be learned in some myths interesting.

Suzanne likes animals. One of her pet cats owes its name to a character in a story that Suzanne had read in school. The story was about a girl named Karni, and Suzanne liked the name so much that she named her calico cat Karni.

Suzanne also has an English springer spaniel named Firebird. He has a shape on his neck and back which looks like a bird, and since her dog is a dark-red color, Suzanne named him Firebird.

Suzanne enjoys the life science classes at her school in Pennsylvania, where she is in the sixth grade.

Checking Comprehension and Skills

Thinking About What You've Read

1. How did the ancient Greeks explain the change from winter to spring?
2. What punishment did Demeter inflict on the earth because of Persephone's disappearance?
3. Did Zeus make the right decision in rescuing Persephone from the underworld? Why?
4. Why did Persephone have to return to the underworld for a few months each year?
5. How did the Ice Man feel about the arrival of the messenger?
6. Do you think the tears in the Ice Man's eyes were tears of happiness or sadness? Explain.
- 7. Compare what happened when the Ice Man and the messenger shook their hair, breathed, and spoke.
- 8. Complete the following analogy: Demeter is to spring, summer, fall as the Ice Man is to _____.
- 9. Compare the explanations of the ancient Greeks and the Chippewas about what causes the seasons to change.

Talking About What You've Read

What is the scientific reason for winter? What specific scientific facts about winter are explained by the myths you just read? Think of the part of each myth that explains each fact. Be prepared to list three facts and the mythical explanations of each of them. Can you make up your own myth to explain the season of winter?

Writing About What You've Read

Write the list of facts. Then write your own mythical explanations of these facts. If you expand your ideas, you could even write your own myth.

- Comprehension Skill: Comparison

Something Told the Wild Geese

by Rachel Field

Something told the wild geese
  It was time to go.
Though the fields lay golden
  Something whispered, "Snow."
Leaves were green and stirring,
  Berries, luster-glossed,
But beneath warm feathers
  Something cautioned, "Frost."
All the sagging orchards
  Steamed with amber spice,
But each wild breast stiffened
  At remembered ice.
Something told the wild geese
  It was time to fly—
Summer sun was on their wings,
  Winter in their cry.

Computer Literacy

Weather conditions, observations, and records for the United States are provided by the National Weather Service. The Weather Service analyzes these reports and makes forecasts with the aid of high-speed computers. Then the information is released to the public via TV, radio, and newspapers.

Computers handle data such as weather forecasts in the form of numbers. A computer program to change Celsius temperatures to Fahrenheit temperatures is given below. The directions are listed in a logical way. First, the question is asked, "What is the Celsius temperature?" Then you type the temperature you want converted. The Celsius temperature is converted to Fahrenheit. Note that the computer uses an asterisk (*) to show multiplication and a slash (/) to show division. The answer is given. Then the question is asked, "Do you want another problem?" The program begins again or ends, depending on your answer.

```
10 PRINT "WHAT IS THE CELSIUS TEMPERATURE?"
20 INPUT C
30 LET F = 1.8 * C + 32
40 PRINT F:
50 PRINT "IS THE FAHRENHEIT TEMPERATURE."
60 PRINT "DO YOU WANT ANOTHER PROBLEM (YES OR NO)?"
70 INPUT A$
80 IF A$ = "YES" THEN GOTO 10
90 END
```

Challenge problem: Can you write a program to convert Fahrenheit temperatures to Celsius? Hint: C = (F − 32)/1.8

When his parents let Ken choose Flicka for his very own horse, they don't realize the difficulty or the satisfaction that the choice will involve. Great changes for both the boy and his horse will result from Ken's struggle to tame Flicka. Read the story of a boy's love for his horse.

My Friend Flicka

by Mary O'Hara

Kennie McLaughlin lives on a ranch in Wyoming with his parents, Nell and Rob, his older brother, Howard, and the ranch hands, Gus and Tim. More than anything else in the world, Kennie wants a colt of his own. To encourage him to improve his schoolwork, his parents agree to let him choose one of the yearlings. He chooses a sorrel with a cream tail and mane and names her Flicka, Swedish for "little girl."

Flicka comes from a line of wild horses. Everyone tries to get Kennie to choose another yearling, one that will become a gentle pet, but Kennie is entranced by Flicka. When the horses on the range are rounded up and brought to the ranch, Flicka is to be separated from the rest so that she can be tamed.

The corral gates were closed, and an hour was spent shunting the ponies in and out through the chutes until Flicka was left alone in the small round corral in which the baby colts were branded. Gus drove the others away, out of the gate and up the saddleback.

But Flicka did not intend to be left. She hurled herself against the poles which walled the corral. She tried to jump them. They were seven feet high. She caught her front feet over the top rung, clung, scrambled, while Kennie held his breath for fear the slender legs would be caught between the bars and snapped. Her hold broke; she fell over backward, rolled, screamed, tore around the corral. Kennie had a sick feeling in the pit of his stomach, and his father looked disgusted.

One of the bars broke. She hurled herself again. Another went. She saw the opening and as neatly as a dog crawls through a fence, inserted her head and forefeet, scrambled through and fled away, bleeding in a dozen places.

As Gus was coming back, just about to close the gate to the upper range, the sorrel whipped through it, sailed across the road and ditch with her inimitable floating leap, and went up the side of the saddleback like a jack rabbit.

From way up the mountain Gus heard excited whinnies as she joined the band. He had just driven up, and the last he saw of them they were strung out along the crest, running like deer.

"Yee whiz!" said Gus, and stood motionless and staring until the ponies had disappeared over the ridge. Then he closed the gate, remounted Rob Roy, and rode back to the corral.

Rob McLaughlin gave Kennie one more chance to change his mind. "Last chance, Son. Better pick a horse that you have some hope of riding one day. I'd have got rid of this whole line of stock if they weren't so fast that I've had the fool idea that someday there might turn out one gentle one in the lot—and I'd have a race horse. But there's never been one so far, and it's not going to be Flicka."

"It's not going to be Flicka," chanted Howard.

"Perhaps she *might* be gentled," said Kennie; and Nell, watching, saw that although his lips quivered, there was fanatical determination in his eyes.

"Ken," said Rob, "it's up to you. If you say you want her, we'll get her. But she wouldn't be the first of that line to die rather than give in. They're beautiful and they're fast, but let me tell you this, young man, they're *loco*!"

Kennie flinched under his father's direct glance.

"If I go after her again, I'll not give up, whatever comes. Understand what I mean by that?"

"Yes."

"What do you say?"

"I want her."

They brought her in again. They had better luck this time. She jumped over the Dutch half door of the stable and crashed inside. The men slammed the upper half of the door shut, and she was caught.

The rest of the band were driven away, and Kennie stood outside of the stable, listening to the wild hoofs beating, the screams, the crashes. His Flicka inside there! He was drenched with perspiration.

"We'll leave her to think it over," said Rob, when dinnertime came. "Afterward, we'll go up and feed and water her."

But when they went back up afterward, there was no

Flicka in the barn. One of the windows, higher than the mangers, was broken.

The window opened into a pasture an eighth of a mile square, fenced in barbed wire six feet high. Near the stable stood a wagon of hay. When they went around the back of the stable to see where Flicka had hidden herself, they found her between the stable and the hay wagon, eating.

At their approach, she leaped away, then headed east across the pasture.

"If she's like her mother," said Rob, "she'll go right through the wire."

"Ay bet she'll go over," said Gus. "She yumps like a deer."

"No horse can jump that," said McLaughlin.

Kennie said nothing because he could not speak. It was, perhaps, the most terrible moment of his life. He watched Flicka racing toward the eastern wire.

A few yards from it she swerved, turned, and raced diagonally south.

"It turned her! It turned her!" cried Kennie, almost sobbing. It was the first sign of hope for Flicka. "Oh, Dad! She has got sense. She has! She has!"

Flicka turned again as she met the southern boundary of the pasture; again at the northern; she avoided the barn. Without abating anything of her whirlwind speed, following a precise, accurate calculation and turning each time on a dime, she investigated every possibility. Then, seeing there was no hope, she raced south toward the range where she had spent her life, gathered herself, and shot into the air.

Each of the three men watching had the impulse to cover his eyes, and Kennie gave a sort of a howl of despair.

Twenty yards of fence came down with her as she hurled herself through. Caught on the upper strands, she turned a complete somersault, landing on her back, her four legs dragging the wires down on top of her, and tangling herself in them beyond all hope of escape.

Kennie followed the men miserably as they walked to the filly. They stood in a circle watching while she kicked and fought and thrashed until the wire was tightly wound and knotted about her, cutting, piercing, and tearing great three-cornered pieces of flesh and hide. At last she was unconscious, streams of blood running on her golden coat and pools of crimson widening and spreading on the grass beneath her.

With the wire cutter which Gus always carried in the hip pocket of his overalls, he cut all the wire away, and they drew her into the pasture, repaired the fence, placed hay, a box of oats, and a tub of water near her, and called it a day.

"I don't think she'll pull out of it," said McLaughlin.

Next morning Kennie was up at five, doing his lessons. At six he went out to Flicka.

She had not moved. Food and water were untouched. She was no longer bleeding, but the wounds were swollen and caked over.

Kennie got a bucket of fresh water and poured it over her mouth. Then he leaped away, for Flicka came to life, scrambled up, got her balance, and stood swaying.

Kennie went a few feet away and sat down to watch her. When he went in to breakfast, she had drunk deeply of the water and was mouthing the oats.

There began then a sort of recovery. She ate, drank, limped about the pasture, stood for hours, with hanging head and weakly splayed-out legs, under the clump of cottonwood trees. The swollen wounds scabbed and began to heal.

Kennie lived in the pasture, too. He followed her around; he talked to her. He, too, lay snoozing or sat under the cottonwoods; and often, coaxing her with hand outstretched, he walked quietly toward her. But she would not let him come near her.

Often she stood with her head at the south fence, looking off to the mountain. It made the tears come to Kennie's eyes to see the way she longed to get away.

Still Rob said she wouldn't pull out of it. There was no use putting a halter on her. She had no strength.

One morning, as Ken came out of the house, Gus met him and said, "De filly's down."

Kennie ran to the pasture, Howard close behind him. The right hind leg, which had been badly swollen at the knee joint, had opened in a festering wound, and Flicka lay flat and motionless, with staring eyes.

"Don't you wish now you'd chosen Doughboy?" asked Howard.

"Go away!" shouted Ken.

Howard stood watching while Kennie sat down on the ground and took Flicka's head on his lap. Though she was conscious and moved a little, she did not struggle nor seem frightened. Tears rolled down Kennie's cheeks as he talked to her and petted her. After a few moments, Howard walked away.

"Mother, what do you do for an infection when it's a horse?" asked Kennie.

"Just what you'd do if it was a person. Wet dressings. I'll help you, Ken. We mustn't let those wounds close or scab over until they're clean. I'll make a poultice for that hind leg and help you put it on. Now that she'll let us get close to her, we can help her a lot."

"The thing to do is see that she eats," said Rob. "Keep up her strength."

But he himself wouldn't go near her. "She won't pull out of it," he said. "I don't want to see her or think about her."

Kennie and his mother nursed the filly. The big poultice was bandaged on the hind leg. It drew out much poisoned matter, and Flicka felt better and was able to stand again.

She watched for Kennie now, and followed him like a dog, hopping on three legs, holding up the right hind leg with its huge knob of a bandage in comical fashion.

"Dad, Flicka's my friend now; she likes me," said Ken.

His father looked at him. "I'm glad of that, Son. It's a fine thing to have a horse for a friend."

Kennie found a nicer place for her. In the lower pasture the brook ran over cool stones. There was a grassy bank, the size of a corral, almost on a level with the water. Here she could lie softly, eat grass, drink fresh running water. From the grass a twenty-foot hill sloped up, crested with overhanging trees. She was enclosed, as it were, in a green, open-air nursery.

Kennie carried her oats morning and evening. She would watch for him to come, eyes and ears pointed to the hill. And one evening Ken, still some distance off, came to a stop, and a wide grin spread over his face. He had heard her nicker. She had caught sight of him coming and was calling to him!

He placed a box of oats under her nose, and she ate while he stood beside her, his hand smoothing the satin-soft skin under her mane. It had a nap as deep as plush. He played with her long, cream-colored tresses, arranged her forelock neatly between her eyes. She was a bit dish-faced, like an Arab, with eyes set far apart. He lightly groomed and brushed her, while she stood turning her head to him whichever way he went.

He spoiled her. Soon she would not step to the stream to drink but he must hold a bucket for her. And she would drink, then lift her dripping muzzle, rest it on the shoulder of his blue chambray shirt, her golden eyes dreaming off into the distance, then daintily dip her mouth and drink again.

When she turned her head to the south, and pricked her ears, and stood tense and listening, Ken knew she heard the other colts galloping on the upland.

"You'll go back there someday, Flicka," he whispered. "You'll be three. You'll be so strong you won't know I'm on your back, and we'll fly like the wind. We'll stand on the very top where we can look over the whole world and smell the snow from Neversummer Range. Maybe we'll see antelope——"

This was the happiest month of Kennie's life.

With the morning, Flicka always had new strength and would hop, three-legged, up the hill to stand broadside to the early sun, as horses love to do.

The moment Ken woke, he'd go to the window and see her there, and when he was dressed and at his table studying, he sat so that he could raise his head and see Flicka.

After breakfast she would be waiting for him and the box of oats at the gate; and for Nell McLaughlin with fresh bandages and buckets of disinfectant; and all three would go together to the brook, Flicka hopping along ahead of them as if she were leading the way.

But Rob McLaughlin would not look at her.

One day all the wounds were swollen again. Presently they opened, one by one, and Kennie and his mother made more poultices.

Still the little filly climbed the hill in the early morning and ran about on three legs. Then she began to go down in flesh and almost overnight wasted away to nothing. Every rib showed; the glossy hide was dull and brittle, and was pulled over the skeleton as if she was a dead horse.

Gus said, "It's de fever. It burns up her flesh. If you could stop de fever, she might get vell."

McLaughlin was standing in his window one morning and saw the little skeleton hopping about, three-legged, in the sunshine, and he said, "That's the end. I won't have a thing like that on my place."

Kennie had to understand that Flicka had not been getting well all this time; she had been slowly dying.

"She still eats her oats," he said mechanically.

They were all sorry for Ken. Nell McLaughlin stopped disinfecting and dressing the wounds. "It's no use, Ken," she said gently. "You know Flicka's going to die, don't you?"

"Yes, Mother."

Ken stopped eating. Howard said, "Ken doesn't eat anything any more. Don't he have to eat his dinner, Mother?"

But Nell answered, "Leave him alone."

Because the shooting of wounded animals is all in the day's work on the Western plains, and sickening to everyone, Rob's voice, when he gave the order to have Flicka shot, was as flat as if he had been telling Gus to kill a chicken for dinner.

"Here's the Marlin, Gus. Pick out a time when Ken's not around and put the filly out of her misery."

Gus took the rifle. "*Ja*, Boss——"

Ever since Ken had known that Flicka was to be shot, he had kept his eye on the rack which held the firearms. His father allowed no firearms in the bunkhouse. The gun rack was in the dining room of the ranch house, and going through it to the kitchen three times a day for meals, Ken's eye scanned the weapons to make sure that they were all there.

That night they were not all there. The Marlin rifle was missing.

When Kennie saw that, he stopped walking. He felt dizzy. He kept staring at the gun rack, telling himself that it surely was there—he counted again and again—he couldn't see clearly—

Then he felt an arm across his shoulders and heard his father's voice.

"I know, Son. Some things are awful hard to take. We just have to take 'em. I have to, too."

Kennie got hold of his father's hand and held on. It helped steady him.

Finally he looked up. Rob looked down and smiled at him and gave him a little shake and squeeze. Ken managed a smile, too.

"All right now?"

"All right, Dad."

They walked in to supper together.

Ken even ate a little. But Nell looked thoughtfully at the ashen color of his face and at the little pulse that was beating in the side of his neck.

After supper he carried Flicka her oats, but he had to coax her, and she would only eat a little. She stood with her head hanging, but when he stroked it and talked to her, she pressed her face into his chest and was content. He could feel the burning heat of her body. It didn't seem possible that anything so thin could be alive.

Presently Kennie saw Gus come into the pasture, carrying the Marlin. When he saw Ken, he changed his direction and sauntered along as if he were out to shoot some cottontails.

Ken ran to him. "When you going to do it, Gus?"

"Ay was goin' down soon now, before it got dark——"

"Gus, don't do it tonight. Wait till morning. Just one more night, Gus."

"Vell, in de morning, den, but it got to be done, Ken. Yer fader gives de order."

"I know. I won't say anything more."

An hour after the family had gone to bed, Ken got up and put on his clothes. It was a warm, moonlit night. He ran down to the brook, calling softly, "Flicka! Flicka!"

But Flicka did not answer with a little nicker; and she was not in the nursery, nor hopping about the pasture. Ken hunted for an hour.

At last he found her down the creek, lying in the water. Her head had been on the bank, but as she lay there, the current of the stream had sucked and pulled at her, and she had no strength to resist; and little by little her head had slipped down until when Ken got there only the muzzle was resting on the bank, and the body and legs were swinging in the stream.

Kennie slid into the water, sitting on the bank, and he hauled at her head. But she was heavy, and the current dragged like a weight; and he began to sob because he had no strength to draw her out.

Then he found leverage for his heels against some rocks in the bed of the stream, and he braced himself against these and pulled with all his might; and her head came up onto his knees, and he held it cradled in his arms.

He was glad that she had died of her own accord, in the cool water under the moon instead of being shot by Gus. Then putting his face close to hers and looking searchingly into her eyes, he saw that she was alive and looking back at him.

And then he burst out crying, and hugged her, and said, "Oh, my little Flicka, my little Flicka."

The long night passed.

The moon slid slowly across the heavens.

The water rippled over Kennie's legs and over Flicka's body. And gradually the heat and fever went out of her. And the cool running water washed and washed her wounds.

When Gus went down in the morning with the rifle, they hadn't moved. There they were, Kennie sitting in water over his hips, with Flicka's head in his arms.

Gus seized Flicka by the head and hauled her out on the grassy bank, and then, seeing Kennie couldn't move, cold and stiff and half-paralyzed as he was, lifted him in his arms and carried him to the house.

"Gus," said Ken through chattering teeth, "don't shoot her, Gus."

"It ain't fur me to say, Ken. You know dat."

"But the fever's left her, Gus."

"Ay wait a little, Ken——"

Rob McLaughlin drove to Laramie to get the doctor, for Ken was in violent chills that would not stop. His mother had him in bed wrapped in hot blankets when they got back.

Ken looked at his father imploringly as the doctor shook down the thermometer.

"She might get well now, Dad. The fever's left her. It went out of her when the moon went down."

"All right, Son. Don't worry. Gus'll feed her, morning and night, as long as she's——"

"As long as I can't do it," finished Kennie happily.

The doctor put the thermometer in his mouth and told him to keep it shut.

All day Gus went about his work, thinking of Flicka. He had not been back to look at her. He had been given no more orders. If she was alive, the order to shoot her was still in effect. But Kennie was ill, and McLaughlin was taking the doctor home and wouldn't be back till long after dark.

After their supper in the bunkhouse, Gus and Tim walked down to the brook. They did not speak as they approached the filly, lying stretched out flat on the grassy bank, but their eyes were straining at her to see if she was dead or alive.

Flicka raised her head as they reached her. She dropped her head, raised it again, and moved her legs and became tense as if struggling to rise. But to do so she must use her right hind leg to brace herself against the earth. That was the damaged leg, and at the first bit of pressure with it, she gave up and fell back.

"We'll swing her on to the other side," said Tim. "Then she can help herself."

"Ja——"

Standing behind her, they leaned over, grabbed hold of her left legs, front and back, and gently hauled her over. Flicka was as lax and willing as a puppy. But the moment she found herself lying on her right side, she began to scramble, braced herself with her good left leg, and tried to rise.

"Yee whiz!" said Gus. "She got plenty strength yet."

"Hi!" cheered Tim. "She's up!"

But Flicka wavered, slid down again, and lay flat. This time she gave notice that she would not try again by heaving a deep sigh and closing her eyes.

Gus took his pipe out of his mouth and thought it over. Orders or no orders, he would try to save the filly. Ken had gone too far to be let down. "Ay'm goin' to rig a blanket sling fur her, Tim, and get her on her feet and keep her up."

There was bright moonlight to work by. They brought down a post-hole digger and set two aspen poles deep into the ground on either side of the filly, then with ropes attached to a blanket hoisted her by a pulley.

Not at all disconcerted, Flicka rested comfortably in the blanket under her belly, touched her feet on the ground, and reached for the bucket of water Gus held for her.

Kennie was sick a long time. He nearly died. But Flicka picked up. Every day Gus passed the word to Nell, who carried it to Ken. "She's cleaning up her oats." "She's out of the sling." "She bears a little weight on the bad leg."

Tim declared it was a real miracle. They argued about it, eating their supper.

"Na," said Gus. "It was de cold water washin' de fever outa her. And more dan dot—it was Ken—you tink it don't count? All night dot boy sits dere and says, 'Hold on, Flicka. Ay'm here wid you. Ay'm standin' by, two of us togedder——'"

Tim stared at Gus without answering while he thought it over. In the silence, a coyote yapped far off on the plains; and the wind made a rushing sound high up in the jack pines on the hill.

Gus filled his pipe.

"Sure," said Tim finally. "Sure. That's it."

Then came the day when Rob McLaughlin stood smiling at the foot of Kennie's bed and said, "Listen! Hear your friend?"

Ken listened and heard Flicka's high, eager whinny.

"She don't spend much time by the brook any more. She's up at the gate of the corral half the time, nickering for you."

"For me?"

Rob wrapped a blanket around the boy and carried him out to the corral gate.

Kennie gazed at Flicka. There was a look of marveling in his eyes. He felt as if he had been living in a world where everything was dreadful and hurting but awfully real; and *this* couldn't be real; this was all soft and happy, nothing to struggle over or worry about or fight for any more. Even his father was proud of him! He could feel it in the way Rob's big arms held him. It was all like a dream and far away. He couldn't, yet, get close to anything.

But Flicka—Flicka—alive, well, pressing up to him, recognizing him, nickering—

Kennie put out a hand, weak and white, and laid it on her face. His thin fingers straightened her forelock the way he used to do, while Rob looked at the two with a strange expression about his mouth, and a glow in his eyes that was not often there.

"She's still poor, Dad, but she's on four legs now."

"She's picking up."

Ken turned his face up, suddenly remembering. "Dad! She did get gentled, didn't she?"

"Gentle as a kitten——"

They put a cot down by the brook for Ken, and boy and filly got well together.

Meet the Author

Mary O'Hara had been a lover of horses ever since she was a child. Eventually she bought a ranch in Wyoming, where she could have her own beloved horses. It was at the ranch that O'Hara got the idea for *My Friend Flicka*, which first appeared as a short story in a magazine; then was expanded into a full-length book, which became a best-seller; and was later made into a popular movie. O'Hara wrote a sequel called *Thunderhead*. This, too, was made into a movie.

Thinking About the Section

Each of the selections in this section describes the unfolding of an event that brings about some kind of change. These are just the kinds of stories that make news headlines.

Suppose that the events outlined in the stories were going to be reported on the evening news broadcast and that you were the reporter sent to cover the stories. What are the important questions you would want to ask in each case? Remember that in order to get the whole story, a good reporter should ask who? what? when? where? and why?

Copy the chart below onto a sheet of paper. Fill in the boxes by answering the questions.

	"Among the Elephants"	"Persephone and Demeter"	"Ice Man and the Messenger"	"My Friend Flicka"
Who are the main characters?				
What events are important?				
When do they occur?				
Where do they occur?				
Why do they occur?				

Writing About the Section

Using the information on the chart above, write a one-paragraph summary of two of the stories. Your paragraphs will be read on the evening news update. Remember that a good summary contains only important information.

Books to Read

The Search for Delicious by Natalie Babbitt, Farrar, Straus © 1969

How can the king discover the real meaning of the word *delicious*? Following orders, Gaylen sets out to question all the king's subjects to find what they think it is. Amusing and adventurous situations crop up as Gaylen tries to uncover only one correct definition for delicious.

Mysteries of Outer Space by Franklin M. Branley, Dutton © 1985

How do you tell time in space? Can color be seen in space? Will space ever end? Find out these answers and many others as the renowned Dr. Branley questions and examines unusual ideas and attitudes about outer space.

What Do You Do When Your Mouth Won't Open? by Susan Beth Pfeffer, Delacorte © 1981

Reesa cannot speak in public. Reesa cannot even speak in class. What is Reesa going to do when she has to read her essay in front of 500 people? See how Reesa overcomes this lifelong fear in a humorous, but sensible, manner.

Balder and the Mistletoe by Edna Barth, Seabury © 1979

According to an old Norse myth, there once lived Balder, the beloved god of light and joy. His untimely death by a dart of mistletoe resulted in the seasons of fall and winter. Discover the significance of mistletoe in today's celebrations of winter holidays.

Word Study Handbook

On the next few pages are some of the strategies you've learned to figure out the meaning and pronunciation of words.

Phonics: Short Vowel Sounds

Strategy 1: I can use what I know about **short vowel sounds.**

> Say these words. Listen to the vowel sounds. What kind of letters are before and after the vowel in dark type in each word?
>
> | Short *a* | Short *e* | Short *i* | Short *o* | Short *u* |
> |-----------|-----------|-----------|-----------|-----------|
> | match | mess | wilt | spot | trudge |
> | panic | exist | pity | comment | muffler |
> | platter | inspect | impress | mascot | sudden |
> | absence | contents | attractive| occupy | adjustment|

Vocabulary and Skill Application

Use your word study strategy to figure out which word belongs in each sentence. Choose the word that makes sense and has the same short vowel sound as the word in parentheses.

1. She carried a bright red _____. (trudge)
   a. muffler   b. shrug   c. scarf

2. That book certainly needs an _____. (mess)
   a. existence   b. editor   c. interpreter

3. I didn't know he was planning to be a _____. (match)
   a. teacher   b. candidate   c. panic

4. There was no _____ that the Tigers would win the soccer game. (spot)
   a. possibility   b. hope   c. mascot

5. I couldn't hear the singer over the _____. (wilt)
   a. piano   b. benefit   c. din

6. Will you come when I _____? (mess)
   a. scream   b. beckon   c. exist

Phonics: Long Vowel Sounds

Strategy 2: I can use what I know about **long vowel sounds.**

Say these words. Listen to the vowel sounds. All have long vowel sounds. Which letter or letters stand for the vowel sound in each word?

Long *a*	Long *e*	Long *i*	Long *o*	Long *u*
taste	he	slide	stole	crude
slay	pity	light	expose	intrude
payment	feature	ideal	oath	humid
painful	foresee	occupy	vocal	nutrition

Vocabulary and Skill Application

Use your word study strategy to figure out which word belongs in each sentence. Choose the word that makes sense and has the same vowel sound as the word in parentheses.

1. Dressing in _____ helps keep a person warm. (taste)
   - a. winter
   - b. layers
   - c. payment

2. My friend and her mother _____ the house next door. (slide)
   - a. occupy
   - b. defy
   - c. rent

3. She _____ about her grades in school. (stole)
   - a. marks
   - b. oaths
   - c. boasts

4. Bill was employed to _____ the machinery. (taste)
   - a. maintain
   - b. waiter
   - c. oil

5. He dreaded the _____ of going to the dentist. (he)
   - a. thought
   - b. feature
   - c. ordeal

6. It was _____ to work with so much noise. (crude)
   - a. exclusive
   - b. futile
   - c. hopeless

7. She won a _____ for her swimming. (he)
   - a. prize
   - b. pastry
   - c. trophy

8. Antarctica is a _____ part of the world. (stole)
   - a. remote
   - b. local
   - c. distant

9. People have struggled long against the _____ forces of nature. (crude)
   - a. harsh
   - b. futile
   - c. brute

Phonics: R-Controlled Vowel Sounds

Strategy 3: I can use what I know about **r-controlled vowel sounds.**

Say these words. Listen to the vowel sounds. What letter comes after the dark vowel in each word?

ba**r**k	he**r**b	bi**r**th	sco**r**n	hu**r**l
cha**r**ge	ale**r**t	twi**r**ling	mo**r**sel	subu**r**bs
a**r**chitect	prese**r**ve	thi**r**sty	pe**r**fo**r**mance	discou**r**aged

Vocabulary and Skill Application

Use your word study strategy to figure out which word belongs in each sentence. Choose the word that makes sense and has the same vowel sound as the word in parentheses.

1. He looked in the refrigerator for a _____. (scorn)
   a. crumb   b. morsel   c. mortal

2. She _____ the key into the lock and opened the door. (herb)
   a. alert   b. inserted   c. put

3. The threat of rain _____ us from taking a long hike. (hurl)
   a. discouraged   b. journeyed   c. prevented

4. His arms were filled with _____ of groceries. (bark)
   a. parcels   b. bards   c. bags

5. The papers on Jim's desk were in an _____ arrangement. (scorn)
   a. ideal   b. orderly   c. ornamental

6. The ice skater received a _____ score for her spins. (herb)
   a. faultless   b. perfect   c. preferred

7. A sunny, mild day is _____ for tomorrow. (scorn)
   a. predicted   b. implored   c. forecast

8. I didn't eat enough breakfast, so I was _____. (bark)
   a. charging   b. hungry   c. starving

9. Tiffany's family made a _____ to see the mountains. (hurl)
   a. surge   b. journey   c. trip

10. Refrigeration helps to _____ fruits and vegetables. (herb)
    a. preserve   b. reserve   c. protect

Phonics: Vowel Sounds
Strategy 4: I can use what I know about **vowel sounds.**

Say these words. Listen to the vowel sounds. What letters stand for the vowel sound in each word?

snowmobile	void	haughty	coop	sprout
bellow	poised	daughter	tycoon	outrage
frown	annoying	straw	cook	cough
shower	loyalty	flaw	stood	mourn

Vocabulary and Skill Application

Use your word study strategy to figure out which word belongs in each sentence. Choose the word that makes sense and has the same vowel sound as the word in parentheses.

1. The children _____ at their new baby brother. (coop)
   a. cooed   b. murmured   c. bloomed

2. A _____ driver never drives too fast. (haughty)
   a. taut   b. cautious   c. careful

3. The ballerina _____ herself on her toes. (void)
   a. embroidered   b. poised   c. balanced

4. When Ted was angry, he seemed to _____. (snowmobile)
   a. frown   b. grow   c. bellow

5. The girl's constant coughing had become _____. (void)
   a. annoying   b. deploying   c. disturbing

6. We went to an amusement park on the _____ of town. (sprout)
   a. edges   b. outskirts   c. flour

7. Cindy _____ in the chair and watched TV. (straw)
   a. sat   b. bawled   c. sprawled

8. David likes to _____ quilts for his friends. (void)
   a. sew   b. embroider   c. poise

Phonics: Consonants and Context

Strategy 5: I can use what I know about **consonants and context.**

Read the sentence and the words. Which of the three words might make sense in the sentence? Which of the three words match the consonants in the unfinished word? Which of the words makes sense and has consonants that match those of the unfinished word? Look at the clue words, keeping it in reserve.

Some people h _ _ rd food in winter, keeping it in reserve.
    a. hoard   b. heard   c. hide

Vocabulary and Skill Application

Use your word study strategy to figure out which word belongs in each sentence. Choose the word that makes sense and has consonants that match the unfinished word.

1. The man used a f _ n _ _ l when he poured oil into his car.
    a. funnel   b. bottle   c. final

2. Becky peeked through her fingers and saw a h _ rr _ d green monster on the TV screen.
    a. hurried   b. horrid   c. horrible

3. It is dangerous to walk barefoot on j _ gg _ d rocks.
    a. jogged   b. pointed   c. jagged

4. The flower beds in the garden were l _ sh.
    a. lash   b. beautiful   c. lush

5. I was f _ _ _ sh _ d after not eating anything all day.
    a. starved   b. famished   c. finished

6. Amy's mother made her pick up the m _ ss in her bedroom.
    a. miss   b. garbage   c. mess

7. The b _ rd sang his own poems to the music of his harp.
    a. bard   b. beard   c. poet

Structure: Syllabication

Strategy 6: I can use what I know about **syllabication.**

A. When a word ends in a consonant and **–le,** divide before the consonant: fum·ble
B. When a word has two consonants between two vowels, divide between the two consonants: sud·den, com·bat
C. When a word has one consonant between two vowels, divide before or after the consonant: pan·ic, si·lent

---

Vocabulary and Skill Application

Use your word study strategy to choose the word that fits each sentence. Choose the word that makes sense and is divided like the word in parentheses.

1. A material familiar to nearly everyone is _____. (pan·ic)
   a. cotton   b. wool   c. denim

2. Melissa's room was a _____ of clothes, games, and toys. (fum·ble)
   a. challenge   b. jumble   c. clutter

3. The monkey swung, chattered, and performed other _____. (com·bat)
   a. capers   b. motions   c. antics

4. The family picked up their mail at the _____ post office. (si·lent)
   a. corner   b. local   c. second

5. One thing that might be handy on a camping trip is a _____. (com·bat)
   a. compass   b. cooler   c. table

6. Sandy fell asleep in the back seat because of the _____ of the car. (si·lent)
   a. motion   b. journey   c. engine

7. Listening to happy music is a way to _____ all cares. (pan·ic)
   a. forget   b. assure   c. banish

558

Structure: Prefixes and Suffixes

Strategy 7: I can use what I know about **prefixes and suffixes.**

A. Add the prefix **un–**   **un** + *tangle* = **un**tangle
B. Add the prefix **im–**   **im** + *possible* = **im**possible
C. Add the prefix **re–**   **re** + *arrange* = **re**arrange
D. Add the prefix **dis–**   **dis** + *courage* = **dis**courage

---

A. Add the suffixes **–able, –al, –ly, –er** without changing the root word:
   enjoy + **able** = *enjoy*able
   mechanic + **al** = *mechanic*al
   bitter + **ly** = *bitter*ly
   wait + **er** = *wait*er
B. Drop the **e** and add the suffix **–able:**
   advise + **able** = *advis*able
C. Change the **y** to **i** and add the suffix **–ly:**
   steady + **ly** = *steadi*ly

Vocabulary and Skill Application

For each underlined word, list the root word, prefix, and/or suffix.

1. Because the room was sparsely decorated, her footsteps began to resound.
2. David tried to untangle his socks as he dug impatiently through the drawer.
3. The composer worked steadily and created music of incomparable beauty.
4. Betsy felt disbelief when she saw that the vase was imperfectly fired and could not be used.
5. Showing no surprise, Chris received his award unemotionally.
6. David was uncertain about writing another book after his failure, but his publisher tried to reassure him.

Structure: Meaningful Word Parts

Strategy 8: I can use what I know about **meaningful word parts**.

> Look at these word parts. What do they mean?
>
> *domus* (house) *liber* (book) *scribere* (write)
> *tele* (at, over, from, or to a distance) *centi* (one hundred)
> *trans* (over, across, through) *geo* (of the earth)

Vocabulary and Skill Application

Complete each sentence by choosing the word that best fits. Use the underlined context words as clues.

1. A person who studies the physical nature and history <u>of the earth</u> is a _____ .
   a. telegrapher   b. centipede   c. geologist
2. A _____ has <u>one hundred</u> legs.
   a. centipede   b. millipede   c. caterpillar
3. With a _____ lens, a person can take pictures <u>at a distance</u>.
   a. postscript   b. telephoto   c. geography
4. The men needed to _____ the supplies <u>through</u> the tunnel.
   a. transport   b. trade   c. carry
5. Dogs make good <u>house</u> pets because they are easily _____.
   a. tamed   b. domesticated   c. sheltered

Etymologies: Word Histories

Strategy 9: I can use what I know about **word histories**.

See Skill Lesson: Learning About Word Histories on pages 302–303.

Word Study: Dictionaries

Strategy 10: I can use what I know about **dictionaries**.

See Skill Lesson: Finding Appropriate Meaning on pages 74–75.

Word Study: Context

Strategy 11: I can use what I know about **context**.

See Skill Lesson: Using Context to Figure Out Unfamiliar Words on pages 158–159.

Glossary

How to Use the Pronunciation Key

After each entry word in this glossary, there is a special spelling, called the **pronunciation.** It shows how to say the word. The word is broken into syllables and then spelled with letters and signs. You can look up these letters and signs in the **pronunciation key** to see what sounds they stand for.

This dark mark (′) is called the **primary accent.** It follows the syllable you say with the most force. This lighter mark (′) is the **secondary accent.** Say the syllable it follows with medium force. Syllables without marks are said with least force.

Full Pronunciation Key

a	hat, cap	**i**	it, pin	**p**	paper, cup	**ə**	stands for:
ā	age, face	**ī**	ice, five	**r**	run, try		a in about
ä	father, far			**s**	say, yes		e in taken
		j	jam, enjoy	**sh**	she, rush		i in pencil
b	bad, rob	**k**	kind, seek	**t**	tell, it		o in lemon
ch	child, much	**l**	land, coal	**th**	thin, both		u in circus
d	did, red	**m**	me, am	**ᴛʜ**	then, smooth		
		n	no, in				
e	let, best	**ng**	long, bring	**u**	cup, butter		
ē	equal, be			**u̇**	full, put		
ėr	her, learn	**o**	hot, rock	**ü**	rule, move		
		ō	open, go				
f	fat, if	**ô**	order, all	**v**	very, save		
g	go, bag	**oi**	oil, toy	**w**	will, woman		
h	he, how	**ou**	house, out	**y**	young, yet		
				z	zoo, breeze		
				zh	measure, seizure		

The contents of the Glossary entries in this book have been adapted from *Scott, Foresman Beginning Dictionary*, Copyright © 1983 Scott, Foresman and Company; *Scott, Foresman Intermediate Dictionary*, Copyright © 1983 Scott, Foresman and Company; and *Scott, Foresman Advanced Dictionary*, Copyright © 1983 Scott, Foresman and Company.

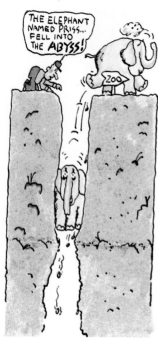

abyss

A

a·bate (ə bāt′), **1** make less; decrease. **2** become less; diminish: *Although the rain has abated somewhat the wind is still blowing very hard.* v., **a·bat·ed, a·bat·ing.**

a·byss (ə bis′), **1** a bottomless or very great depth; a very deep crack in the earth: *The mountain climber stood at the edge of a cliff overlooking an abyss four thousand feet deep.* **2** anything too deep or great to be measured. *n., pl.* **a·byss·es.**

ac·cus·tomed (ə kus′təmd), usual; familiar; customary: *By Monday I was well again and was back in my accustomed seat in class. adj.*

aer·i·al (er′ē əl *or* ar′ē əl), **1** a long wire or set of wires or rods used in television or radio for sending out or receiving electromagnetic waves; antenna. **2** having to do with or done by aircraft: *aerial photography.* **1** *n.,* **2** *adj.*

af·front (ə frunt′), **1** word or act intended to show disrespect; open insult: *To be called a coward is an affront.* **2** insult openly; offend purposely: *The boy affronted his sister by calling her names.* **1** *n.,* **2** *v.* [*Affront* came into English over 600 years ago from French *afronter,* meaning "to strike on the forehead."]

ag·gres·sion (ə gresh′ən), **1** the first step in an attack or a quarrel; unprovoked attack: *A country that sends its army to occupy another country is guilty of aggression.* **2** practice of making assaults or attacks on the rights or territory of others. *n.*

ag·i·tate (aj′ə tāt), **1** move or shake violently: *The slightest wind will agitate the leaves of some trees.* **2** disturb or excite very much: *He was agitated by the unexpected news of his friend's illness.* v., **ag·i·tat·ed, ag·i·tat·ing.** [*Agitate* comes from Latin *agitatum,* meaning "moved to and fro."] —**ag′i·tat′ed·ly,** *adv.*

ag·i·ta·tion (aj′ə tā′shən), a violent moving or shaking: *The agitation of the sea almost turned the little boat over. n.*

ag·ri·cul·ture (ag′rə kul′chər), farming; cultivating the soil to make the crops grow. *n.* [*Agriculture* comes from Latin *agricultura,* Latin *ager* meaning "field" and *cultura* meaning "cultivation."]

air·borne (er′bôrn′ *or* ar′bôrn′), supported by the air; off the ground: *Within seconds the plane was airborne. adj.*

a·lert (ə lėrt′), **1** keen and watchful; wide-awake: *A good hunting dog is alert to every sound and movement in the field.* **2** quick in action; nimble: *A sparrow is very alert in its movements. adj.* —**a·lert′ly,** *adv.*

a·light[1] (ə līt′), **1** get down; get off; dismount: *She alighted from the bus.* **2** come down from the air and lightly settle; come down from flight: *The bird alighted on our window sill.* v., **a·light·ed** *or* **a·lit** (ə lit′), **a·light·ing.** [*Alight*[1] comes from Old English *ālīhtan,* meaning "to get down."]

a·light[2] (ə līt′), **1** on fire; lighted: *Is the kindling alight?* **2** lighted up; aglow: *Her face was alight with happiness. adj.* [*Alight*[2] comes from Old English *ālīht,* meaning "lighted up."]

al·ter·nate (ôl′tər nāt *for 1,2;* ôl′tər nit *for 3,4*), **1** arrange by turns: *We alternated work and pleasure.* **2** take turns: *The two of us will alternate in setting the table.* **3** first one and then the other by turns. **4** every other: *Our dairy no longer delivers milk daily, but only on alternate days.* **1,2** *v.,* **al·ter·nat·ed, al·ter·nat·ing;** **3,4** *adj.*

al·ti·tude (al′tə tüd *or* al′tə tyüd), **1** height above the earth's surface: *What altitude did the airplane reach?* **2** height above sea level: *The altitude of Denver is 5300 feet. n.*

am·pu·tate (am′pyə tāt), cut off (all or part of a leg, arm, etc.) by surgery. v., **am·pu·tat·ed, am·pu·tat·ing.** [*Amputate* comes from Latin *amputatum,* meaning "cut around, pruned."]

an·ces·tor (an′ses′tər), person from whom one is descended, such as one's great-grandparents: *Their ancestors came to America in 1812. n.*

an·ces·tral (an ses′trəl), of or having to do with ancestors: *England was the ancestral country of the Pilgrims. adj.*

a·new (ə nü′ *or* ə nyü′), once more; again: *I made so many mistakes I had to begin the work anew. adv.*

an·noy·ance (ə noi′əns), **1** a feeling of uneasiness, irritation, etc. **2** something that angers, disturbs, or troubles: *The heavy traffic on our street is an annoyance. n.*

an·tic·i·pa·tion (an tis′ə pā′shən), a looking forward to; an expectation: *In anticipation of a cold winter, they cut extra firewood. n.*

an·ti·cli·max (an′ti klī′maks), an abrupt descent from the important to the unimportant. *n., pl.* **an·ti·cli·max·es.**

anx·i·e·ty (ang zī′ə tē), uneasy thoughts or fears about what may happen; troubled, worried, or uneasy feeling: *We* all felt anxiety when the airplane was caught in the storm. *n., pl.* **anx·i·e·ties.**

ap·pren·tice (ə pren'tis), **1** person learning a trade or art. In return for instruction the apprentice agrees to work for the employer a certain length of time with little or no pay. **2** beginner; learner. *n.*

ar·chi·tec·ture (är'kə tek'chər), **1** science or art of planning and designing buildings. **2** style or special manner of building: *Greek architecture made much use of columns. n.*

a·ris·to·crat (ə ris'tə krat), **1** person who has a high rank in society because of birth or title. **2** person like an aristocrat in tastes, opinions, and manners. **3** anything that has style or a grand manner. *n.*

ar·ti·fi·cial (är'tə fish'əl), **1** made by human skill or labor; not natural: *At night, you read by artificial light.* **2** made as a substitute or imitation; not real: *We made artificial paper flowers. adj.* —**ar'ti·fi'cial·ly,** *adv.*

as·sem·bly (ə sem'blē), **1** a coming together. **2** a putting together; fitting together: *the assembly of parts to make an automobile.* **3** the complete group of parts required to put something together: *the tail assembly of an airplane. n., pl.* **as·sem·blies.**

as·sim·i·la·tion (ə sim'ə lā'shən), **1** an absorbing or a being absorbed: *the assimilation of food.* **2** a making or a becoming like the people of a nation or a society in customs, viewpoint, character, etc. *n.*

as·sort·ment (ə sôrt'mənt), collection of various kinds: *These scarves come in an assortment of colors. n.*

ath·lete (ath'lēt'), person trained in exercises of physical strength, speed, and skill. Baseball players, runners, boxers, and swimmers are athletes. *n.* [*Athlete* comes from Greek *athlon,* meaning "a prize, a contest."]

at·tend·ant (ə ten'dənt), person who waits on another, such as a servant or follower; aide. *n.*

ax·is (ak'sis), a straight line about which an object turns or seems to turn. The axis of the earth is an imaginary line through the North Pole and the South Pole. *n.*

ax·le (ak'səl), bar or shaft on which a wheel turns. *n.*

az·ure (azh'ər), **1** the blue color of the unclouded sky. **2** having this color; sky-blue. **1** *n.,* **2** *adj.*

B

ban·ish (ban'ish), **1** force (a person) to leave a country; exile: *The king banished some of his enemies.* **2** force to go away; drive away; expel. *v.*

bard (bärd), **1** poet and singer of long ago: *The bard sang his own poems to the music of his harp.* **2** any poet. *n.*

bar·ren (bar'ən), **1** not able to produce offspring: *a barren fruit tree, a barren animal.* **2** not able to produce much: *a barren desert. adj.*

bar·ri·er (bar'ē ər), **1** something that stands in the way; something stopping progress or preventing approach; obstacle: *A dam is a barrier holding back water.* **2** something that separates or keeps apart. *n.*

ba·zaar or **ba·zar** (bə zär'), **1** street or streets full of small shops and booths in Oriental countries. **2** place for the sale of many kinds of goods. **3** sale of things contributed by various people, held for some charity or other special purpose. *n.* [*Bazaar* comes from Persian *bāzār.*]

be·drag·gled (bi drag'əld), **1** wet and hanging limp: *She tried to comb her bedraggled hair.* **2** soiled by being dragged in the dirt. *adj.*

ben·e·fit (ben'ə fit), **1** anything which is for the good of a person or thing; advantage: *Good roads are of great benefit to travelers.* **2** performance at the theater, a game, etc., to raise money for a worthy cause. *n.*

be·witch (bi wich'), put under a spell; use magic on; charm: *The wicked fairy bewitched the princess and made her fall into a long sleep. v.*

bore·dom (bôr'dəm), weariness caused by dull, tiresome people or events. *n.*

bow¹ (bou) **1** bend the head or body in greeting, respect, worship, or submission: *The people bowed before the queen. Let us bow our heads in prayer.* **2** a bending of the head or body in this way. **3** show by bowing: *The actors bowed their thanks at the end of the play.* **1,3** *v.,* **2** *n.*

bow² (bō), **1** a weapon for shooting arrows. **2** a slender rod with horsehairs stretched on it, for playing a violin, cello, etc. **3** to curve; bend. **4** something curved; curved part: *A rainbow is a bow.* **5** a looped knot: *The gift had a bow on top.* **1,2,4,5** *n.,* **3** *v.* —**bow'like',** *adj.*

bow³ (bou), the forward part of a ship, boat, or aircraft. *n.*

a hat	oi oil	ə stands for:
ā age	ou out	a in about
ä far	u cup	e in taken
e let	ù put	i in pencil
ē equal	ü rule	o in lemon
ėr term	ch child	u in circus
i it	ng long	
ī ice	sh she	
o hot	th thin	
ō open	ᴛʜ then	
ô order	zh measure	

bow² (def. 3) The branches were broken and **bowed** by snow and ice.

cascade

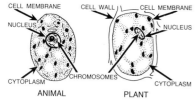

cell
two types, greatly magnified

centipede—about 1 in.
long

brag·gart (brag′ərt), person who brags; boaster. *n.*

brute (brüt), **1** an animal without power to reason. **2** like an animal; without power to reason. **3** a cruel or coarse person. **4** without feeling. 1,3 *n.*, 2,4 *adj.*

buf·fet (buf′it), knock about, strike, or beat back: *The waves buffeted the small boat. v.*

C

cal·ci·um (kal′sē əm), a soft, silvery-white metallic element. It is a part of limestone, chalk, milk, bone, shells, teeth, etc. *n.*

cal·en·dar (kal′ən dər), table showing the months, weeks, and days of the year. A calendar shows the day of the week on which each day of the month falls. *n.* [*Calendar* comes from Latin *kalendarium,* meaning "account book," *kalendae* calends (the day bills were due)]

cap·sule (kap′səl), **1** a small case or covering. Medicine is often given in capsules made of gelatin. **2** the enclosed front section of a rocket made to carry instruments, astronauts, etc., into space. *n.*

cas·cade (ka skād′), **1** a small waterfall. **2** fall, pour, or flow in a cascade: *The water cascaded off the roof in the thunderstorm.* 1 *n.*, 2 *v.*, **cas·cad·ed, cas·cad·ing.**

case[1] (kās), **1** any special condition of a person or thing; instance; example: *a case of poverty. A case of chicken pox kept me away from school.* **2** a matter for a court of law to decide: *The case will be brought before the court tomorrow. n.*

in any case, no matter what happens; anyhow. **in case,** if it should happen that; if.

case[2] (kās), **1** thing to hold or cover something: *a typewriter case.* **2** put in a case; cover with a case: *He cased the books for shipping.* 1 *n.*, 2 *v.*

cas·u·al (kazh′ü əl), **1** happening by chance; not planned or expected; accidental: *Our long friendship began with a casual meeting at a party.* **2** informal in manner; offhand: *Some people mistook his casual behavior for rudeness. adj.* —**cas′u·al·ly,** *adv.* —**cas′u·al·ness,** *n.*

cel·e·brate (sel′ə brāt), **1** observe (a special time or day) with the proper ceremonies or festivities: *We celebrated her birthday with cake, ice cream, and presents.* **2** praise; honor: *Her books are celebrated all over the world. v.,* **cel·e·brat·ed, cel·e·brat·ing.**

cel·e·bra·tion (sel′ə brā′shən), **1** special services or activities in honor of a particular person, act, time, or day: *A Fourth of July celebration often includes a display of fireworks.* **2** act of celebrating: *celebration of a birthday. n.*

cell (sel), **1** a small room in a prison, convent, or monastery. **2** the basic unit of living matter of which all plants and animals are made. *n.*

centi-, *combining form.* **1** 100: *Centigrade = 100 degrees.* **2** 100th part of: *Centimeter = 100th part of a meter.* [*Centi* comes from Latin *centum* meaning "hundred."]

cen·ti·pede (sen′tə pēd), a bug with many pairs of legs, the front pair of which are clawlike and contain poison glands. *n.* [*Centipede* comes from Latin *centipeda, centum* meaning "hundred," and *pedem* meaning "foot."]

cen·tu·ry (sen′chər ē), **1** each 100 years. **2** period of 100 years. *n.* [*Century* comes from Latin *centura,* meaning "hundred."]

char·ac·ter·is·tic (kar′ik tə ris′tik), **1** marking off or distinguishing one person or thing from others. **2** a special quality or feature; whatever distinguishes one person or thing from others; trait: *An elephant's trunk is its most noticeable characteristic.* 1 *adj.,* 2 *n.*

charge (chärj), **1** ask as a price; demand payment: *The grocer charged 75 cents a dozen for eggs.* **2** give a task, duty, or responsibility to: *My parents charged me to take good care of the baby.* **3** rush with force; attack: *A herd of elephants charged the hunters.* **4** an attack: *The charge drove the enemy back.* 1,2,3 *v.,* **charged, charg·ing;** 4 *n.*

clar·i·fy (klar′ə fī), make clearer; explain: *The teacher's explanation clarified the difficult instructions. v.,* **clar·i·fied, clar·i·fy·ing.**

clog (klog), fill up; choke up: *Grease clogged the drain. v.,* **clogged, clog·ging.**

cob·ble·stone (kob′əl stōn′), a naturally rounded stone formerly much used in paving. *n.*

col·lapse (kə laps′), **1** fall in; shrink together suddenly: *Sticking a pin into the balloon caused it to collapse.* **2** a falling in; sudden shrinking together: *A heavy flood caused the collapse of the bridge.* 1 *v.,* **col·lapsed, col·laps·ing;** 2 *n.*

col·lide (kə līd′), hit or strike violently together; crash. *v.* [*Collide* comes from Latin *collidere, com-* meaning "together" and *laedere* meaning "strike."]

co·los·sal (kə los′əl), of huge size; gigantic: *Skyscrapers are colossal structures. adj.*

com·mis·sion (kə mish′ən), **1** a written order giving certain powers, rights, and duties. **2** a written order giving rank or authority in the armed forces: *A captain in the United States Army has a commission signed by the President. n.*

com·mu·nal (kə myü′nl, kom′yə nəl), **1** of a community; public. **2** owned jointly by all; used or participated in by all members of a group or community. *adj.* —**com′mu·nal·ly,** *adv.*

com·mu·ni·ty (kə myü′nə tē), all the people living in the same place and subject to the same laws; people of any district or town: *This lake provides water for six communities. n., pl.* **com·mu·ni·ties.**

com·plaint (kəm plānt′), **1** a voicing of dissatisfaction; finding fault: *His letter is filled with complaints about the food at camp.* **2** a cause for annoyance: *Her main complaint is that she has too much work to do. n.*

com·pose (kəm pōz′), **1** make up; form: *The ocean is composed of salt water.* **2** put together. To compose a story or poem is to construct it from words. To compose a piece of music is to invent the tune and write down the words. To compose a picture is to arrange the things in it artistically. **3** make calm: *Stop crying and compose yourself.* **4** settle; arrange. *v.,* **com·posed, com·pos·ing.**

com·pul·sion (kəm pul′shən), **1** use of force; force: *A contract signed under compulsion is not legal.* **2** impulse that is hard to resist: *Some people have a compulsion to gamble. n.*

con·cept (kon′sept), idea of a thing or class of things; general notion; idea: *the concept of equal treatment under law. n.*

con·cep·tion (kən sep′shən), **1** idea; thought; notion: *Her conception of the problem was different from mine.* **2** act of forming an idea or thought. *n.*

con·fide (kən fīd′), **1** tell as a secret: *He confided his troubles to his brother.* **2** show trust by telling secrets: *She always confided in her friend. v.,* **con·fid·ed, con·fid·ing.**

con·flict (kon′flikt) a fight or struggle, especially a long one. *n.* [*Conflict* comes from Latin *confligere,* meaning "to clash."]

con·front (kən frunt′), **1** meet face to face; stand facing. **2** face boldly; oppose: *We crept downstairs with baseball bats in hand to confront the prowler.* **3** bring face to face: *The teacher confronted the student with his failing grade. v.*

con·serve (kən sėrv′ *for 1;* kon′sėrv′ *for 2*), **1** keep from harm or decay; keep from loss or from being used up;

preserve: *She conserved her strength for the end of the race.* **2** Often, **conserves,** *pl.,* fruit preserved in sugar, often as jam. **1** *v.,* **con·served, con·serv·ing; 2** *n.* —**con·serv′·er,** *n.* [*Conserve* comes from Latin *con servare, con* meaning "with" and *servare* meaning "to preserve."]

con·sist·en·cy (kən sis′tən sē), degree of firmness or stiffness: *Frosting for a cake must be of the right consistency to spread easily without dripping. n.*

con·ta·gious (kən tā′jəs), **1** spreading by contact; catching: *Mumps is a contagious disease.* **2** easily spreading from one person to another: *Yawning is often contagious. adj.* —**con·ta′gious·ly,** *adv.* —**con·ta′gious·ness,** *n.* [*Contagious* comes from Latin *con,* meaning "with" and *tag,* a form of *tangere,* meaning "to touch."]

con·temp·tu·ous (kən temp′chü əs), showing disdain; scornful: *a contemptuous look. adj.* —**con·temp′tu·ous·ly,** *adv.*

con·tents (kon′tents). See def. 1 of **content**[1]. *n.pl.*

con·tent[1] (kon′tent), **1** Often, **contents,** *pl.* what is contained in anything; all things inside: *The contents of the box fell out in my lap.* **2** facts and ideas stated; what is written in a book or said in a speech: *I didn't understand the content of her speech. n.*

con·tent[2] (kən tent′), **1** give satisfaction; please; make easy in mind: *Nothing contents me when I'm in a bad mood.* **2** satisfied; pleased; easy in mind; contented: *Will you be content to wait until tomorrow?* **1** *v.,* **2** *adj.*

coop (küp *or* kùp), a small cage or pen for chickens, rabbits, etc. *n.*

cop·per (kop′ər), **1** a reddish-brown metal, easy to work with. **2** a thing made of this metal such as a copper kettle. **3** reddish-brown. **1** *n.,* **2,3** *adj.*

cour·ti·er (kôr′tē ər), person often present at a royal court; court attendant. *n.*

crim·son (krim′zən), **1** a deep red. **2** deep-red. **1** *n.,* **2** *adj.*

cru·cial (krü′shəl), very important or decisive; critical: *This is a crucial game, for it will decide the championship. adj.* —**cru′cial·ly,** *adv.*

cul·ti·vate (kul′tə vāt), **1** prepare and use (land) to raise crops by plowing it, planting seeds, and taking care of the growing plants. **2** help (plants) grow by labor and care. *v.,* **cul·ti·vat·ed, cul·ti·vat·ing.**

cul·ture (kul′chər), **1** fineness of feelings, thoughts, tastes, manners, etc.; refinement. **2** growth of bacteria in a special medium for scientific use. *n.*

a hat	oi oil	ə stands for:
ā age	ou out	a in about
ä far	u cup	e in taken
e let	ù put	i in pencil
ē equal	ü rule	o in lemon
ėr term	ch child	u in circus
i it	ng long	
ī ice	sh she	
o hot	th thin	
ō open	ŦH then	
ô order	zh measure	

565

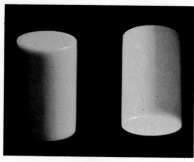

cylinders

cun·ning (kun′ing), **1** clever in deceiving; sly: *The cunning fox outwitted the dogs and got away.* **2** clever; skillful: *With cunning hand the sculptor shaped the little statue.* *adj.* —**cun′ning·ly,** *adv.*

cyl·in·der (sil′ən dər), **1** any long, round object, solid or hollow, with flat ends. Rollers and tin cans are cylinders. **2** a vessel or container having the form of a cylinder that may serve as the piston chamber of an automobile engine or the barrel of a pump. *n.*

D

dan·de·li·on (dan′dl ī′ən), a common weed with deeply notched leaves and bright-yellow flowers that bloom in the spring. *n.* [*Dandelion* comes from Middle French *dent de lion,* meaning "lion's tooth"; from its toothed leaves.]

de·ci·pher (di sī′fər), **1** make out the meaning of. **2** change (something in cipher or code) to ordinary language; decode: *The spy deciphered the secret message. v.*

de·fy (di fī′), **1** set oneself openly against (authority); resist boldly: *defy the law.* **2** withstand; resist: *Our boat defied the high waves. v.,* **de·fied, de·fy·ing.**

dem·on·strate (dem′ən strāt), **1** explain by carrying out experiments, or by using samples or specimens; show how (a thing) is done: *The science teacher demonstrated the use of a magnet in class.* **2** show the merits of (a thing for sale); advertise or make known by carrying out a process in public. *v.* **dem·on·strat·ed, dem·on·strat·ing.**

dem·on·stra·tion (dem′ən strā′shən), **1** a showing or explaining something by using samples or specimens. **2** a showing of the merits of a thing for sale: *the demonstration of a new vacuum cleaner. n.*

dense (dens), closely packed together; thick: *a dense forest, a dense fog. adj.,* **dens·er, dens·est.** —**dense′ly,** *adv.*

de·ploy (di ploi′), spread out or place (anything), especially in a planned or strategic position: *A fleet of ships was deployed over the area in which the astronauts were expected to land. v.* —**de·ploy′ment,** *n.*

der·rick (der′ik), **1** machine for lifting and moving heavy objects. A derrick has a long arm that swings at an angle from the base of an upright post or frame. **2** a towerlike framework over an oil well that holds the drilling and hoisting machinery. *n.*

derrick

des·ert[1] (dez′ərt), **1** a dry, barren region that is usually sandy and without trees. **2** not inhabited or cultivated; wild. 1 *n.,* 2 *adj.*

de·sert[2] (di zėrt′), go away and leave a person or a place, especially one that should not be left; forsake. *v.*

de·sert[3] (di zėrt′). Usually, **deserts,** *pl.* what one deserves; suitable reward or punishment. *n.*

des·ti·na·tion (des′tə nā′shən), place to which a person or thing is going or is being sent. *n.*

de·ten·tion (di ten′shən), **1** act of delaying; holding back: *They were held in detention at the border.* **2** a keeping in custody. *n.*

de·throne (di thrōn′), put off a throne or a high position; remove from ruling power: *The rebels dethroned the weak king. v.,* **de·throned, de·thron·ing.**

de·vot·ed (di vō′tid), very loyal; faithful: *devoted friends. adj.* —**de·vot′ed·ly,** *adv.*

di·a·gram (dī′ə gram), drawing or sketch showing important parts of something. A diagram may be an outline, a plan, a figure, a chart, or a combination of any of these, made to show clearly what something is, how it works, or the relation between the parts. *n.*

dis·cour·age (dis kėr′ij), **1** take away the courage of; lessen the hope or confidence of; dishearten. **2** try to prevent by disapproving; frown upon. **3** prevent or hinder. *v.*

dis·cour·age·ment (dis kėr′ij mənt), **1** condition of being or feeling discouraged. **2** something that discourages. **3** act of discouraging. *n.*

dis·in·fect·ant (dis′in fek′tənt), substance used to destroy disease germs. Alcohol and iodine are disinfectants. *n.*

dis·lodge (dis loj′), drive or force out of a place or out of a position, etc.: *She used a crowbar to dislodge a heavy stone. v.,* **dis·lodged, dis·lodg·ing.**

dis·po·si·tion (dis′pə zish′ən), one's habitual ways of acting toward others or of thinking about things; nature: *His cheerful disposition made him popular. n.*

dis·tinct (dis tingkt′), not the same; separate: *She asked me about it three distinct times. adj.* —**dis·tinct′ly,** *adv.*

dis·tort (dis tôrt′), **1** pull or twist out of shape; change the normal appearance of: *Rage distorted his face.* **2** to twist out of a natural, normal, or original condition or shape. *v.*

do·mes·tic (də mes′tik), of the home, household, or family affairs: *domestic problems, a domestic scene. adj.* [*Domestic* comes from Latin *domus,* meaning "house."]

dom·i·cile (dom′ə sīl), **1** a dwelling place; house; home. **2** place of permanent residence. A person may have several residences, but only one legal domicile at a time. **3** settle in a domicile. **4** dwell; reside: *They domiciled in Italy part of the year.* 1,2 *n.,* 3,4 *v.,* **dom·i·ciled, dom·i·cil·ing.** [*Domicile* comes from Latin *domus,* meaning "house."]

dom·i·nate (dom′ə nāt), control or rule by strength or power: *She spoke with the authority needed to dominate the meeting. v.,* **dom·i·nat·ed, dom·i·nat·ing.**

drone (drōn), **1** make a deep, continuous humming sound: *The bees droned among the flowers.* **2** talk or say in a monotonous voice: *Several people in the audience fell asleep as the speaker droned on. v.,* **droned, dron·ing.**

du·pli·cate (dü′plə kit *or* dyü′plə kit *for 1;* dü′plə kāt *or* dyü′plə kāt *for 2*), **1** one of two things exactly alike; an exact copy: *I mailed the letter, but kept a duplicate.* **2** make an exact copy of; repeat exactly: *duplicate a picture, duplicate a mistake.* 1 *n.,* 2 *v.,* **du·pli·cat·ed, du·pli·cat·ing.** [*Duplicate* comes from Latin *duplicatum,* meaning "made double," *du* meaning "two," and "plicare," meaning "to fold."]

dwell (dwel), make one's home; live: *They dwell in the city. v.,* **dwelt** or **dwelled, dwell·ing. —dwell′er,** *n.* **dwell on** or **dwell upon, 1** think, write, or speak about for a long time: *Her mind dwelt on the pleasant day she had spent in the country.* **2** put stress on: *The speaker dwelt on the great need for teachers.*

dy·nam·ic (dī nam′ik), **1** of energy or force in motion. **2** active; energetic; forceful: *a dynamic personality, dynamic weather patterns. adj.* **—dy·nam′i·cal·ly,** *adv.*

E

ec·o·log·i·cal (ek′ə loj′ə kəl *or* ē′kə loj′ə kəl), of or about the relationship of living things to their environment and to each other: *ecological studies. adj.* **—ec′o·log′i·cal·ly,** *adv.*

ed·i·tor (ed′ə tər), **1** person who prepares another person's writings for publication. **2** person in charge of a newspaper, magazine, etc.: *She is the editor of our school paper. n.* [*Editor* can be traced back to Latin *ex-,* meaning "out," and *dare,* meaning "to give."]

eer·ie (ir′ē), causing fear because of strangeness or weirdness: *a dark and eerie old house. adj.,* **eer·i·er, eer·i·est.** Also, **eery.**

ef·fi·cient (ə fish′ənt), able to produce the effect wanted without waste of time, energy, etc.; capable: *An efficient worker deserves good pay. adj.* **—ef·fi′cient·ly,** *adv.*

el·e·men·tar·y (el′ə men′tər ē *or* el′ə men′trē), of or dealing with the simple, necessary parts to be learned first; having to do with first principles: *Addition, subtraction, multiplication, and division are taught in elementary arithmetic. adj.*

em·bar·rass·ment (em bar′əs mənt), **1** condition of being self-conscious; uneasiness; shame: *He blushed in embarrassment at such a stupid mistake.* **2** thing that embarrasses: *Forgetting the name of an old friend is a great embarrassment. n.*

em·ber (em′bər), piece of wood or coal still glowing in the ashes of a fire. *n.*

em·broi·der (em broi′dər), **1** ornament (cloth, leather, etc.) with a pattern of stitches: *embroider a shirt with a colorful design.* **2** make (an ornamental design or pattern) on cloth, leather, etc., with stitches: *I embroidered silver stars on my blue jeans. v.*

en·force (en fôrs′), **1** force obedience to; cause to be carried out: *Monitors help enforce school regulations.* **2** compel: *We have laws to enforce people to pay income taxes. v.,* **en·forced, en·forc·ing. —en·force′a·ble,** *adj.*

en·light·en (en līt′n), give truth and knowledge to; inform; instruct: *The book enlightened me on the subject of medicine. v.*

en·rich (en rich′), make rich or richer: *An education enriches your mind. Adding vitamins or minerals to food enriches it. Fertilizer enriches the soil. v.*

en·to·mol·o·gy (en′tə mol′ə jē), branch of zoology that deals with insects. *n.*

e·qua·tion (i kwā′zhən), statement of the equality of two quantities. EXAMPLES: $(4×8) + 12 = 44$. $C = 2\pi r$. *n.*

es·sen·tial (ə sen′shəl), needed to make a thing what it is; very important; necessary: *Good food and enough rest are essential to good health. adj.*

a hat	oi oil	ə stands for:
ā age	ou out	a in about
ä far	u cup	e in taken
e let	ů put	i in pencil
ē equal	ü rule	o in lemon
ėr term	ch child	u in circus
i it	ng long	
ī ice	sh she	
o hot	th thin	
ō open	ŦH then	
ô order	zh measure	

eerie—an **eerie** face

embroider

exclamations

expedition
The **expedition** climbed the mountain peak.

falcon—Falcons are trained to perch on a glove or cover around the hand.

es·ti·mate (es′tə mit or es′tə māt for 1; es′tə māt for 2), **1** judgment or opinion about how much, how many, how good, etc.: *My estimate of the length of the room was 15 feet.* **2** form a judgment or opinion (about how much, how many, how good, etc.): *We estimated that it would take four hours to weed the garden.* 1 *n.,* 2 *v.,* **es·ti·mat·ed, es·ti·mat·ing.**

ex·cla·ma·tion (ek′sklə mā′shən), something said suddenly as the result of surprise or strong feeling. *Oh! Hurrah! Well!,* and *Look!* are common exclamations. *n.*

ex·er·tion (eg zėr′shən), strenuous action; strong effort: *Our exertions kept the fire from spreading. n.*

ex·ile (eg′zīl or ek′sīl), **1** force to leave one's country or home as a punishment; banish: *Napoleon was exiled to Elba.* **2** person who is exiled: *She has been an exile for ten years.* 1 *v.,* **ex·iled, ex·il·ing;** 2 *n.*

ex·ist (eg zist′), **1** having being; be: *Travel in space has existed for only a few years.* **2** be real; have being in space or time. *v.*

ex·ist·ence (eg zis′təns), **1** being: *When we are born, we come into existence.* **2** a being real: *Most people today do not believe in the existence of ghosts. n.*

ex·pe·di·tion (ek′spə dish′ən), journey for some special purpose, such as exploration, scientific study, or for military purposes. *n.*

ex·ploit (ek′sploit), a bold, unusual act; daring deed: *This book tells about the exploits of Robin Hood. n.*

ex·qui·site (ek′skwi zit or ek skwiz′it), very lovely; beautiful; delicate: *These violets are exquisite. adj.* [*Exquisite* comes from Latin *ex-,* meaning "out" and *quaerere,* meaning "seek."] —**ex′qui·site·ly,** *adv.*

ex·ten·sion (ek sten′shən), **1** a stretching out; a lengthening: *the extension of one's arm, the extension of a road.* **2** an enlarged part; addition: *The new extension to our school will make room for more students. n.*

F

fair[1] (fer or far), **1** not favoring one more than others; just; honest: *a fair judge.* **2** according to the rules: *fair play.* **3** not good and not bad; average: *a fair student.* **4** not dark; light: *A blond person has fair hair and skin.* **5** not cloudy or stormy; clear; sunny: *The weather will be fair today.* **6** pleasing to see; beautiful: *a fair lady.* **7** in a just manner; honestly: *to play fair.* 1–6 *adj.* 7 *adv.*

fair[2] (fer or far), **1** a showing of farm products and goods of a certain region: *Prizes were given for the best livestock at the county fair.* **2** a gathering of buyers and sellers, often held at the same time and place every year: *a trade fair, an art fair.* **3** sale of articles; bazaar: *Our school held a fair to raise money for library books. n.*

fal·con (fôl′kən, fal′kən, or fô′kən), **1** hawk trained to hunt and kill birds and small game. In the Middle Ages, hunting with falcons was a popular sport. **2** a swift-flying hawk having a short, curved bill and long claws and wings. *n.*

fam·ished (fam′isht), very hungry; starving: *We were famished after not eating anything for ten hours. adj.*

fa·nat·i·cal (fə nat′ə kəl), enthusiastic beyond reason; extremely eager. *adj.* —**fa·nat′i·cal·ly,** *adv.*

fare (fer or far), **1** the money that a person pays to ride in a taxi, bus, train, airplane, etc. **2** passenger. **3** food: *plain and simple fare.* **4** get along; get on; do: *She is faring well in school.* **5** turn out; happen: *It will fare hard with her if she ignores parking tickets.* **6** OLD USE. go; travel: *fare forth on a journey.* 1–3 *n.,* 4–6 *v.,* **fared, far·ing.**

fate (fāt), power supposed to fix beforehand and control what is to happen. Fate is beyond any person's control. *n.*

fa·tigue (fə tēg′), weariness caused by hard work or effort: *I felt extreme fatigue after studying for four hours. n.*

fe·ro·cious (fə rō′shəs), **1** very cruel; savage; fierce: *The bear's ferocious growl terrified the hunter.* **2** INFORMAL. intense: *a ferocious headache. adj.* —**fe·ro′cious·ly,** *adv.* —**fe·ro′cious·ness,** *n.* [*Ferocious* comes from Latin *ferocem,* meaning "fierce."]

fer·vent (fėr′vənt), showing great warmth of feeling; very intense; very earnest: *She made a fervent plea for more food and medical supplies for the earthquake victims. adj.* —**fer′vent·ly,** *adv.*

fes·ter (fes′tər), form pus; become poisoned or inflamed: *The neglected wound festered and became very painful. v.*

fidg·et (fij′it), move about restlessly; be uneasy: *Many people fidget if they have to sit still a long time. v.*

fi·nan·cial (fə nan′shəl or fī nan′shəl), **1** having to do with money matters: *Their financial affairs are in bad condition.* **2** having to do with the management of large sums of money. *adj.* —**fi·nan′cial·ly,** *adv.*

flange (flanj), **1** a raised edge or rim on a wheel used to keep it in place.

Railroad cars have wheels with flanges to keep them on the track. **2** something that braces or holds. *n.*

flaw (flô), a slight defect; fault; blemish: *A flaw in the dish caused it to break. n.*

flu·id (flü′id), any liquid or gas; something that will flow. Water, mercury, air, and oxygen are fluids. *n.*

for·mal (fôr′məl), **1** according to set customs or rules: *a formal invitation, a formal education.* **2** done with the proper forms; clear and definite. *adj.* —**for′mal·ly,** *adv.*

for·ti·fy (fôr′tə fī), build forts or walls to protect a place against attack. *v.* [*Fortify* comes from Latin *fortis,* meaning "strong," and *facere,* meaning "to make."]

for·tress (fôr′tris), place built with walls and defenses; large fort or fortification. *n., pl.* **for·tress·es.**

foun·da·tion (foun dā′shən), part on which the other parts rest for support; base: *the foundation of a house. n.*

frag·ile (fraj′əl), easily broken, damaged, or destroyed; delicate; frail: *Be careful; that thin glass is fragile. adj.* [*Fragile* comes from Latin *frangere,* meaning "to break."]

frank[1] (frangk), free in expressing one's real thoughts, opinions, and feelings; not hiding what is in one's mind; not afraid to say what one thinks; open: *She was frank in telling me that she did not like my new hat. v.* —**frank′ly,** *adv.* —**frank′ness,** *n.*

frank[2] (frangk), INFORMAL. frankfurter. *n.*

fret (fret), be peevish, unhappy, discontented, or worried: *The baby frets in hot weather. Don't fret over your mistakes. v.,* **fret·ted, fret·ting.**

fright·ful (frīt′fəl), **1** likely to frighten; dreadful; terrible: *a frightful experience.* **2** ugly; shocking. *adj.* —**fright′ful·ly,** *adv.*

fun·nel (fun′l), **1** a tapering tube with a wide, cone-shaped mouth. A funnel is used to prevent spilling in pouring liquids, powder, grain, etc., into containers with small openings. **2** anything shaped like a funnel: *a funnel of smoke. n.*

fu·tile (fyü′tl), not successful; useless: *He fell down after making futile attempts to keep his balance. adj.* —**fu′tile·ly,** *adv.*

G

gape (gāp), **1** open wide: *A deep hole in the earth gaped before us.* **2** open the mouth wide; yawn. **3** stare with the mouth open: *The crowd gaped at the daring tricks performed by the tightrope walkers. v.,* **gaped, gap·ing.**

geo-. *combining form.* earth; of the earth: *Geology = science of the (crust of the) earth.* [The form *geo-* comes from Greek *gē,* meaning "the earth."]

ge·og·ra·phy (jē og′rə fē), **1** study of the earth's surface, climate, continents, countries, peoples, industries, and products. **2** the surface features of a place or region: *the geography of Ohio. n.* [*Geography* comes from Greek *geōgraphia, gē* meaning "earth," and *graphein* meaning "describe."]

gnash (nash), strike or grind together: *I gnashed my teeth in rage. v.*

gos·sip (gos′ip), **1** idle talk, not always true, about other people and their private affairs. **2** repeat what one knows or hears about other people and their private affairs. **3** person who gossips a good deal. 1,3 *n.,* 2 *v.*

grief (grēf), great sadness caused by trouble or loss; heavy sorrow. *n.*

grove (grōv), group of trees standing together. *An orange grove is an orchard of orange trees. n.*

gul·ly (gul′ē), a narrow gorge; small ravine; ditch made by heavy rains or running water. *n., pl.* **gul·lies.**

gus·to (gus′tō), hearty enjoyment; keen relish: *The hungry boy ate his dinner with gusto. n.*

gy·ro·scope (jī′rə skōp), instrument consisting of a heavy, rotating wheel so mounted that its axis can turn freely in one or more directions. A spinning gyroscope tends to resist any change in the direction of its axis, no matter which way its base is turned. Gyroscopes are used to keep ships and airplanes steady. *n.*

H

hab·it (hab′it), tendency to act in a certain way; usual way of acting; custom; practice. *n.* [*Habit* comes from Latin *habere,* meaning "to have, hold."]

hab·i·tat (hab′ə tat), place where an animal or plant naturally lives or grows. *n.* [*Habitat* comes from Latin *habere,* meaning "to have, hold."]

hap·less (hap′lis), unlucky; unfortunate. *adj.* —**hap′less·ly,** *adv.* —**hap′less·ness,** *n.*

hatch[1] (hach), **1** bring forth (young) from an egg or eggs: *A hen hatches chickens.* **2** arrange; plan. **3** plan secretly; plot: *The spies hatched a scheme to steal government secrets. v.*

a hat	oi oil	ə stands for:
ā age	ou out	a in about
ä far	u cup	e in taken
e let	ù put	i in pencil
ē equal	ü rule	o in lemon
ėr term	ch child	u in circus
i it	ng long	
ī ice	sh she	
o hot	th thin	
ō open	ᴛʜ then	
ô order	zh measure	

funnel
funnel of a tornado

gape
the **gaping** mouth of a hippopotamus

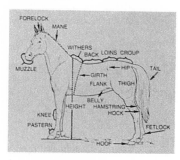

horse (def. 1)

hatch² (hach), **1** an opening in a ship's deck or in the floor or roof of a building, etc. A ship's cargo is loaded through the hatch. The escape hatch in an airplane permits passengers to get out in an emergency. **2** a trapdoor covering such an opening. *n., pl.* **hatch·es.**

haugh·ti·ly (hô′tl ē), in a scornful or overly proud manner: *glance haughtily. adv.*

heave (hēv), **1** lift with force or effort: *She heaved the heavy box into the station wagon.* **2** lift and throw: *The sailors heaved the anchor overboard.* **heaved** or **hove, heav·ing.**

heist (hīst), SLANG. **1** rob or steal. **2** a robbery or theft. **1** *v.,* **2** *n.*

heli-, *combining form.* spiral. [The form *heli-* comes from Greek *helikos,* meaning "a spiral."]

hel·i·cop·ter (hel′ə kop′tər), aircraft without wings that is lifted from the ground and kept in the air by horizontal propellers. *n.* [*Helicopter* comes from Greek *helikos,* meaning "a spiral," and *pteron,* meaning "wing."]

her·ald (her′əld), person who carries messages and makes announcements; messenger. In former times, a herald was an official who made public announcements and carried messages between rulers, etc. *n.*

he·red·i·ty (hə red′ə tē), **1** the passing on of physical or mental characteristics from parent to offspring by means of genes. **2** qualities of body and mind that have come to offspring from parents. *n., pl.* **he·red·i·ties.**

hi·er·ar·chy (hī′ə rär′kē), organization of persons or things arranged one above the other according to rank, class, or grade. *n.* [*Hierarchy* comes from a medieval Latin word *hierarchia,* and can be traced back to Greek *hieros,* meaning "sacred," and *archein,* meaning "to rule."]

hoard (hôrd), **1** save and store away: *A squirrel hoards nuts for the winter. The wealthy woman hoarded her money.* **2** what is saved and stored away; things stored: *They have a hoard of candy.* **1** *v.,* **2** *n.* —**hoard′er,** *n.*

hor·mone (hôr′mōn), substance formed in certain glands, which enters the bloodstream and affects or controls the activity of some organ or tissue. Adrenalin and insulin are hormones. *n.*

hor·ti·cul·ture (hôr′tə·kul′chər), **1** science or art of growing flowers, fruits, vegetables, and plants. **2** cultivation of a garden. *n.* [*Horticulture* comes from Latin *hortus,* meaning "garden," and English *culture.*]

horse (hôrs), **1** a large, four-legged mammal with solid hoofs, and a mane and tail of long, coarse hair. Horses are used for riding and for carrying and pulling loads. **2** a full-grown male horse. *n., pl.* **hors·es** or **horse.**

hu·mid (hyü′mid), slightly wet; moist; damp: *The air is very humid near the sea. adj.*

hum·mock (hum′ək), **1** a very small, rounded hill; knoll; hillock. **2** a bump or ridge in a field of ice. *n.*

I

i·de·al (ī dē′əl), **1** a perfect type; model to be imitated; what one would wish to be: *a person with high ideals.* **2** just as one would wish; perfect: *A warm, sunny day is ideal for a picnic.* **1** *n.,* **2** *adj.*

im·mi·gra·tion (im′ə grā′shən), **1** a coming into a country or region to live there: *There has been immigration to America from many countries.* **2** the persons who immigrate; immigrants: *The immigration of 1956 included many people from Hungary. n.*

im·plore (im plôr′), **1** beg earnestly for; plead. **2** beg (a person) to do something or not to do something: *I implored my parents to let me go on the trip. v.,* **im·plored, im·plor·ing.** —**im·plor′ing·ly,** *adv.*

im·pov·er·ished (im pov′ər isht), very poor; lacking wealth and resources. *adj.*

im·print (im′print), **1** mark made by pressure; print: *Your foot made an imprint in the sand.* **2** mark; impression: *Suffering left its imprint on her face. n.*

im·pu·ri·ty (im pyůr′ə tē), unclean thing; thing that makes something else impure or dirty: *Filtering the water removed some of its impurities. n., pl.* **im·pu·ri·ties.**

in·cip·i·ent (in sip′ē ənt), just beginning; in an early stage: *I hope this incipient cold doesn't become worse. adj.*

in·dom·i·ta·ble (in dom′ə tə bəl), that cannot be conquered; unyielding. *adj.* —**in·dom′i·ta·bly,** *adv.* [*Indomitable* comes from Latin *in,* meaning "not," and *domitare,* meaning "to tame."]

in·dus·try (in′dəs trē), any branch of business, trade, or manufacture: *the automobile industry. Industries dealing with steel, copper, coal, and construction employ millions of people. n., pl.* **in·dus·tries.**

in·jus·tice (in jus′tis), **1** lack of justice; being unjust. **2** an unjust act: *It is an injustice to send an innocent person to jail.* *n.*

in·sert (in sėrt′ *for 1;* in′sėrt′ *for 2*), **1** put in; set in: *He inserted the key into the lock. She inserted a letter into the misspelled word.* **2** something put in or set in: *The newspaper had an insert of several pages of pictures.* 1 *v.,* 2 *n.*

in·ser·tion (in sėr′shən), act of inserting: *The insertion of one word can change the meaning of a whole sentence.* *n.*

in·sist·ent (in sis′tənt), **1** continuing to make a strong, firm demand or statement: *In spite of the rain she was insistent on going out.* **2** impossible to overlook or disregard; compelling attention or notice; pressing; urgent: *Her insistent knocking on the door woke us up,* *adj.* —**in·sist′ent·ly,** *adv.*

in·spec·tion (in spek′shən), **1** a looking over; examination: *An inspection of the roof showed no leaks.* **2** a formal or official examination: *The soldiers lined up for their daily inspection by their officers.* *n.*

in·ter·mit·tent (in′tər mit′nt), stopping for a time and beginning again; pausing at intervals: *The pilot watched for an intermittent red light, flashing on and off every 15 seconds.* *adj.* —**in′ter·mit′tent·ly,** *adv.*

in·tern·ment (in tėrn′mənt), confinement within a country or place, especially during wartime. *n.*

in·tri·cate (in′trə kit), **1** with many twists and turns; puzzling, entangled, or complicated: *An intricate knot is very hard to tie or untie. A mystery story usually has a very intricate plot.* **2** very hard to understand; complicated: *The directions were so intricate that I made several errors.* *adj.* —**in′tri·cate·ly,** *adv.* [*Intricate* comes from Latin *in-,* meaning "in" and *tricae,* meaning "hindrances."]

in·trude (in trüd′), **1** force oneself in; come unasked and unwanted: *Do not intrude upon the privacy of your neighbor.* **2** thrust oneself in where one is uninvited or has no right to go. **3** thrust or force in or upon. *v.,* **in·trud·ed, in·trud·ing.** —**in·trud′er,** *n.* [*Intrude* comes from Latin *in-,* meaning "in" and *trudere,* meaning "to thrust."]

in·ves·ti·gate (in ves′tə gāt), look into thoroughly; search into carefully; examine closely: *Detectives investigate crimes to find out who did them.* *v.,* **in·ves·ti·gat·ed, in·ves·ti·gat·ing.**

in·volve (in volv′), **1** have as a necessary part, condition, or result; take in; include: *Housework involves cooking, washing dishes, sweeping, and cleaning.* **2** bring (into difficulty, danger, etc.): *One foolish mistake can involve you in a good deal of trouble.* **3** entangle; complicate: *Long, involved sentences are hard to understand.* **4** take up the attention of; occupy: *She was involved in working out a puzzle.* *v.,* **in·volved, in·volv·ing.**

ir·re·deem·a·ble (ir′i dē′mə bəl), **1** not able to be redeemed or bought back. **2** impossible to save; beyond remedy; hopeless: *an irredeemable error.* *adj.*

is·sue (ish′ü), **1** send out; put forth: *This magazine is issued every week.* **2** something sent out: *That newsstand sells the latest issues of all the popular magazines and newspapers.* 1 *v.,* **is·sued, is·su·ing;** 2 *n.*

J

jeep (jēp), a small, powerful, general-purpose motor vehicle in which power is transmitted to all four wheels. It was originally designed for use by the United States Army. *n.* [*Jeep* comes from a fast way of pronouncing the abbreviation *G.P.,* which stands for *General Purpose* Car.]

jos·tle (jos′əl), shove, push, or crowd against; elbow roughly: *We were jostled by the big crowd at the entrance to the circus.* *v.,* **jos·tled, jos·tling.**

K

kelp (kelp), **1** a large, tough, brown seaweed. **2** ashes of seaweed, used as a source of iodine. *n.*

ker·nel (kėr′nl), **1** the softer part inside the hard shell of a nut or inside of a fruit. **2** a grain or seed like that of wheat or corn. *n.*

kid·nap (kid′nap), steal (a child); carry off (a person) by force. *v.,* **kid·napped, kid·nap·ping** or **kid·naped, kid·nap·ing.**

L

lad·en (lād′n), **1** loaded; burdened: *a ship laden with goods.* **2** a past participle of **lade.** *The camels were laden with bundles of silk.* 1 *adj.,* 2 *v.*

la·goon (lə gün′), **1** pond or small lake connected with a larger body of water. **2** shallow water separated from the sea by low ridges of sand. *n.* [*Lagoon* comes from Latin *lacus,* meaning "a lake, pond."]

a hat	oi oil	ə stands for:
ā age	ou out	a in about
ä far	u cup	e in taken
e let	u̇ put	i in pencil
ē equal	ü rule	o in lemon
ėr term	ch child	u in circus
i it	ng long	
ī ice	sh she	
o hot	th thin	
ō open	ᵺ then	
ô order	zh measure	

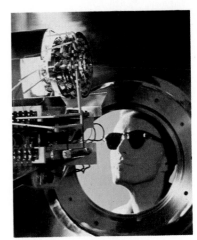

inspect—After this engine is tested and **inspected** it will be used in a spacecraft.

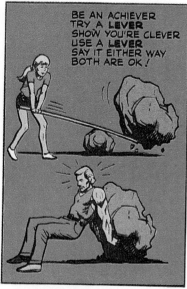

leverage

lead[1] (lēd), **1** show the way by going along with or in front of: *She led the horses to water.* **2** be first among: *She leads the class in spelling.* **3** guidance or direction; leadership: *The scientists followed the lead of the director of the expedition.* 1,2 *v.,* 3 *n.*

lead[2] (led), **1** made of lead: *a lead pipe.* **2** a long, thin piece of graphite used in pencils. 1 *adj.,* 2 *n.*

leg·ume (leg′yüm *or* li gyüm′), plant which bears pods containing a number of seeds. Beans and peas are legumes. Legumes can absorb nitrogen from the air. *n.*

lev·er·age (lev′ər ij *or* lē′vər ij), **1** advantage or power gained by using a lever. **2** a bracing against in order to increase power or force. *n.*

lev·i·tate (lev′ə tāt), rise or float in the air. *v.,* **lev·i·tat·ed, lev·i·tat·ing.** —**lev′i·ta′tion,** *n.*

lev·i·ty (lev′ə tē), lightness of mind, character, or behavior; lack of proper seriousness or earnestness: *Giggling in class shows levity. n., pl.* **lev·i·ties.**

li·brar·y (lī′brer′ē), collection of books, magazines, films, recordings, etc., either public or private. *n.* [Library comes from Latin *liber* meaning "book."]

li·bret·to (lə bret′ō), *n., pl.,* **-bret·tos, -bret·ti** (-bret′ē). **1** the words of an opera or other long musical composition. **2** book containing the words. [*Libretto* comes from Italian diminutive of *libro,* which comes from Latin *liber,* meaning "book."]

light[1] (līt), **1** that by which we see; form of radiant energy that acts on the retina of the eye. **2** cause to give light: *She lighted the lamp.* **3** set fire to: *She lighted the candles.* 1 *n.,* 2,3 *v.*

light[2] (līt), **1** easy to carry; not heavy: *a light load.* **2** having little weight for its size: *Feathers are light.* **3** easy to bear. *adj.*
light in the head, 1 dizzy. **2** silly; foolish. **make light of,** treat as of little importance.

loy·al·ty (loi′əl tē), loyal feeling or behavior; faithfulness. *n., pl.* **loy·al·ties.**

lush (lush), **1** tender and juicy; growing thick and green: *Lush grass grows along the river banks.* **2** characterized by abundant growth; producing abundantly. *adj.* —**lush′ly,** *adv.* —**lush′ness,** *n.*

lyr·ic (lir′ik), **1** a short poem expressing emotion. A love poem, a patriotic song, and a hymn might all be lyrics. **2** Usually, **lyrics,** *pl.* the words for a song. *n.*

M

mag·is·trate (maj′ə strāt), **1** a government official who has power to apply the law and put it in force. **2** a local government official with limited powers. *n.*

mag·net (mag′nit), stone or piece of metal that has the property, either natural or induced, of attracting iron or steel. *n.*

mag·net·ic (mag net′ik), having the properties of a magnet: *the magnetic needle of a compass. adj.* —**mag·net′i·cal·ly,** *adv.*

main·tain (mān tān′), **1** keep; keep up; carry on: *maintain a business, maintain a family.* **2** keep supplied, equipped, or in repair: *The company employs people to maintain the machinery. v.*

ma·lev·o·lent (mə lev′ə lənt), wishing evil to happen to others; showing ill will; spiteful. *adj.* —**ma·lev′o·lent·ly,** *adv.* [*Malevolent* comes from Latin *male,* meaning "badly," and *velle,* meaning "to wish."]

ma·ni·a (mā′nē ə), **1** kind of mental illness marked by great excitement and uncontrolled activity. **2** unusual or unreasonable fondness; craze: *a mania for dancing. n., pl.* **ma·ni·as.**

man·u·al (man′yü əl), of the hands; done with the hands: *manual labor; manual alphabet. adj.* —**man′u·al·ly,** *adv.*

mar·quee (mär kē′), a rooflike shelter over an entrance, especially of a theater or hotel. Theater marquees usually display the names of shows being featured. *n.*

mas·cot (mas′kot), animal, person, or thing supposed to bring good luck: *The team used a stray dog as a mascot. n.*

ma·tri·arch (mā′trē ärk), **1** mother who is the ruler of a family or tribe. **2** a highly respected elderly woman. *n.* [*Matriarch* comes from Latin *mater, matris* meaning "mother" + English *(patri)arch.*]

maze (māz), **1** network of paths through which it is hard to find one's way: *A guide led us through a maze of caves.* **2** confusion; muddle: *I couldn't find what I wanted in the maze of papers on the desk. n.* [*Maze* comes from Middle English *mazen,* meaning "to confuse."]

me·di·e·val (mē′dē- ē′vəl *or* med′ē- ē′vəl), of or belonging to the Middle Ages (the years from about A.D. 500 to about 1450). *adj.* Also, **mediaeval.**

mess (mes), **1** a dirty or untidy mass or group of things; dirty or untidy condition: *Please clean up the mess in your room.* **2** make dirty or untidy: *She messed up her book by scribbling in it.* **3** confusion or difficulty: *His business affairs are in a mess.* **4** make a failure of; spoil: *He messed up his chances of winning the race.* **5** an unpleasant or unsuccessful affair or state of affairs: *She made a mess of her final examinations.* **6** group of people who take meals together regularly, especially such a group in the armed forces. **7** meal of such a group: *The officers ate early mess.* 1,3,5-7 *n., pl.,* **mess·es;** 2,4 *v.*

me·te·or (mē′tē ər), mass of stone or metal that enters the earth's atmosphere from outer space with enormous speed; shooting star. Meteors become so hot from rushing through the air that they glow and often burn up. *n.*

me·thod·i·cal (mə thod′ə kəl), **1** done according to a plan; systematic; orderly: *a methodical check of one's work.* **2** acting according to a method: *A scientist is usually a methodical person. adj.* —**me·thod′i·cal·ly,** *adv.*

midst (midst), **1** the middle part; middle. **2** position or condition of being surrounded, especially by a number of persons: *a traitor in our midst, a stranger in their midst. n.*

mi·grate (mī′grāt), **1** move from one place to settle in another: *Pioneers from New England migrated to all parts of the United States.* **2** go from one region to another with the change in the seasons: *Most birds migrate to warmer countries in the winter. v.,* **mi·grat·ed, mi·grat·ing.**

mi·gra·tion (mī grā′shən), **1** a migrating. **2** number of people or animals migrating together. *n.*

min·now (min′ō), **1** a very small freshwater fish related to the carp. **2** any very tiny fish. *n., pl.* **min·nows** or **min·now.**

mi·nor (mī′nər), **1** less important; smaller; lesser: *a minor fault. Your paper is good; it contains only a few minor errors.* **2** person under the legal age of responsibility (18 or 21 years). **3** in music: **a** less by a half step than the corresponding major interval: *a minor chord.* 1,3 *adj.,* 2 *v.*

mi·rage (mə räzh′), an optical illusion, usually in the desert, at sea, or on a paved road, in which some distant scene appears to be much closer than it actually is. It is caused by the refraction of light rays from the distant scene by air layers of different temperatures. Travelers on the desert may see a mirage of palm trees and water. *n.*

mi·ser (mī′zər), person who loves money for its own sake; one who lives poorly in order to save money and keep it. *n.* [*Miser* comes from Latin *miser,* meaning "wretched, miserable."]

mi·ser·ly (mī′zər lē), of, like, or suited to a miser; stingy. *adj.*

mold¹ (mōld), **1** a hollow shape in which melted metal is poured to harden into shape. **2** the shape or form which is given by a mold. **3** make or form into shape. 1,2 *n.,* 3 *v.* Also, **mould.** —**mold′a·ble,** *adj.* —**mold′er,** *n.*

mold² (mōld), a woolly or furry growth, often greenish in color, that appears on food when left too long in a warm, moist place. *n.* Also, **mould.**

mold³ (mōld), loose earth; fine, soft, rich soil. *n.* Also, **mould.**

mon·u·ment (mon′yə mənt), something set up to honor a person or an event. A monument may be a building, pillar, arch, statue, tomb, or stone. *n.*

mor·sel (môr′səl), **1** a small portion of food. **2** piece; fragment. *n.*

mot·to (mot′ō), **1** a brief sentence adopted as a rule of conduct: *"Think before you speak" is a good motto. n., pl.* **mot·toes** or **mot·tos.** [*Motto* comes from Latin *muttum,* meaning "grunt, word."]

muf·fler (muf′lər), anything used to deaden sound. An automobile muffler, attached to the exhaust pipe, deadens the sound of the engine's exhaust. *n.*

mus·sel (mus′əl), shellfish which resembles a clam. Sea mussels have dark-blue shells and can be eaten. *n.*

muz·zle (muz′əl), **1** the nose, mouth, and jaws of a four-footed animal. **2** a cover or cage of straps or wires to put over the head and mouth of an animal to keep it from biting or eating. **3** put such a muzzle on. 1,2 *n.,* 3 *v.,* **muz·zled, muz·zling.**

N

nor′·east·er (nôr′ēs′tər), wind or storm that blows from the northeast. *n.* Also, **northeaster.**

nu·mer·ous (nü′mər əs *or* nyü′mər əs), **1** very many: *The child asked numerous questions.* **2** in great numbers. *adj.*

O

ob·struc·tion (əb struk′shən), **1** thing that blocks; something in the way; obstacle: *The old path was blocked by such obstructions as boulders and fallen trees.* **2** a blocking or hindering: *the obstruction of justice. n.*

a hat	**oi** oil	**ə** stands for:
ā age	**ou** out	a in about
ä far	**u** cup	e in taken
e let	**ú** put	i in pencil
ē equal	**ü** rule	o in lemon
ėr term	**ch** child	u in circus
i it	**ng** long	
ī ice	**sh** she	
o hot	**th** thin	
ō open	**ᵀH** then	
ô order	**zh** measure	

percussion

oc·cu·pant (ok′yə pənt), **1** one that takes up space in: *The occupants of the car stepped out as I approached.* **2** person in actual possession of a house, office, etc. *n.*

om·i·nous (om′ə nəs), unfavorable; threatening: *Those black clouds look ominous. adj.* —**om′i·nous·ly,** *adv.*

op·ti·mist (op′tə mist), **1** person who looks on the bright side of things. **2** person who believes that everything in life will turn out for the best. *n.*

or·der·ly (ôr′dər lē), **1** in order; with regular arrangement, method, or system: *an orderly arrangement of dishes on shelves, an orderly mind.* **2** keeping order; well-behaved or regulated: *an orderly class.* **3** a hospital attendant who keeps things clean and in order. 1,2 *adj.,* 3 *n., pl.* **or·der·lies.**

or·na·ment (ôr′nə mənt *for 1;* ôr′nə-ment *for 2*), **1** something pretty or decorative; something to add beauty: *Lace, jewels, vases, and statues are ornaments.* **2** add beauty to; make more pleasing or attractive; adorn; decorate. 1 *n.,* 2 *v.*

or·na·men·tal (ôr′nə men′tl), **1** of or for ornament; used as an ornament: *ornamental plants.* **2** decorative: *ornamental designs in wallpaper. adj.*

out·skirts (out′skėrts′), the outer parts or edges of a town, district, etc.; outlying parts: *We have a farm on the outskirts of town. n. pl.*

P

pad·dock (pad′ək), a small, enclosed field near a stable or house, used for exercising animals or as a pasture. *n.* [*Paddock* is a variant of *parrock,* which comes from Old English *pearroc.* Related to *park.*]

pag·eant·ry (paj′ən trē), a splendid show; gorgeous display; pomp. *n., pl.* **pag·eant·ries.**

palm¹ (päm), **1** the inside of the hand between the wrist and the fingers. **2** conceal in the hand: *The magician palmed the nickel.* 1 *n.,* 2 *v.*

palm² (päm), **1** any of a group of trees or shrubs which grow in warm climates. Most palms have tall trunks, no branches, and many large leaves at the top. **2** leaf or stalk of leaves of a palm tree, used as a symbol of victory or triumph. *n.*

pan·el (pan′l), a strip or surface that is different in some way from what is around it. A panel is often used for decoration. Panels may be in a door or other woodwork, on large pieces of furniture, or made as parts of a piece of clothing. *n.*

pan·to·mime (pan′tə mīm), **1** a play without words, in which the actors express themselves by gestures. **2** gestures without words. **3** express by gestures. 1,2 *n.,* 3 *v.,* **pan·to·mimed, pan·to·mim·ing.**

par·cel (pär′səl), **1** bundle of things wrapped or packed together; package: *She had her arms filled with parcels of gifts.* **2** lot; pack: *The peddler had a whole parcel of odds and ends in his sack. n.*

par·ti·cle (pär′tə kəl), **1** a very little bit: *I got a particle of dust in my eye.* **2** any of the extremely small units of matter of which all atoms are composed. *n.*

pas·try (pā′strē), pies, tarts, or other baked food made with dough rich in butter or other shortening. *n., pl.* **pas·tries.**

path·o·gen (path′ə jən), anything capable of producing disease, especially a living microorganism or virus *n.* [*Pathogen* comes from Greek *pathos,* meaning "disease."]

pa·tient (pā′shənt), having or showing a willingness to put up with waiting, pain, trouble, etc. *adj.* —**pa′tient·ly,** *adv.*

pat·tern (pat′ərn), **1** arrangement of forms and colors; design: *the pattern of a wallpaper.* **2** a model or guide for something to be made: *I used a paper pattern in cutting the cloth for my coat. n.*

peace (pēs), **1** freedom from strife of any kind; condition of quiet, order, and security. *n.* [*Peace* came into English over 800 years ago from French *pais,* which came from Latin *pax,* meaning "peace."]

at peace, 1 not in a state of war. **2** not quarreling.

hold one's peace, be silent.

-pede, *combining form.* footed: *centipede = hundred footed.* [-*pede* comes from Latin *pedem,* meaning "foot."]

ped·es·tal (ped′i stəl), **1** base on which a column or a statue stands. **2** base of a tall vase or lamp. *n.* [*Pedestal* comes from Middle French *piedestall* and from Italian *piedestallo, pie di stallo,* meaning "foot of stall."]

place on a pedestal, accord a very high place to; idolize.

per·cus·sion (pər kush′ən), the striking of one body against another with force; stroke; blow. A percussion instrument, such as a drum or cymbal, is played by striking it to produce tones. *n.*

per·se·ver·ance (pėr′sə vir′əns), a sticking to a purpose or an aim; never giving up what one has set out to do: *By perseverance I finally learned to swim. n.*

pet·ri·fy (pet′rə fī), **1** turn into stone. **2** paralyze with fear, horror, or surprise.

v. [*Petrify* comes from the Greek *petra*, meaning "rock."]

petro-, *combining form.* **1** rock; rocks, as in *petrology*. **2** petroleum, as in *petrochemical*. [*Petro-* comes from Greek *petra*, meaning "rock."]

phan·tom (fan'təm), **1** image in the mind which seems to be real: *phantoms of a dream*. **2** a vague, dim, or shadowy appearance; ghost. *n.*

phar·ma·cy (fär'mə sē), store where drugs and medicines are prepared or sold. *n., pl.* **phar·ma·cies.** [*Pharmacy* comes from Greek *pharmakon*, meaning "medicine."]

phys·i·cal (fiz'ə kəl), **1** of the body: *physical exercise, physical strength*. **2** of matter; material: *The tide is a physical force. adj.* —**phys'i·cal·ly**, *adv.* [*Physical* comes from Latin *physica*, meaning "natural science," which comes from Greek *phyein*, meaning "produce."]

phys·ics (fiz'iks), science that deals with matter and energy and the relationships between them. Physics includes the study of mechanics, heat, light, sound, electricity, magnetism, and atomic energy. *n.*

pi·az·za (pē az'ə *for 1;* pē ät'sə *or* pē-az'ə *for 2*), **1** a large porch along one or more sides of a house. **2** an open public square in Italian towns; courtyard. *n., pl.* **pi·az·zas.**

pil·lar (pil'ər), **1** a slender, upright structure; column. Pillars are used as supports or ornaments for a building. **2** anything slender and upright like a pillar. *n.*

plat·form (plat'fôrm), **1** a raised level surface. There usually is a platform beside the track at a railroad station. A hall usually has a platform for speakers. **2** any horizontal flat surface, usually higher than the surrounding area. *n.*

plat·ter (plat'ər), a large, shallow dish for holding or serving food, especially meat and fish. *n.*

plunge (plunj), **1** throw or thrust with force into a liquid, place, or condition: *plunge one's hand into water*. **2** throw oneself (into water, danger, a fight, etc.): *She plunged into the lake to save the drowning swimmer. v.,* **plunged, plung·ing.**

point (point), **1** a sharp end. **2** a tiny round mark; a punctuation mark; dot. **3** direct (a finger, weapon, etc.); aim: *Point the arrow at the target.* **1,2** *n.,* **3** *v.* [*Point* comes from Latin *pungere*, meaning "to pierce, prick."]

poise (poiz), **1** mental balance, composure, or self-possession: *He has perfect poise and never seems embarrassed*. **2** the way in which the body, head, etc., are held; carriage.

3 balance: *Poise yourself on your toes.* **1,2** *n.,* **3** *v.,* **poised, pois·ing.**

pol·lu·tant (pə lüt'nt), something that pollutes, *n.*

pol·lute (pə lüt'), make dirty; defile: *The water at the beach was polluted by refuse. v.,* **pol·lut·ed, pol·lut·ing.** [*Pollute* comes from Latin *pollutum*, meaning "soiled."]

pome·gran·ate (pom'gran'it), the reddish-yellow fruit of a small tree. It has thick skin, and red pulp and seeds having a pleasant, slightly sour taste. *n.*

pop·u·lar (pop'yə lər), **1** liked by most people. **2** of the people. *adj.* [*Popular* comes from Latin *populus*, meaning "people."]

pop·u·la·tion (pop'yə lā'shən), people of a city, country, or district. *n.* [*Population* comes from Latin *populus*, meaning "people."]

por·ce·lain (pôr'sə lin), very fine earthenware; china: *Teacups are often made of porcelain. n.*

pos·si·bil·i·ty (pos'ə bil'ə tē), something that may exist, happen, or be done under certain conditions or circumstances: *There is a possibility that the train may be late. n., pl.* **pos·si·bil·i·ties.**

poul·tice (pōl'tis), a soft, moist mass of mustard, herbs, etc., applied to the body as a medicine. *n.*

pre·scribe (pri skrīb'), **1** lay down as a rule to be followed; order, direct: *Good citizens do what the laws prescribe.* **2** order as a medicine or treatment: *The doctor prescribed penicillin.* **3** give medical advice; issue a prescription. *v.,* **pre·scribed, pre·scrib·ing,** —**pre·scrib'er**, *n.* [*Prescribe* comes from Latin *prae-*, meaning "before," and *scribere*, meaning "write."]

pred·e·ces·sor (pred'ə ses'ər), **1** person holding a position or office before another. **2** thing that came ahead of or earlier than another. *n.*

pre·oc·cu·py (prē ok'yə pī), take up all the attention of; absorb: *The problem of how to pay her debts preoccupied her mind. v.,* **pre·oc·cu·pied, pre·oc·cu·py·ing.**

pres·ent¹ (prez'nt), **1** being in the place or thing in question; at hand, not absent. **2** at this time; being or occurring now. *adj.*

pre·sent² (pri zent' *for 1;* prez'nt *for 2*), **1** give: *They presented flowers to their teacher.* **2** thing given; gift: *a birthday present.* **1** *v.,* **2** *n.*

pre·serve (pri zėrv'), **1** keep from harm or change; keep safe; protect. **2** keep up; maintain. *v.,* **pre·served, pre·serv·ing.**

a hat	**oi** oil	**ə** stands for:
ā age	**ou** out	a in about
ä far	**u** cup	e in taken
e let	**u̇** put	i in pencil
ē equal	**ü** rule	o in lemon
ėr term	**ch** child	u in circus
i it	**ng** long	
ī ice	**sh** she	
o hot	**th** thin	
ō open	**ᴛʜ** then	
ô order	**zh** measure	

primitive
Primitive cave dwellers drew this picture on a cave wall.

pupa of a butterfly

pri·mar·y (prī′mer′ē), **1** first in time or order; original; fundamental: *the primary causes of unemployment.* **2** first in importance; chief: *A balanced diet is primary to good health. adj.* [Primary comes from Latin *primus,* meaning "first."]

prim·i·tive (prim′ə tiv), **1** of early times; of long ago: *Primitive people often lived in caves.* **2** very simple; such as people had early in human history: *A primitive way of making fire is by rubbing two sticks together.* **3** person living in a primitive society or in primitive times. 1,2 *adj.* 3 *n.* —**prim′i·tive·ly,** *adv.* —**prim′i·tive·ness,** *n.* [Primitive comes from Latin *primus,* meaning "first."]

prin·ci·ple (prin′sə pəl), **1** a truth that is a foundation for other truths: *the principles of democratic government.* **2** a fundamental belief. **3** a rule of action or conduct. *n.*

proc·ess (pros′es, prō′ses), **1** set of actions, changes, or operations occurring or performed in a special order toward some result: *the process of breathing, a new manufacturing process.* **2** course of action; procedure. *n.*

pro·fes·sion·al (prə fesh′ə nəl), **1** making a business or trade of something which others do for pleasure: *a professional ballplayer, professional musicians.* **2** undertaken or engaged in by professionals rather than amateurs: *a professional ball game. adj.* —**pro·fes′sion·al·ly,** *adv.*

prog·ress (prog′res *for 1,3;* prə gres′ *for 2,4*), **1** an advance or growth; development; improvement: *the progress of science, showing rapid progress in one's studies.* **2** get better; advance; develop: *We progress in learning step by step.* **3** a moving forward; going ahead: *make rapid progress on a journey.* **4** move forward; go ahead: *The building of the new school progressed quickly during the summer.* 1,3 *n.,* 2,4 *v.*

pro·mo·tion (prə mō′shən), an advance in rank or importance: *The clerk was given a promotion and an increase in salary. n.*

prov·ince (prov′əns), one of the main divisions of a country. Canada is made up of provinces instead of states. *n.*

punc·tu·ate (pungk′chü āt), **1** use periods, commas, and other marks in writing or printing to help make the meaning clear. **2** interrupt now and then: *a speech punctuated with cheers. v.,* **punc·tu·at·ed, punc·tu·at·ing.**

pu·pa (pyü′pə), **1** stage between the larva and the adult in the development of many insects. **2** insect in this stage. Most pupae are inactive and some, such as those of many moths, are enclosed in a tough case or cocoon. *n., pl.* **pu·pae** (pyü′pē), **pu·pas.** [Pupa comes from Latin *pupa,* meaning "girl, doll." The pupa was called this because it looks somewhat like the adult insect.]

puz·zle (puz′əl), **1** a hard problem: *How to get all my things into one trunk is a puzzle.* **2** problem or task to be done for fun: *This puzzle has seven pieces of wood you fit together.* **3** make unable to answer, solve, or understand something; perplex: *How the cat got out puzzled us.* **4** be perplexed. **5** exercise one's mind on something hard: *They puzzled over their arithmetic.* 1,2 *n.,* 3-5 *v.,* **puz·zled, puz·zling.** —**puz′zled·ly,** *adv.*—**puz′zling·ly,** *adv.*

puzzle out, find out by thinking or trying hard; *puzzle out the meaning of a sentence.*

R

ra·dar (rā′där), instrument for determining the distance, direction, speed, etc., of unseen objects by the reflection of radio waves. *n.* [Radar comes from the words *(ra)dio (d)etecting (a)nd (r)anging.* It was formed from the first two letters of *radio* and the first letter of the words *detecting, and, ranging.*]

ra·di·ant (rā′dē ənt), shining; bright; beaming: *a radiant smile. adj.* —**ra′di·ant·ly,** *adv.*

ra·ti·o (rā′shē ō), **1** the relationship in quantity or size between two or more things. "They have sheep and cows in the ratio of 10 to 3" means that they have ten sheep for every three cows. **2** quotient expressing this relation. *n., pl.* **ra·ti·os.**

realm (relm), **1** kingdom. **2** region or sphere in which something rules or prevails. *n.*

re·cep·tion (ri sep′shən), a gathering to receive and welcome people: *Our school gave a reception for our new principal. n.*

re·cord (ri kôrd′ *for 1;* rek′ərd *for 2,3*), **1** set down in writing so as to keep for future use: *Listen to the speaker and record what she says.* **2** the thing written or kept. **3** the best yet done; best amount, rate, or speed yet reached: *Who holds the record for the high jump?* 1 *v.,* 2,3 *n.* [Record came into

English about 700 years ago from French *recorder,* which came from Latin *recordari,* meaning "remember, call to mind," which comes from *re-,* meaning "back," and *cordis,* meaning "heart."]
—**re·cord′a·ble,** *adj.*

off the record, not to be recorded or quoted.

re·flex (rē′fleks), **1** an involuntary action in direct response to a stimulation of some nerve cells. Sneezing and shivering are reflexes. **2** not voluntary; not controlled by the will; coming as a direct response to a stimulation of some sensory nerve cells. 1 *n., pl.* **re·flex·es;** 2 *adj.*

re·hearse (ri hėrs′), **1** practice (a play, part, etc.) for a public performance: *We rehearsed our parts for the school play.* **2** drill or train by repetition. *v.,* **re·hearsed, re·hears·ing.**

re·ject (ri jekt′), **1** refuse to take: *She rejected our help. He tried to join the army but was rejected because of poor health.* **2** throw away as useless or unsatisfactory: *Reject all apples with soft spots. v.*

re·mote (ri mōt′), **1** far away; far off: *The North Pole is a remote part of the world.* **2** out of the way; secluded: *Mail comes to this remote village only once a week. adj.* —**re·mote′ly,** *adv.*

rep·re·sent·a·tive (rep′ri zen′tə tiv), **1** person appointed or elected to act or speak for others: *She is the club's representative at the convention.* **2 Representative,** member of the United States House of Representatives, or of a similar body, such as certain state legislatures. *n.*

re·sist·ance (ri zis′təns), act of striving against or resisting; opposition: *The clerk showed no resistance to the robber. n.*

re·source (ri sôrs′ *or* rē′sôrs), **1** any supply that will meet a need. We have resources of money, of knowledge, of strength, etc. **2 resources,** *pl.* the actual and potential wealth of a country: *natural resources, human resources. n.*

res·taur·ant (res′tər ənt *or* res′tə ränt′), place to buy and eat a meal. *n.* [*Restaurant* comes from Latin *restaurare,* meaning "restore."]

re·venge (ri venj′), harm done in return for a wrong; returning evil for evil: *a blow struck in revenge. n.*

ridge (rij), **1** the line where two sloping surfaces meet. **2** a long, narrow chain of hills or mountains: *the Blue Ridge of the Appalachian Mountains. n.*

riv·et (riv′it), a metal bolt with a head at one end, the other end being hammered into a head after insertion. Rivets fasten heavy steel beams together. *n.*

S

sa·li·ent (sā′lē ənt), standing out; easily seen or noticed; prominent; striking: *the salient points in a speech. Sharp mountain peaks were salient features in the landscape. adj.* —**sa′li·ent·ly,** *adv.*

saun·ter (sôn′tər), walk along slowly and happily; stroll: *People sauntered through the park on summer evenings. v.*

scaf·fold·ing (skaf′əl ding), a temporary structure for holding workers and materials. *n.*

scale¹ (skāl), **1** the dish or pan of a balance. **2** Usually, **scales,** *pl.* balance; instrument for weighing. *n.* [*Scale¹* came into English about 700 years ago from Icelandic *skal.*]

scale² (skāl), **1** one of the thin, flat, hard plates forming the outer covering of some fishes, snakes, and lizards. **2** any of various usually flattened outgrowths of the body wall of an insect (as those on the wings of most moths and butterflies). **3** to remove scales from. 1,2 *n.,* 2 *v.,* **scaled, scal·ing.** [*Scale²* came into English about 600 years ago from French *escale,* meaning "scale, husk."]

scale³ (skāl), **1** series of steps or degrees; scheme of graded amounts. **2** series of marks made along a line at regular distances to use in measuring. **3** (in music) a series of tones ascending or descending in pitch according to fixed intervals. **4** climb. 1-3 *n.,* 4 *v.* [*Scale³* comes from Latin *scalae,* meaning "ladder."]

scheme (skēm), **1** program of action; plan. **2** a plot: *a scheme to cheat the government.* **3** devise plans, especially underhanded or evil ones; plot: *They schemed to bring the jewels into the country without paying duty.* 1,2 *n.,* 3 *v.,* **schemed, schem·ing.**

scorn (skôrn), **1** look down upon; think of as mean or low; despise: *Most people scorn tattletales.* **2** a feeling that a person, animal, or act is mean or low; contempt: *Most pupils feel scorn for those who cheat.* 1 *v.,* 2 *n.*

scrounge (skrounj), INFORMAL. **1** search about for what one can find. **2** beg; get by begging: *scrounge a meal. v.,* **scrounged, scroung·ing.** —**scroung′er,** *n.*

scroun·gy (skroun′jē), SLANG. scruffy; bedraggled; tacky; seedy. *adj.*

scull (skul), one of a pair of oars used, one on each side, by a single rower. *n.*

scaffolding—used to bring materials to the various floors of a building under construction

a hat	oi oil	ə stands for:
ā age	ou out	a in about
ä far	u cup	e in taken
e let	ů put	i in pencil
ē equal	ü rule	o in lemon
ėr term	ch child	u in circus
i it	ng long	
ī ice	sh she	
o hot	th thin	
ō open	ᵺH then	
ô order	zh measure	

shimmer
The **shimmer** of the moonlight on the water made a golden pathway.

snowmobiles

seal[1] (sēl), **1** stamp for marking things to show ownership or authenticity. **2** close tightly; shut. **3** thing that fastens or closes. **4** give a sign that (a thing) is true. 1,3 *n.*, 2,4 *v.* [*Seal*[1] came into English about 700 years ago from French *seel*, and can be traced back to Latin *signum*, meaning "a sign."] —**seal′a·ble**, *adj.* —**seal′er**, *n.*

seal[2] (sēl), **1** a flesh-eating sea mammal with large flippers, living usually in cold regions. **2** hunt seals. 1 *n.*, *pl.* **seals** or **seal**; 2 *v.* [*Seal*[2] comes from Old English *seolh*.] —**seal′like′**, *adj.*

sen·sa·tion (sen sā′shən), **1** action of the senses; power to see, hear, feel, taste, smell, etc.: *An unconscious person is without sensation.* **2** a general or indefinite feeling, such as discomfort, anxiety, or doubt. **3** a strong or excited feeling. *n.*

sen·ti·nel (sen′tə nəl), person stationed to keep watch and guard against surprise attacks. *n.* [*Sentinel* is from French *sentinelle*, which comes from Italian *sentinella*, and can be traced back to Latin *sentire*, meaning "to perceive, to feel."]

stand sentinel, act as a sentinel; keep watch.

se·rene (sə rēn′), **1** peaceful; calm: *serene happiness, a serene smile.* **2** not cloudy; clear; bright: *a serene sky. adj.* —**se·rene′ly,** *adv.*

ser·pent (sėr′pənt), snake, especially a big snake. *n.* [*Serpent* comes from Latin *serpentem*, meaning "a creeping thing."]

shank (shangk), **1** the part of the leg between the knee and the ankle. **2** the corresponding part in animals. **3** the whole leg. *n.*

sheathe (shēᴛ͟H), **1** put (a sword, etc.) into a case or covering. **2** enclose; encase; envelop: *a mummy sheathed in linen. v.,* **sheathed, sheath·ing.**

shim·mer (shim′ər), **1** gleam faintly: *Both the sea and the sand shimmered in the moonlight.* **2** a faint gleam or shine. 1 *v.,* 2 *n.*

shoal (shōl), **1** place in a sea, lake, or stream where the water is shallow. **2** sandbank or sandbar that makes the water shallow, expecially one which can be seen at low tide: *The ship was wrecked on the shoals. n.*

shrug (shrug), **1** raise (the shoulders) as an expression of dislike, doubt, indifference, or impatience: *She shrugged and walked away.* **2** a raising of the shoulders in this way: *A shrug was her only reply.* 1 *v.,* **shrugged, shrug·ging;** 2 *n.*

si·mul·ta·ne·ous·ly (sī′məl tā′nē əs-

lē), at once; at the same time; together. *adv.*

skep·ti·cal (skep′tə kəl), inclined to doubt; not believing easily. *adj.* —**skep′ti·cal·ly,** *adv.*

slide (slīd), **1** move smoothly along a surface. **2** act of sliding. **3** a smooth surface for sliding on. **4** a small, thin sheet of glass on which objects are placed in order to look at them under a microscope. 1,2 *v.,* 3,4 *n.*

snow·mo·bile (snō′mō bēl), tractor or other vehicle for use in snow. Some snowmobiles have skis or runners in front. *n.*

soap·stone (sōp′stōn), a soft rock that feels somewhat like soap, used for griddles, hearths, etc. *n.*

soft·ware (sôft′wer′, sôft′war′), program for a computer system. *n.*

sol·emn (sol′əm), serious; grave; earnest: *to speak in a solemn voice. I gave my solemn promise to do better. adj.* —**sol′emn·ly,** *adv.*

sor·rel (sôr′əl), **1** reddish-brown. **2** a reddish brown. **3** a horse having this color. 1 *adj.,* 2,3 *n.*

sparse (spärs), thinly scattered; occurring here and there: *a sparse population, sparse hair. adj.,* **spars·er, spars·est. sparse′ly,** *adv.*

spe·cies (spē′shēz), group of animals or plants that have certain permanent characteristics in common and are able to interbreed. Wheat is a species of grass. The lion is one species of cat. *n.,* *pl.* **spe·cies.**

splin·ter (splin′tər), **1** a thin, sharp piece of wood, bone, glass, etc.: *I have a splinter in my hand. The mirror broke into splinters.* **2** split or break into thin, sharp pieces. 1 *n.,* 2. *v.*

spring·board (spring′bôrd), a flexible board used to give added spring in diving, jumping, and vaulting. *n.*

spume (spyüm), **1** frothy matter; foam; froth. **2** to foam or froth. 1 *n.,* 2 *v.,* **spumed, spum·ing.**

squint (skwint), **1** to look with the eyes partly closed. **2** a looking with partly closed eyes. **3** a sidelong look. **4** to look sideways. 1,4 *v.,* 2,3 *n.*

stance (stans), **1** position of the feet of a player when making a stroke in golf or other games. **2** manner of standing; posture: *an erect stance. n.*

ster·e·o·typed (ster′ē ə tīpt′ *or* stir′ē ə-tīpt′), fixed or settled in form; conventional: *"It gives me great pleasure to be with you tonight" is a stereotyped opening for a speech. adj.*

sti·fle (stī′fəl), **1** stop the breath of; smother. **2** keep back; suppress; stop: *stifle a cry, stifle a yawn, stifle business activity, stifle a rebellion. v.,* **sti·fled, sti·fling.**

stor·age (stôr′ij), **1** act or fact of storing goods: *the storage of storm windows in summertime.* **2** place for keeping, preserving, or saving for future use. *n.*

stren·u·ous (stren′yü əs), **1** very active: *We had a strenuous day moving into our new house.* **2** full of energy; vigorous. *adj.* —**stren′u·ous·ly,** *adv.*

struc·ture (struk′chər), **1** something built; a building or construction. Dams, bridges, and tunnels are very large structures. **2** anything composed of parts arranged together: *The human body is a wonderful structure.* **3** arrangement of parts, elements, etc.: *the structure of a molecule, the structure of a flower, sentence structure, the structure of a story.* *n.*

stu·di·o (stü′dē ō, styü′dē o), **1** workroom of a painter, sculptor, photographer, etc. **2** place where motion pictures are made. **3** place from which a radio or television program is broadcast. *n., pl.* **stu·di·os.** [*Studio* comes from Latin *studium,* meaning "study."]

sub·mit (səb mit′), yield oneself to the power, control, or authority of some person or group; surrender: *They submitted to the will of the authorities.* *v.,* **sub·mit·ted, sub·mit·ting.**

sub·stance (sub′stəns), what a thing consists of; matter; material: *Ice and water are the same substance in different forms.* *n.*

sub·urb (sub′ėrb′), district, town, or village just outside or near a city: *Many people who work in the city live in the suburbs.* *n.*

suf·fo·cate (suf′ə kāt), **1** kill by stopping the breath. **2** keep from breathing; hinder in breathing. **3** gasp for breath; choke. **4** die for lack of oxygen; be smothered. *v.,* **suf·fo·cat·ed, suf·fo·cat·ing.**

sum·mit (sum′it), the highest point; top: *the summit of a mountain.* *n.*

surge (sėrj), **1** a swelling wave; sweep or rush of waves: *Our boat was upset by a surge.* **2** something like a wave: *A surge of anger swept over him.* *n.*

sur·pass (sər pas′), **1** do better than; be greater than; outperform: *She surpasses her sister in arithmetic.* **2** be too much or too great for; go beyond. *v.* —**sur·pass′ing·ly,** *adv.*

sur·plus (sėr′pləs *or* sėr′plus), amount over and above what is needed; extra quantity left over; excess: *The bank keeps a large surplus of money in reserve.* *n.* [*Surplus* comes from French *sur,* meaning "over," and "plus," meaning "more."]

sym·pa·thy (sim′pə thē), a sharing of another's sorrow or trouble: *We feel sympathy for a person who is ill.* *n., pl.* **sym·pa·thies.**

T

tal·on (tal′ən), claw of an animal, especially a bird of prey: *The eagle seized a chicken with its talons.* *n.*

tear[1] (tir), **1** drop of salty liquid coming from the eye. **2** fill with tears; shed tears. **1** *n.,* **2** *v.*

tear[2] (ter *or* tar), **1** pull apart by force: *tear a box open.* **2** pull hard; pull violently: *Tear out the page.* **3** a torn place: *She has a tear in her jeans.* **1,2** *v.,* **3** *n.*

tech·nol·o·gy (tek nol′ə jē), science of the mechanical and industrial arts: *I studied engineering at a school of technology.* *n.* [*Technology* comes from Greek *technē,* meaning "art," and *logia,* -logy.]

te·di·ous (tē′dē əs *or* tē′jəs), long and tiring; boring; wearisome: *A boring talk that you cannot understand is tedious.* *adj.* —**te′di·ous·ly,** *adv.*

teem·ing (tē′ming), full of; alive with: *ponds teeming with fish, cities teeming with people.* *adj.*

tele-, *combining form.* **1** over a long distance: *Telescope = instrument for looking over a long distance.* **2** television: *Telecast = broadcast over television.* [The form *tele-* comes from Greek *tēle,* meaning "far."]

tel·e·phone (tel′ə fōn), **1** apparatus, system, or process for sending sound or speech to a distant point over wires by means of electrical impulses. **2** talk through a telephone. **1,** *n.,* **2** *v.* [*Telephone* comes from the Greek *tēle,* meaning "far."]

ther·mal (thėr′məl), **1** of or having to do with heat; thermic. **2** warm; hot. **3** a rising current of warm air. **1,2** *adj.,* **3,** *n.* [*Thermal* comes from Greek *thermē,* meaning "heat."]

ther·mo·stat (thėr′mə stat), an automatic device for regulating temperature: *Most furnaces and ovens are controlled by thermostats.* *n.*

thor·ough (thėr′ō), **1** being all that is needed; complete. **2** doing all that should be done; very careful: *The doctor was very thorough in examining the patient.* *adj.* —**thor′ough·ly,** *adv.* —**thor′ough·ness,** *n.*

thread·bare (thred′ber′ *or* thred′bar′), **1** having the nap worn off; worn so much that the threads show: *a threadbare coat.* **2** wearing clothes worn to the threads; shabby: *a threadbare beggar.* **3** old and worn. *adj.*

to·ken (tō′kən), **1** a mark or sign (of something): *His actions are a token of his sincerity.* **2** sign of friendship; keepsake: *She received many birthday tokens.* **3** having only the appearance of; serving as a symbol; nominal; partial: *a token payment, token resistance.* **1-2** *n.,* **3** *adj.*

a	hat	oi	oil	ə	stands for:
ā	age	ou	out		a in about
ä	far	u	cup		e in taken
e	let	ú	put		i in pencil
ē	equal	ü	rule		o in lemon
ėr	term	ch	child		u in circus
i	it	ng	long		
ī	ice	sh	she		
o	hot	th	thin		
ō	open	ᴛʜ	then		
ô	order	zh	measure		

trophy—She proudly displayed her **trophy**.

ukulele

tome (tōm), a book, especially a large, heavy book. *n.*

tor·rent (tôr'ənt), **1** a violent, rushing stream of water: *The mountain torrent dashed over the rock.* **2** a heavy downpour: *The rain came down in torrents during the thunderstorm. n.*

tough (tuf), **1** bending without breaking: *Leather is tough: cardboard is not.* **2** hard to cut, tear, or chew: *The steak was so tough I couldn't eat it.* **3** strong; hardy: *Donkeys are tough little animals and can carry big loads.* **4** hard; difficult: *Dragging the load uphill was tough work.* **5** hard to influence; stubborn: *a tough customer. adj.,* —**tough'ly,** *adv.* —**tough'ness,** *n.*

trade·mark (trād'märk'), a mark, picture, name, word, symbol, design, or letters, used to identify and distinguish a product or merchandise as belonging to a specific manufacturer or seller. A registered trademark is legally protected, and may be used only by the owner. *n.*

trance (trans), **1** state of unconsciousness somewhat like sleep. **2** a dreamy, absorbed condition that is like a trance: *She sat in a trance, thinking of her past life. n.*

tran·scribe (tran skrīb'), to write out or type out in full. *v.* [*Transcribe* comes from *transcribere, trans* meaning "over," and *scribere* meaning "write."]

trans·fix (tran sfiks'), make motionless or helpless (with amazement, terror, grief, etc.). *v.*

treat·ment (trēt'mənt), **1** act or process of easing or curing: *My cold won't respond to treatment.* **2** thing done to bring about some special result. *n.*

trel·lis (trel'is), frame of light strips of wood or metal crossing one another with open spaces in between, especially one supporting growing vines. *n., pl.* **trel·lis·es.**

tres·pass (tres'pəs), go on somebody's property without any right: *We put up "No Tresspassing" signs to keep hunters off our land. v.*

tri·fle (trī'fəl), **1** thing having little value or importance. **2** a small amount; little bit: *He was a trifle late. n.*

tro·phy (trō'fē), **1** any prize, cup, etc., awarded to a victorious person or team: *The champion kept her tennis trophies on the mantelpiece.* **2** a spoil or prize of war. **3** anything serving as a remembrance. *n., pl.* **tro·phies.**

troupe (trüp), troop, band, or company, especially a group of actors, singers, or acrobats. *n.*

trudge (truj), **1** go on foot; walk. **2** walk wearily or with effort. *v.,* **trudged, trudg·ing.**

tu·ber (tü'bər *or* tyü'bər), the thick part of an underground stem. A potato is a tuber. *n.*

tus·sock (tus'ək), a tuft of growing grass or the like. *n.*

ty·coon (tī kün'), an important businessman. *n.* [*Tycoon* is from Japanese *taikun,* which came from Chinese *tai,* meaning "great," and *kium,* meaning "lord."]

tyr·an·ny (tir'ə nē), **1** cruel or unjust use of power: *Cinderella escaped the tyranny of her stepsisters. The colonists rebelled against the king's tyrannies.* **2** government by an absolute ruler. *n., pl.* **tyr·an·nies.**

U

u·ku·le·le (yü'kə lā'lē), a small guitar having four strings. *n.* [*Ukulele* comes from Hawaiian *ukulele,* which originally meant "leaping flea."]

un·a·bridged (un'ə brijd'), not shortened or condensed; complete: *an unabridged book. adj.*

un·doubt·ed·ly (un dou'tid lē), beyond question; certainly. *adv.*

V

val·or (val'ər), bravery; courage. *n.* [*Valor* is from Latin *valor,* meaning "value, courage," which comes from *valere,* meaning "be strong."]

van·quished (vang'kwisht), conquered; defeated; overcome. *adj.*

va·por (vā'pər), **1** moisture in the air that can be seen, such as steam, fog, mist, etc., usually due to the effect of heat upon a liquid. **2** gas formed from a substance that is usually a liquid or a solid. *n.*

veer (vir), **1** change in direction; shift; turn: *The wind veered to the south. The talk veered to ghosts.* **2** change the direction of: *We veered our boat. v.*

veil (vāl), **1** piece of very thin material worn to protect or hide the face. **2** piece of material worn so as to fall over the head and shoulders. **3** anything that screens or hides: *a veil of clouds. n.*

ven·dor (ven'dər), seller; peddler. *n.* Also, **vender.**

vet·er·an (vet'ər ən), person who has served in the armed forces. *n.*

vi·a (vī'ə *or* vē'ə), by way of; by a route that passes through: *She is going from New York to Paris via London. prep.*

vi·per (vī′pər), any of various poisonous snakes with a pair of large, hollow fangs and often having a thick, heavy body. *n.*

viv·id (viv′id), **1** strikingly bright; strong and clear; brilliant: *Dandelions are a vivid yellow.* **2** full of life; lively: *a vivid description of an experience.* **3** strong and distinct: *I have a vivid memory of the fire. adj.* —**viv′id·ly,** *adv.* —**viv′id·ness,** *n.*

void (void), **1** an empty space; vacuum. **2** a feeling of emptiness or great loss: *The death of his dog left a void in the boy's life.* **3** emptiness; vacancy. *n.*

vol·u·ble (vol′yə bəl), tending to talk much; fond of talking: *a voluble speaker, adj.*

vol·ume (vol′yəm), **1** book: *We own a library of five hundred volumes.* **2** book forming part of a set or series: *You can find what you want to know in the ninth volume of this encyclopedia. n.*

W

war·rant (wôr′ənt *or* wor′ənt), **1** that which gives a right; authority. **2** a written order giving authority for something: *a warrant to search the house.* **3** declare positively; certify: *I'll warrant they won't try that again.* 1,2 *n.,* 3 *v.*

wig·wam (wig′wom *or* wig′wôm), hut made of bark, mats, or skins laid over a dome-shaped frame of poles, used by certain North American Indians. *n.* [*Wigwam* comes from its North American Indian name.]

wind[1] (wind), **1** air in motion. The wind varies in force from a slight breeze to a strong gale. **2** a strong wind; gale: *Winds blowing at ninety miles an hour toppled a tree onto our roof.* **3** air filled with some smell: *The deer caught the wind of us and ran off.* **4** follow by scent; smell. **5** power of breathing; breath: *A runner needs good wind.* **6** put out of breath; cause difficulty in breathing: *Walking up the steep hill winded me.* **7 winds,** *pl.* wind instruments. 1-3,5,7 *n.,* 4,6 *v.,* **wind·ed, wind·ing.**

wind[2] (wīnd), **1** move this way and that; go in a crooked way; change direction; turn: *A brook winds through the woods.* **2** to fold, wrap, or place about something: *She wound her arms around her new puppy.* **3** to cover with something put, wrapped, or folded around: *The patient's arm is wound with bandages.* **4** roll into a ball or on a spool: *We took turns winding yarn.* **5** twist or turn around something: *The*

vine winds around a pole. **6** make (some machine) go by turning some part of it: *wind a clock. v.,* **wound, wind·ing;** —**wind′a·ble,** *adj.* —**wind′er,** *n.*

wind[3] (wīnd), blow: *wind a fanfare on a trumpet. v.,* **wind·ed** *or* **wound, wind·ing.**

with·ers (wiᴛʜ′ərz), the highest part of a horse's or other animal's back, between the shoulder blades. See **horse** for diagram. *n. pl.* [origin uncertain]

wreath (rēth), a ring of flowers or leaves twisted together: *They hung a wreath on the door. She made a wreath of daisies. n., pl.* **wreaths** (rēᴛʜz).

Y

year·ling (yir′ling), animal that is one year old. *n.*

yearn (yėrn), feel a longing or desire; desire earnestly: *I yearned for home. v.*

Z

zo·ol·o·gist (zō ol′ə jist), an expert in zoology. *n.*

zo·ol·o·gy (zō ol′ə jē), the science of animals; the study of animals and animal life. Zoology is a branch of biology. *n.* [The form *zoo-* comes from Greek *zōion,* meaning "animal."]

a hat	oi oil	ə stands for:
ā age	ou out	a in about
ä far	u cup	e in taken
e let	u̇ put	i in pencil
ē equal	ü rule	o in lemon
ėr term	ch child	u in circus
i it	ng long	
ī ice	sh she	
o hot	th thin	
ō open	ᴛʜ then	
ô order	zh measure	

wigwam
Part of the wigwam is cut away to show the framework.

John Rice, page 286; Statue of Liberty Centennial Commission, page 297; Claudia Sargent, page 302; Richard Del Rosso, pages 326–327, 440–441, 444–445, 448–449; Elliot Kreloff, pages 333, 335, 338, 339, 342; Meryl Henderson, pages 346–347, 348–349, 351, 354–355; Mike O'Reilly, pages 361, 364, 366, 371; Allen Davis, pages 392–393, 396–397, 399; Susan David, page 404; Betsy Day, pages 406–423; Jim Deigan, pages 426–427; Joe Dawes, pages 434, 435, 436; Janet Bohn, page 480; Nancy Didion, pages 486, 527; Rodica Prato, pages 508–509; Anthony Accardo, pages 523, 524, 525, 526; Howard Post, pages 532, 539, 545

Glossary:
Bow—NOAA; Cascade—William B. Parker; Expedition—Jonathan Wright © National Geographic Society from their film "Journey to the Outer Limits"; Falcon—Arabian American Oil Company; Funnel—NOAA; Gape—H. Armstrong Roberts; Inspect—Hughes Aircraft Corp.; Primitive—Courtesy of The American Museum of Natural History, New York; Pupa—Lynn M. Stone; Scaffold—Uris Building Corporation; Shimmer—William B. Parker; Snowmobiles—Bill Lingard/National Film Board of Canada; Trophy—Robert Farbin

Photographs
Pages 16–17, 174–181, 432, 434, 455–463, Michal Heron; Page 32, Richard Mewton. Courtesy of Greenwillow Books; Pages 60–61, © Dan McCoy/Rainbow; Pages 65, 67, 72, Courtesy of Senator Daniel K. Inouye; Page 69, United States Signal Corps; Page 76, Photograph of Richard H. Ebright. Courtesy of Mrs. D. F. Muth. Spot photograph by John Gerlach/DRK Photo; Pages 79 (top), 80, 82 (top, left and right; bottom, right), Copyright © 1985 Dwight R. Kuhn; Page 79 © Breck Kent/Animals Animals (bottom); Page 82, E. R. Degginger/Animals Animals (bottom, left); Pages 86–87, 89–90, 93, 95–96, Courtesy of American Foundation for the Blind; Pages 100–101, "Invitation to the Sideshow" (La Parade), Georges Pierre Seurat, 1888. The Metropolitan Museum of Art. Bequest of Stephen C. Clark, 1960; Page 102, The Bridgeman Art Library, Art Resource; Page 109, Courtesy of the estate of Pura Belpré White; Pages 113–116, Courtesy of Levi Strauss and Co.; Page 118, Jerry Jacka; Page 141, Historical Pictures Service, Chicago; Pages 144–145, Dennis Brack/Black Star; Page 170, Alexander Limont. Courtesy of E. P. Dutton, Inc.; Pages 184–185, Michael Melford/The Image Bank; Page 200, Watson. Courtesy of The Scribner Book Companies, Inc.; Pages 230–231, Adam Woolfitt/Woodfin Camp & Associates; Page 233, M. P. L. Fogden/Bruce Coleman; Page 237, S. C. Bisserat/Bruce Coleman; Pages 238, 240–241, 244–247, Robert Frerck/Odyssey Productions; Pages 242–243, Charmayne McGee; Page 249, John Lei/Omni Photo Communications; Pages 251, 255–257, 260–261, Rick Smolen/Woodfin Camp & Associates; Page 262, Copyright © 1981 Rick Smolen/Woodfin Camp & Associates; Page 265, Johnny Johnson/DRK Photo; Page 266, Esther Hautzig; Pages 269, 274, 277, Tass from Sovfoto; Page 280, Courtesy of Macmillan Publishing Company; Pages 284–285, © Peter B. Kaplan; Page 293, © Joe Azzara/The Image Bank; Page 294, Michael George; Page 299, Library of Congress (top), Culver Pictures (bottom); Page 300, Naoki Okamoto/Black Star; Page 305, Photograph by Byron/The Byron Collection, The Museum of the City of New York; Pages 308–311, Library of Congress; Page 315, David Burnett/Woodfin Camp & Associates; Pages 318–321, Paul Conklin; Page 324, Langston Hughes—UPI, Copyright © 1980 George Hall/Woodfin Camp & Associates; Page 356, Cox Studios, Courtesy of Macmillan Publishing Company; Page 358, Peter Miller/Photo Researchers; Pages 376–377, "The Notch in the White Mountains," Thomas Cole, 1839. National Gallery of Art, Washington, D.C. Andrew W. Mellon Fund; Page 380, Stephen J. Krasemann/Peter Arnold, Inc. (left), Grant Heilman Photography (right); Page 381, Cary Wolinsky/Stock, Boston; Page 387, Courtesy of IBM; Page 389, Alpha; Page 390, Rene Burri/Magnum; Page 402, Photograph by Ellan Young. Courtesy of E. P. Dutton, Inc.; Page 423, The Illustrated London News Pictures Library; Page 428, David W. Hamilton/The Image Bank; Page 449, Photograph by Georgia Litwack. Courtesy of Norton Juster; Pages 466–467, Jeff Rotman; Pages 469–470, Peter Veit; Pages 475, 478, 480, 483, NASA; Pages 487, Copyright © 1980 and 492, Copyright © 1978, David Hoadley; Page 488, Stephanie Maze; Page 490, NOAA; Pages 498–499, 501, Mitchell Funk; Pages 502, 504, 505 (left), Calvin Sperling; Page 505, Timothy Johns (right); Page 510, © Vic Cox/Peter Arnold, Inc. (top), Peter Quidley (bottom); pages 514, 519, 521, Iain and Oria Douglas-Hamilton; Page 530, Copyright © 1974 Bill Carter/The Image Bank; Page 550, Marian Stephenson. From Something About the Author, vol. 2

Cover Artist
Nathan Greene